THE FUTURE OF THE EUROPEAN LAW OF CIVIL PROCEDURE

THE FUTURE OF THE EUROPEAN LAW OF CIVIL PROCEDURE

Coordination or Harmonisation?

Edited by
Fernando GASCÓN INCHAUSTI
Burkhard HESS

INTERSENTIA

Intersentia Ltd
8 Wellington Mews
Wellington Street | Cambridge
CB1 1HW | United Kingdom
Tel.: +44 1223 736 170
Email: mail@intersentia.co.uk
www.intersentia.com | www.intersentia.co.uk

Distribution for the UK and Ireland:
NBN International
Airport Business Centre, 10 Thornbury Road
Plymouth, PL6 7PP
United Kingdom
Tel.: +44 1752 202 301 | Fax: +44 1752 202 331
Email: orders@nbninternational.com

Distribution for Europe and all other countries:
Intersentia Publishing nv
Groenstraat 31
2640 Mortsel
Belgium
Tel.: +32 3 680 15 50 | Fax: +32 3 658 71 21
Email: mail@intersentia.be

Distribution for the USA and Canada:
Independent Publishers Group
Order Department
814 North Franklin Street
Chicago, IL 60610
USA
Tel.: +1 800 888 4741 (toll free) | Fax: +1 312 337 5985
Email: orders@ipgbook.com

The Future of the European Law of Civil Procedure. Coordination or Harmonisation?

Artwork on cover: Gurgen Bakhshetyan – Shutterstock

ISBN 978-1-78068-859-6
D/2020/7849/9
NUR 822

British Library Cataloguing in Publication Data. A catalogue record for this book is available from the British Library.

CONTENTS

LIST OF CASES

NATIONAL COURTS

BELGIUM

ENGLAND

FRANCE

GERMANY

USA

COURT OF JUSTICE OF THE EUROPEAN UNION

EUROPEAN COURT OF HUMAN RIGHTS

LIST OF AUTHORS

Dominik Düsterhaus
Référendaire, Court of Justice of the European Union

Fernando Gascón Inchausti
Professor of Law, Complutense University of Madrid – Instituto de Derecho Europeo e Integración Regional (IDEIR)

Burkhard Hess
Executive Director, Max Planck Institute, Luxembourg; Professor of Law, Universities of Heidelberg and Luxembourg

Stefan Huber
Professor of Law, University of Tübingen

Christoph A. Kern
Professor of Law, University of Heidelberg

Stephanie Law
Senior Research Fellow, Max Planck Institute, Luxembourg

Patricia Llopis Nadal
Lecturer in Law, University of Valencia

Janek T. Nowak
Max Planck Institute, Luxembourg; KU Leuven, Belgium; MCI Innsbruck, Austria

Marta Requejo Isidro
Senior Research Fellow, Max Planck Institute, Luxembourg

Vincent Richard
Senior Research Fellow, Max Planck Institute, Luxembourg

Elisabetta Silvestri
Professor of Law, University of Pavia

Michael Stürner
Professor of Law, University of Konstanz

María Luisa Villamarín López
Professor of Law, Complutense University of Madrid

Enrique Vallines García
Senior Research Fellow, Max Planck Institute, Luxembourg

INTRODUCTION

Fernando Gascón Inchausti and Burkhard Hess

The harmonisation of civil proceedings within the European Union has become one of the trending topics among scholars of procedural law and private international law.[1] The reasons for this interest are as numerous as they are obvious. It is unquestionable that the globalisation of legal relations – economic and personal – has increased cross-border litigation, forcing an interplay between different procedural systems, which has become necessary for many purposes: for example, when it comes to serving abroad the document instituting the proceedings; in order to obtain the cooperation of another Member State's court to gather evidence; to request a protective measure that must be immediately effective in another jurisdiction; or to promote the recognition and/or enforcement of a judgment in a Member State other than the one in which it was issued.

For decades now, the institutions of the European Union have been aware of this phenomenon and of the need to have rules that allow for the additional obstacles that this diversity entails to be effectively overcome, in order to ensure an adequate resolution of cross-border disputes. This is, indeed, one of the aims that legitimise the progressive construction of a European Area of Civil Justice, as proclaimed in Articles 67 and 81 TFEU.

However, there seems to be a paradigm shift in the manner of dealing with this issue. Initially, the European law-maker chose to face this matter from the perspective of international judicial cooperation, which in turn has been based for 20 years on the notions of mutual trust and mutual recognition. This approach was probably the only one possible, although it has placed the rules on civil procedure approved by the European Union in a kind of "no man's land". It is not procedural law in a *classical* or *traditional* sense – at least, not in its entirety – since it is basically intended to coordinate the national

---

1 B. Hess, "Ein einheitliches Prozessrecht?", (2016) 6(1) *International Journal of Procedural Law* 55–85; B. Hess/X.E. Kramer (eds.), *From common rules to best practices in European Civil Procedure*, Baden-Baden, Nomos, 2017; M. Weller/C. Althammer (eds.), *Mindeststandards im Europäischen Zivilprozessrecht*, Tübingen, Mohr Siebeck, 2016; B. Hess/M. Bergstrom/E. Storskrubb, *EU civil justice: current issues and future outlook*, Oxford, Hart, 2016.

procedural legislation of the Member States in cross-border scenarios, but not to regulate civil proceedings as such – except very tangential aspects, such as the exequatur procedure, where it subsists. Rather, it is EU law – based on the fundamental values of the European Union, such as access to justice, fair trial, equal treatment or the best interests of the child, among others – that performs this function. This dimension of EU civil procedural law as EU law explains that it is strongly influenced by the developments that EU law itself has experienced in the last years.

The developments of EU law, in fact, have subjected national procedural legislation to important challenges, which in turn have also had an impact on the procedural law of the EU. At a general and higher level, the adoption of the Charter of Fundamental Rights has allowed the Court of Justice of the European Union to analyse the practical problems in applying the European civil procedure rules from a fundamental rights perspective:[2] this constitutional dimension of EU procedural law has, in turn, repercussions on the domestic procedural law-makers, having to endure as the Court of Justice establishes that an internal legal provision is contrary to the Charter (as in the *Alder* case[3]). In this vein, the European law-maker's concern to reach an adequate protection of the rights of each party to the proceedings is clear. In the field of recognition and enforcement, for instance, EU legislation has created a creditor-friendly environment, which has been reinforced by the instruments of the second generation and with the broader suppression of exequatur proceedings in the Brussels I bis Regulation; this *pro actore* approach is also supported by the legal option to reinforce the obligation of the debtor to defend himself in the Member State of origin, as stressed by the Court of Justice, among others, in *Diageo Brands*.[4] But the rights of the defendant have also been reinforced, as has been highlighted by the case law of the Court of Justice regarding enforcement of default judgments rendered after fictitious service of the claim, and by the EU legislation itself, with the prominent example of Article 43 of the Brussels I bis Regulation, which requires service of the enforceable title on the defendant before enforcement proceedings are permitted in the requested Member State. A similar balance between effective access to the court by the plaintiff and the right of the defendant party to a fair

---

2 All EU instruments of procedural law must be interpreted so as to fully implement the guarantees of Article 47 of the Charter; C-112/13 Judgment of the Court, 11 September 2014, *A v. B and others*, EU:C:2014:2195, para. 51; C-559/14, Judgment of the Court, 25 May 2015, *Rudolfs Meroni v. Recoletos Limited*, EU:C:2016:349, paras. 42–45.

3 C-325/11, Judgment of the Court, 19 December 2012, *Alder Krystyna Alder and Ewald Alder v. Sabina Orlowska and Czeslaw Orlowski*, EU:C:2012:824.

4 C-681/13, Judgment of the Court, 16 July 2015, *Diageo Brands BV v. Simiramida-04 EOOD*, EU:C:2015:471.

trial underlies the Service Regulation and the provisions on service included in many other EU instruments.[5]

The influence of EU *substantive* law on national procedural law is even more decisive: the case of consumer law is paradigmatic, and this was clearly highlighted by the so-called "Luxembourg Report on European Procedural Law".[6] At this level a double phenomenon has developed, brought about almost exclusively by the Court of Justice: on the one hand, the attribution to European standards of consumer protection of a strongly imperative nature; and on the other hand, the need to give full effect to these mandatory protective rules, especially in the area of unfair contract terms. The impact of the case law of the Court of Justice in some national procedural systems has been clear and has made the dialogue between national judges and the Court of Justice, through preliminary rulings, a source of transformation of national procedural rules and of harmonisation in the manner of applying or interpreting the existing ones. However, it has not been the only example. "Horizontal" harmonisation in matters such as intellectual property, antitrust damages claims, data protection or confidential information is a good example of the fact that EU procedural law is to be found also beyond the traditional instruments of judicial cooperation in civil matters and cross-border litigation. It is undeniable that its purpose is – also – to interfere in the internal legislation of the Member States, even if this entails complicated symbiosis or hybridisation. The 2018 proposal of the EU Commission for a Directive on representative actions for the protection of the collective interests of consumers seems to point in the same direction.[7]

These developments have put on the table the option of harmonisation as a new and complementary approach to the previous one – i.e., coordination – when it comes to consolidating the European Area of Civil Justice. Once again, the "Luxembourg Report on European Procedural Law", addressing the situation of national procedural legislation in relation to the EU procedural regulations,[8]

---

5 F. Gascón Inchausti, "Service of Proceedings on the Defendant as a Safeguard of Fairness in Civil Proceedings: in Search of Minimum Standards from EU Legislation and European Case-Law", (2017) 13(3) *Journal of Private International Law* 475–518.

6 B. Hess/S. Law (eds.), *Implementing EU Consumer Rights by National Procedural Law*, C.H. Beck/Hart, 2019; also available at: *An evaluation study of national procedural laws and practices in terms of their impact on the free circulation of judgments and on the equivalence and effectiveness of the procedural protection of consumers under EU consumer law – Strand 2 Procedural Protection of Consumers*, Report prepared by a Consortium of European universities led by the Max Planck Institute Luxembourg for Procedural Law as commissioned by the European Commission (JUST/2014/RCON/PR/CIVI/0082): https://ec.europa.eu/newsroom/just/item-detail.cfm?item_id=612847.

7 COM/2018/0184 final – 2018/089 (COD).

8 B. Hess/P. Ortolani (eds.), *Impediments of National Procedural Law to the Free Movement of Judgments*, Oxford, Hart, 2019, also available as: *An evaluation study of national procedural laws and practices in terms of their impact on the free circulation of judgments and on the equivalence and effectiveness of the procedural protection of consumers under*

reveals considerable divergences that exist, perhaps not in the essential, but certainly in many technical aspects. In the end, the functioning of the interplay between European and domestic procedural law determines the realisation of effective judicial protection for litigants. The regulations approved so far on judicial cooperation under the umbrella of Article 81 TFEU have contributed to some extent to aligning some aspects of national procedural legislation, although not significantly.[9] If the differences between the national systems of civil justice can be said to constitute hurdles to the proper functioning of cross-border litigation, and if there are already instances of horizontal harmonisation in specific sectors of civil procedure, then the scenario seems ready to consider moving forward on the path of a more straightforward harmonisation. In this regard, one should not forget that Article 81(2)(f) enables the Union to adopt legislative measures aimed at the "elimination of obstacles to the proper functioning of civil proceedings, if necessary by promoting the compatibility of the rules on civil procedure applicable in the Member States."

Two initiatives, in fact, have helped to foster this interest in the harmonisation of national civil procedural legislation in the European Union. On the one hand are the works promoted by the European Parliament, which culminated in 2017 with a proposal for a Directive on common minimum standards of civil procedure in the European Union;[10] and on the other hand is the project promoted jointly by the European Law Institute and UNIDROIT to elaborate a set of European Rules of Civil Procedure, which is already in a very advanced phase of development. It is still too early to know what the real impact of each endeavour will be. Nevertheless, it is unquestionable that the launching of both initiatives has a special value, as it marks a qualitative leap at a methodological and strategic level for the future developments of civil procedural law in the EU. Procedural harmonisation has ceased to be a taboo that ran up against the wall of the procedural autonomy of the Member States. The debate, rather, seems to be centred now on the *how* and on the *how much* of that harmonisation.

The chapters of this book have been undertaken in this framework. They are the fruits of the reflections on a seminar held at the Max Planck Institute Luxembourg for Procedural Law on 19 July 2018 jointly with the members

---

EU consumer law – Strand 1 Mutual Trust and Free Circulation of Judgments, at: https://publications.europa.eu/en/publication-detail/-/publication/531ef49a-9768-11e7-b92d-01aa75ed71a1/language-en.

9 A. Nylund/B. Krans (eds.), *The European Union and National Civil Procedure*, Cambridge, Intersentia, 2016.

10 European Parliament resolution of 4 July 2017 with recommendations to the Commission on common minimum standards of civil procedure in the European Union (2015/2084(INL), available at: http://www.europarl.europa.eu/doceo/document/TA-8-2017-0282_EN.html?redirect.

of a research project funded by the Spanish Ministry of Science and Innovation and with prominent scholars in the field of European civil procedure and private international law.

The three chapters in the first Part focus on the possible methodological approaches for this harmonisation. *Stefan Huber* analyses in a general plan the various tools that the European law-makers can use if they want to promote procedural harmonisation. *Stephanie Law* and *Janek T. Nowak*, on the other hand, present an impressive analysis of the role of the Court of Justice as promoter of procedural harmonisation based on the categories of EU law and seeking a reasonable balance between the traditional procedural autonomy of the Member States and the principles of effectiveness and equivalence. The constitutional dimension of European procedural law as a starting point for harmonisation is, lastly, the focus of the contribution of *Dominik Düsterhaus*.

The second Part aims to confront the reader with the current *status quo*; that is, what is the real level of harmonisation already reached today – firstly, in a "vertical" manner, through the regulations on international judicial cooperation (*Fernando Gascón Inchausti*) and, more particularly, in the field of provisional and protective relief, through the European Account Preservation Order (*María Luisa Villamarín López*). This is also done horizontally, through the promotion of harmonised standards in terms of access to information and evidence, promoted by the Directives on intellectual property rights and competition damages (*Enrique Vallines García*), and regarding the protection of confidential information, present in the Directive on trade secrets (*Patricia Llopis Nadal*) and in the field of data protection (*Marta Requejo Isidro*).

Looking to the future is the objective of the third Part, in which the two aforementioned initiatives are analysed. On the one hand, the ELI-UNIDROIT project is presented in general terms by *Elisabetta Silvestri*. The working methodology and the type of rules that are being elaborated are illustrated thereafter in relation to two specific topics, namely access to information and evidence (*Michael Stürner*) and the provisions on judgments and appeals (*Christoph A. Kern*). The proposed Directive on minimum standards, finally, is elaborated upon and criticised in two separate contributions by *Fernando Gascón Inchausti* and *Vincent Richard*.

The future of procedural law in the European Union and, more specifically, the paradigm shift from coordination to harmonisation, is an exciting topic that will undoubtedly continue to generate much debate and discussion. The creation of a common European code of civil procedure is not only still an unattainable Utopia but also possibly remains undesirable, as *Elisabetta Silvestri* points out in her final remarks. Nevertheless, moving forward along the path of harmonisation, either sectorally or as a formula to make cross-border litigation more effective, is an approach that is already on the table. This book aims to contribute to this collective conversation, pointing out the progress made, as well as its limits – some inescapable; others convenient.

PART I

METHODOLOGICAL APPROACHES

INITIAL REMARKS ON THE METHODOLOGICAL APPROACHES TO PROCEDURAL HARMONISATION

Stefan HUBER

Model laws, minimum standards, directives, recommendations – the variety of instruments designed to harmonise law has almost become confusing. In order to clarify the picture, the present contribution first gives an overview of the different instruments that might be suitable for harmonising civil procedure (section 1). In a second step, it will be analysed which types of instruments have already been used on the European level, and major weak and strong points of these instruments will be discussed (section 2). This leads finally to the question which type of instrument might be suitable for future challenges (section 3).

1. INSTRUMENTS DESIGNED TO HARMONISE PROCEDURAL LAW

Different types of instruments are to be distinguished.

On the one hand, there are hard law instruments, such as conventions and, at the European level, directives and regulations. All these instruments are characterised by their binding character.[1]

[1] For conventions, see R. Goode/H. Kronke/E. McKendrick/J. Wool, *Transnational Commercial Law*, 2nd edn. Oxford University Press, 2012, p. 1 et seq.; regarding directives and regulations, see Art. 288(2), (3) TFEU (ex Art. 249 TEC).

On the other hand, there is a vast variety of soft law instruments. Their common element is the absence of any binding effect.[2] This means that they have to convince the addressees by their substance. Within this huge category of soft law, another distinction might be made between those instruments which are addressed to private actors, those which are addressed to national legislators and, thirdly, all other instruments.

The first subcategory comprises, first and foremost, model contracts, model terms and conditions and codes of conduct. The INCOTERMS, published by the International Chamber of Commerce,[3] are an example of model terms and conditions, which have found wide acceptance by the market.[4]

The most important instrument of the second subcategory – soft law designed for national legislators – is the model law. A prominent and very successful example is the UNCITRAL model law on arbitration[5] – a model law in the field of procedure. The last important reform of the German Arbitration Law also followed this model.[6]

Minimum standards are less detailed than model rules. They do not propose specific rules, but only lay down a common fundament, by which the national laws should be construed. According to Burkhard Hess, minimum standards are not as general and fundamental as constitutional principles, but are less precise than procedural principles.[7]

Another soft law instrument designed for national legislators is the legislative guide. This instrument is sometimes used by international organisations such as UNCITRAL in order to offer guidelines for national legislators in fields of law where reforms seem desirable. One recent example is the UNCITRAL legislative guide on secured transactions.[8] Legislative guides might also comprise model rules, but, in general, they describe the different problems that need to be resolved in detail and propose several

2 U. Schneider/M. Nietsch, "Internationale Rechtsangleichung" in H.-P. Mansel/T. Pfeiffer/H. Kronke/C. Kohler/R. Hausmann (eds.), *Festschrift für Erik Jayme*, Sellier, 2004, pp. 1361–1376 (at 1363).

3 Available at: https://cdn.iccwbo.org/content/uploads/sites/3/2010/01/ICC-Introduction-to-the-Incoterms-2010.pdf.

4 R. Goode/H. Kronke/E. McKendrick/J. Wool, *Transnational Commercial Law*, 2nd edn., Oxford University Press, 2012, p. 175.

5 Available at: https://uncitral.un.org/sites/uncitral.un.org/files/media-documents/uncitral/en/07-86998_ebook.pdf.

6 This approach is expressly mentioned in the explanatory memorandum of the Schiedsverfahrens-Neuregelungsgesetz, Bundestagsdrucksache 13/5274, p. 1. For this reason, the Federal Court of Justice referred to the UNCITRAL model law when interpreting the German rules on arbitration, BGH NJW-RR 2011, pp. 570–571 (at 571).

7 B. Hess, *Harmonized Rules and Minimum Standards in the European Law of Civil Procedure*, European Parliament Publication Office, 2016, p. 8.

8 Available at: https://uncitral.un.org/sites/uncitral.un.org/files/media-documents/uncitral/en/09-82670_ebook-guide_09-04-10english.pdf.

alternative rules. As such, there is no unique model. Recommendations which are designed for national legislators might be classified as the light version of a legislative guide.

The third subcategory comprises all those soft law instruments which are not specifically designed for national legislators or for private actors, but that might be used by legislators, judges and private actors. The UNIDROIT principles of international commercial contracts[9] are construed in this sense. Best practices guides might be classified within this subcategory, as well. In the legal context, they lay down recommendations with the objective of ensuring the uniform and efficient application of harmonised rules.[10]

In the area of procedural law, one category of soft law is obviously not a suitable tool for harmonising the national systems: soft law designed for private actors. This type of soft law can only have positive effects if the area of law that is concerned is based on the principle of party autonomy, so that the private actors are in a position to choose the soft law rules. However, party autonomy is not sufficiently recognised in the field of state court proceedings.[11] This leads to the second section: An overview of the harmonising instruments that have already been used at the European level in the area of civil procedure.

2. THE EUROPEAN EXPERIENCE

At the EU level, the most effective instrument for harmonising law is the regulation. For harmonising procedural law, this instrument is, however, very limited. The European legislator only has competence to adopt regulations for disputes with cross-border implications.[12] Procedural rules for purely national cases do not fall within the competence of the European legislator.[13] Certainly, it might be discussed how purely national cases should be defined and how they can be distinguished from cases with cross-border implications. Does, for example, the theoretical possibility of cross-border enforcement

---

9 Available at: https://www.unidroit.org/english/principles/contracts/principles2016/principles2016-e.pdf.

10 Cf., for example, the Recommendations to assist arbitral institutions and other interested bodies with regard to arbitration under the UNCITRAL Arbitration Rules, available at: https://uncitral.un.org/en/texts/arbitration/explanatorytexts/recommendations/arbitral_institutions_2010.

11 R. Fentiman, *Foreign Law in English Courts: Pleading, Proof and Choice of Law*, Clarendon Press, 1998, p. 29; C. Chainais/F. Ferrand/L. Mayer/S. Guinchard, *Procédure civile*, Dalloz, 2018, n° 60; H. Schack, *Internationales Zivilverfahrensrecht*, C.H. Beck, 2017, n° 57.

12 Cf. Art. 81 TFEU.

13 B. Hess, *Europäisches Zivilprozessrecht*, C.F. Müller, 2010, §2 n° 11 (concerning Art. 65 Treaty of Rome, which did not undergo substantial change in this respect when becoming Art. 81 in the Treaty of Amsterdam).

indicate the transnational character of the entire proceedings?[14] But independently from the precise criterion, there is a distinction to be made between purely national cases and cases with cross-border implications, which makes it impossible to harmonise the entire procedural law on a horizontal level by regulations. In any case, at present, there seems to be no political consensus for such a project.

However, regulations establishing a comprehensive set of procedural rules for specific proceedings, such as the regulation establishing a European small claims procedure, might develop the character of a model law for the purely national level, if the content is sufficiently convincing. Unfortunately, this is very doubtful for the European small claims procedure, which covers disputes up to €5,000 and which obliges the defendant to conduct the proceedings in writing even if the defendant prefers an oral hearing.[15]

In 2017, the European Parliament pursued a more comprehensive approach by proposing the so-called Minimum Standards Directive.[16] The direct field of application would also be limited to cross-border cases;[17] but it would concern any type of procedure. A directive seems indeed to be the perfect instrument for setting out minimum standards, as it leaves the Member States the flexibility to implement higher standards of procedural fairness and efficiency. The question, however, is how we measure whether a rule implements a higher degree of procedural fairness or maybe a lower degree. In the case of directives aimed at consumer protection, it is clear that a rule providing for more consumer protection guarantees a higher standard. However, in the case of procedural fairness, the interests of the two parties have to be balanced. The text of the proposed directive for minimum standards of civil procedure accordingly mentions the possibility for the Member States to adopt standards which are more favourable for the litigants.[18] At first glance, this sounds convincing; it is, however, obvious that there are many procedural rules that are only favourable to one of the parties, either to the claimant or to

---

14 For such an idea, see the reform process of the European Small Claims procedure, especially the European Commission's Proposal for a Regulation of the European Parliament and of the Council amending Regulation (EC) No. 861/2007 of the European Parliament and of the Council of 11 July 2007 establishing a European Small Claims Procedure, and Regulation (EC) No. 1896/2006 of the European Parliament and of the Council of 12 December 2006 creating a European order for payment procedure, COM(2013) 794 final, p. 6.

15 S. Huber, "Die Reform des europäischen Verfahrens für geringfügige Forderungen", *Recht der internationalen Wirtschaft* (*RIW*) 2018, 625–631 (628).

16 European Parliament resolution of July 2017 with recommendations to the Commission on common minimum standards of civil procedure in the European Union (2015/2084(INL)), P8_TA(2017)0282 (Art. 7); cf. the contribution of Fernando Gascón Inchausti in this volume, Chapter 4.

17 Cf. Arts. 2 and 3 of the proposed directive.

18 Cf. Art. 2 of the proposed directive.

the defendant. This is, for example, true for rules limiting the claimant's right to modify its claim unilaterally. A higher protection of the defendant's rights weakens the claimant's right to effective proceedings. As such, it is difficult to say that procedural rules are more favourable "for the litigants".

In addition to regulations and directives, there are recommendations.[19] In 2013, the Commission adopted the collective redress recommendation.[20] Here, the Commission formulated guidelines for national legislators in order to promote civil proceedings where an individual action is of no interest. The success of this, however, has been quite limited. The recommendation has no binding effect,[21] and the Member States did not really implement the recommendations. Some Member States, such as Austria, have not adopted any instrument of collective redress at all.[22] Other Member States that have adopted such instruments have deviated from the recommendation in fundamental aspects: the Netherlands, for example, has adopted an instrument of collective redress on the basis of an opt-out mechanism,[23] although the Commission's recommendation clearly recommends an opt-in mechanism.[24] As the success has been quite limited, the European legislator is currently discussing the project of a binding directive establishing an instrument of collective redress.[25]

Since 2011, there is a new actor on the European scene: the European Law Institute.[26] This independent organisation is currently carrying out a project

---

19 Cf. Art. 288(1) TFEU.

20 Commission Recommendation of 11 June 2013 on common principles for injunctive and compensatory collective redress mechanisms in the Member States concerning violations of rights granted under Union Law (2013/396/EU).

21 Following the distinction described above, recommendations are to be categorised as soft law, due to their non-binding character, cf. Art. 288 (4) TFEU.

22 As there are no specific legal instruments based on the idea of collective redress, the practice uses general instruments, such as the assignment of claims or joinder of cases, in order to bundle several claims; cf. the Report from the Commission to the European Parliament, the Council and the European Economic and Social Committee on the implementation of the Commission Recommendation of June 2013 on common principles for injunctive and compensatory collective redress mechanisms in the Member States concerning violations of rights granted under Union law (2013/396/EU), COM(2018) 40 final, of 25.1.2018, p. 3.

23 C. Hodges/S. Voet (eds.), *Delivering Collective Redress: New Technologies*, Hart Publishing, 2018, p. 125 et seq.

24 Cf. n° 21 of the Commission Recommendation mentioned above in n. 20; Portugal also applies an "opt-out" principle; C. Hodges/S. Voet (eds.), *Delivering Collective Redress: New Technologies*, Hart Publishing, 2018, p. 13.

25 European Commission's Proposal for a Directive of the European Parliament and of the Council on representative actions for the protection of the collective interests of consumers, and repealing Directive 2009/22/EC, COM(2018) 184 final; see as well the Report on the proposal by the European Parliament of 7.12.2018, A8-0447/2018.

26 For more information, see the homepage of the ELI, available at: https://www.europeanlawinstitute.eu/.

called "From Transnational Principles to European Rules of Civil Procedure".[27] This soft law project is also referred to in the Parliament's recommendation to adopt a directive on minimum standards of civil procedure.[28] The advantage of the European Law Institute is its independence from the legislative procedure within the European Union. The model rules can be elaborated by working groups that are composed of experts (cf. the contributions of *Elisabetta Silvestri*, *Michael Stürner* and *Christoph A. Kern* in this volume (Chapters 9, 10 and 11 respectively).

A new instrument for harmonising procedural standards is the European survey of the national legal systems. This survey not only analyses the status quo, but it also formulates recommendations on how Member States could act in order to improve their national systems.[29]

3. INSTRUMENTS FOR FUTURE CHALLENGES

The question is: Which instruments might be suitable for future challenges? Talking about future challenges, a distinction should be made between law-making on the one hand and applying existing legal rules on the other. Currently, it seems convincing to put an emphasis on the application of the European rules of civil procedure that have already been adopted.[30] Certain specific instruments are not even known by those for whom the instruments have been designed. This is, for example, the case of the regulation establishing a European small claims procedure.[31] It is interesting to see that

27 In cooperation with UNIDROIT, more information available at: https://www.europeanlawinstitute.eu/projects-publications/current-projects-feasibility-studies-and-other-activities/current-projects/civil-procedure/.

28 European Parliament resolution of July 2017 with recommendations to the Commission on common minimum standards of civil procedure in the European Union (2015/2084(INL)), P8_TA(2017)0282, p. 1.

29 Cf. the EU justice scoreboard at: https://ec.europa.eu/info/policies/justice-and-fundamental-rights/effective-justice/eu-justice-scoreboard_en; for a critical analysis, see A. Dori, *The EU Justice Scoreboard – Judicial Evaluation as a new Governance Tool*, MPI Luxembourg Working Paper 2 (2015); C. Kern, "Statistical Methods in Comparative Civil Procedure – Chances and Risks" in L. Cadiet/B. Hess/M. Requejo Isidro (eds.), *Approaches to Procedural Law*, Studies of the Max Planck Institute Luxembourg for International, European and Regulatory Procedural Law Vol. 9, Nomos, 2017, pp. 121–143.

30 Cf. J. Basedow, "Kohärenz im Internationalen Privat- und Verfahrensrecht der Europäischen Union – Eine einleitende Orientierung" in J. von Hein/G. Rühl (eds.), *Kohärenz im internationalen Privat- und Verfahrensrecht der Europäischen Union*, Mohr Siebeck, 2016, pp. 3–23 (23).

31 Regulation (EU) 2015/2421 of the European Parliament and of the Council of 16 December 2015 amending Regulation (EC) No 861/2007 establishing a European Small Claims Procedure, and Regulation (EC) No 1896/2006 creating a European order for payment procedure; cf. the observation of D. Einhaus, "Die revidierte EuGFVO im System des europäischen Zivilverfahrensrechts", *RIW* 2018, pp. 631–634.

the European legislator has adopted a reform of this instrument in order to promote its application and that, by this reform, the European legislator has created new obligations for the Member States in order to ensure that the citizens are informed about the instrument.[32] In addition, the European legislator has strengthened the duties of the Member States to assist the citizens who would like to bring a claim under this regulation. In so doing, the European legislator has integrated best practice rules in a regulation, a promising way to ensure the effective application of regulations. Another general area where best practice instruments could be helpful concerns the use of electronic devices in the context of civil proceedings. As instruments of binding character don't seem to be suitable for these questions, which depend on the objective possibilities in the different Member States, a recommendation might be the best instrument.

As far as law-making is concerned, the *acquis* should be an important cornerstone. The European legislator should adopt a general regulation comprising all those rules of civil procedure that are relevant for more than one existing instrument.[33] This would make the *acquis* more coherent and more visible. In such a form, the existing procedural rules might really gain the character of model rules for reforms at the national level.

If the objective is more ambitious in the sense of horizontal comprehensive harmonisation, a soft law instrument adopted by an independent organisation seems to be the only possible way. Soft law instruments might be very successful if national legislators feel the need for reforms to cope with new situations. Currently, we can observe a real competition between certain Member States in order to attract transnational cases.[34] Dispute resolution, not only by arbitral courts, but also by state courts, has evolved into an interesting market. In this context, soft law instruments, such as model rules, might be used as orientation in order to modernise the judiciary system. All this shows that the circumstances for successful soft law instruments in the field of civil procedure might be quite good at present.

---

[32] Cf. Art. 11 of Regulation (EU) 2015/2421 (cf. note 20) and its recital (20). Nevertheless sceptical about the use of the small claims procedure in the future C. Hodges/S. Voet (eds.) *Delivering Collective Redress: New Technologies*, Hart Publishing, 2018, p. 19.

[33] B. Hess, *Europäisches Zivilprozessrecht*, C.F. Müller, 2010, §13 n° 3.

[34] Cf. the brochures of Germany and England emphasising the benefits of their national legal systems. The brochures are available at: https://www.lawmadeingermany.de/Law-Made_in_Germany_EN.pdf (D); https://www.eversheds-sutherland.com/documents/LawSocietyEnglandAndWalesJurisdictionOfChoice.pdf (GB); cf. also the brochure "Continental law", published by a French-German initiative, at: https://www.drb.de/fileadmin/DRB/pdf/Buendnis_deutsche_Recht/Broschuere_Kontinentales_Recht.pdf.

PROCEDURAL HARMONISATION BY THE EUROPEAN COURT OF JUSTICE

Procedural Autonomy and the Member States' Perspective

Stephanie LAW and Janek T. NOWAK

1. INTRODUCTION

The interrelation of national and European civil procedure can be examined from various perspectives. On the one hand, one might assess the emergence of a body of European civil procedural rules. The law of European civil procedure has recently celebrated its half century, 50 years having passed since the Brussels Convention of 1968 was signed. This field of law has been propelled forward with various legislative endeavours, supplemented by the case law of the European Court of Justice (ECJ), and perhaps most significantly, the entry into force of the Treaty of Amsterdam in 1999, which brought with it the aim of establishing an Area of Freedom, Security and Justice (AFSJ) encompassing a "genuine European area of justice" through judicial cooperation in civil matters.[1] On the other hand, one might instead examine the impact of European Union (EU) law on national civil procedure. The debate on the influence of substantive EU law on national civil procedure has emerged only more recently. Nevertheless, it has been at the forefront of political and academic debates in European civil procedure for at least 20 years.

This chapter focuses on the latter, namely on the influence of EU substantive law on national civil procedure. Other contributions to this edited collection focus on the role of the Union legislative institutions in this field as regards *inter alia*, the development of a framework of specific regulations providing for EU-wide procedures, for the core of cross-border civil procedure (that is, jurisdiction and applicable law, amongst other concerns[2]) and the procedural rules applicable in sector-specific, vertical fields. This chapter does not examine those areas in which the EU has made either soft or hard law regarding national or European procedural rules. Rather, it analyses the grey areas in which the Member States remain competent to maintain and apply their own rules of national civil procedure but where this body of domestic law might be influenced by the application of rules found in EU substantive legislation.

Various authors have indicated in this regard that the case law of the ECJ on national procedural law, in particular in the context of national procedural autonomy, may lead to the harmonisation of national procedural law.[3]

---

1 European Council, "Presidency Conclusions – Tampere", 15–16 October 1999.

2 For a brief overview, see B. Hess, "Procedural Harmonisation in a European Context" in X.E. Kramer and C.H. Rhee (eds.), *Civil Litigation in a Globalising World* (Springer, 2012), pp. 159–173, pp. 161–168, and for an overview of the constitutional dimensions underpinning, see S. Prechal, "The European *acquis* of Civil Procedure: Constitutional Aspects" (2014) 19 *Uniform Law Review* 179. See also, the contribution of V. Richard in this volume.

3 See, for example, J.H. Jans, "Harmonization of national procedural law via the back door? Preliminary comments on the ECJ's judgment in Janecek in a comparative context" in M. Bulterman, L. Hancher, A. McDonnell and H. Sevenster (eds.), *Views of European law from the mountain: Liber amicorum Piet Jan Slot* (Kluwer Law International, 2009), p. 267, at p. 275; M. Tulibacka, "Europeanization of civil procedures: in search of a

It may, then, not come as a surprise that the case law of the ECJ on national procedural law is part and parcel of this volume on procedural harmonisation in the European Union. In examining the role of the ECJ in the harmonisation of civil procedure in the EU, this chapter aims to provide an analysis that stems from both the top down, that is, from the perspective of the ECJ's role (on the one hand, the ECJ's interpretation of substantive rules, and on the other, its determination as to whether those rules generate limits to national procedural autonomy), and from the bottom up, that is, the impact of the ECJ's case law on the national procedural cultures.

Adopting a critical analysis of the framework of the "procedural autonomy of the Member States" versus the "principles of equivalence and effectiveness as limitations to procedural autonomy", we engage in an assessment of these contested concepts, the evolution of the ECJ's case law and its impact on the national systems of civil procedure. To this end, we unpack the notion of procedural autonomy, assess the principles of effectiveness and equivalence identified by the ECJ as limits to procedural autonomy, and take a closer look at the concrete functioning of these principles in the legal orders of the Member States. In drawing some conclusions, we will also comment on the limitations of case law that aims to systematise in this field, and the political dimensions underpinning the ECJ's endeavours.

2. EU LAW RIGHTS AND NATIONAL REMEDIES: THE LEGAL AND POLITICAL CONTEXT

The procedural autonomy of the Member States is a difficult and contested concept; its content and limitations have been challenged and its very existence has even been called into question.[4] On one reading, it is advanced that the Member States are procedurally autonomous and it is this autonomy that precludes the EU legislature from enacting legislation dealing with the same procedural aspects. On another, national procedural autonomy does not exist as autonomy as such. On another still, Member States are not autonomous but rather retain procedural competences. And on yet another,

coherent approach", (2009) 46 *C.M.L. Rev.* 1527, 1535–1540; W. Van Gerven, "Bridging the gap between Community and national laws: Towards a principle of homogeneity in the field of legal remedies?", (1995) 32 *C.M.L. Rev.* 679, 697–698. For an overview of the harmonising effects of the case law of the Court, see M. Dougan, *National Remedies Before the Court of Justice: Issues of Harmonisation and Differentiation* (Hart Publishing, 2004), pp. 227–387.

4 M. Bobek, "Why There Is No Principle of Procedural Autonomy of the Member States" in B. de Witte and H.-W. Micklitz (eds.) *The European Court of Justice and the Autonomy of the Member States* (Intersentia, 2011), pp. 305–324; W. Van Gerven, "Of Rights, Remedies and Procedures" (2000) 37 *C.M.L. Rev.* 501; C.N. Kakouris, "Do the Member States possess Judicial Procedural 'Autonomy'?" (1997) 34 *C.M.L. Rev.* 1389.

the Member States can only be deemed to be procedurally autonomous where the EU has not legislated for procedural rules.

To better understand the concept of procedural autonomy, and the role it plays in shaping the institutional relationship between the EU and the Member States, it is necessary firstly to examine the EU's legislative and political framework. It is submitted that the concept of procedural autonomy is more complex than any of the readings set out above. In order to begin to understand it better, it is necessary to examine first the limited legislative competences of the EU as regards civil procedure as well as the division of labour between the EU and the Member States as to the judicial and administrative institutions by which EU law can be applied and enforced (effectively and uniformly) and the procedural rules applicable.

2.1. THE TREATY FRAMEWORK OF THE EU AND MEMBER STATES' COMPETENCES

The EU is not only a legal but also a political and economic (and increasingly, social and cultural) endeavour. It is neither an international organisation nor a state;[5] it cannot be said, either, to be a fully-fledged federation. It is complex and dynamic, as regards its structure and institutions, its powers, its rules and its relationship with the Member States. The legal competences held by the EU institutions are based on the principle of conferral, that is, on the transfer of powers from the Member States to the EU; these competences might be attributed expressly by the Treaties[6] or implied.[7] This framework gives rise to two sets of related considerations, both of which are relevant to the analysis of procedural autonomy. Firstly, the Union's competences are limited in certain fields including that of civil procedure. The Member States have exhibited a general reluctance to broadly empower the EU in this field, while the Union legislature (as well, initially, as the ECJ) was also reluctant to engage in such an endeavour.[8] Secondly, there is a division of labour as regards,

---

5 A. von Bogdandy, "Neither an International Organization Nor A Nation State: The EU as a Supranational Federation" in E. Jones, A. Menon and S. Weatherill (eds.), *The Oxford Handbook of the European Union* (OUP, 2012), pp. 761–771.

6 See T.C. Hartley, *The Foundations of European Union Law*, 8th edn. (OUP, 2014), pp. 112–113.

7 S. Law, "European Agreement on Road Transport, Commission of the European Communities v Council of the European Communities, 31st March 1971 ([1971] ECR 263), OXIO 310" in J. d'Aspremont, C. Brölmann and I. Scobbie (eds.), *Oxford International Organizations (OXIO)* (OUP, March 2018).

8 M. Dougan, "The Vissicitudes of Life at the Coalface: Remedies and Procedures for Enforcing Union Law Before the National Courts" in P.P. Craig and G. de Búrca (eds.), *The Evolution of EU Law*, 2nd edn. (OUP, 2011), pp. 407–438, p. 435.

on the one hand, the making of EU law and on the other, the institutions and rules applicable to its application and enforcement.

As to the latter consideration, the Treaties neither encompass the powers for the EU to legislate for, nor provide, mechanisms and institutions by which EU law and the rights that individuals derive from EU law can be enforced. This results in a system which is centralised (in terms of law-making by the EU legislature) and decentralised (in terms of the enforcement of such rules) and which is reliant on the Member States and the national institutions to execute what has been legislated by the EU institutions.[9] This decentralisation generates potential challenges where, while there is an EU right, national procedural rules present an obstacle to its enforcement, or where there exists no national remedy by which the right can be enforced. This is examined below in Section 4.3.

As to the former consideration, competence to legislate and enact EU law is a complex issue. As the existence of the EU's competences is largely established in the Treaties, the Treaty structure also shapes their scope and operation. A number of key provisions are identifiable. Fundamentally Article 5 Treaty on the European Union (TEU) dictates that the EU's policy determinations and legislative choices must be made in line with the principles of conferral,[10] proportionality[11] and subsidiarity.[12] It is determined by the express or implied attribution of powers from the Member States to the EU, and the nature of those competences (whether shared between the Member States and the EU or exclusively held by the EU) via the principle of conferral. The Union can act only within the limits of the competences conferred on it by the Member States in the Treaties or on an implied basis. The principle of subsidiarity, which operates where the competence is shared,[13]

[9] A key dimension of Pescatore's understanding of integration: P. Pescatore, *Le droit de l'intégration: Emergence d'un phénomène nouveau dans les relations internationales selon l'expérience des Communautés Européennes* (Bruylant, 2005).

[10] Art. 5(2) TEU provides that the EU is competent to act only within the limits of the competences conferred on it by the Member States in the Treaties for the purpose of achieving particular aims and objectives. In respect of European private law matters, Case C-376/98, *Germany v. Parliament and Council*, EU:C:2002:326, para. 84, which will be discussed further below, is significant. The case highlights that private law directives should aim "to contribute to the proper functioning of the internal market and achieve a high level of consumer protection by approximating laws".

[11] Art. 5(4) TEU establishes that Union action must be proportional; in terms of the principle of proportionality, the ECJ has identified a relatively broad discretion on the part of the Union such that only if the Union action is "manifestly inappropriate" will it be conceived as disproportionate (Case C-344/04, *The Queen, on the application of International Air Transport Association (IATA) and European Low Fares Airline Association (ELFAA) v Department for Transport*, EU:C:2006:10, para. 83).

[12] Art. 5(3) TEU provides that the EU can only act on the basis that regulation at the EU level is more appropriate than at the national level.

[13] The areas of exclusive EU competences are set out in Art. 3 TFEU.

suggests that fundamentally, every competence should be exercised at the most appropriate level.[14] The principles of proportionality and subsidiarity are reflected also in the Article 4(3) TEU[15] principle of sincere cooperation, which provides a Treaty basis for the Member States' obligation to ensure the effective enforcement of EU law. It provides for the duty of the Member States to ensure the full effectiveness (*effet utile*) of EU law, so that the primacy and direct effect of EU law is not undermined. Article 19(1) TEU creates an obligation on Member States as regards the provision of remedies, establishing that the "Member States shall provide remedies sufficient to ensure the effective legal protection in the fields covered by Union law" and ensure sufficient remedies are available when EU rights are violated.[16] Relatedly Article 47 of the Charter of Fundamental Rights (CFREU) aims to promote access to justice, establishing a right to effective judicial protection, via the right to a fair trial and to an effective remedy.

The EU's competence to legislate for primary or secondary law to regulate specific matters is largely dependent on the contours of that particular area of law, again as established via the Treaties. Consumer protection is an area of shared competence.[17] EU law that aims to facilitate consumer protection may be legislated for as measures that promote the interests of consumers, per Article 169 TFEU; in the alternative, consumer protection might be indirectly advanced via Article 114 Treaty on the Functioning of the European Union (TFEU), which allows for the approximation of national laws for the purposes of facilitating the establishment and functioning of the internal market.[18] Consumer legislation may also be introduced within the field of competition law, an area of exclusive competence,[19] to the extent that consumer protection rules are concerned with precluding unfair competition.[20]

To reiterate, this chapter does not aim at examining the areas in which the EU legislature has legislated for procedural rules, including in the field

---

14 This understanding rests to a certain degree on the construction of the EU as a system that is characterised by a variety of federalism (see eg R. Schütze, *From Dual to Cooperative Federalism: The Changing Structure of European Law* (OUP, 2009). The nature of the European legal system is much debated and we will not venture into these debates now.

15 The operation of proportionality and subsidiarity are governed by Protocol (no. 2) of the Lisbon Treaty on the application of the principles of subsidiarity and proportionality.

16 Art. 19(1) TEU provides: "Member States shall provide remedies sufficient to ensure effective legal protection in the fields covered by Union law".

17 Art. 4(2)(f) TFEU.

18 As will be seen below, the Union has a clear preference as to the legitimacy basis engaged; that is to say, most consumer law legislation has been made on the basis of the internal market provision now found in Art. 114 TFEU.

19 Art. 3 (1)(b) TFEU.

20 Generally, the Union is obliged to ensure consistency in its law and policies per Art. 7 TFEU; this is established in particular as regards consumer protection in Art. 12 TFEU. Consumer and competition law and policy is one of the areas in which there is a significant need for consistency.

of cross-border civil procedure. The competence of the EU to legislate for European rules of civil procedure (or procedural rules applicable to cross-border civil or commercial legal relationships) is discussed elsewhere in this collection. Here, it is worth simply noting that the Treaty confers a competence in Article 81 TFEU concerning judicial cooperation in civil matters, by which the "Union shall develop judicial cooperation in civil matters having cross-border implications, based on the principle of mutual recognition of judgments and of decisions in extrajudicial cases" for the development of the Area of Freedom, Security and Justice.[21] The EU's competence in the field of procedural matters is not non-existent, but it is limited, particularly due to the cross-border requirement for the exercise of this power. While EU directives and regulations establishing substantive rights tend not to harmonise national rules of civil procedure, substantive EU legislation may infrequently provide for rules of procedure that ultimately impact national civil procedure.[22] It is in this sphere that the principle of procedural autonomy comes to the fore and in which the ECJ has recognised that national rules of procedure may impact the possibility for individuals to exercise, rely upon and effectively benefit from the rights derived from EU law within their national systems. The EU has no general or overarching power to legislate for procedural rules.[23] In light of the absence of a general competence for the EU institutions and their limited judicial and administrative capabilities, the EU must rely on national enforcement mechanisms (administrative and judicial, public and private) in order to ensure that EU law is observed in a uniform manner across the Member States. The Member States must ensure that this is done not only in line with the Treaty obligations set out above but also in line with the related obligations established by the ECJ;[24] this case law is examined in the following section.

2.2. THE CASE LAW OF THE ECJ: THE JUDICIAL PROTECTION OF EU LAW

The ECJ has jurisdiction (to give preliminary references) as regards the interpretation of the Treaties and the validity and interpretation of the acts

---

21 There is reference to the development of both the internal market and the AFSJ in Art. 3(3) TEU and Art. 3(2) TEU respectively. There is furthermore a link between Art. 19(1) TEU (Member States shall provide remedies to ensure effective judicial protection), Art. 47 CFREU (effective judicial protection), the private enforcement of consumer law and the development by the EU of the AFSJ.

22 See eg, Art. 7, Unfair Contract Terms Directive 93/13/EEC.

23 Its competences are rather limited to the adoption of procedural rules in specific areas of regulation in which the Union does have competence.

24 Predominantly via the preliminary reference procedure in Art. 267 TFEU, which provides a mechanism for communication, if not dialogue, between the national courts and the ECJ as regards the interpretation of Union law.

of the Union's institutions, bodies, offices and agencies.[25] Fundamentally, it has distinguished the EU from other international legal regimes as "its own legal system, which, on the entry into force of the treaty, became an integral part of the legal systems of the Member States".[26] The characterisation of the EU as a new legal order[27] is said to encompass the *sui generis* character of the ECJ itself, and in particular, applies to its interpretative role.[28] The ECJ, in its foundational case law, recognised the principle of the primacy and direct effect[29] of EU law,[30] as well as the notion that individuals, as benefactors of EU law, have rights which they are entitled to enforce.[31] To this end, it has long been recognised that the people of Europe are "interested parties" in the construction of an EU legal order; in *Van Gend en Loos*, the ECJ highlights that the

> Treaty is more than an agreement which merely creates mutual obligations between the Contracting States ... confirmed by the Preamble to the Treaty which refers not only to governments but to peoples ... the nationals of the States brought together in the Community are called upon to cooperate in the functioning of this community through the intermediary of the European Parliament and the Economic and Social Committee.[32]

Individuals enjoy rights as European citizens, expressly conferred by the EU Treaties and via the obligations imposed on individuals, Member States and

25 Art. 267 TFEU.

26 Case C-6/64, *Flaminio Costa v. ENEL*, EU:C:1964:66.

27 Opinion of the Court: *Opinion 1/91 on the Draft Treaty on a European Economic Area* EU:C:1991:490.

28 See A. Stone Sweet, *The Judicial Construction of Europe* (OUP, 2004), and also A. Stone Sweet and M. McCown, "Discretion and Precedent in European Law" in O. Wiklund (ed.), *Judicial Discretion in European Perspective* (Kluwer, 2003), pp. 84–115, p. 92: "the legal system, as it is understood by the actors that use it, is a product of judicial discretion. Most obviously, the Court supplemented Art. 234 with supremacy, direct effect, and related 'constitutional' doctrines".

29 Case C-26/62, *Van Gend en Loos v. Netherlands Inland Revenue Administration*, EU:C:1963:1. Via the principle of direct effect, the ECJ has broadened the body of parties that can become engaged in the legal dimension of integration, extending these participants beyond public institutions to private individuals, companies and other interest groups; L. Azoulai and R. Dehousse, "The ECJ and the Legal Dynamics of Integration" in S. Weatherill *et al* (eds.), *The Oxford Handbook of the European Union* (OUP, 2012), pp. 350–364, p. 356.

30 Positivism shaping Union law – similarly be reflected in the notion of the EU as an independent, functionalist order; as expressed unforgettably in Case C-6/64, *Costa v. ENEL*, EU:C:1964:66, n. 26 above, p. 593; "the EEC Treaty has created its own legal system which, on entry into force of the treaty, became an integral part of the legal systems of the Member States, which their courts are bound to apply ... [as an] independent source of law".

31 Case C-26/62, *Van Gend en Loos*, EU:C:1963:1, n. 29 above, and Case C-6/64, *Costa v. ENEL*, EU:C:1964:66, n. 26 above.

32 Case C-26/62, *Van Gend en Loos*, EU:C:1963:1, n. 29 above, para. 12.

EU institutions by secondary EU law.[33] With this case, the ECJ established that as well as the role of Member States in facilitating the public enforcement of EU law, individuals have a role to play in the private enforcement of those rights,[34] both in relation to the compliance of public authorities with EU law and that of individuals, confirming the vertical and horizontal direct effect of (certain) Union law.

These cases shape the interface between national and EU law, and the positive and negative obligations of national courts and tribunals. Indeed, from the principle of direct effect in *Van Gend en Loos*, the national courts (and administrative organisations[35]) are confined by the operation of the supremacy principle[36] and specifically, the doctrine established in *Simmenthal*[37] whereby EU law must be fully implemented in the national legal systems from its date of entry into force, requiring that national norms conflicting with EU law must be set aside.[38] Moreover, the national courts are limited by the principles set out in *Marleasing*[39] (on the basis of which national law must be interpreted and applied, insofar as possible, so as to avoid a conflict with an EU norm) and *Von Kolson*[40] (which imposes an obligation on the national courts to interpret national law in such a manner that it conforms with EU law).[41] These principles are intended to ensure that individual rights can be enforced and that remedies are available to individuals when they are violated.

Taken together, these principles shape the role and obligations of the national judge. National courts and tribunals are obliged to promote the

33 Case C-26/62, *Van Gend en Loos*, EU:C:1963:1, para. 112.

34 Case C-26/62, *Van Gend en Loos*, EU:C:1963:1, para. 12.

35 Case C-103/88, *Fratelli Costanzo SpA v Comune di Milano*, EU:C:1989:256, paras. 31–33.

36 Case C-6/64, *Costa v. ENEL*, EU:C:1964:66, n. 26 above, p. 594: "It follows from all these observations that the law stemming from the treaty, an independent source of law, could not, because of its special and original nature, be overridden by domestic legal provisions, however framed, without being deprived of its character as community law and without the legal basis of the community itself being called into question".

37 Case C-106/77, *Amministrazione delle Finanze dello Stato v. Simmenthal SpA*, EU:C:1978:49.

38 Per Case C-198/01, *Consorzio Industrie Fiammiferi (CIF) v. Autorità Garante della Concorrenza e del Mercato*, EU:C:2003:430, paras. 49–50. It is irrelevant whether the national authority has the power not to apply the national law which is contrary to EU law; that national authority must not apply that law where it is necessary to ensure EU law's full effect.

39 Case C-106/89, *Marleasing SA v. La Comercial Internacional de Alimentacion SA*, EU:C:1990:395.

40 Case C-14/83, *Sabine Von Colson and Elisabeth Kamann v Land Nordrhein-Westfalen*, EU:C:1984:153.

41 For an overview of the ECJ's case law deriving from Case C-106/77, *Simmenthal*, EU:C:1978:49, n 37 above, on the relationship between the primacy of EU law and national procedural autonomy, see the Opinion of AG Wahl in Case C-378/17, *The Minister for Justice and Equality and Commissioner of the Garda Síochána v. Workplace Relations Commission*, EU:C:2018:698, paras. 45 et seq, a case concerning the compatibility of an Irish law that divides jurisdiction between the High Court and a statutory body.

uniform implementation of Union law[42] in line with national arrangements and the principle of sincere cooperation. National courts must ensure that the rights that individuals derive from EU law can be protected. This might require that national courts must set aside incompatible or conflicting national rules (in so far as the national legislature has not otherwise amended them in implementing Union law[43]), and must be empowered to do so where national rules are incompatible on the basis of the supremacy of EU law, in order to ensure the full scope and effect of Union law.[44] Moreover, the Member States must ensure that remedies are available for individuals in so far as they are not established in Union law. A key example is to be found in *Francovich*, in which the ECJ, engaging systematic reasoning, identified an obligation to repair loss from the need to ensure the full effectiveness of EU law[45] and the rights conferred thereby on individuals[46] (the satisfaction of which the Court considered would otherwise be undermined if individuals could not obtain a remedy). The ECJ case law reinforces the decentralised enforcement framework established by the Treaties; the EU relies or piggybacks on the Member States and their institutions to ensure that individual rights derived from EU law can be enforced in line with the aforementioned principles identified from the Treaties and developed in the ECJ's jurisprudence, to ensure that adequate remedies are available when those rights are violated.[47]

---

42 Alongside the principle of indirect administration which required that "Member States shall adopt all measures of national law necessary to implement legally binding Union acts" per Art. 291(1) TFEU. This is true for directives and regulations; Case C-6/64, *Costa v. ENEL*, EU:C:1964:66, n. 26 above – Union (then Community) law cannot be undermined or overridden by "domestic legal provisions, however framed" (Case C-6/64, *Costa v. ENEL* EU:C:1964:66, para. 594).

43 Case C-106/77, *Simmenthal*, EU:C:1978:49, n. 37 above, para. 24: at paras. 21–22, the ECJ held that "every national court must, in a case within its jurisdiction, apply Community law in its entirety and protect rights which the latter confers on individuals and must accordingly set aside any provision of national law which may conflict with it, whether prior or subsequent to the Community rule". The national courts should not apply conflicting provisions.

44 Case C-213/89, *The Queen v Secretary of State for Transport, ex parte Factortame Ltd and others*, EU:C:1990:257, para. 20: "The Court has also held that any provision of a national legal system and any legislative, administrative or judicial practice which might impair the effectiveness of Community law by withholding from the national court having jurisdiction to apply such law the power to do everything necessary at the moment of its application to set aside national legislative provisions which might prevent, even temporarily, Community rules from having full force and effect are incompatible with those requirements, which are the very essence of Community law (judgment of 9 March 1978 in Simmenthal, cited above, paragraphs 22 and 23".

45 Case C-106/77, *Simmenthal*, EU:C:1978:49, n. 37 above. See now, Art. 19(1) TFEU, which provides that "Member States shall provide remedies sufficient to ensure effective legal protection in the fields covered by Union law".

46 Case C-26/62, *Van Gend en Loos*, EU:C:1963:1, n. 29 above, and Case C-6/64, *Costa v. ENEL* EU:C:1964:66, n. 26 above.

47 Primarily via Art. 19(1) TFEU and the cases of Case C-213/89, *Factortame*, EU:C:1990:257, n. 44 above, and Joined Cases C-6/90–C-9/90, *Andrea Francovich and Danila Bonifaci and others v. Italian Republic*, EU:C:1991:428.

3. UNPACKING PROCEDURAL AUTONOMY: LEGISLATIVE AND JUDICIAL PRACTICES

The meaning, scope and even existence of the concept of national procedural autonomy have long been contested. The concept of autonomy is in itself disputed and difficult, and arises in a vast breadth of fields of thought, with divergent iterations in moral, social and political philosophy. Broadly, it has been conceived of as concerning a capacity for self-governance or determination, that is, governing by one's own laws.[48] While there is a fruitful analysis to be undertaken on the relationship between autonomy broadly,[49] the interrelations of the EU and the Member States as regards the character of the EU order generally, and procedural autonomy as a pertinent reflection of this characterisation, as well the strengthening of the democratic legitimacy of the Union, such a discussion extends far beyond this chapter. For the moment, it is necessary to recognise only broadly that the way in which we conceive of and understand the relationship between the EU and the Member States - particularly as regards issues that relate to the competences of each, including that of procedural autonomy - is also shaped by our way in which we conceive of the autonomy of each legal order.[50] Moreover, the discussion of procedural autonomy is also one that brings the question of the democratic legitimacy of the Union institutions to the fore.

In the following paragraphs, the key component parts of the concept, as identified by the ECJ, will be examined. It is worth noting that an iteration of the principle of procedural autonomy was first identifiable in the 1968 case of *Lück*,[51] concerning (then) Article 95 EEC which required certain conduct on the part of the Member States but did not establish the specific rules

[48] See, amongst others, J. Feinberg, "Autonomy" in J. Christman (ed.), *The Inner Citadel: Essays on Individual Autonomy* (OUP, 1989), pp. 27–53.

[49] J. Cohen, "Deliberation and Democratic Legitimacy" in J. Bohman and W. Rehg (eds.), *Deliberative Democracy* (MIT Press, 2002), pp. 67–92.

[50] For a brief overview, and an indication of some relevant readings, see also J. Dickson and P. Eleftheriadis, "Introduction: The Puzzles of European Union Law" in J. Dickson and P. Eleftheriadis (eds.), *Philosophical Foundations of European Union Law* (OUP, 2012), pp. 1–22, the contributions in the edited volume and pp. 10–12 on the discussion of democracy especially. See further M. Avbelj, "National Procedural Autonomy: Concept, Practice and Theoretical Queries" in A. Lazowski and S. Blockmans (eds.), *Research Handbook on EU Institutional Law* (Elgar, 2016), pp. 421–440, pp. 435–440.

[51] Case 34/67, *Lück v. Hauptzollamt Köln-Rheinau*, EU:C:1968:24, p. 251: "Although Article 95 of the Treaty has the effect of excluding the application of any national measure incompatible with it, the Article does not restrict the powers of the competent national courts to apply, from among the various procedures available under national law, those which are appropriate for the purpose of protecting the individual rights conferred by Community law".

that should apply in the place of national law.[52] The typical iteration of the principle of procedural autonomy, however, is that found in the ECJ's 1976 case of *Rewe-Zentralfinanz*:

> In the absence of Community rules on this subject, it is for the domestic legal system of each Member State to designate the courts having jurisdiction and to determine the procedural conditions governing actions at law intended to ensure the protection of the rights which citizens have from the direct effect of Community law.[53]

The ECJ has also identified limitations to this notion of autonomy; these national rules must not undermine the principles of the effectiveness and equivalence of EU law, discussed further below. Thus, four "bricks" have been identified by the ECJ since the 1960s: 1) for the Member States to identify relevant institutions, procedures and remedies; 2) in the absence of EU procedural rules; 3) governing actions intended to ensure the protection of citizens' rights; and 4) as derived from the direct effect of EU law.

In its early case law, the ECJ held that the determination of how EU rights should be protected and how a violation of those rights should be dealt with is for the national legal systems.[54] In the 1971 case of *International Fruit Company*, reiterated and affirmed in later case law, the ECJ established that where EU primary law requires that certain measures are taken by a Member State, it is for that state to determine the national institutions that are empowered to take such measures:

> Under Article [4(3) TEU – sincere cooperation] the Member States are obliged to take all appropriate measures … to ensure fulfilment of the [Treaty] obligations, it is for them to determine which institutions within the national system shall be empowered to adopt the said measures.[55]

In this case, the ECJ did not refer to an absence of EU rules setting out the relevant procedural conditions. Rather, the ECJ's express reference to an absence of EU procedural rules was rather made in the 1976 cases of *Rewe* and *Comet*, the judgments in which were both rendered on 16 December 1976. In each judgment, the ECJ set out a classic statement, which has come to be known

---

52 It originally emerged as a scholarly concept explaining the character of the (now) Union regime and its relationship with the national legal systems – J. Rideau, "Le rôle des États membres dans l'application du droit communautaire" (1972) 18 *Annuaire Français de Droit International* 864–903.

53 Case C-33/76, *Rewe-Zentralfinanz eG and Rewe-Zentral AG v. Landwirtschaftskammer für das Saarland*, EU:C:1976:188, para. 5.

54 Case C-6/60, *Jean E. Humblet v. Belgian State*, EU:C:1960:48.

55 Joined Cases C-51/71–54/71, *International Fruit Company, NV and others v. Produktschap voor groenten en fruit*, EU:C:1971:128, para. 3.

as the principle of the procedural autonomy of the Member States.[56] The ECJ provided that

> in the absence of Community rules on this subject, it is for the domestic legal system of each Member State to designate the courts having jurisdiction and to determine the procedural conditions governing actions at law intended to ensure the protection of the rights which citizens have from the direct effect of Community law, it being understood that such conditions cannot be less favourable than those relating to similar actions of a domestic nature.[57]

The principle of procedural autonomy operates only where the EU legislature has not promulgated EU procedural rules; when it comes into play, it shapes the legislative and judicial framework that regulates the relationship between the EU and national institutions. Given the decentralised enforcement system and the division of labour that exists, the national institutions – usually, ultimately, courts in the context of private enforcement – are necessarily the key and primary enforcers of EU law and are tasked with ensuring its full *effet utile*. In order to do this, these national institutions are obliged to utilise national rules and mechanisms of procedure; given the lack of EU provisions, there is no choice. However, to the extent that these rules or mechanisms undermine the principles of the effectiveness or equivalence of EU law, they must not be applied but rather amended in line with states' obligations in the application of EU law.[58] The principle of procedural autonomy is not a political concept but one which guides the identification of the obligations of the Member States to apply national law in the absence of EU law provisions.

It is worth noting that the wording of the ECJ seems to have changed in its recent case law. While previously, it has made reference to the notion that the procedural rules of the Member States should apply in order to "ensure the protection of the rights which citizens have from the direct effect of [Community] law", in the 2018 judgments of *Aquino*[59] and

56 Case C-201/02, *The Queen, on the application of Delena Wells v. Secretary of State for Transport, Local Government and the Regions*, EU:C:2004:12, para. 67.

57 Case C-33/76, *Rewe*, EU:C:1976:188, n. 53 above, para. 5; Case C-45/76, *Comet*, EU:C:1976:191, para. 13.

58 The principle of supremacy of EU law dictates that the entry into force of EU law automatically renders any incompatible rule of national law inapplicable; Case C-106/77, *Simmenthal*, EU:C:1978:49, n. 37 above, paras. 17 *et seq.*

59 Case C-3/16, *Lucio Cesare Aquino Lucio Cesare Aquino v. Belgische Staat*, EU:C:2017:209, para. 48: "It should be recalled here that, according to settled case-law of the Court, in the absence of EU rules on the matter, it is for the national legal order of each Member State to establish procedural rules for actions intended to safeguard the rights of individuals, in accordance with the principle of procedural autonomy on condition, however, that those rules are not less favourable than those governing similar domestic situations (principle of equivalence) and that they do not make it excessively difficult or impossible in practice to exercise the rights conferred by EU law (principle of effectiveness)".

Karel de Grote,[60] the ECJ no longer makes reference to the notion of direct effect. The reference to the doctrine of direct effect is significant for a number of reasons. The principle of direct effect (as well as the supremacy of EU law) shapes the concept of national procedural autonomy; where the EU has legislated for procedural rules, it is these principles that necessitate their applicability in the national legal systems. The principle of direct effect also provides the basis on which individuals, as citizens of the Union, can rely on the rights they derive from EU law before the courts of the Member States in line with the principle of sincere cooperation, either against the state or against an individual.[61] Together, as noted above, these principles are foundational to the development of the Union legal order, shaping the relationship between the Union and national institutions, and the furtherance of integration on the one hand, and the preservation of national sovereignty on the other. Where reference is no longer made to direct effect in the context of a determination concerning limitations to national procedural autonomy, it indicates – per Cadiet[62] – that the basis upon which the protection of rights that individuals derive from EU law is made, is extended beyond the direct effect of EU law. While it cannot be discounted that the lack of reference to direct effect in these recent cases is simply an inconsistency on the part of the ECJ and not a choice, as such, it must be considered that this goes to the heart of the construction of the Union legal order, and relationship between it and the Member States.

The term "procedural autonomy" was only used explicitly for the first time in the 1990s by an Advocate General (AG), and then subsequently in the 2000s in a judgment of the ECJ.[63] It emerged rather as a scholarly concept, from a 1972 article by Rideau.[64] The ECJ continues to engage different

---

60 Case C-147/16, *Karel de Grote – Hogeschool Katholieke Hogeschool Antwerpen VZW v Susan Romy Jozef Kuijpers*, EU:C:2018:320, para. 33: "In the absence of EU legislation, the procedural rules governing appeal proceedings for safeguarding the rights that individuals derive from EU law fall within the internal legal order of the Member States by virtue of the principle of procedural autonomy of those Member States. However, those rules must not be less favourable than those governing similar domestic actions (principle of equivalence); nor may they be framed in such a way as to make it in practice impossible or excessively difficult to exercise the rights conferred by EU law (principle of effectiveness) (see, by analogy, the judgment of 30 May 2013, *Asbeek Brusse and de Man Garabito*, C-488/11, EU:C:2013:341, [n. 90 below] paragraph 42 and the case-law cited)".

61 Joined Cases C-430/93 and C-431/93, *Jeroen van Schijndel and Johannes Nicolaas Cornelis van Veen v. Stichting Pensioenfonds voor Fysiotherapeuten*, EU:C:1995:441, paras. 13–14.

62 L. Cadiet, "L'autonomie procédurale dans la jurisprudence de la Cour de justice de l'Union européenne: Réflexions naïves d'un Huron au Palais du Kirchberg", presentation given at the conference celebrating the 50th Anniversary of the European Law of Civil Procedure, 27 and 28 September 2018, Court of Justice of the European Union.

63 Case C-201/02, *Wells*, EU:C:2004:12, n. 56 above, para. 67.

64 J. Rideau, "Le rôle des États membres dans l'application du droit communautaire" (1972) 18 *Annuaire Français de Droit International*, pp. 864–903.

wordings, albeit in line with the settled case law of the Court; it refers at once to the procedural autonomy of the Member States[65] and to the principle of the procedural autonomy of the Member States.[66] The principle of procedural autonomy might therefore largely understood to mean that in the absence of harmonised EU rules of procedure, substantive EU rules and the rights deriving therefrom must be enforced in the national legal systems in line with national procedures and remedies.

There is a lack of agreement on the most appropriate term for the role of the Member States in civil procedure. The ECJ and many scholars use the term "procedural autonomy". However, the notion of autonomy is a complex one. Two perspectives might be adopted. On the one hand, when the concept is phrased as above it is possible to see why the notion of autonomy, as such, is difficult to grasp. There is no sense of autonomy or freedom per se, given that the absence of EU activity is a prerequisite. This would suggest that the term procedural competence is rather more appropriate. It is not clear that what the Member States possess is really autonomy. It has been suggested that the term "procedural competence" or "procedural primacy" are more appropriate.[67] On the other hand, one might assess the concept of procedural autonomy from the perspective that it constitutes a right on the part of the Member States to identify the pertinent institutions and procedural rules to be used and applied to enforce rights derived from EU law. Where the competence is rather understood as a right on the part of the Member States, deriving from the competences reserved, it is more conceivable to refer to the notion of autonomy. To this end, the autonomy of the Member States is the starting point, and the above-mentioned component parts constitute limitations to it.

3.1. LIMITATIONS ON PROCEDURAL AUTONOMY

As explained above, the principle of procedural autonomy only comes into play when the EU legislature has not legislated for rules of procedure. As noted above, there are limited fields in which the EU has competence and in which the EU legislature has adopted measures which aim to harmonise national rules of civil procedure, due to the contours of Article 81 TFEU which requires the existence of a cross-border dimension. The first limitation must therefore be understood to be a legislative one. Beyond measures adopted as private

65 Case C-246/17, *Ibrahima Diallo v. État belge*, EU:C:2018:499.

66 Case C-572/16, *INEOS Köln GmbH v. Bundesrepublik Deutschland*, EU:C:2018:100.

67 See amongst others, D.-U. Galetta, *Procedural Autonomy of EU Member States: Paradise Lost? A Study on the "Functionalized Procedural Competence" of EU Member States* (Springer, 2010).

international law instruments, relevant areas (of civil procedure)[68] in which measures that aim to harmonise national civil procedural rules are adopted might rather be limited to European regulations on Europe-wide instruments,[69] sector-specific instruments, discussed elsewhere in this volume, or provisions included in substantive secondary law, which have eventually come to be understood – through ECJ case law – as influencing national rules of civil procedure.[70] Herein, the focus shifts to the limitations identified by the ECJ in its considerable, yet largely incoherent, case law.

Prima facie, the scope for procedural autonomy is potentially wide, given that the EU's competences in the field of civil procedure, and particularly national civil procedure, are limited. When the principle of procedural autonomy does come into play, the application of national procedural rules is subject to two limitations, namely those of equivalence and effectiveness. These limitations operate to ensure that the Member States' obligations can be honoured in their implementation and application of EU law and are not undermined by national procedure. Again, the ECJ set these limitations out in the *Rewe* case, where it held that the national rules and procedures applicable to actions brought on the basis of a right derived from EU law, or "conditions cannot be less favourable than those relating to similar actions of a domestic nature" or "impossible in practice to exercise the rights which national courts are obliged to protect".[71]

The requirements of equivalence and effectiveness have been developed and refined over the last 40 years by the ECJ, and identified as general principles of Union law.[72] Alongside the principle of effective judicial protection, it is suggested that the application of these principles no longer simply constitutes an application of a minimum set of criteria as regards national procedural rules; rather the application of these principles has come to constitute a mechanism for judicial review. That is to say, together with the preliminary reference procedure, which provides the basis of the ECJ's interpretative jurisdiction, these limitations afford the ECJ an opportunity to review national procedural rules and mechanisms, including available remedies. The ECJ is essentially engaged in a review process where the EU system must rely on the Member States to apply and enforce rights deriving from EU law.

---

68 Not to speak, e.g., of criminal procedure.

69 E.g. Regulation 1896/2006 creating a European Order for Payment Procedure, OJ 2006 L 399/1 and Regulation 2015/2421 establishing a European Small Claims Procedure, OJ L 341/1.

70 E.g. Arts. 6 and 7 of the Directive 1993/13/EC on Unfair Contract Terms in Consumer Contracts.

71 Case C-33/76, *Rewe*, EU:C:1976:188, n. 53 above, para. 5.

72 Case C-261/95, *Rosalba Palmisani v. Istituto nazionale della previdenza sociale (INPS)*, EU:C:1995:351 – recognised as general principles of community law and confirmed as such in a number of cases (eg Case C-147/16, *Karel de Grote*, EU:C:2018:320, n. 60 above, and Case C-518/17, *Stefan Rudigier*, EU:C:2018:757).

The notion that the principles of equivalence and effectiveness are applied as a two-step test to limit the principle of procedural autonomy is dominant in the literature. The ECJ's reasoning has previously adopted this approach, beginning with an assessment of equivalence and followed by effectiveness, where there is no issue of discrimination between national and EU actions. Increasingly however, the ECJ jumps directly to assess the principle of effectiveness without examining the principle of equivalence. If the assessment of these principles is made in a two-stage process, effectiveness is understood to be part of equivalence. In the latter approach, effectiveness is understood instead to be a self-standing principle.[73] Even where the ECJ does refer to both principles, it tends only to make a passing reference to equivalence. Where the reference only amounts to a passing reference, the ECJ's scope of review is expanded; that is to say, the national rules of procedure can be either incompatible with the principle of equivalence or that of effectiveness. There is no requirement of incompatibility with both principles but merely with one.

3.2. NON-DISCRIMINATION: THE PRINCIPLE OF EQUIVALENCE

The principle of equivalence derives from the principle of non-discrimination; in the context of procedural law, this necessitates the equality of claims in national and EU law,[74] which requires that Member States ensure that EU law is applied in a way that avoids unequal treatment or discrimination between economic actors. That is to say, EU rights should not be treated less favourably than rights deriving from national law; the actions and procedural conditions available as regards the protection of national rights should also be available to ensure the protection of rights deriving from EU law. The equivalence principle does not, however, require that the "Member States … extend their most favourable rules to all actions brought in a certain field of law",[75] nor does it dictate the content of national procedural rules or practice. Recently AG Wahl – who has adopted a rather strict approach as regards the amendment of national procedural rules for EU consumer

[73] M. Bobek, "Why There Is No Principle of Procedural Autonomy of the Member States" in B. de Witte and H.-W. Micklitz (eds.), *The European Court of Justice and the Autonomy of the Member States* (Intersentia, 2011), pp. 305–324, p. 312.

[74] Case C-94/71, *Schlüter & Maack v. Hauptzollamt Hamburg-Jonas*, EU:C:1972:45, paras. 10–11.

[75] Case C-118/08, *Transportes Urbanos y Servicios Generales SAL v Administración del Estado*, EU:C:2010:39, para. 34.

protection aims – has described the equivalence principle as applying in the following way:

> the national rule at issue must be applied without distinction, that is, in the same way irrespective of whether the action is based on rights which individuals derive from EU law or is based on an infringement of national law, where the purpose and cause of action are similar.[76]

If we go beyond the notion that the ECJ (or indeed the national court) simply "knows when it sees" when the principle of equivalence has been undermined by the application of national procedural rules, the necessary assessment requires that the judge undertakes a comparative analysis. This necessitates that he or she engages in a two-stage process. Firstly, the satisfaction of the principle of equivalence requires that the judge determines whether there exists comparable actions in national and EU law,[77] based on the identification of an appropriate comparator.[78] If such actions exist, the rules applicable must then be identified and the favourability of the national procedural rules to each action must be assessed; moreover, the purpose of the action, the cause of action and their essential characteristics must be examined.[79] The comparison of actions in national and EU law for the purpose of identifying their equivalence brings with it a number of problems. Firstly, it is necessary that the ECJ identifies the correct comparator, which requires that it examines the pertinent national procedural rules and procedural culture in which they operate. This determination is particularly challenging as few national procedures remain entirely national in light of the (even limited) interventions of the EU in procedural law.[80] If the task is to fall to the ECJ, in comparing national and EU claims and the procedural rules applicable, the ECJ must necessarily firstly interpret the rules applicable to those actions.

---

76 Case C-378/17, *The Minister for Justice and Equality and Commissioner of the Garda Síochána*, EU:C:2018:698, n. 41 above, Opinion of AG Wahl, para. 97.

77 Case C-93/12, *ET Agrokonsulting-04 ET Agrokonsulting-04-Velko Stoyanov v. Izpalnitelen direktor na Darzhaven fond "Zemedelie" – Razplashtatelna agentsia*, EU:C:2013:432, para. 39.

78 The difficulties in identifying the correct comparator are clear from Case C-378/17, *The Minister for Justice and Equality and Commissioner of the Garda Síochána*, EU:C:2018:698, n. 41 above, Opinion of AG Wahl, paras. 95–104, as regards claims in discrimination in employment (where "their purpose, cause and essential characteristics may differ depending on the source of discrimination" at para. 99).

79 Case C-261/95, *Palmisani*, EU:C:1997:351, n. 72 above, paras. 34 et seq.

80 See e.g. Case C-261/95, *Palmisani*, EU:C:1997:351, n. 72 above, paras. 34 et seq. The ECJ identified a difficulty in finding the correct comparator as the claim being litigated – an employment discrimination claim concerning pregnant workers – has been harmonised by EU law. To identify the correct comparator, it would be necessary to look to discrimination in employment matters outside of the scope of pregnant workers.

While the ECJ can interpret EU rules, it is consistently reiterated that the interpretation of national laws is for the national courts and not for the ECJ.[81] The ECJ will face difficulties in interpreting national rules, and in comparing those rules with EU rules, to the extent that its knowledge of the former is less than the latter. It is inevitably difficult for the ECJ to identify and assess such rules in detail, particularly as comparison requires an in-depth knowledge of the system, not only of the rules but also of context, and of procedural cultures.[82]

The ECJ's approach seems to be somewhat incoherent, particularly as regards where the task of making such an assessment falls. On the one hand, the ECJ has highlighted that the determination of compliance with the principle of equivalence is for the national court, as it "alone has direct knowledge of the procedural rules governing actions in the field of employment law ... [and] must consider both the purpose and the essential characteristics of allegedly similar domestic actions".[83] Indeed, following *van Schijndel*,[84] the ECJ held that the assessment of compatibility should be made with reference to "the procedure as a whole, as well as the operation and any special features of that procedure before the different national courts".[85] For this reason, more recently AG Wahl has acknowledged that "it is for the referring court, which has direct knowledge of the detailed procedural rules applicable, to ascertain whether the actions concerned are similar" and stated that consequently the ECJ should only challenge the national court's determination in exceptional circumstances, where its "assessment proves to be manifestly flawed".[86] This approach would tie in with that of Bobek, who has noted that while equivalence tends "towards the Member States' national regime, effectiveness [pushes]

---

81 M. Bobek, "Why There Is No Principle of Procedural Autonomy of the Member States" in B. de Witte and H.-W. Micklitz (eds.), *The European Court of Justice and the Autonomy of the Member States* (Intersentia, 2011) pp. 305–324, p. 312.

82 V. Gessner *et al*, "Introduction to the Patchwork of Legal Cultures in Europe" in V. Gessner *et al* (eds.), *European Legal Cultures* (Dartmouth, Aldershot, 1996), pp. 245–269. See also A. Adinolfi, "The 'Procedural Autonomy' of Member States and the Constraints Stemming from the ECJ's Case Law" in B. de Witte and H.-W. Micklitz (eds.), *The European Court of Justice and the Autonomy of the Member States* (Intersentia, 2011), pp. 281–304, p. 286. The relevance of national legal traditions and cultures to domestic rules has of course been recognised in a wide variety of cases; to take one example, as regards default interests, both the AG and the Court in *Aziz* highlighted the significance of the specificities of the national regimes, Opinion of AG Kokott, para. 86 (noting, "The purposes lawfully pursued by default interest may be different from one Member State to the next. It is not the spirit and purpose of Directive 93/13 to level out differences between national legal cultures") and *Aziz* Judgment, para. 74.

83 Case C-326/96, *B.S. Levez v. T.H. Jennings (Harlow Pools) Ltd.*, EU:C:1998:577, paras. 43–44.

84 Joined Cases C-430/93 and C-431/93, *van Schijndel*, EU:C:1995:441, n. 61 above, para. 19.

85 Case C-326/96, *Levez*, EU:C:1998:577, n. 83 above, para. 44.

86 Case C-378/17, *The Minister for Justice and Equality and Commissioner of the Garda Síochána*, EU:C:2018:698, Opinion of AG Wahl, para. 99.

towards a harmonised Euro-standard" giving rise to difficulties in identifying the correct balance between Union and Member States' interests.[87]

On the other hand, the ECJ has suggested that the equivalence test is to be applied by it not with reference to the individual case before it but in the abstract.[88] Nevertheless, the ECJ has made concrete determinations in particular cases, finding, for example, that the principle of equivalence does not apply or is not satisfied on the facts, or that certain national rules should be used as the applicable comparator when assessing equivalence.[89] The ECJ has also drawn the conclusion that national procedural rules are incompatible with the principle of equivalence (more often than not also alongside a finding of incompatibility with the principle of effectiveness). For example, in the case of *Asbeek Brusse*, the ECJ highlighted that if a national court has the power to raise points of national law *ex officio* in a *res judicata* situation, it must also be empowered to raise similar points of EU law.[90] In the *Levez* case, the ECJ examined the principle of equivalence as regards time-limits in national procedural law. An employee had brought a claim for damages for arrears in payment which had been denied to her in breach of EU equal pay rules. The English system provided for a two-year time-limit on such claims. The ECJ found that while this procedural rule was not incompatible with the principle of effectiveness, it did not seem to satisfy the principle of equivalence. The case of *Levez* indeed suggests a similar approach applied by the ECJ as regards the determination of the compatibility of national procedural rules with effectiveness and equivalence; that is to say, it suggests a context-specific balancing approach by the national court between equivalence and procedural autonomy.[91] It is worth noting that the ECJ mostly relies on the information provided by the national court in the reference for a preliminary ruling; as such, this would limit the ECJ's approach to the single case before it. Often, this leads to the ECJ finding that there is nothing in the file submitted by the national court to suggest a violation. This suggests that it is not always possible for the ECJ to engage in a thorough examination of the equivalence

---

87 M. Bobek, "Why There Is No Principle of Procedural Autonomy of the Member States" in B. de Witte and H.-W. Micklitz (eds.), *The European Court of Justice and the Autonomy of the Member States* (Intersentia, 2011) pp. 305–324, p. 319 and p. 312, respectively.

88 Case C-78/98, *Preston and others v. Wolverhampton Healthcare NHS Trust and others; Fletcher and others v. Midland Bank plc*, EU:C:2000:247, para. 62. The ECJ held that "It follows that the various aspects of the procedural rules cannot be examined in isolation but must be placed in their general context. Moreover, such an examination may not be carried out subjectively by reference to circumstances of fact but must involve an objective comparison, in the abstract, of the procedural rules at issue".

89 P. Craig and G. de Búrca, *EU Law: Text, Cases and Materials* (OUP, 2015), pp. 247–248.

90 Case C-488/11, *Dirk Frederik Asbeek Brusse and Katarina de Man Garabito v. Jahani BV*, EU:C:2013:341.

91 Case C-326/96, *Levez*, EU:C:1998:577, n. 83 above, paras. 43–52.

of the national and EU actions. It is therefore difficult to identify the approach to comparison that has been adopted by the ECJ.[92]

3.3. THE PRINCIPLE OF EFFECTIVENESS

From the notion of "impossible in practice" (in *Rewe*[93]), the ECJ has since established that national procedural rules must not render the enforcement of rights derived from EU law "virtually impossible or excessively difficult".[94] This shift generates a considerable degree of discretion on the part of the court; that is to say, "virtually impossible or excessively difficult" is not a set standard, like the notion of impossible or impossibility. Rather, this determination is one of a political nature but it is one that might shape the standards to which adherence should occur in the national system, in order to ensure that the principle of effectiveness is not undermined. While the ECJ has identified the notions of equivalence and effectiveness as general principles of EU law, this status has been challenged in the scholarship. In particular, it has been asserted that given the discretion that exists in relation to it, effectiveness "has no internal limits",[95] and as such cannot be categorised as a legal principle. This lack of internal limits stems from the evolution of the effectiveness test in the ECJ's case law; that is to say, from impossible (an objective and certain criterion) to virtually impossible or excessively difficult.[96] With this notion of effectiveness, the ECJ aims to ensure the possibility to pursue the goal that has been established by substantive EU law rules, namely an "obligation of result" on the part of the Member States.

3.3.1. The Ex Officio Application of EU Law

With the aim, as Bobek asserts, to attribute a "shape" to effectiveness,[97] the ECJ sets out a contextualised, balancing approach, to be adopted by the national

---

92 The few exceptions are identifiable from the Opinions of the AG. See e.g. Case C-62/93, *BP Soupergaz Anonimos Etairia Geniki Emporiki-Viomichaniki kai Antiprossopeion v. Greek State*, EU:C:1995:223, paras. 52 et seq.

93 Case C-33/76, *Rewe*, EU:C:1976:188, n. 53 above, para. 5.

94 Case C-199/82, *Amministrazione delle Finanze dello Stato v. San Giorgio*, EU:C:1983:318, para. 14.

95 M. Bobek, "Why There Is No Principle of Procedural Autonomy of the Member States" in B. de Witte and H.-W. Micklitz (eds.), *The European Court of Justice and the Autonomy of the Member States* (Intersentia, 2011), pp. 305–324, p. 11.

96 Case C-199/82, *Amministrazione delle Finanze dello Stato v. SpA San Giorgio*, EU:C:1983:318, n. 94 above, para. 14.

97 M. Bobek, "Why There Is No Principle of Procedural Autonomy of the Member States" in B. de Witte and H.-W. Micklitz (eds.), *The European Court of Justice and the Autonomy of the Member States* (Intersentia, 2011), pp. 305–324, p. 11.

courts on a case-by-case basis. It is worth examining how effectiveness has been assessed by the courts in two instances, firstly as regards the *ex officio* application of EU law in the national courts, that is, the invocation by the courts of EU law (or as it has been transposed into national law) of their own motion.[98] The ECJ found initially in *Rewe*, that national courts should be obliged to apply EU law *ex officio* where there is a similar obligation with regards to the application of national law.[99] This was extended in *van Schijndel*, when the ECJ found a *possibility* for *ex officio* application to exist as regards the application of EU law where a similar *possibility* existed as regards national law.[100] *Van Schijndel* concerned the power of the national courts to examine EU law *ex officio* as regards the compatibility of a compulsory pension fund with EU competition law. The parties had not raised any issue of EU law and argued that the appeal court, the judgment of which they were challenging, ought to have raised the issue of its own motion. Starting from the principle of procedural autonomy, in respect of which Dutch law did not allow the national court to raise an issue of law of its own motion, the ECJ examined this rule from the perspective of its compatibility with the principles of equivalence and effectiveness. Finding no issue of equivalence, the ECJ turned to the principle of effectiveness and as above, examined the Dutch rule with reference to the procedure as a whole, balancing the interests that the national rule sought to protect (including the rights of the defence, legal certainty and the proper conduct of procedure) against the effectiveness of the protection of EU rights.[101] Another interest of the national system in this case derived from the adversarial nature of civil proceedings, that is, it being for the parties to the proceedings to raise issues of law. As a result, the ECJ considered that EU law could not be understood to require national courts to raise issues of law of their own motion where this would oblige them to abandon their passive role.[102]

Following *van Schijndel*, in the case of *Peterbroeck*,[103] the ECJ found that the application of the effectiveness principle requires that the relevant and disputed rule of national law should be examined with "reference to the role of that provision in the procedure, its progress and its special features, viewed as a whole"; that is to say, continued to provide that account should also be taken of "the basic principles of the domestic judicial system, such as protection of the rights of the defence, the principle of legal certainty and the

---

98 See S. Law, "General Structure of Procedural Consumer Protection" and B. Hess and P. Taelman, "Consumer Actions before National Courts" in B. Hess and S. Law (eds.), *The Impact of National Procedures on the Protection of Consumers under EU Law* (Beck/Hart/Nomos, 2019), pp. 1–55 and pp. 89–150, respectively.

99 Case C-33/76, *Rewe*, EU:C:1976:188, n. 93 above, para. 5.

100 Joined Cases C-430/93 and C-431/93, *van Schijndel*, EU:C:1995:441, n. 61 above.

101 Joined Cases C-430/93 and C-431/93, *van Schijndel*, EU:C:1995:441, n. 61 above, paras. 19–20.

102 Joined Cases C-430/93 and C-431/93, *van Schijndel*, EU:C:1995:441, n. 61 above, paras. 21–22.

103 Case C-312/93, *Peterbroeck, Van Campenhout & Cie SCS v. Belgian State*, EU:C:1995:437.

proper conduct of procedure".[104] In the case of *Peterbroeck* however, the ECJ did not consider that the principle of judicial passivity was compatible with that of effectiveness. Instead, while still making reference to the interests inherent in the operation of the national procedural system, including those of legal certainty and the need to ensure the proper conduct of proceedings, the ECJ found the Belgian procedural rule, which precluded both the parties and the national court from raising a point of EU law after a 60-day period, to be incompatible with the principle of effectiveness. The different outcomes of the two cases reflect the notion that the assessment by the ECJ is to be made on a case-by-case basis in light of the specificities and interests of the national procedural system as balanced with the interests in the protection of the EU right, and not in the abstract. While the ECJ has confirmed its reasoning in *van Schijndeli*,[105] it has also found that the national court may indeed be empowered or even obliged to raise an issue of EU law *ex officio* where EU law is deemed to be part of public policy.[106] This evolution of the ECJ's case law is identifiable, for example, in the context of EU consumer – and more broadly, competition – law.[107] In this substantive law context also, the ECJ has recognised that in respect of equivalence, consumer protection rules must be deemed to have the same status as rules of public policy and thus capable of being raised *ex officio* in the same way as rules of national public policy.[108]

3.3.2. *Res Judicata, Finality of Decisions and the Review of Compliance with EU Law*

An important aspect of the ECJ's case law on national procedural law concerns the finality of judicial and administrative decisions. The ECJ

[104] Joined Cases C-430/93 and C-431/93, *van Schijndel*, EU:C:1995:441, n. 61 above, para. 19.

[105] Joined Cases C-222/05-C-225/05, *J. van der Weerd and Others v. Minister van Landbouw, Natuur en Voedselkwaliteit*, EU:C:2007:318. As the parties had a reasonable opportunity to raise the issue of EU law themselves (concerning Directive 85/511/European Commission on the control of foot and mouth disease), but did not, the national courts could not be required to do so; the ECJ found that neither EU law nor the principles of equivalence or effectiveness required the national court to raise the allegation of the infringement of EU law of its motion.

[106] Case C-126/97, *Eco Swiss China Time Ltd v. Benetton International NV*, EU:C:1999:269, para. 37.

[107] From Joined Cases C-240/98 to C-244/98, *Océano Grupo Editorial SA v. Roció Murciano Quintero* (C-240/98), *and Salvat Editores SA v. José M. Sánchez Alcón Prades* (C-241/98), *José Luis Copano Badillo* (C-242/98), *Mohammed Berroane* (C-243/98) *and Emilio Viñas Feliú* (C-244/98), EU:C:2000:346, in which a power was recognised to the recognition of an obligation on the part of the national court; followed up by Case C-473/00, *Cofidis SA v. Jean-Loius Fredout*, EU:C:2002:705. See further, Case C-243/08, *Pannon GSM*, EU:C:2009:350 (see further A. Ancery and M. Wissink, "ECJ 4 June 2009, Pannon GSM Zrt. v. Erzsébet Sustikné Győrfi" (2010) 18 *European Review of Public Law* 307).

[108] See e.g. Case C-497/13, *Froukje Faber v. Autobedrijf Hazet Ochten BV*, EU:C:2015:357 and Case C-147/16, *Karel de Grote*, EU:C:2018:320, n. 60 above, paras. 33–37.

has been very careful in not extending the application of the principle of primacy to final judicial and administrative decisions that are in breach of EU law. It sought to avoid challenging directly the finality of such decisions either by providing for an indirect means of redress, such as the principle of Member State liability,[109] or by excluding the need for any special review,[110] underscoring how EU law is part and parcel of the legal orders of the Member States.[111] In doing so, the ECJ has attributed great significance to the principle of legal certainty – which underpins the notion of finality – finding that the finality of decisions could be upheld and need not be reopened,[112] unless exceptional circumstances are at play.[113] All in all, and as will be examined further below,[114] the situations in which the ECJ itself finds that a national decision or judgment should be reopened seem to be exceptional and dependent on the particular circumstances of those cases.

3.3.3. *Availability of National Remedies and Procedural Autonomy*

A related limitation to national procedural autonomy, which shapes the role of the institutions of the national procedural systems, concerns the availability of remedies in national law. As noted above, the protection of EU rights in line with national procedures and remedies runs into difficulties where national law does not provide for appropriate remedies by which the effective application of Union law (or indeed recourse for its violation) can be ensured. The ECJ initially found that the national systems need not create new remedies where they do not exist under national law, holding that the Treaty "was not intended to create new remedies in the national courts to ensure the observance of Community law other than those already laid down by national law".[115] Following its finding that the Treaties did not require the introduction of new remedies in national law,[116] the ECJ has limited this conclusion, particularly where the availability of a remedy is deemed to derive directly from the pertinent rule of EU law.[117] The ECJ's case law has nevertheless

---

109 Judgment of 30 September 2003, *Gerhard Köbler v. Republik Österreich*, Case C-224/01, EU:C:2003:513.

110 Case C-234/04, *Rosmarie Kapferer v. Schlank & Schick GmbH*, EU:C:2006:178.

111 Judgment of 24 October 2018, *XC and Others v. Generalprokuratur*, C-234/17, EU:C:2018:853.

112 Compare amongst many others, Case C-224/97, *Erich Ciola v. Land Vorarlberg*, EU:C:1999:212 and Case C-119/05, *Lucchini*, EU:C:2007:434, n. 148 below; with Case C-234/04, *Kapferer*, EU:C:2006:178, n. 110 above, para. 21 and para. 72.

113 Case C-453/00, *Kühne & Heitz NV v. Produktschap voor Pluimvee en Eiere*, EU:C:2004:17, para. 28.

114 See below, section 6.

115 Case C-158/80, *Rewe v. Hauptzollamt Kiel*, EU:C:1981:163, para. 44.

116 Case C-158/80, *Rewe v. Hauptzollamt Kiel*, EU:C:1981:163, para. 44.

117 Case C-199/82, *Amministrazione delle Finanze dello Stato v. SpA San Giorgio*, EU:C:1983:318, n. 94 above, para. 12, concerning the availability of the repayment of charges paid in breach

been rather inconsistent as regards the need for the creation or introduction of national remedies.[118] A number of cases in which the ECJ has identified a need for new remedies include, for example, the repayment of charges paid in breach of EU law.[119] Other cases have concerned the procedural rules to be applied as regards the remedies available for the violation of EU rules of non-discrimination.[120]

Fundamentally, the ECJ recognised in *Factortame I* that the full *effet utile* of EU law, in line with the supremacy of EU law (per *Simmenthal*),[121] may necessitate the creation of a new procedural remedy in the national system. This finding obliged the English court to introduce a procedural remedy of interim relief, where a general principle of English law precluded the availability of interim relief against the Crown, in respect of a violation of EU law.[122] The ECJ established that national procedural autonomy could not operate in the context of EU law to provide a blanket prohibition of interim relief but nevertheless left the determination of the conditions for providing such a remedy to the national court.[123] The ECJ's earlier findings have been developed in its subsequent case law. In *Francovich*, the ECJ established that certain – judicially-harmonised – rules should apply to determine the basis on which damages for the breach of Union law should be available.[124] Moreover, it found

of EU law. The ECJ held that the remedy of repayment "is a consequence of, and an adjunct to, the rights conferred on individuals by the Community provisions prohibiting charges", finding also that the national court is obliged to assess evidence it deems relevant, even where national rules would not allow for it.

118 See Case C-338/91, *H. Steenhorst-Neerings v. Bestuur van de Bedrijfsvereniging voor Detailhandel, Ambachten en Huisvrouwen*, EU:C:1993:857, para. 23; Case C-410/92, *Johnson II*, EU:C:1994:401, para. 26, in which the ECJ held that there is a need to refer to the specificities of the case of the operation of the procedural rules.

119 M. Dougan, "Cutting Your Losses in the Enforcement Deficit: A Community Right to the Recovery of Unlawfully Levied Charges?" (1998) 1 *Cambridge Yearbook of European Law Studies* 233.

120 Case C-177/88, *Elisabeth Johanna Pacifica Dekker v. Stichting Vormingscentrum voor Jong Volwassenen (VJV Centrum) Plus*, EU:C:1990:383, para. 26; the ECJ held that the relevant EU law "nevertheless requires that, where a Member State opts for a sanction forming part of the rules on civil liability, any infringement of the prohibition of discrimination suffices in itself to make the person guilty of it fully liable".

121 Case C-106/77, *Simmenthal*, EU:C:1978:49, n. 37 above, in which the ECJ held that the national law that precluded the suspension of proceedings and the possibility to assess compliance and constitutionality of national legislation and EU law before the Italian constitutional court, should be disapplied to allow for such a possibility.

122 Case C-213/89, *Factortame*, EU:C:1990:257, n. 44 above, paras. 19–23. This was later on also extended to cases outside of the scope of EU law. See below, section 10.

123 No such remedy is available as regards administrative bodies; Joined Cases C-453/03-C-194/04, *ABNA*, EU:C:2005:741.

124 Joined Cases C-6/90-C-9/90, *Francovich*, EU:C:1991:428, n. 47 above, para. 51: there is "a right to reparation where three conditions are met: the rule of law infringed must be intended to confer rights on individuals; the breach must be sufficiently serious; and there must be a direct causal link between the breach of the obligation resting on the State and the damage sustained by the injured parties".

that state liability, established on the basis of those (judicially) harmonised conditions, could arise where a Member State has failed to implemented EU law in the national legal system.[125] The application of those conditions is nevertheless a matter for the national courts in the case before it. Fundamentally, the ECJ has deemed that national remedies for violations of EU rights must be adequate (and sanctions must be proportional and dissuasive), as well as satisfy the principles of equivalence and effectiveness.[126] The basis on which remedies which might otherwise be unavailable are made available for breaches of EU rights[127] derives from the effectiveness of EU law, the full *effet utile* of EU law, and relatedly its primacy or supremacy. As Craig and de Búrca set out, the current situation can be said to reflect the need for the national courts to "strike an appropriate, proportionality-based, case-by-case balance between the requirement of effective judicial protection for EU law rights and the application of legitimate national procedural and remedial rules".[128]

The ECJ has highlighted that procedural autonomy is limited by the principles of effectiveness and equivalence, in order to avoid divergent applications of Union norms across the Member States, and thus promote a uniform level of protection throughout the Union, and with this aim it has gradually "scratched away" at the understanding that the rigid procedural autonomy of the Member States remains intact in light of the principles of equivalence and effectiveness.[129] This is the case in theory if not in practice.[130] The determination of the procedure and means by which the

---

125 Joined Cases C-6/90-C-9/90, *Francovich*, EU:C:1991:428, n. 47 above, para. 33.

126 Case C-14/83, *Von Colson*, EU:C:1984:153, n. 40 above.

127 Case C-208/90, *Theresa Emmott v. Minister for Social Welfare and the Attorney General*, EU:C:1991:333 (concerning the retrospective payment of a disability benefit in the period of a non-implementation of a directive; the ECJ held that "given the particular nature of directives" the Member State could not invoke a time-limit against an individual action until the proper implementation of the directive on which the individual sought to rely until); Case C-271/91, *Marshall v. Southampton and South-West Hampshire Area Health Authority* (*Marshall II*), EU:C:1993:335 (in which the ECJ held that interest should form part of the repayment necessary to restore equality).

128 P. Craig and G. de Búrca, *EU Law: Text, Cases and Materials* (OUP, 2015), p. 239.

129 To the extent that national rules "cannot be less favourable than those relating to similar actions of a domestic nature nor render virtually impossible or excessively difficult the exercise of rights conferred by Community law" (Case C-33/76, *Rewe*, EU:C:1976:188, n. 53 above, para. 5); the limitation – essentially based on the principle of equivalence and effectiveness to be applied, "by reference to the role of that provision in the procedure, its progress and its special features, viewed as a whole, before the various national instances. In the light of that analysis the basic principles of the domestic judicial system, such as protection of the rights of the defence, the principle of legal certainty and the proper conduct of procedure, must, where appropriate, be taken into consideration" (Case C-312/93, *Peterbroeck*, EU:C:1995:437, n. 103 above, para. 14).

130 M. Avbelj, "National Procedural Autonomy: Concept, Practice and Theoretical Queries" in A. Lazowski and S. Blockmans (eds.), *Research Handbook on EU Institutional Law* (Edward Elgar, 2016), pp. 421–440, p. 432.

ex officio application of EU law might be made, or by which national remedies should be available for violations of EU law, where otherwise they would not, nevertheless remains for the Member States, in so far as the national procedural rules adhere to the principles of effectiveness and equivalence.[131] This suggests that what might seem to be attempts by the ECJ to harmonise national rules of procedure may in fact be less extensive in practice than they *prima facie* appear. However, it could be said that the application of the principles of equivalence and effectiveness, alongside the principle of effective judicial protection and that of the full *effet utile* of Union law, no longer constitutes an application of minimum criteria as regards national procedural rules, but rather a mechanism for judicial review. In engaging in an assessment of the limitations of the application of procedural autonomy in line with the principles of effectiveness and equivalence, the ECJ is essentially engaging in a review process.[132] That is to say, it is engaged in a review of national procedures and remedies applicable where the EU system must rely on the Member States to apply and enforce rights deriving from EU law.

4. PROCEDURAL AUTONOMY AND THE RELATIONSHIP BETWEEN THE NATIONAL LEGAL SYSTEM AND THE EU

Here it is worth drawing some preliminary conclusions before examining how the ECJ's case law concretely affects the national procedural law. The ECJ's case law concerning procedural autonomy, and its limitations, is – as discussed above – incoherent and messy. The ECJ has defined national procedural autonomy as a principle that shapes the relationship between national and EU institutional law but in reality, it is difficult to define and has few contours. Given the limits of the Treaties' legal and political framework, as discussed above, the limits of the Union's competences and the division of labour between the EU institutions and the national courts and administrative bodies in enforcement, it falls to the ECJ to apply Union law and to promote its application in a uniform way across the Member States, while ensuring that national procedural laws and practices do not undermine this objective by undermining the principles of effectiveness or equivalence.

---

131 Case C-432/05, *Unibet (London) Ltd and Unibet (International) Ltd v. Justitiekanslern*, EU:C:2007:163, paras. 40–41.

132 L. Cadiet, "L'autonomie procédurale dans la jurisprudence de la Cour de justice de l'Union européenne: Réflexions naïves d'un Huron au Palais du Kirchberg", presentation given at the conference celebrating the 50th Anniversary of the European Law of Civil Procedure, 27 and 28 September 2018, Court of Justice of the European Union.

Procedural autonomy therefore exists as a concept due to the absence of EU rules of civil procedure and in light of the ECJ's case law; this brings us back to the question of whether the pertinent concept is indeed that of autonomy of the Member States.[133] We question whether this is really the case;[134] as stated above, procedural autonomy only comes to the fore where the EU has not legislated for procedural rules. The principles of equivalence especially, and effectiveness are – at least in theory – limitations to all rules of national procedure. Relatedly, the question of the ECJ's "judicial activism" in the field of procedure comes to the fore. If the ECJ indeed no longer refers to the principle of direct effect, it is arguably utilising the principles of effectiveness and equivalence together to constitute the practical expression of both the principles of supremacy and direct effect.[135] It is possible to identify different approaches to procedural autonomy, from a strong emphasis on autonomy, to an increased focus on the twin requirements in light of the national courts' obligations as regards loyal cooperation, and then later a turn to an emphasis on effectiveness instead of equivalence. More recently, a fundamental rights dimension has emerged.[136] This is reflective of the development of a balancing approach, which requires an analysis of the specific context in which the rule applies, with assessment made of the national rule, its content, scope and purpose, in light of the importance of the EU law. This context-specific approach means that the focus is on the specific national rule in the specific national context and limits the spillover effects of the judgment of the ECJ.[137]

---

133 M. Avbelj, "National Procedural Autonomy: Concept, Practice and Theoretical Queries" in A. Lazowski and S. Blockmans (eds.), *Research Handbook on EU Institutional Law* (Edward Elgar 2016), pp. 421–440, p. 435.

134 See also M. Bobek, "Why There Is No Principle of Procedural Autonomy of the Member States" in B. de Witte and H.-W. Micklitz (eds.), *The European Court of Justice and the Autonomy of the Member States* (Intersentia, 2011), pp. 305–324, p. 319, where the author challenges the notion of understanding the doctrine of procedural autonomy of the Member States in a rigid way; that is to say, the notion of a definitive national procedural autonomy.

135 See J. Rideau, "Ordre juridique de l'Union européenne" *Fascicule 191 du Jurisclasseur Europe Traité* (LexisNexis, 2014) and L. Cadiet, "L'autonomie procédurale dans la jurisprudence de la Cour de justice de l'Union européenne: Réflexions naïves d'un Huron au Palais du Kirchberg", presentation given at the conference celebrating the 50th Anniversary of the European Law of Civil Procedure, 27 and 28 September 2018, Court of Justice of the European Union.

136 This fundamental rights dimension will not be discussed further here for reasons of space; however, it is worth highlighting one particular case of the ECJ. In Case C-93/12, *Agrokonsulting*, EU:C:2013:432, n. 77 above, concerning whether national jurisdiction rules conferring jurisdiction on a single court for all disputes relating to decisions of an administrative authority responsible for payments of aid under the CAP satisfied the principles of effectiveness and equivalence and Art. 47 CFR, the ECJ seems to suggest that the observance of all requirements – equivalence, effectiveness, effective judicial protection and the principle of loyal cooperation – "must be analysed by reference to the role of the rules concerned in the procedure viewed as a whole, to the conduct of that procedure and to the special features of those rules, before the various national instances" (para. 38).

137 See below, section 7.

That is to say, the ECJ might give guidance to the national court on what effectiveness and equivalence require but will often leave it to the national court to determine in light of the facts of the case, following which the concrete application of these principles remains unknown. It is on this that we will shed further light in the next sections.

5. PROCEDURAL HARMONISATION VIA THE ECJ: INTRODUCING THE MEMBER STATES' PERSPECTIVE

The argument defended in the remaining part of this contribution is that the harmonising powers attributed to the case law of the Court of Justice should be qualified in various respects. First, when considering the concrete function of the case law on national procedural autonomy, a harmonising effect is far from self-evident. Indeed, a decision taken by the Court in this context is foremostly aimed at solving an issue of procedural law that has emerged in a particular case in a particular Member State.[138] Given the differences between the procedural systems of the Member States, which we as procedural lawyers accept to exist (for example, to explain why harmonisation is so difficult),[139] it then seems slightly contradictory to infer general rules from decisions given in relation to particular problems in particular procedural law systems.[140] The same goes to a large extent for decisions in which the Court of Justice provides for an interpretation of EU law instruments that contain procedural rules, and which have harmonisation as their object. The differences in procedural law that exist in the Member States mean that the interpretation of such an instrument remains largely context-specific, depending on how the EU law instrument interacts with national procedural rules. Second, when looking at the harmonisation question from the point of view of a Member State, it appears that the harmonising effect of the case law of the Court of Justice may not always be visible or, even to the contrary, that the Court's case law leads to the fragmentation of national procedural law.[141] Third, when comparing the effects of the case law of the Court between different Member States, it appears that it strengthens the differences between the Member States rather than bringing their procedural systems closer together.[142]

Further to this, attention should be given to the pressure that the Court's case law exerts on national courts and decision-makers, leading them to extend

---

138 See below, section 6.
139 M. Tulibacka, "Europeanization of civil procedures: In search of a coherent approach", (2009) 46 *C.M.L. Rev.* 1527, 1532–1533.
140 See below, section 7.
141 See below, sections 7–9.
142 See below, sections 8–9.

the Court's decisions beyond the scope of EU law.[143] While such harmonising effect is not required by EU law but the consequence of a choice by the Member State, it should not be overlooked. Moreover, one may wonder to what degree a Member State is completely acting out of its own will in such a case.

This chapter provides several examples illustrating these different aspects of the Court's case law. It will appear that the case law thus paints a rather diverse picture of harmonisation, fragmentation and disintegration.

6. THE IMPORTANCE OF THE SPECIFIC CASE

When considering the harmonising effects of decisions of the Court of Justice in the area of procedural law, one must always obtain knowledge about the procedural context in which the case was given. This necessitates an exercise in comparative law, comparing the procedural law of the Member State in relation to which the decision was given and the procedural law of the Member State of "reception".[144] Overall, unless the Court is exclusively interpreting a notion of EU law, preliminary rulings are an exercise in comparative law.[145] This is especially so with regard to procedural law, since most decisions given in this context amount to a *de facto* review of rules of national procedural law. The interpretation of the principle of effectiveness by the Court is *per se* nothing other than a compatibility review of national procedural law in light of EU law. It only takes the form of an interpretation because the Court has no jurisdiction to review the compatibility of national law with EU law in the context of the preliminary reference procedure.[146]

Thus, before one seeks to draw inferences from a Court's decision for one's own national legal system, or for all Member States' legal systems, one must first familiarise itself with the procedural law of the Member State in relation to which the decision was given and the procedural law(s) of the Member State(s). If not, one risks attaching effects to a decision of the Court that do not exist. Even the speculative phrase, often used in comments on the Court's case law, that "This decision may have as a consequence that ..." is, in a lot of instances, not accurate at best. Further to this, one should not overlook

143 See below, section 10.

144 Van Gerven rightly pointed out that comparative law has a true practical application in the context of the EU legal system. See, W. Van Gerven, "Bridging the gap between Community and national laws: Towards a principle of homogeneity in the field of legal remedies?" (1995) 32 *C.M.L. Rev.* 679, 695–697.

145 On the use of comparative law by the Court of Justice, see K. Lenaerts and K. Gutman, "The comparative law method and the Court of Justice of the European Union" in M. Adenas and D. Fairgrieve (eds.), *Courts and Comparative Law* (OUP, 2015), pp. 141, 143.

146 K. Lenaerts, I. Maselis and K. Gutman (J.T. Nowak (ed.)), *EU Procedural Law* (OUP, 2014), p. 233.

the fact that the Court's case law on national procedural law is mostly about solving a particular problem of procedural law in a particular context and not about imposing a general standard for the whole of the EU. Thus, apart from having to consider the specificity of national procedural law, one should also take into account the particulars of the specific case.

It is in this regard instructive to consider the Court's case law on *res judicata*,[147] and the academic debate around that case law, in particular in regard of the decision in *Lucchini*.[148] Various commentators have responded quite dramatically to this decision, *inter alia* considering it "an unprecedented attack on the principle of legal certainty".[149] Yet, in every decision where the finality of court decisions is somehow at stake, the Court is at pains to highlight the value it attaches to the finality of judicial decisions,[150] underscoring the importance of the principle of *res judicata* for both the EU legal order and the legal orders of the Member States.[151] Is the Court just paying lip service to *res judicata* or does it actually mean it when it says that it respects *res judicata*? We believe it is the latter.

The first question is which concept of *res judicata* the Court is referring to. Kornezov points out that at least three different conceptions of the scope of the principle of *res judicata* could be distinguished in the Member States.[152] In the minimal conception of *res judicata*, the preclusive effects of a judgment do not extend beyond what has actually been considered by the judge, namely the claims brought and the factual grounds relied upon. The scope of *res judicata* does not extend to alternative claims that could have been brought in light of the factual grounds or to connected but alternative factual grounds. Moreover, the same claim based on the same factual grounds could be brought again if the legal ground relied upon were different. This is what is called the "triple identity test"[153] and forms the minimal core of *res judicata*: it does not

147 See also above, section 3.3.2.

148 Judgment of 18 July 2007, *Ministero dell'Industria, del Commercio e dell'Artigianato v. Lucchini SpA*, C-119/05, EU:C:2007:434.

149 P. Bříza, "Lucchini, SpA – Is there anything left of res judicata principle?" (2008) 27(1) *Civil Justice Quarterly* 40, 50.

150 Judgment of 24 October 2018, *XC*, C-234/17, EU:C:2018:853, n. 111 above, para. 52; Judgment of 6 October 2009, *Asturcom*, C-40/08, EU:C:2009:615, para. 37; Judgment of 3 September 2009, *Fallimento Olimpiclub*, C-2/08, EU:C:2009:506, para. 23; Judgment of 16 March 2006, *Kapferer*, C-234/04, EU:C:2006:178, n. 110 above, para. 21.

151 Judgment of 10 July 2014, *Impresa Pizzarotti*, C-213/13, EU:C:2014:2067, para. 58 and case law cited.

152 A. Kornezov, "Res judicata of national judgments incompatible with EU law: Time for a major rethink?" (2014) 51 *C.M.L. Rev.* 809, 818.

153 A. Kornezov, "Res judicata of national judgments incompatible with EU law: Time for a major rethink?" (2014) 51 *C.M.L. Rev.* 809, 818. The approach was changed by the legislator in Belgium in 2015 and a judgment of the French Cour de Cassation from 2006 (Cass. fr. 7 July 2006, *Césaréo*) did more or less the same for France. (Perhaps one could still refer

allow a final court decision on points expressly decided to be reopened. In the maximalist conception of *res judicata*, parties are obliged to concentrate their disputes to a maximum extent. The preclusive effects of *res judicata* extend to claims not brought but available in light of the factual grounds presented and factual grounds not presented but part of the wider dispute (merger theory). It goes without saying that in this conception of *res judicata* the same claim and the same factual grounds cannot be relied upon again in light of a different legal ground. The maximalist approach does not only imply a prohibition on the reassessment of the first court's express findings but also a prohibition on continuing the dispute for connected issues not expressly decided by the first court. In between those two extremes, mixed approaches to the scope of *res judicata* are possible: inclusion of all alternative claims, inclusion of all alternative causes of action, or inclusion of all alternative legal grounds.[154]

Given this diversity between the Member States, what does it mean when one states that the Court has ended the finality of national judgments? Does it mean that the Court has stated that every judgment that contains a violation of EU law should be open to review? Or that EU law does not allow particular preclusive effects, for example claim preclusion that is the result of the application of the merger theory? The recent judgment of the Court in *XC* implies that it is certainly not the former.[155] In that judgment, the Court held that EU law does not require Member States to extend an exceptional procedure for the reopening of final judgments – where the European Court of Human Rights or the Member State supreme court has established a violation of the European Convention on Human Rights – to final judgments that contain a violation of a fundamental right guaranteed by EU law, whether or not in light of subsequent case law of the Court of Justice.[156] Consequently, since a violation of the Charter of Fundamental Rights is

to the triple identity test in a different form. For Jeuland and Cadiet, the triple identity test encompasses identity of parties, object and cause, the latter being factual and not legal. See L. Cadiet and E. Jeuland, *Droit judiciaire privé* (LexisNexis, 2017), 624–628.) The requirement that also the legal grounds relied upon should be the same is thus no longer applicable. For Belgium, see J.-F. van Drooghenbroeck, "La concentration des écritures: Rédaction des conclusions et extension de l'autorité de la chose jugé" in J.-F. van Drooghenbroeck, *Le Code judiciaire en pot-pourri* (Larcier, 2016), pp. 115, 119–153. For France, see A. Posez, "Le principe de concentration des moyens, ou l'autorité retrouvée de la chose jugée", *Revue trimestrielle de croit civile* 2015, 283–310, especially n° 2.

154 For an overview of various conceptions of the *res judicata* principle, see Y. Sinai, "Reconsidering res judicata: A comparative perspective" (2011) 21 *Duke Journal of Comparative & International Law* 353–400; E. Schopflocher, "What is a single cause of action for the purposes of the doctrine of res judicata?" (1942) 21 *Oregon Law Review* 319–364.

155 Judgment of 24 October 2018, *XC*, C-234/17, EU:C:2018:853, n. 111 above.

156 Judgment in *XC*, n. 111 above, para. 59.

as such not sufficient to put in question the authority of a final judgment in criminal proceedings, it is safe to say that a violation of EU law in the course of administrative or civil court proceedings does not justify the reopening of a final judgment.

What the Court did in *Lucchini* was thus the latter. Lucchini had applied for aid from the Italian authorities for the modernisation of its steel plants. The European Commission investigated the planned aid and issued a decision holding it incompatible with the internal market. In the meantime, Lucchini had started proceedings in the Italian courts to obtain a subsidy from the Italian state. The Italian state disputed the grant of the subsidy but not on account of its incompatibility with the rules on state aid. Moreover, neither the Commission Decision nor the relevant state aid rules were raised by the Italian courts of their own motion. After having lost the case on appeal, the Italian state deemed that the questions of law raised were dealt with properly and therefore did not start cassation proceedings against the judgment. The judgment of the Court of Appeal of Rome became final.[157]

Under Italian law, the finality of a judgment does not only preclude the reopening of matters expressly dealt with but also the examination in other proceedings of matters which could have been raised in earlier proceedings but were not.[158] Applying this rule to the judgment of the Rome Court of Appeal, it meant that the court had also implicitly ruled on the compatibility of the measure with EU state aid law and thus the measure could no longer be challenged on that account – or any other. However, on the basis of the division of powers between the EU and the Member States, the European Commission has exclusive jurisdiction to rule on the compatibility of aid measures with the internal market. The application of the Italian rules on *res judicata* led in this case thus to a violation of the division of powers between the EU and the Member States, causing the Italian court to transgress its jurisdiction.[159] This led the Court to decide that this particular preclusive effect of the judgment of the Rome Court of Appeal could not be maintained in subsequent proceedings in which the legality of the aid measure was contested in light of EU state aid law.[160]

Now, is this an "unprecedented attack on the principle of res judicata"?[161] The answer is clearly no. First, it only concerns a particular conception of res judicata that is not at all shared amongst the Member States of the European Union. The core of *res judicata* remains respected: the finality

157 Judgment in *Lucchini*, n. 148 above, paras. 19–29 and 58.
158 Judgment in *Lucchini*, para. 59.
159 Judgment in *Lucchini*, para. 59.
160 Judgment in *Lucchini*, paras. 62–63.
161 P. Bříza, "Lucchini, SpA – Is there anything left of res judicata principle?" (2008) 27(1) *Civil Justice Quarterly* 40, 50.

of the judgment of the Rome Court of Appeal with regard to the issues expressly ruled upon was not at all put into question. Second, one should also look at the particular issue in this case. The extensive preclusive effect of the Italian *res judicata* rules was rejected because it led the Italian court to transgress its jurisdiction in violation of the division of powers between the EU and the Member States in matters of state aid. The problem was thus not a mere wrongful application of EU law but a violation of rules on exclusive jurisdiction in an international context. This is not an insignificant detail.[162]

Rules on exclusive jurisdiction are protected in most legal orders by an obligation imposed on courts to raise a violation of these rules of their own motion.[163] They have special status because they determine the judicial organisation of the state and cannot be disposed of by the parties. Exclusive jurisdiction rules receive even stronger protection in an international context. Article 45(1)(e)(ii) Brussels I^{bis} Regulation allows for the refusal of recognition or enforcement of a final judgment originating in another Member State when the judgment was given in violation of the rules on exclusive jurisdiction laid down in Section 6 of Chapter II of the Brussels I^{bis} Regulation. Note that under the Brussels Convention, courts were even required to refuse recognition or enforcement of their own motion for this reason.[164] A limitation on the preclusive effects of *res judicata* is thus acceptable when the exclusive jurisdiction of a state is violated – why then not when the exclusive jurisdiction of the EU is violated?

What the *Lucchini* judgment shows is that we must be careful with attributing harmonising effects to the case law of the Court of Justice on national procedural law. First, the national procedural context should be taken into account, which requires a comparative law exercise. There is no uniform conception of *res judicata* amongst the Member States of the EU. The same goes for the powers of the judge, evidence, legal aid, the availability of remedies, etc. The *Lucchini* case is, in this regard, only relevant for Member States which adhere to a wider conception of the scope of *res judicata*. Second, the actual problem should be taken into account as well. In *Lucchini*, the Court of Justice did not decide that the preclusive effects based on a large conception of *res judicata* were problematic *per se*. It did so because they caused the Member State to violate the exclusive jurisdiction of the European Commission to declare aid compatible with the internal market. *Lucchini* is thus only

---

162 This is the real issue in *Lucchini*, n. 148 above. See in this regard, X. Groussot and T. Minssen, "Res judicata in the Court of Justice case law: Balancing legal certainty with legality?" (2007) 3 *European Constitutional Law Review* 385, 414.

163 See, for example, Article 27 Brussels I^{bis} Regulation.

164 Cf. European Commission, *Proposal for a Council Regulation (EC) on jurisdiction and the recognition and enforcement of judgments in civil and commercial matters*, COM(1999) 348 final, [1999] O.J. 1999, C 376/1 E, explanations accompanying Section 2 of Chapter 10.

relevant for such situations. It does not say anything about whether such preclusive effects are also problematic when the Member State court actually had jurisdiction but has wrongfully applied EU law. It may, however, be relevant for other matters pertaining to the exclusive jurisdiction of the EU institutions.[165]

It is with this approach that one should evaluate the harmonising effects of a judgment of the Court of Justice on national procedural law. When it comes to *Lucchini*, it means that EU law does not allow for extensive preclusive effects if this would affect the exclusive jurisdiction of the European Commission in matters of state aid. There is thus a harmonised rule, but its effect is quite limited. This is so because not all Member States adhere to a conception of *res judicata* that has caused the problem and because the situations in which such a conception of *res judicata* would be problematic are extremely limited.

7. SOLVING A PARTICULAR PROBLEM IN A PARTICULAR MEMBER STATE

We have already stated in section 6 of this chapter that the Court's case law on national procedural autonomy mainly deals with solving a specific issue in a specific Member State. This appears clearly from the Court's case law on time-limits. Apart from the general standard that time-limits must be reasonable, it is impossible to find a harmonised rule on the length of time-limits in relation to particular claims in the Court's case law. In every case, the Court assesses whether the applicable time-limits are not discriminatory or whether they make the enforcement of rights deriving from EU law virtually impossible. Whether a time-limit is 60 days, 90 days or four years does not make a difference in this regard.[166] Time-limits may thus differ between the Member States for the same type of claim without there being any problem of equivalence or effectiveness.[167] The application of the principles of equivalence and effectiveness does not have much harmonising effect in this regard, apart from a very loose common standard.[168]

One may point out that the example of time-limits is a convenient one, since the possibilities for the Member States are virtually endless. This would be

---

165 X. Groussot and T. Minssen, "Res judicata in the Court of Justice case law: Balancing legal certainty with legality?" (2007) 3 *European Constitutional Law Review* 385, 416.

166 Cf. Judgment of 17 June 2004, *Recheio-Cash & Carry SA v. Fazenda Pública/Registo Nacional de Pessoas Colectivas, and Ministério Público*, Case C-30/02, EU:C:2004:373, para. 20.

167 See, for example, Opinion of Advocate General R.J. Colomer of 11 december 2003, *Recheio-Cash & Carry*, C-30/02, EU:C:2003:666, para. 41, fn. 58.

168 This may not be without problems. See in this regard, V. Couronne, "L'autonomie procédurale des états membres de l'Union européenne à l'épreuve du temps" (2010) 46(3/4) *Cahiers de droit européen* 273, 307.

much less the case with procedural themes for which fewer possible variations exist, for example the powers of the judge. But even in those cases the wider procedural context plays a role, as the case of *Duarte Hueros* shows us.[169]

Duarte Hueros concerns the case of a Spanish citizen seeking redress for lack of conformity of goods purchased in accordance with the guarantees laid down in Directive 1999/44/EC on certain aspects of the sale of consumer goods and associated guarantees.[170] Ms Duarte Hueros returned a car she had bought from a seller because water leaked in through the roof into the car. The seller could not have the problem fixed, following which Ms Duarte Hueros asked the vehicle to be replaced. Upon refusal by the seller, Ms Duarte Hueros brought proceedings before the referring judge, seeking rescission of the contract of sale and an order that Autociba and Citroën España SA (the latter as the manufacturer of the vehicle), be held jointly and severally liable to repay the purchase price of the vehicle.[171]

The judge before whom the case was brought considered that the lack of conformity was too minor to grant the rescission of the contract on the basis of the Directive. A reduction in the sales price was considered to be a more appropriate remedy in light of the Directive. However, the judge found himself limited by Spanish procedural law because, in his interpretation,[172] judges do not have the power to grant a remedy different from the type of relief sought by the claimant. Moreover, it appeared that Ms Duarte Hueros could not bring the alternative claim in new proceedings because of the broad scope of the *res judicata* principle under Spanish law. Neither could she alter her claim in the course of the proceedings because Spanish procedural law provides for a strong application of the principle of immutability of the claim. As a result of this, Ms Duarte Hueros would be left without redress in this case.[173]

The Court of Justice found that the combined application of the rules of the Spanish Civil Procedure Act made the exercise of the rights conferred upon Ms Duarte Hueros by the Directive extremely difficult and virtually impossible. It held in this regard the following:[174]

> In those circumstances, as the Advocate General observed in point 31 of her Opinion, it must be held that the Spanish legislation at issue in the main proceedings does not appear to comply with the principle of effectiveness, in so far as, in proceedings

---

169 Judgment of 3 October 2013, *Soledad Duarte Hueros v. Autociba SA and Automóviles Citroën España SA*, Case C-32/12, EU:C:2013:637.

170 Directive 1999/44/EC of the European Parliament and of the Council of 25 May 1999 on certain aspects of the sale of consumer goods and associated guarantees ([1999] O.J. L 171/12).

171 Judgment in *Duarte Hueros*, n. 169 above, paras. 17–19.

172 See below.

173 Judgment in *Duarte Hueros*, n. 169 above, paras. 20–22.

174 Judgment in *Duarte Hueros*, para. 41.

> brought by consumers in cases where the goods delivered are not in conformity with the contract of sale, it makes the enforcement of the protection which Directive 1999/44 seeks to provide to those consumers excessively difficult, if not impossible.

Note that, in the interpretation of the referring judge, there were three particularities that led to the incompatibility with the principle of effectiveness, namely the strict application of the principle of immutability of claims, the wide scope of *res judicata*, and the absence of powers for the judge to grant an alternative remedy. While the Advocate General had argued in her opinion that the focus should be on these other issues,[175] the Court of Justice took up the suggestion of the Spanish judge and held that the lack of power for the judge to grant the alternative remedy of its own motion was contrary to the principle of effectiveness.

The type of the relief sought in case of a defective product is not an issue that is limited to the Spanish legal order.[176] Also in other legal orders the question has emerged whether a judge can grant one of the other remedies listed in Article 3 of the Directive if the type of remedy applied for by the consumer is not appropriate in light of the defect complained of. This is the reason why the judgment in *Duarte Hueros* has received attention in the Belgian[177] and Dutch[178] legal orders. The question was thus whether EU law now gave judges the power, or imposed an obligation, to grant an alternative remedy of their own motion if the type of relief applied for by the consumer would not be appropriate considering the defect complained of.

Taking the issue in isolation, this may indeed have been the question the Court has answered. However, when the Court analyses an issue of national procedural law in light of the principle of effectiveness, it does so against the wider procedural context of that rule. Thus,

> each case which raises the question whether a national procedural provision renders the exercise of rights conferred on individuals by the Community legal order impossible or excessively difficult must be analysed by reference to the role of that

---

175 Opinion of Advocate General J. Kokott of 28 February 2013, *Duarte Hueros*, Case C-32/12, EU:C:2013:128, n. 169 above, para. 52.

176 Cf. Belgian Cour de Cassation, 23 January 2015, N° C.13.0034.N, *Rechtskundig Weekblad* 2016–17, 503.

177 S. Jansen and F. Peeraer, "Hof van Justitie beschermt keuzerecht consument bij gebrekkige zaak", De Juristenkrant, 6 November 2013, 2; S. Jansen, "De bevoegdheid van de nationale rechter om een prijsvermindering ambtshalve toe te wijzen", *Revue de droit commercial belge* 2014, 156, 159.

178 A. Hartkamp, "Ambtshalve toepassing van het Europees consumentenrecht. Een nieuw hoofdstuk: de richtlijn consumentenkoop", *Ars Aequi* 2006, 222–226; A.F.G. Ancery, "De reikwijdte van de plicht tot ambtshalve ingrijpen sterk ingeperkt?", *Tijdschrift voor Consumentenrecht & Handelspraktijken* 2014, 153–156.

> provision in the procedure, its progress and its special features, viewed as a whole, before the various national instances. In that context, it is necessary to take into consideration, where relevant, the principles which lie at the basis of the national legal system, such as the protection of the rights of the defence, the principle of legal certainty and the proper conduct of the proceedings.[179]

This means that the issue was not whether judges have the power to provide an alternative remedy of their own motion when it appears that the remedy applied for by the consumer is not appropriate, but rather whether judges have the power to provide an alternative remedy of their own motion when it appears that the remedy applied for by the consumer is not appropriate *if* the consumer is not allowed to amend his or her claim in the course of the proceedings *and* the scope of the *res judicata* effect of the judgment in the pending case would prevent the consumer from introducing the alternative claim in a new procedure.

These are two different questions and it was only the second question that was put to the Court. Looking at this from the perspective of the Belgian or Dutch legal order, the issue is now wholly irrelevant. Under Belgian civil procedure,[180] consumers would be allowed to amend their claims in the course of proceedings[181] and would not be precluded from bringing the alternative claim if the court rejected the initial claim.[182] (If the claim was still in time of course. But this is a question of prescription and not preclusion, which is a different matter and was not part of the discussion in *Duarte Hueros*.) The same goes for Dutch civil procedure, where parties are allowed to amend their claims in the course of the proceedings.[183] *Duarte Hueros* therefore does not concern the Belgian and Dutch legal orders and Belgian and Dutch judges are not required to implement the Court's decision. Quite to the contrary; *Duarte Hueros* does not even give them the power to do so if national procedural law would not allow them to raise an alternative claim of

---

179 Judgment of 21 February 2008, *Tele2 Telecommunication GmbH v. Telekom-Control-Kommission*, C-426/05, EU:C:2008:13, para. 55.

180 S. Jansen and F. Peeraer, "Hof van Justitie beschermt keuzerecht consument bij gebrekkige zaak", *De Juristenkrant*, 6 November 2013, p. 2.

181 Article 807 Belgian Judicial Code.

182 Article 23 Belgian Judicial Code.

183 A.F.G. Ancery, "De reikwijdte van de plicht tot ambtshalve ingrijpen sterk ingeperkt?", *Tijdschrift voor Consumentenrecht & Handelspraktijken* 2014, 153, 154. Contrary to Ancery, Hartkamp is also of the opinion that the Dutch res judicata rules would allow the alternative claim being brought in fresh proceedings. See A. Hartkamp, "Ambtshalve toepassing van het Europees consumentenrecht. Een nieuw hoofdstuk: de richtlijn consumentenkoop", *Ars Aequi* 2006, 222, 226. This does not matter, however, for the purposes of the relevance of *Duarte Hueros* for the Dutch legal order. The fact that a consumer is allowed to adapt his or her claims (certainly in first instance proceedings) suffices in light of *Duarte Hueros*, n. 169 above.

their own motion: the conditions for the application of the judgment in *Duarte Hueros* are simply not met. This can be illustrated by a judgment of the Belgian Cour de Cassation, in which a judgment of the Court of Appeal was annulled because it had violated the disposition principle by awarding a price reduction of its own motion whereas the applicant, a consumer, had only claimed the rescission of the contract.[184] This is a perfectly valid decision in light of *Duarte Hueros*. The analysis of the wider procedural context limits, thus, to a great extent the significance of the judgment and its purported intrusiveness for national procedural law. It is not relevant for many Member States and carries thus much less importance than one might believe when considering the relevant doctrine.[185] This was also rightly stressed by Ancery in his (Dutch language) case not under the judgment.[186]

This example illustrates how a decision of the Court with regard to the principle of effectiveness is in the first place addressed to the Member State in which the question has emerged. Because the answer given by the Court is determined by the wider procedural law context, it is generally very difficult to extend the impact of a Court's judgment beyond that legal order. Only when it appears that the procedural context in another Member State is largely

184 Belgian Cour de Cassation, 23 January 2015, N° C.13.0034.N, *Rechtskundig Weekblad* 2016–17, 503. Note that the consumers had claimed rescission with complete reimbursement and, failing that, a price reduction at a lower amount. The Court of Appeal rejected the rescission claim but then awarded a price reduction by way of damages that was higher than the amount claimed secondarily to rescission. The fact that the consumer had introduced a subsidiary claim already changes the procedural context compared to *Duarte Hueros*, demonstrating again the importance of the wider procedural context and how one small detail may change everything.

185 See, for example, S. Jansen, "Price reduction as a consumer sales remedy and the powers of national courts: Duarte Hueros" (2014) 51 *C.M.L. Rev.* 975, 990, who highlights the obligation for national courts to grant the alternative remedy and does only raise the wider procedural context to a limited extent. The same imbalance can be found in A. Hartkamp, "Ambtshalve toepassing van het Europees consumentenrecht. Een nieuw hoofdstuk: de richtlijn consumentenkoop", *Ars Aequi* 2006, 222, 226. In M. Jull Sørensen, "In the name of effective consumer protection and public policy!" (2016) *European Review of Private Law* 791, 807–808, the procedural context is almost disregarded completely. More importantly, the Dutch Report *Ambtshalve Toetsing III*, which provides Dutch judges with guidelines on how to apply the case law of the Court of Justice regarding the application of EU law by national courts of their own motion, does not mention any of these qualifying conditions. It states that the application of *Duarte Hueros* would not lead to problems in the Dutch legal order because they know the concept of "partial rescission", which corresponds *de facto* to price reduction. This is, however, not the point and goes beyond the obligation flowing from *Duarte Hueros*. See LOVCK & T, *Ambtshalve toetsing III* (2018), 15–16, to be consulted at: https://www.rechtspraak.nl/SiteCollectionDocuments/rapport-at-III-31-juli-2018.pdf.

186 A.F.G. Ancery, "De reikwijdte van de plicht tot ambtshalve ingrijpen sterk ingeperkt?", *Tijdschrift voor Consumentenrecht & Handelspraktijken* 2014, 153–156. (Note that Ancery is one of the authorities in the Netherlands on the subject, having written his PhD thesis on the application of EU law by Dutch courts of their own motion: A.F.G. Ancery, *Ambtshalve toepassing van EU-recht* (Kluwer, 2012), p. 246.

similar or the same, the judgment may also be binding for that Member State. This qualifies to a great extent the *erga omnes* effect of a preliminary ruling of the Court of Justice:[187] it has only *erga omnes* effect for the same situations. As soon as the procedural context differs, the same question may generate a completely different answer. Thus, when it comes to the question whether a judge is obliged to raise an alternative remedy based on Directive 1999/44/EC, the answer depends on the availability in the legal order concerned of means for the consumer to introduce the alternative claim. This means that there will not be a single or similar rule on the powers of the judge in this regard applicable throughout the European Union. The harmonising effect of the judgment is thus limited to similar situations. That being said, one could say that the judgment nevertheless leads to a convergence of standards throughout the European Union, namely that a consumer must not be penalised for having introduced the wrong claim and that there must be a possibility for him or her to introduce the alternative claim. This is surely true. But then we enter a discussion about what we understand by harmonisation[188] and the level on which one appreciates the harmonising effects of the case law of the Court. If it is about creating a common loose standard (procedural law must allow for consumers to have the alternative claim heard), then the decision in *Duarte Hueros* has indeed a large harmonising effect throughout the EU. If it is about creating a single rule or largely similar rules for the whole of the EU (the judge can raise an alternative claim), then the decision does not have great harmonising effects.

If we look at the judgment from a Spanish perspective, the decision surely has a harmonising effect in the sense that it brings Spain into line with a general European standard. The judgment results in Spanish consumers now having a level of protection that is largely similar to other European consumers, without there being necessarily a single rule. The same result will thus be achieved through different procedural design, which is basically the essence of procedural autonomy.

That being said, the judgment leads at the same time to fragmentation. According to the referring judge, the Spanish Civil Procedure Act prevents him from granting the alternative claim of price reduction if the claim to rescind the contract would not be justified in light of the defect complained of. This is so because, according to the referring judge, Article 218.1 CPA reflects "the principle that judicial decisions must be commensurate with the requests made by the parties".[189] Provided that this is a correct presentation of Spanish

---

[187] K. Lenaerts, I. Maselis and K. Gutman (J.T. Nowak (ed.)), *EU Procedural Law* (OUP, 2014), p. 244.

[188] Cf. M. Tulibacka, "Europeanization of civil procedures: in search of a coherent approach" (2009) 46 *C.M.L. Rev.* 1527, 1534; D. Vignes, "The harmonisation of national legislation and the EEC" (1990) *E.L. Rev.* 358–374.

[189] Judgment in *Duarte Hueros*, n. 169 above, para. 21.

procedural law, it means that the Court's decision in *Duarte Hueros* gives the referring judge the power to grant the alternative remedy and that Spanish courts in the future will have a larger power to introduce remedies of their own motion in cases falling within the scope of Directive 1999/44/EC compared to cases that do not fall within the scope of the Directive. On a more structural level, the decision of the Court has, as a consequence, that a dual regime is being created within the civil procedural framework of one single Member State, fragmenting the rules on the powers of the judge to act of her or his own motion. There is no longer one rule for all civil cases. Henceforth, there are two regimes: one for cases concerning Directive 1999/44/EC and one for all other cases.

The decision of the Court thus leads at the same time to harmonisation and fragmentation: harmonisation between the Member States on the possibility for consumers to have their claims based on Directive 1999/44/EC heard by a court, and fragmentation of the civil procedure rules on the powers of the judge within Spain and the Member States who find themselves in the same situation.

Before moving to the next issue, we should add a disclaimer here. For our argument, we worked on the basis of the judgment of the Court and the opinion of the Advocate General. We thus accepted Spanish law as it was presented by the referring national judge. During the seminar, it appeared however that the presentation of national procedural law by the referring judge was nuanced or contradicted by Spanish participants of the seminar.[190] This is part of a wider problem in relation to the Court's case law on national procedural law, namely that referring judges sometimes present their own interpretation of national procedural law to the Court rather than the accepted interpretation of national procedural law in that Member State.[191] This leads to the Court delivering preliminary rulings that merely have a virtual existence because they give a solution for a problem that only existed in the mind of the referring judge and not in the legal order referring Member State. Conversely, such judgments may then spark off a debate in other legal orders on how to implement them;[192] the irony of it all being that the judgment may cause

190 See also, R. Miquel Sala, "Verbraucherschutz auf Kosten der Dispositionsmaxime: War das erforderlich?" (2014) 3 *Journal of European Consumer and Market Law* 178–182.

191 The same appeared to have happened in regard of the case of *Sales Sinués*: Judgment of 14 April 2016, *Sales Sinués*, C-381/14 and C-385/14, EU:C:2016:252. See in this regard, S. Voet, "Actions for collective redress" in B. Hess (ed.), *An evaluation study of national procedural laws in terms of their impact on the free circulation of judgments and on the equivalence and effectiveness of the procedural protection of consumers under EU consumer law.* Report prepared by a consortium of European universities led by the MPI Luxembourg for Procedural Law as commissioned by the European Commission (JUST/2014/RCON/PR/CIVI/0082) – Strand 2: Procedural protection of consumers (Publications Office of the European Union, 2017), p. 251, 262–264.

192 See nn. 177 and 178 for references to the debate in the Belgian and Dutch legal doctrine.

effects in legal orders apart from the one legal order in which it was intended to have an effect. That being said, this does not detract from our analysis above. The case law of the Court of Justice regarding the principle of effectiveness does not necessarily entail harmonising effects, or only to a limited extent, and may even lead to fragmentation within a single Member State.

8. HARMONISATION WITHIN ONE MEMBER STATE

The principle of equivalence obliges Member States to treat claims based on EU law no less advantageously than claims based on national law.[193] This means for example that a damages claim against a Member State for a violation of EU law should not have a prescription period[194] that is inferior to the prescription period of a damages claim against the same Member State for a violation of national law.[195] Note that the principle of equivalence does not work both ways; it does not oppose to the application of a more favourable procedural regime to claims based on EU law.[196]

The principle of equivalence does not say anything about the content of a Member State procedural rule. It only entails an obligation for the Member States not to discriminate against claims based on EU law. Thus, contrary

193 K. Lenaerts, I. Maselis and K. Gutman (J.T. Nowak (ed.)), *EU Procedural Law* (OUP, 2014), pp. 118–119. See above, section 3.2.

194 The Court takes a large approach to procedural law issues, blurring the distinction between substantive law and procedural law on many occasions. (See W. Van Gerven, "Bridging the gap between Community and national laws: Towards a principle of homogeneity in the field of legal remedies?" (1995) 32 *C.M.L. Rev.* 679, 693–694.) In relation to prescription periods, it is clear that the Court looks at them through a procedural lens, even though some Member States consider prescription periods to be part of substantive law.

195 Generally, no dissimilar conditions such apply between such procedures. Cf. Judgment of 26 January 2010, *Transportes Urbanos y Servicios Generales*, Case C-118/08, EU:C:2010:39, n. 75 above.

196 While part of the Court's formula may suggest otherwise ("that a national rule be applied without distinction to procedures based on EU law and those based on national law"), it should be read together with the requirement that procedural rules must not be "less favourable than those governing similar domestic situations". (Taken from Judgment of 20 September 2018, *ESO KSI Slovensko s.r.o. v Ján Danko and Margita Danková*, Case C-448/17, EU:C:2018:745, paras. 37–38.) Moreover, it is inherent in the functioning of the principle of effectiveness that a more advantageous procedural rule can apply to claims based on EU law. On a proper construction, the principle of equivalence is thus only concerned with procedural rules that treat claims based on EU law les advantageous than equivalent claims based on national law and does not aim at equal or analogous treatment. Situations in which claims based on national law are treated less advantageously than similar claims based on EU law should be addressed by national constitutional law. See for an example in regard to Belgium, M.E. Storme, "De wet van 2 augustus 2002 inzake betalingsachterstand en de discriminatie inzake de verhaalbaarheid van advocatenkosten" (2003) 40 *Tijdschrift voor Privaatrecht* 1077, 1085–1086.

to the principle of effectiveness, there will be no evaluation of the actual procedural rule. The only effect that may follow from an application of the principle of equivalence is that Member States will have to extend the scope of a certain procedural rule to encompass claims based on EU law. This means that the principle of equivalence as such does not harmonise the procedural laws of the Member States. It will not lead to the imposition of a common rule or a common standard throughout the Member States. The result of its application is determined by the existing procedural rules in the Member States. It cannot add something that is not already there.

The fact that the Court applies the principle of equivalence consistently in a certain way does not alter that conclusion, even when this leads to similar outcomes in different Member States. The similarity is in that case not the result of the application of the principle of equivalence but of the pre-existing presence of similar procedural rules in the different Member States. For example, the fact that judges in various Member States apply EU competition law of their own motion is the result of a pre-existing obligation for judges in those Member States to apply national rules of public policy of their own motion. The principle of equivalence does not add anything to that procedural rule; it only states that the same treatment should be given to EU competition law.[197] The procedural law framework is thus already harmonised without EU law intervention.

The only harmonising effect that can be ascribed to the principle of equivalence is that claims based on EU law and claims based on Member State law are being treated in an equivalent way inside of a single Member State. This means that the procedural standard for EU law claims is at least equal to the procedural standard applicable to claims based on Member State law. This diminishes the fragmentation within the legal order of a particular Member State. At the same time, however, this may confirm differences in procedural laws between the Member States, making them applicable also in relation to claims based on EU law.

Let us go back to the example of a procedural rule that obliges national courts to apply national rules of public policy of their own motion and imagine the following situation. In Member State A, such a rule exists. In Member State B, such a rule does not exist. Courts in both Member States are not applying EU competition law of their own motion because courts in Member State A do not consider EU competition law to be a matter of public policy while courts in Member State B do not apply the law *ex officio*, which includes EU competition law. Consequently, EU competition law is applied in the same

[197] Judgment of 14 December 1995, *van Schijndel and van Veen*, Cases C-430/93 and C-431/93, EU:C:1995:441, n. 61 above, para. 22; Judgment of 4 June 2009, *T-Mobile Netherlands BV and Others v. Raad van bestuur van de Nederlandse Mededingingsautoriteit*, Case C-8/08, EU:C:2009:343, para. 49.

manner in both Member States. Now, let us apply the principle of equivalence to these two Member States, with the understanding that the Court of Justice has ruled that EU competition law must be treated in the same way as national rules of public policy. This results in courts in Member State A having to apply EU competition law of their own motion whereas courts in Member State B may continue not to apply EU competition law of their own motion. The consequence of the application of the principle of equivalence is thus the opposite of harmonisation: EU competition law is being treated differently in Member State A compared to Member State B as the result of the principle of equivalence. It does not harmonise procedural rules but extends the differences that exist between Member States in respect of claims based on national law to claims based on EU law: fragmentation instead of harmonisation.

9. THE PRINCIPLE OF SINCERE COOPERATION – INTENSIFYING THE FRAGMENTING EFFECTS OF THE PRINCIPLE OF EQUIVALENCE

A principle that is often overlooked in connection to the case law of the Court of Justice on national procedural law is the principle of sincere cooperation.[198] This is not justified since it can lead to procedural obligations for Member State courts that do not exist as such in Member State law. At the same time, it cannot be equated to the principle of effectiveness since some connection to Member State law must exist. It applies in matters where national procedural law leaves a discretion to the judge and transforms this discretion into an obligation.[199] The idea behind it is that a national court must do everything in its power to secure the effective application of EU law.[200] In terms of effect on national procedural law, it can be placed in between the principles of equivalence and effectiveness. It exists 'alongside' these two principles.[201]

The starting point is the principle of equivalence. If the national court has been given the discretion to take a certain course of action in relation to a claim

198 J.T. Lang, "The principle of loyal cooperation and the role of the national judge in Community, union and EEA law" (2006) 7(4) *ERA Forum* 476–501.

199 A. Wallerman, "Towards an EU law doctrine of the exercise of discretion in national courts? The member states' self-imposed limits on national procedural autonomy" (2016) 53 *C.M.L. Rev.* 339, 355.

200 It is the result of the application of Article 4(3) TEU to national courts. See in regard of the application of Article 4(3) TEU to national courts, Judgment of 13 November 1990, *Marleasing*, C-106/89, EU:C:1990:395, para. 8.

201 A. Wallerman, "Towards an EU law doctrine of the exercise of discretion in national courts? The member states' self-imposed limits on national procedural autonomy" (2016) 53 *C.M.L. Rev.* 339, 340.

based on national law, that discretion must also exist in relation to a similar claim based on EU law. The principle of equivalence, however, does not oblige the national court to exercise that discretion. Enter the principle of sincere cooperation. The application of this principle may require the national court to exercise the discretion allotted to it under national procedural law in cases involving EU law. The consequence is that an obligation is imposed upon the national court that did not exist under national procedural law. The origin of the obligation must still be a rule of national procedural law – in the absence of a rule allotting discretion to the national court no obligation can be created through the principle of sincere cooperation – but the transformation of a discretionary power into an obligation changes the nature of that rule to such an extent that it creates a different procedural regime, *de facto* amounting to a new rule.

The Court of Justice has applied the principle of sincere cooperation in this way to impose an obligation to reopen final (judicial) decisions contrary to EU law[202] and to enlarge the *ex officio* obligations of national courts in relation to EU law.[203] We will focus on this latter case law. A case in point here is *van Schijndel and van Veen*,[204] on whether a Dutch appeal court was under an obligation to apply Article 101 TFEU of its own motion if, for this purpose, it had to take facts into account on which the parties had not relied.

In that case, the Court of Justice set out the general framework following which national courts are required to raise points of EU law of their own motion. This can be summarised as follows:

- If national law obliges national courts to raise points of mandatory national law of their own motion when the parties failed to do so, the principle of equivalence requires them to do the same for mandatory rules of EU law;[205]
- If national law only confers a discretion on national courts to raise points of mandatory national law of their own motion when the parties failed to do so, the principle of sincere cooperation requires them to exercise that discretion in order to "ensure the legal protection which persons derive from the direct effect of provisions of [EU] law";[206]

---

202 Judgment of 13 January 2004, *Kühne & Heitz*, C-453/00, EU:C:2004:17, n. 113 above, para. 28; Judgment of 10 July 2014, *Impresa Pizzarotti*, C-213/13, EU:C:2014:2067, para. 62. Note that it concerns each the reopening of final decisions given in a context in which a last instance courts failed to make a reference for a preliminary ruling to the Court of Justice in breach of Article 267 TFEU.

203 Judgment of 14 December 1995, *van Schijndel and van Veen*, Cases C-430/93 and C-431/93, EU:C:1995:441, n. 61 above, para. 14.

204 See above, section 3.3.1.

205 Judgment in *van Schijndel and van Veen*, para. 13.

206 Judgment in *van Schijndel and van Veen*, para. 14.

- National courts are not obliged to raise points of EU law of their own motion if this would require "going beyond the ambit of the dispute defined by the parties themselves and relying on facts and circumstances other than those on which the party with an interest in application of those provisions bases his claim".[207]

It should be pointed out that the principle of equivalence is not limited to mandatory national law. If national procedural law would require courts to raise points of law of their own motion regardless of their mandatory nature, the same applies for rules of EU law. It is, however, not clear whether this also goes for the application of the principle of sincere cooperation, namely whether national courts have an obligation to raise of their own motion points of *EU law* that are not of a mandatory nature if those courts merely have a discretion to raise of their own motion points of *national law* that are not of a mandatory nature. Note that while in certain Member States the courts always have to raise the applicable law (e.g., Germany, the Netherlands), this is/was at the time of the judgment not always clear in other Member States (e.g., France, Belgium, Luxembourg). That being said, it is clear that for rules of a mandatory nature, a discretion under national law becomes an obligation under EU law. The notion "mandatory rules" is a bit unclear but encompasses surely rules of public policy. The Court of Justice has held in this regard that Article 101 TFEU[208] and Article 6 UCTD[209] should be equated to national rules of public policy for this purpose.

The Court's decision in *van Schijndel and van Veen* combines the principle of equivalence and the principle of sincere cooperation in order to impose on national judges who have the discretion to raise mandatory rules an obligation to raise rules of EU law of equal standing.[210] This is an interesting

[207] Judgment in *van Schijndel and van Veen*, n. 61 above, para. 22.

[208] Judgment of 4 June 2009, *T-Mobile*, C-8/08, EU:C:2009:343, n. 197 above, para. 49; Judgment of 13 July 2006, *Vincenzo Manfredi v. Lloyd Adriatico Assicurazioni SpA* (C-295/04), *Antonio Cannito v Fondiaria Sai SpA* (C-296/04) and *Nicolò Tricarico* (C-297/04) and *Pasqualina Murgolo* (C-298/04) *v. Assitalia SpA*, C-295/04 to C-298/04, EU:C:2006:461, para. 31.

[209] Judgment of 17 May 2018, *Karel de Grote*, C-147/16, EU:C:2018:320, n. 60 above, para. 35 and case law cited.

[210] It is, however, unfortunate that the Court of Justice no longer mentions the principle of sincere cooperation alongside the principle of equivalence in later case law, creating the impression that an obligation to exercise discretion merely flows from the principle of equivalence. This is, however, not in line with the goals of that principle. See also, A. Wallerman, "Towards an EU law doctrine of the exercise of discretion in national courts? The member states' self-imposed limits on national procedural autonomy" (2016) 53 *C.M.L. Rev.* 339, 353. Even more curious is that the Court gives the impression in more recent case law that the obligation to exercise the discretion may follow from a combined application of the principles of equivalence and effectiveness. See, for example, Judgment of 10 July 2014, *Impresa Pizzarotti*, C-213/13, EU:C:2014:2067, para. 62.

combination in light of the harmonisation question. We have seen in the previous section that the application of the principle of equivalence may lead to fragmentation instead of harmonisation of the procedural treatment of EU law, in that it extends the differences in procedural law that exist between Member States for the application of national law to the application of EU law. When adding the application of the principle of sincere cooperation to that, it appears that the Court's case law not only confirms the differences between the Member States but also intensifies those differences, pushing the procedural systems of the Member States further away from each other. Moreover, while the application of the principle of equivalence leads to a harmonisation within a single Member State of the procedural treatment of claims based on national law and claims based on EU law, the combination with the application of the principle of sincere cooperation leads again to fragmentation within that same Member State, creating two different regimes in regard of the origin of the claim.

One could point out that this is merely a theoretical concern, especially in relation to the raising of points of law of public policy by national courts of their own motion. This is generally true. Given their importance, the raising of rules of public policy will in principle be an obligation for a national court if it does not have to go beyond the ambit of the dispute as defined by the parties or the facts relied upon by the parties in support of their claim. However, we see that in the Belgian legal order, national courts have a discretion and not an obligation to raise rules of public policy of their own motion in relation to facts that are part of the file but have not been directly relied upon by the parties in support of their claims.[211] The principle of sincere cooperation can thus have a fragmenting effect here. Where it can also have such an effect is in relation to the powers of the French Cour de Cassation to raise pleas in law of its own motion. We will take up this example to develop our fragmentation argument further.

In accordance with Article 620 of the French Code of Civil Procedure (Code de procedure civile (CPC)), the French Court of Cassation has the power but not the obligation to raise pleas of pure law (*moyens de pur droit*) of its own motion.[212] These are pleas that do not require any assessment of the facts and solely focus on the correct application of the law in light of the facts established by the lower judge.[213] It is not entirely clear under French law under

---

211 Belgian Cour de Cassation, 17 March 2016, N° C.15.0235.N: "a judge has the possibility but not the obligation to raise points of law of public policy in relation to facts that are part of the case (file) but have not been directly relied upon by the parties in support of their claims."

212 Article 620 CPC: "La Cour de cassation peut rejeter le pourvoi en substituant un motif de pur droit à un motif erroné ; elle le peut également en faisant abstraction d'un motif de droit erroné mais surabondant. Elle peut, sauf disposition contraire, casser la décision attaquée en relevant d'office un moyen de pur droit."

213 J. Boré and L. Boré, *La cassation en matière civile* (Dalloz, 2008), p. 498.

which conditions the Cour de Cassation decides to exercise this discretionary power. It is, however, without question that the Cour de Cassation uses this power to raise points of law related to public policy rules.[214] There exists thus a power for the French Cour de Cassation to raise points of law related to public policy rules of its own motion. The application of the judgment in *van Schijndel and van Veen* to the situation of the French Cour de Cassation consequently results in an obligation for that court to raise of its own motion pleas in law based on EU rules of a public policy nature.[215] This fragments the power of the French Cour de Cassation to raise points of pure law of its own motion, as it would have an obligation to exercise its discretion for EU rules of public policy but not for national rules of public policy.

Enter the Belgian Cour de Cassation. This court is very similar to the French Cour de Cassation and, equally, cannot enter into the merits of the case. In contrast to the French Cour de Cassation, the Belgian Cour de Cassation does not have the power to raise pleas of pure law of its own motion in civil matters.[216] The application of the judgment in *van Schijndel and van Veen* did not change this. In the absence of any power under national law in this regard, there is also no power or obligation under EU law to do so.

When we compare the powers of the French Cour de Cassation and the Belgian Cour de Cassation to raise points of pure law of their own motion, a difference already existed before the application of the *van Schijndel and van Veen* judgment. The principle of equivalence confirmed this difference in relation to the application of EU rules of public policy. With the application of the principle of sincere cooperation, however, the difference between these two courts became stronger in relation to the procedural treatment of EU rules of public policy. While the Belgian Cour de Cassation continued not to have any powers in this regard, the French Cour de Cassation moved from a position of only having discretion to a position of having an obligation. The

---

214 J. Boré and L. Boré, *La cassation en matière civile* (Dalloz, 2008), p. 503.

215 See in this regard, G. Canivet and J.G. Huglo, "L'obligation pour le juge judiciare national d'appliquer d'office le droit communautaire au regard des arrêts *van Schijndel* et *Peterbroeck*", *Europe*, April 1996, Chron. No. 4, 2. Delicostopoulos and Szyczczak have pointed out that such instances will be rare (J. Delicostopoulos and E.M. Szyczczak, "Intrusions into national procedural autonomy: the French paradigm" (1997) 22 *European Law Review* 141, 147, as is with all points of pure law. See, however, the overview provided by the 2006 annual report of the French Cour de Cassation, which demonstrates an established practice in this regard: Cour de Cassation, *La Cour de cassation et la construction juridique européenne – Rapport annuel 2006* (La documentation française, 2007), 139–145. More recently, the French Cour de Cassation has raised points of law of its own motion based on the Product Liability Directive (Directive 85/374/EEC), considering it a matter of public policy: French Cour de Cassation, 7 July 2017, N° 15-25.651.

216 P. Gérard, H. Boularbah and J.-F. van Drooghenbroeck, *Pourvoi en cassation en matière civile* (Bruylant, 2012), pp. 24–25 and 115–120.

judgment in *van Schijndel and van Veen* thus pushed two Member States with closely connected procedural systems further away from each other instead of bringing them together. The difference between having no power and having an obligation is much stronger than the difference between having no power and having a discretionary power. The case law of the Court of Justice on national procedural law intensified here the existing fragmentation of procedural rules between Member States, rather than limiting it.

10. SPONTANEOUS HARMONISATION BY THE MEMBER STATES

The Court's case law on national procedural law only finds application within the scope of EU law. This means that its decisions on national procedural law do not extend beyond cases in which EU law is at stake. From a procedural point of view, EU law cases could thus be separated from national law cases, provided that the standard applicable in EU law cases is not inferior to the standard applied in national law cases. The procedural systems of the Member States are, however, constructed with the idea of coherence in mind. They aim at providing a uniform set of procedural rules for cases tried by their courts, covering both claims based on national law and claims based on EU law. The ideal of coherence may be put under pressure when the Court of Justice rules on an aspect of national procedural law that affects EU law. If the Court determines that the national procedural rule is not in line with EU law requirements, a different procedural rule would henceforth have to be applied for proceedings involving a claim based on EU law. This, however, undermines the coherence of the procedural system. Member States may then be tempted or pressurised into extending the application of the case law of the Court of Justice beyond the scope of EU law, affecting their regulatory autonomy for procedural law matters.[217] The (threat of) fragmentation of procedural law may lead in this way to a spontaneous harmonisation of the EU law procedural regime and the national law procedural regime within a single Member State.[218]

A well-known example is the *Factortame* case,[219] in which the Court held that interim relief should be available against the Crown in order to suspend

217 J.T. Nowak, "Considerations on the impact of EU Law on national civil procedure: Recent examples from Belgium" in V. Lazic and S. Stuij (eds.), *International dispute resolution. Short studies in private international law* (TMC Asser Press, 2018), pp. 1–41.

218 M. Eliantonio, "The future of national procedural law in Europe: Harmonisation vs. judge-made standards in the field of administrative justic" (2009) 13(3) *Electronic Journal of Comparative Law* 1, 2.

219 Judgment of 19 June 1990, *Factortame*, C-213/89, n. 44 above, EU:C:1990:257.

national rules that a national court suspects to be contrary to EU law pending the outcome of the ECJ preliminary reference procedure connected with this question. In the aftermath of that case, the principle of interim relief against the Crown was extended beyond the scope of EU law and also made available in case of violations of national law by the Crown.[220] More recently, the Belgian Constitutional Court had to rule on the conditions under which the Belgian state could be held liable for wrongful applications of Belgian law by a Belgian court.[221] Instead of developing a particular Belgian doctrine on this matter, the Belgian Constitutional Court held that national judges should apply the *Köbler*[222] criteria developed by the Court of Justice. It justified this move by referring to the principle of equality, namely that similar situations should not be treated differently.[223] From a procedural law perspective, this reflects the idea of coherence within a procedural law system, the Constitutional Court underlining the necessity to harmonise the guarantees recognised by EU law and national law.[224]

These are just two examples of spontaneous adaptations of national procedural rules in light of EU law. Such adaptations limit the fragmenting effects of the case law of the Court of Justice on national procedural law and may provide a blueprint for a further coming together of the procedural laws of the Member States. It is important to note that these adaptations consisted of extending a standard set by the Court of Justice to purely national situations, which demonstrates the growing influence of the Court of Justice on national procedural systems but at the same time raises the question whether it is appropriate for the Court to be regulating national procedural law, from the perspective of the division of competences between the EU and the Member

---

220 J. McKendrick, "Modifying procedural autonomy: Better protection for Community rights" (2000) 4 *European Review of Private Law* 565, 585.

221 Belgian Constitutional Court, 30 June 2014, N° 99/2014.

222 Judgment of 30 September 2003, *Köbler*, C-224/01, EU:C:2003:513, n. 109 above.

223 *Ibid.*, para. B.22: "Afin de respecter le principe d'égalité, il appartient au juge de la responsabilité de tenir compte de tels éléments afin de déterminer si la faute commise par une juridiction statuant en dernier ressort, en dehors du champ d'application du droit de l'Union européenne, constitue une violation suffisamment caractérisée des règles de droit applicables."

224 *Ibid.*, B.21: "compte tenu de la nécessité d'harmoniser les garanties reconnues par le droit de l'Union européenne, d'une part, et par le droit interne, d'autre part, la Cour tient compte de la jurisprudence de la Cour de justice". This logic also lies at the basis of the seminal judgment of the Court of Justice in *Associação Sindical dos Juízes Portugueses*. The judgment has received until now not the attention it deserves. It may, however, be as ground-breaking as *Van Gend en Loos*, n. 29 above, or *Costa v. ENEL*, n. 26 above, especially for national procedural law. The Court of Justice effectively confirms that national procedural law should always take EU law requirements into account, as every rule on court organisation or on the conduct of proceedings will also serve the application of EU law. The idea of within or outside the scope of EU law does not play a role in this regard: Judgment of 27 February 2018, *Associação Sindical dos Juízes Portugueses v Tribunal de Contas*, C/64/16, EU:C:2018:117.

States, the division of powers between the EU institutions,[225] but also from a democratic point of view. Is it for the courts or the legislator to regulate procedural law?

11. CONCLUDING REMARKS

The aim of this chapter was to put into perspective the harmonisation powers that have been ascribed to the Court's case law on national procedural law, in particular the case law on national procedural autonomy. What may appear as an act of harmonisation at first sight may lead to the complete opposite result when bringing national procedural law into the equation. It shows the importance of a contextual analysis of the Court's case law on national procedural law by applying a comparative law perspective.

The conclusions of this exercise can be summarised as follows:

- The first part of this chapter aimed to unpack the concept of procedural autonomy which is deemed to govern the relationship between the EU and the Member States in the context of civil procedure; moreover the concept has come to shape the role of the ECJ, in – paradoxically – on the one hand, identifying the principle of national procedural autonomy in itself, and on the other, making inroads into this principle. We have identified where national procedural rules and practices undermine these principles of effectiveness and equivalence.
- To this end, we have attempted to unpack the notion of procedural autonomy, as well as the limitations to it identified by the ECJ, namely effectiveness and equivalence.
- Fundamentally, when we talk of national procedural autonomy, we must question – in light of a short analysis of the legal and political framework shaping the EU's competences and endeavours in the field of civil procedure – whether what we are talking about is really autonomy.
- In the literature, the concept of procedural autonomy is often placed in direct opposition to the principles of effectiveness and equivalence; in light of an assessment of the case law of the ECJ, this formulation rather seems to be inconsistent, particularly as the ECJ frequently examines only the compliance of the national procedural rule or practice with the principle of effectiveness.
- Against this background, we have set out the key case law of the ECJ as regards its construction of the principle of procedural autonomy, the principle of

225 M. Dougan, *National Remedies Before the Court of Justice: Issues of Harmonisation and Differentiation* (Hart Publishing, 2004), p. 392.

equivalence and effectiveness, and as regards the latter, more specifically, national rules and practices pertaining to the *ex officio* examination of EU law, the availability of remedies at the national level and the principle of *res judicata*.

- When one talks about the harmonising effect of the Court's case law, one must define clearly what this means. Does it mean rule harmonisation or standard harmonisation? Moreover, does it mean harmonisation between all Member States, a few Member States or within one Member State, between claims based on national law and claims based on EU law? Harmonisation is a layered concept and the case law of the Court may not reflect all these layers.
- In many instances, the case law of the Court on national procedural law may have fragmentation effects, either within a single Member State or between Member States. The principle of equivalence may buttress or strengthen the differences between Member States whereas the principle of effectiveness may cause fragmentation within the national system. The principle of sincere cooperation may even lead to fragmentation in both situations.
- The issue of fragmentation is the result of the fact that the Court's case law only applies to issues within the scope of EU law. Member States are not required by EU law to extend interpretations of the principle of effectiveness to the whole of their national procedural law. Member States may also not want to do this in order to preserve their regulatory autonomy in this regard. It may, however, be challenging to maintain different procedural regimes within one Member State. This is especially so since the procedural systems of the Member States are built on the idea of coherence. In a bid to maintain such coherence, some Member States may then apply the case law of the Court also outside the scope of the EU law. The 2014 judgment of the Belgian Constitutional Court serves as a good example in this regard. This amounts to a reverse application of the principle of equivalence, and raises important questions about the role of the Court of Justice as a regulator of national procedural law.[226]

[226] M. Dougan, *National Remedies Before the Court of Justice: Issues of Harmonisation and Differentiation* (Hart Publishing, 2004), p. 395: "[O]n might ultimately feel pressed towards the conclusion that remedial harmonisation … is a task to which the Court is inherently unsuited."

CONSTITUTIONALISATION OF EUROPEAN CIVIL PROCEDURE AS A STARTING POINT FOR HARMONISATION?

Dominik DÜSTERHAUS*

1. INTRODUCTION

Constitutionalisation may be concisely defined as the incremental re-shaping of statutory law by means of its judicial interpretation in the light of constitutional principles and values.[1] Within the different fields of EU law,

* All views expressed are personal to the author.

1 As B. Hess, "Die Konstitutionalisierung des europäischen Privat- und Prozessrechts", *Juristenzeitung* [JZ] 2005, 540, defines the term of constitutionalisation.

this concept can be approached either broadly[2] or broken down into more specific aspects, notably a purely judicial-protection-based perspective, dealing with how Article 47 of the EU Charter of Fundamental Rights (CFR) infuses, amends or supplements the statutory law, at both EU and domestic levels. This is the perspective I have adopted for the present contribution.

Two characteristic features of how the European Court of Justice (ECJ) deals with EU law appear to favour its constitutionalisation. These are the affinity towards teleological interpretation[3] and the Court's constructive use of precedent,[4] which allows the incremental creation of constitutional principles by way of de-contextualisation of specific considerations. Does this also apply to procedural rights? This contribution will argue that, within the limits of its jurisdiction, when dealing with procedural issues under Article 47 CFR the ECJ certainly fosters a common standard of procedural rights by construing primary and secondary law in a way that ensures its compliance as well as that of domestic rules and practices with the requirements of fair, effective and expedient judicial protection.

The European Court of Justice may not aim at constitutionally harmonising civil procedure across the EU and individual, case-specific judgments are certainly no blue-prints for future procedural legislation, even less so where they concern other fields of EU law. Still, insofar as they all implement and further characterise the guarantees enshrined in Article 47 CFR, they are indeed a useful starting point for legislative harmonisation. The argument in this chapter develops as follows. In the first instance, the defining aspects of fair trial in civil matters will be recalled (section II); secondly, the scope of ECJ involvement with procedural issues will be outlined (section III); and thirdly, the Court's method of constitutionalisation as understood by this author will be described (section IV).

2. THE CONCEPT OF FAIR TRIAL UNDER ECHR AND EU LAW

While this chapter specifically addresses the EU law guarantees as interpreted by the ECJ, there is no way around a brief exposition of the ECHR requirements for civil proceedings, which have previously been the prime benchmark for EU law interpretation and are still good law within the scope of Article 47 CFR.[5]

---

2 For an example of this approach, focusing on the implementation of principles and values of EU integration, see D. Düsterhaus, "Does the European Court of Justice constitutionalise EU Private International Law?" (2017) 6(2) *Cambridge International Law Journal* 159.

3 B. Hess (n. 1 above) 540.

4 D. Düsterhaus, "Eppur Si Muove! The Past, Present, and (possible) Future of Temporal Limitations in the Preliminary Ruling Procedure" (2018) 36 *Yearbook of European Law* 1.

5 Pursuant to Article 52(3) CFR. See in detail section 4 below, as well as P. Gilliaux, *Droit(s) européen(s) à un procès équitable* (Bruylant, 2012).

2.1. ARTICLE 6(1) ECHR

As further detailed in ECtHR case law, Article 6(1) ECHR[6] covers an important number of procedural guarantees in civil matters. As regards *access to a Court*,[7] they include the right to commence civil proceedings,[8] legal aid where necessary,[9] protection against disproportionate court fees,[10] even recourse to electronic filing, where available.[11]

As far as the topical *fair hearing* itself is concerned, the requirement of fairness implies that the parties must be given sufficient and adequate opportunity to present their views on both the legal and factual aspects of the case.[12] The ECtHR generally takes a holistic approach and dispenses with an abstract definition. It may nevertheless be understood that the requirement of fairness provides parties with a right to present all observations and evidence that they consider relevant to their case, and puts on courts a "duty to conduct a proper examination of the submissions, arguments and evidence adduced by the parties, without prejudice to its assessment whether they are relevant to its decision".[13] It also involves a duty for the court to communicate, on its own initiative, all documents that it has at its disposal, so that parties are given an effective opportunity to comment on all available information.[14]

Alongside these general considerations, the ECtHR has further characterised specific guarantees.

The right to *adversarial proceedings* requires that the parties are given an opportunity to have knowledge of and comment on the observations filed or

---

6 "In the determination of his civil rights and obligations or of any criminal charge against him, everyone is entitled to a fair and public hearing within a reasonable time by an independent and impartial tribunal established by law. Judgment shall be pronounced publicly but the press and public may be excluded from all or part of the trial in the interests of morals, public order or national security in a democratic society, where the interests of juveniles or the protection of the private life of the parties so require, or to the extent strictly necessary in the opinion of the court in special circumstances where publicity would prejudice the interests of justice."

7 ECtHR *Naït-Liman v. Switzerland*, Appl. No. 51357/07, §§114–115. Of special interest in connection with transnational litigation should be that, depending on the circumstances, a court which declines to take international jurisdiction may or may not infringe Article 6(1) ECtHR. See, on the one hand, ECtHR *Arlewin v. Sweden*, Appl. No. 22302/10, and, on the other, ECtHR *Naït-Liman v. Switzerland*, Appl. No. 51357/07.

8 "The right to a fair hearing, as guaranteed by Article 6 (1) ECHR, must be construed in the light of the rule of law, which requires that all litigants should have an effective judicial remedy enabling them to assert their civil rights" (ECtHR *Al-Dulimi and Montana Management Inc. v. Switzerland*, Appl. No. 5809/08, §126).

9 ECtHR *Steel and Morris v. UK*, Appl. No. 68416/01.

10 ECtHR *Weissman v. Romania*, Appl. No. 63945/00.

11 ECtHR *Lawyer Partners AS v. Slovakia*, Appl. No. 54252/07.

12 ECtHR *Bricmont v. Belgium*, Appl. No. 9938/82.

13 ECtHR *Perez v. France*, Appl. No. 47287/99, §80.

14 ECtHR *Kerojärvi v. Finland*, Appl. No. 17506/90, §42.

evidence adduced by the other party[15] or relevant information at the court's disposal.[16] For *equality of arms* to be guaranteed, there must be a reasonable opportunity to present one's case and evidence under conditions not placing one at a substantial disadvantage *vis-à-vis* the opponent.[17] There must be adequate information of the proceedings[18] and, of course, *effective service*,[19] which is the source of abundant and quite diverse ECtHR case law.

Article 6(1) ECHR does not provide for specific forms of service of documents[20] and allows the Contracting States to organise their legal systems in a manner which facilitates expeditious and efficient judicial proceedings, including provision for the possibility of issuing default judgments.[21] However, if court documents, including summonses to hearings, are not served in person, with a proof of delivery,[22] an applicant could be unduly prevented from defending himself in the proceedings.[23]

The *right to an oral hearing*[24] does not constitute an absolute obligation, notably considering that some cases are better dealt with in writing.[25] Also, the right to be present at a trial can be waived, provided that the waiver is made of one's own free will, either expressly or tacitly; it is established in an unequivocal manner; that there are minimum safeguards commensurate to its importance; and that it does not run counter to any important public interest.[26] And of course there is a right to be assisted by a lawyer.[27]

Judgments must be *adequately reasoned*, meaning that courts must indicate with sufficient clarity the grounds on which they base their decision.[28] Parties can expect to receive a specific and explicit reply to the arguments which are

---

15 ECtHR *Lobo Machado v. Portugal*, Appl. No. 15764/89, §31.

16 ECtHR *Ruiz Mateos v. Spain*, Appl. No. 12952/87.

17 ECtHR *Ankerl v. Switzerland*, Appl. No. 17748/91. See also ECtHR *Krčmár v. Czech Republic*, Appl. No. 35376/97, §39; ECtHR *Dombo Beheer v. Netherlands*, Appl. No. 14448/88, §33.

18 ECtHR *Colozza v. Italy*, Appl. No. 9024/90, §28.

19 ECtHR *Beer v. Austria*, Appl. No. 30428/96, §18; ECtHR *Övüs v. Turkey*, Appl. No. 42981/04; ECtHR *Miholapa v. Latvia*, Appl. No. 61655/00, §29; ECtHR *Gospodinov v. Bulgaria*, Appl. No. 62722/00, §40.

20 ECtHR *Lay Lay Company Ltd. v. Malta*, Appl. No. 30633/11, §60; ECtHR *Aždajić v. Slovenia*, Appl. No. 71872/12, §48.

21 ECtHR *Aždajić v. Slovenia*, Appl. No. 71872/12, §48.

22 ECtHR *Godorozea v. Moldova*, Appl. No. 17023/05, §31.

23 ECtHR *Weber v. Germany*, Appl. No. 4769/02; ECtHR *Aždajić v. Slovenia*, Appl. No. 71872/12, §48. See also ECtHR *Dilipak and Karakaya v. Turkey*, Appl. Nos. 7942/05 and 24838/05, §§76–80, as well as the assessment by F. Gascón Inchausti, "Service of proceedings on the defendant as a safeguard of fairness in civil proceedings: in search of minimum standards from EU legislation and European case-law" (2017) 13(3) *Journal of Private International Law* 475, 482.

24 ECtHR *Jussila v. Finland*, Appl. No. 73053/01.

25 ECtHR *Schuler-Zgraggen v. Austria*, Appl. No. 14518/89.

26 ECtHR *Sejdovic v. Italy*, Appl. No. 56581/00.

27 ECtHR *Poitrimol v. France*, Appl. No. 14032/88, §34.

28 ECtHR *Hadjanastassiou v. Greece*, Appl. No. 12945/87.

decisive for the outcome of the proceedings.[29] This allows them to see whether they have indeed been given a fair hearing. It also enables them to make effective use of the possibilities for appeal.[30] Whilst the Convention does not compel the Contracting States to set up courts of appeal in civil cases, where such courts do exist, the guarantees of Article 6 must be complied with, *inter alia*, by ensuring to litigants an effective access to the courts.[31] As expressly stated in Article 6(1), the hearing and the pronouncement of the judgment must be public in principle.[32] Moreover, there is ample case law on the requirement of *adjudication by an impartial*[33] *and independent*[34] *tribunal*, as well as on *trial within a reasonable time.*[35]

Finally, Article 6(1) ECHR also guarantees the *enforcement of a civil judgment.*[36] There must be no interferences by national law with that right, unless the interference or the refusal to take positive measures is justified, in line with the principle of proportionality. The ECHR nevertheless accommodates reasonable conditions that a judgment must fulfill, in line with international standards, for its recognition and enforcement.[37]

2.2. THE CFR PERSPECTIVE

Article 47 CFR codifies the requirements concerning the access to, and conduct of, judicial proceedings under EU law which the ECJ has over time recognised under the general principles of effective judicial protection and fair trial.[38] As the Explanations relating to the Charter[39] state, the first paragraph of Article 47 CFR is based on Article 13 of the ECHR (effective remedy), while the second paragraph corresponds to Article 6(1) of the ECHR.

---

29 ECtHR *Deryan v. Turkey*, Appl. No. 41721/04, §33.

30 ECtHR *Hirvisaari v. Finland*, Appl. No. 49684/99, §30.

31 ECtHR *Andrejeva v. Latvia*, Appl. No. 55707/00, §97.

32 ECtHR *Levages Prestations Services v. France*, Appl. No. 21920/93, §44; *Poitrimol v France*, Appl. No. 14032/88, §§13–15.

33 ECtHR *Micallef v. Malta*, Appl. No. 17056/06.

34 ECtHR *Baka v. Hungary*, Appl. No. 20261/12.

35 ECtHR *Sürmeli v. Germany*, Appl. No. 75529/01.

36 ECtHR *Hornsby v. Greece*, Appl. No. 42338/98; ECtHR *Abaluta v. Romania*, 38196/05.

37 P. Kinsch, "Enforcement as a Fundamental Right", *Nederlands Internationaal Privaatrecht* [2014] 540. In the context of EU law compare with the distinct situation of different time-limits for the execution of judicial decisions among the Member States, Case C-379/17, *Società Immobiliare Al Bosco* [EU:C:2018:806].

38 For an overview see D. Ritleng, "L'encadrement des procedures devant le juge national par le droit à un procès équitable" in Picheral (ed.), *Le droit à un procès équitable au sens du droit de l'Union européenne* (Paris, 2012), 103; H. Jarass, "Bedeutung der EU-Rechtsschutzgewährleistung für nationale und EU-Gerichte", *Neue Juristische Wochenschrift* 2011, 1393.

39 OJ 2007 C-303/17 of 14 December 2007.

Just like the requirements laid down in Articles 6(1) and 13 ECHR,[40] the provisions of Article 47 CFR[41] differ from substantive rights in purpose and operational mode: Fair trial requirements as laid down in Articles 47(2) CFR and 6(1) ECHR are meant to secure the judicial assertion of rights, whereas specific shortcomings in this connection may call for a remedy within the meaning of Articles 13 ECHR and 47(1) CFR. While under Article 52(3) CFR the protection of the rights enshrined in the Charter may be no less than the guarantees under the ECHR, this does not hinder their autonomous interpretation, not least because the Charter may, pursuant as well to its Article 52(3), always grant more extensive protection than the ECHR.

Indefinitely more challenging than the interplay of these sources of procedural rights is their judicial implementation with regard to the European Union's attributed powers and composite legal order. To what extent does domestic procedural law come within the scope of EU law and the Court's fundamental rights jurisdiction? The following exploration may help appreciate the challenges and merits of procedural constitutionalisation in this context.

3. THE SCOPE OF PROCEDURAL CONSTITUTIONALISATION UNDER EU LAW

Procedural law is not a *domaine réservé* of the Member States. As Koen Lenaerts has aptly put it, each Member State "contributes its own judicial system for the sake of ensuring the effective application and enforcement of EU law".[42] Whilst the national courts guarantee, within their spheres of competence, procedural fairness as required *inter alia* by EU law, it is the Court of Justice which, when asked to do so, determines what the EU standard of procedural fairness is by interpreting Articles 19(1), (2) TEU and 47 CFR, as well as any act having a bearing on the matter. In this connection, notably the growing body of transnational procedural law comes to mind.[43]

---

40 M. Safjan and D. Düsterhaus, "A Union of Effective Judicial Protection – Addressing a Multilevel Challenge Through the Lens of Article 47 CFR" (2014) 33(1) *Yearbook of European Law* 3–41.

41 "Everyone whose rights and freedoms guaranteed by the law of the Union are violated has the right to an effective judicial remedy before a tribunal"; "everyone is entitled to a fair and public hearing within a reasonable time by an independent and impartial tribunal previously established by law" and has "the possibility of being advised, defended and represented"; "legal aid shall be made available to those who lack sufficient resources insofar as such aid is necessary to ensure effective access to justice."

42 K. Lenaerts, "The Rule of Law and the Coherence of the Judicial System of the European Union" (2007) 44(6) *C.M.L. Rev.* 1625–1659, 1625.

43 See below, section 3.3.

3.1. THE ELUSIVE SCOPE OF ARTICLE 47 CFR

Where EU law applies, procedures must comply with the requirements of effective judicial protection as defined by the Court of Justice.[44] Whether this is the case may be assessed, on the one hand, from an institutional point of view. As the Court has recently confirmed in *ASJP*, Article 19(1) TEU not only lays down the structural complementarity of the European Union's judicial architecture but also allows for the scrutiny of whether national judiciaries institutionally comply with the EU standard of effective judicial protection.[45]

On the other hand, procedural fairness is, of course, a key guarantee bestowed upon individuals by Article 47 CFR. However, because of the latter's narrow scope of application, the Court's confirmation of the institutional dimension of effective judicial protection in *ASJP* was of utmost importance. Indeed, while Article 47 CFR is a binding,[46] directly applicable and effective[47] provision of EU law, it may still not be relevant in any given case coming before the ECJ, for its jurisdiction over the Charter is not unconditional. The Court can only adjudicate on Article 47 CFR in respect of legal situations falling within the scope of EU law. This covers the actions of the EU institutions, bodies and agencies, as well as those of the Member States insofar as they are implementing EU law, i.e. applying, transposing, executing, derogating from, or simply infringing provisions other than those of the Charter. While nothing stands in the way of respecting Article 47 CFR outside the so-determined scope of EU law, this will not establish ECJ jurisdiction. Numerous failed preliminary ruling references on arguably insufficient judicial protection bear witness to this fact.[48] In practice, the requirement under Article 51 CFR to be implementing EU law for the Charter rights to bite results in a complex

44 M. Safjan and D. Düsterhaus (n. 40 above).

45 Case C-64/16 *Associação Sindical dos Juízes Portugueses v. Tribunal de Contas* [EU:C:2018:117].

46 See Article 6(1) TEU.

47 "Article 47 of the Charter on the right to effective judicial protection is sufficient in itself and does not need to be made more specific by provisions of EU or national law to confer on individuals a right which they may rely on as such", Case C-414/16 *Egenberger* [EU:C:2018:257].

48 See, e.g. Case C-457/09 *Chartry* [EU:C:2011:101] as well as Case C-213/10 *F-Tex SIA* [EU:C:2012:215], Case C-483/11 *Boncea* [EU:C:2011:832], Case C-492/11 *Di Donna* [EU:C:2013:225], Case C-499/12 *Gentile* [EU:C:2013:77], Case C-555/12 *Loreti* [EU:C:2013:174], Case C-73/13 *T* [EU:C:2013:299], Case C-224/13 *Lorrai*, [EU:C:2013:750], Case C-258/13 *Sociedade Agrícola e Imobiliária da Quinta de S. Paio* [EU:C:2013:810], Case C-371/13 *SC Schuster & Co.*, [EU:C:2013:748], Case C-28/14 Pańczyk [EU:C:2014:2003], Case C-45/14 *Bálazs and Papp*, [EU:C:2014:2021], Case C-380/15 *Garzón Ramos* [EU:C:2016:112], Case C-407/15 *Ripanu* [EU:C:2016:167], Case C-520/15 *Aiudapds* [EU:C:2016:124], Case C-532/15 *Eurosaneamientos* [EU:C:2016:932], Case C-321/16 *Pardue* [EU:C:2016:871], Case C-508/16 *Boudjellal*, [EU:C:2017:6], Case C-589/16 *Filippi* [EU:C:2018:417], Case C-131/17 *Hélder José Cunha Martins* [EU:C:2017:902], Case C-177/17 *Demarchi Gino Sas* [EU:C:2017:656], Case C-344/17 *IJDF Italy* [EU:C:2017:924].

collocation of EU, ECHR and domestic procedural fundamental rights. In civil proceedings, in the course of which Member State and ECHR guarantees have to be observed as well, Article 47 CFR is engaged

- where substantive EU law is the litigation object[49] or frames procedural obligations,[50]
- where EU law sets out common/specific procedural rules,[51]
- where jurisdiction is examined on the basis of EU law rules,[52]
- where service is (to be) effected pursuant to Regulation 1393/2007,[53]
- where a judgment is to be certified for the purpose of cross-border enforcement,[54] or such enforcement is contested,[55]
- where evidence is gathered abroad,[56]
- where EU law makes specific procedural provision for the domestic adjudication of cross-border disputes.[57]

In a nutshell, the fields in which Article 47 CFR may have a bearing on procedural rules and practices are thus the following. First, there is the enforcement of substantive EU law in the absence of common procedural rules, comprising situations where effective judicial protection serves the enforcement of EU law (section 3.2.1 below), as well as those where the guarantees enshrined in Article 47 CFREU may constitute limits to such enforcement (3.2.2 below). Next in line is the Member State implementation or application of procedural provisions under secondary law, specifically in

49 Case C-279/09 *DEB* [EU:C:2010:811].

50 See, in the field of consumer protection, e.g. Case C-169/14 *Sánchez Morcillo and Abril Garcia* [EU:2014:2099]. As regards fundamental freedoms, see Case C-291/09 *Francesco Guarnieri & Co* [EU:C:2011:217].

51 E.g. the Patent Court Rules or incidental provisions of the IP directive (Directive 2004/48/EC of the European Parliament and of the Council of 29 April 2004 on the enforcement of intellectual property rights, OJ 2004 L 157) and anti-trust private enforcement directive (Directive 2014/104/EU of the European Parliament and of the Council of 26 November 2014 on certain rules governing actions for damages under national law for infringements of the competition law provisions of the Member States and of the European Union, OJ 2014 L 349).

52 Notably the Brussels I(a) Regulation, see Case C-112/13 *A v. B and Others* [EU:C:2014:2195].

53 Case C-354/15 *Henderson* [EU:C:2017:157].

54 Case C-300/14 *Imtech Marine Belgium* [EU:C:2015:825].

55 Case C-156/12 *GREP* (order) [EU:C:2012:342].

56 Council Regulation (EC) No. 1206/2001 of 28 May 2001 on cooperation between the courts of the Member States in the taking of evidence in civil or commercial matters (OJ 2001 L 174, p. 1).

57 See Council Directive 2003/8/EC of 27 January 2003 to improve access to justice in cross-border disputes by establishing minimum common rules relating to legal aid for such disputes (OJ 2003 L 26) at issue in Case C-670/15 *Šalplachta* [EU:C:2017:594] or Directive 2008/52/EC of the European Parliament and of the Council of 21 May 2008 on certain aspects of mediation in civil and commercial matters (OJ 2008 L 136).

the field of judicial cooperation (section 3.3). Whilst the varying degree of autonomy left to the Member States across these fields does not alter the requirements of effective judicial protection,[58] it still affects the way these requirements are met in practice.

3.2. IN THE ABSENCE OF EU RULES GOVERNING THE MATTER

Even where EU legislation does not lay down a specific procedural rule in order to guarantee effective judicial protection, Member State action under EU law is framed by its requirements, both in order to effectively enforce that law and to ensure that its enforcement does not itself interfere with Article 47 CFR.

3.2.1. Effective Judicial Protection Serving the Effectiveness of EU Law

As one of the classics[59] of EU law currently[60] reads,

> in the absence of European Union rules governing the matter, it is for the domestic legal system of each Member State to designate, with due observance of [the obligation to provide effective judicial protection and the principles of effectiveness and equivalence], the courts and tribunals with jurisdiction and to lay down the detailed procedural rules governing actions brought to safeguard rights which individuals derive from EU law.

Thus, where there is such a right, the rules for its enforcement must comply with Article 47 CFR and the principles of equivalence and effectiveness (the "*Rewe* principles").

"In the absence of EU rules governing the matter" does not mean, however, that procedural autonomy and its limits, i.e. equivalence, effectiveness and/or autonomous review under Article 47 CFR, come into play only where the applicable EU law contains no procedural rules.[61] They may also operate alongside such rules insofar as specific aspects are not governed by them[62] or they leave Member States with considerable discretion, in the exercise of which Article 47 CFR can provide guidance.[63] Moreover, Member

58 See P. van Cleynenbreugel, "Case note on *Samba Diouf*" (2012) 49 *C.M.L. Rev.* 327–348, 345 and the Opinion of Advocate General Cruz Villalón in this case, notably point 32.

59 Building upon a first statement in this sense in Case 33/76, *Rewe-Zentralfinanz and Rewe-Zentral* [EU:C:1976:188] para. 5.

60 Case C-176/17 *Profi Credit Polska* [EU:C:2018:711].

61 Case C-214/16 *King* [2017] EU:C:2017:914. Compare with Case C-510/13 *E.ON. Földgáz Trade* [EU:C:2015:189] and Case C-403/16 *El Hassani* [EU:C:2017:960].

62 Case C-73/16 *Puškár* [EU:C:2017:725].

63 Case C-69/10 *Samba Diouf* [EU:C:2011:524].

State legislation is often scrutinised both under detailed secondary law requirements and with regard to effectiveness and effective judicial protection.[64]

According to the Court, the requirements of equivalence and effectiveness "embody" the general obligation on the Member States to ensure judicial protection of an individual's rights under EU law. They apply both as regards the designation of the courts and tribunals having jurisdiction to hear and determine actions based on EU law and as regards the definition of detailed procedural rules.[65] It should be stressed, however, that within the remit of Article 47 CFR its specific requirements must always be the yardstick for national procedural rules.[66] Whether these requirements superpose the *Rewe* principles, infuse them with their specific purpose or leave them unaltered may notably turn on the procedural and legislative context. In a previous publication,[67] this author has co-identified five scenarios of descending intertwinement between effective judicial protection and the *Rewe* principles, i.e. exclusivity,[68] superposition,[69] coexistence,[70] infusion[71] and autonomy.[72] Their diverging scope and content notwithstanding, all these judgments impart the emerging EU standard of fair and effective protection.[73] But, then again, effective judicial protection by national courts does not always serve the purpose of furthering the effectiveness of such rights. It can also be a safeguard against undue enforcement of EU law.

3.2.2. *Effective Judicial Protection vs Effectiveness of EU Law*

As regards the requirement of a right guaranteed by EU law within the meaning of Article 47 of the Charter, it should be borne in mind that it covers

64 See for example Case C-415/11 *Aziz* [EU:C:2013:164].

65 M. Safjan and D. Düsterhaus (n. 40 above).

66 Joined Cases C-317/08 to C-320/08 *Alassini and Others* [EU:C:2010:146], para. 49.

67 M. Safjan and D. Düsterhaus (n. 40 above).

68 The reasons vary, compare e.g. Case C-243/09 *Fuß v. Stadt Halle* [EU:C:2010:609], Case C-279/09 *DEB* [EU:C:2010:811] and Case C-685/15 *Online Games* [EU:C:2017:452].

69 See, on the one hand, Case C-510/13 E.ON. *Földgáz Trade* [EU:C:2015:189], para. 50 with reference to Case C-12/08, *Mono Car Styling* [EU:C:2009:466], para. 49 and, on the other, Case C-169/14 *Sánchez Morcillo and Abril García v. BBVA* [EU:C:2014:2099]. An analogous reasoning can be found in Case C-61/14 *Orizzonte Salute* [EU:C:2015:655], as well as in Case C-495/14 *Tita* [EU:C:2016:230].

70 Joined Cases C-317/08 to C-320/08 *Alassini and Others* [EU:C:2010:146], Case C-93/12 *Agrokonsulting-04*, [EU:C:2013:432], Case C-205/15 *Toma* [EU:C:2016:499], Case C-483/16 *Sziber* [EU:C:2018:367].

71 Case C-536/11 *Donau Chemie* [EU:C:2013:366], Case C-439/08 *VEBIC*, [EU:C:2010:739].

72 Case C-413/12 *ACICL* [EU:C:2013:800], Case C-567/13, *Baczó* [EU:C:2015:88], Case C-49/14 *Finanmadrid* [EU:C:2016:98] para. 54, Case C-470/12 *Photovost' s.r.o.* [EU:C:2014:101], Case C-570/13 *Gruber* [EU:C:2015:231], Case C-32/14 *ERSTE Bank Hungary* [EU:C:2015:637].

73 Which does not necessarily go beyond the floor level of ECHR guarantees as interpreted by the ECtHR. Where it does, this may be mandated by the substantive rules at issue, rather than being a matter of procedural law. See in this regard AG Szpunar's opinion in Case C-49/14, *Finanmadrid* [EU:C:2016:98].

not only positive entitlements but also the situation of those who seek to defend themselves against the enforcement of EU law.[74] The latter may find its limits in Article 47 CFR insofar as access to court must be guaranteed also in order to contest an obligation stemming from EU law and because all parties to judicial proceedings under that law are entitled to a fair trial.[75] This does not mean, however, that their position ultimately prevails.[76] Whether the protection afforded in any given procedural situation complies with the rights enshrined in Article 47 CFR depends on an assessment of its context. Limitations may be justified[77] both in light of the opposing rights of all parties and the need for an effective enforcement of EU law, which have to be weighed in the balance. In its interpretation of these requirements, the ECJ notably relies on the concept of fair trial as defined under the ECHR.

The Court's involvement with domestic procedural rules and practices is not, however, confined to assessing their compatibility with EU law. Instead, in view of the fact that the emerging common law of civil procedure is, and will be, tailored after the image of domestic rules in the field, which are compared, discarded or, eventually, adopted as common rules, a judgment upholding a domestic procedural provision or practice contributes to this standard.

3.3. PROCEDURAL RIGHTS AND CIVIL JUDICIAL COOPERATION

Because, within their scope, the directly applicable EU judicial cooperation provisions oust domestic rules rather than allowing for procedural autonomy and fundamental rights pluralism,[78] one would expect procedural issues to be increasingly determined under Article 47 CFR and the auspices of the ECJ,

---

74 Case C-682/15 *Berlioz Investment Fund SA* [EU:C:2017:373].

75 M. Safjan and D. Düsterhaus (n. 40 above).

76 Contrast insofar, on the one hand, Case C-418/11 *Texdata Software GmbH* [EU:C:2013:588], Case C-682/15 *Berlioz Investment Fund SA* [EU:C:2017:373], para. 59, Case C-662/13 *Surgicare* [EU:C:2015:89] para. 33, Case C-419/14 *WebMindLicenses Kft.* [EU:C:2015:832], para. 91, Case C-437/13 *Unitrading* [EU:C:2014:2318] and, on the other hand, Case C-455/06 *Heemskerk and Schaap* [EU:C:2008:650] paras. 46–47, Case C-500/10, *Belvedere Costruzioni* [EU:C:2012:186], Case C-472/11 *Banif Plus Bank* [EU:C:2013:88] para. 29, Case C-119/15 *Biuro podróży "Partner"* [EU:C:2016:987].

77 Case C-418/11 *Texdata* [EU:C:2013:588] paras. 84–87.

78 D. Düsterhaus, "Procedural Primacy and Effective Judicial Protection: A Trilogue, Case C-112/13 *A v. B and Others*, EU:C:2014:2195" (2012) 23(2) *Maastricht Journal of European & Comparative Law* 317. Pursuant to Case C-399/11 *Melloni* [EU:C:2013:107], para. 60, in a situation where action of the Member States is entirely determined by European Union law, national courts may not apply diverging national standards of protection of fundamental rights.

with a focus on facilitating cross-border litigation. But, then again, many of these instruments are merely complementary to existing domestic provisions as well as to the common enforcement regime of the Brussels I Regulation.[79] Moreover, for the time being, few actually concern genuine procedural issues and, where necessary, refer to national law instead and thus leave room for procedural autonomy and fundamental rights pluralism.

It is thus not surprising that only roundabout 20 judgments in this field since 2009 contain a reference to the CFR. And indeed they almost exclusively concern the right to effective judicial protection in Article 47 of the Charter.[80] While these judgments set out some topical considerations, the place of fundamental rights in EU civil judicial cooperation remains undefined.[81] Could it be that, due to their technical, "rigid"[82] nature, procedural rules are rightly met by the Court's cautious reticence[83] to entertain fundamental rights considerations? In this vein, consider the *Weber v. Weber* case, in which the referring Oberlandesgericht Munich asked whether the right of access to justice may allow derogation from the obligation to stay proceedings in cases of *lis pendens*.[84] While the ECJ did not answer this question, Advocate General Jääskinen opined that an interpretation of Article 27(1) of Brussels I in the light of the Charter cannot amend the scope of that article. He found it to be a purely technical provision, the application of which should raise no issue as regards Article 47 of the Charter, since the parties benefit, in all Member States, from access to justice and a fair hearing before the court first seised.[85]

It is nevertheless submitted that the judicial protection guarantees of Article 47 are indeed informing the Court's civil judicial cooperation case law, be that in diverse ways. Let me name three.

---

79 Council Regulation (EC) No 44/2001 of 22 December 2000 on jurisdiction and the recognition and enforcement of judgments in civil and commercial matters (OJ 2001 L 12, p. 1), now recast by Regulation (EU) No 1215/2012 of the European Parliament and of the Council of 12 December 2012 on jurisdiction and the recognition and enforcement of judgments in civil and commercial matters (OJ 2012 L 351, p. 1) [Brussels Ia].

80 A notable exception, although so far confined to Brussels IIa, is the child's fundamental right under Article 24(3) of the Charter to maintain on a regular basis a personal relationship and direct contact with both parents, see Case C-403/09 PPU *Detiček* [EU:C:2009:810].

81 See D. Düsterhaus, "Effective remedies and fair trial in civil matters: How to Promote Justice within the Confines of EU Powers", in S. Iglesias Sánchez et al. *Fundamental Rights in the AFSJ* (CUP, forthcoming).

82 J. Bomhoff, *Judicial Discretion in European Law on Conflicts of Jurisdiction* (The Hague, Sdu Uitgevers, 2005), 21.

83 See in detail M. Safjan, D. Düsterhaus and A. Guérin, "La Charte des droits fondamentaux de l'Union européenne et les ordres juridiques nationaux, entre mise en œuvre et mise en balance" [2016] *Revue trimestrielle de droit européen* (RTDE) 219.

84 Case C-438/12 *Weber v. Weber* [EU:C:2014:212].

85 Opinion of 30 January 2014 in Case C-438/12 *Weber v. Weber* [EU:C:2014:43].

Firstly, ever since the ECJ infused the Brussels cosmos with fundamental rights considerations in 1980,[86] it has become settled case law that, under Brussels I, proceedings leading to the delivery of judicial decisions must take place in such a way that the rights of the defence are observed.[87] The application of EU rules of judicial cooperation thus triggers Article 47 CFR. In this connection, the Court found, for example, in *GREP*[88] that the right to be exempt from paying the costs of procedure and/or lawyer's fees, which Article 47 of the Charter confers, applies to an action which challenges a decision of enforceability ordering conservatory attachment measures.

Secondly, the emergence of common procedural rules in the EU obviously builds upon the idea of access to and fairness of judicial proceedings. The mandate under Article 67(4) TFEU to facilitate access to justice must therefore be read in the light of Article 47 CFR.

Thirdly, even in the absence of legislative harmonisation of procedural provisions, the judicial protection guarantees of the Charter can become directly applicable as absolute limits to national procedural autonomy so as to avoid the persistence of diverging and, in any case, insufficient standards in the Member States.[89] But the content and scope of procedural fundamental rights in the civil branch of EU judicial cooperation are not easy to chart and their implementation is particularly challenging.

Granted, compliance with the inalienable core of procedural fundamental rights is generally easily discernible. However, beyond these core rights, procedural fairness cannot be assessed *in abstracto*. In all cases, the specific aspects of access to justice ("effective remedy") and fair trial ("fair hearing"), which Article 47 CFR juxtaposes in its first two paragraphs must be weighed in the balance,[90] as ultimately required under Article 52(1) CFR. This is why the considerations set out in a specific judgment on the interpretation of Article 47 CFR may not suffice as such to establish an EU-wide standard.

Moreover, while the conditions laid down in the different judicial cooperation instruments framing cross-border enforcement call for an interpretation (in the light[91]) of[92] Article 47 CFR, the latter is not the sole

---

86 Case 125/79 *Denilauler* [EU:C:1980:130], para. 13.

87 See Case C-394/07 *Gambazzi*, [EU:C:2009:219], para. 23; Case C-327/10 *Hypoteční banka* [EU:C:2011:745], para. 48.

88 Case C-156/12 *GREP GmbH v. Freitstaat Bayern* (order) [EU:C:2012:342].

89 D. Düsterhaus, "Judicial Coherence in the AFSJ – Squaring mutual trust with effective judicial protection" (2015) 8(2) *Review of European Administrative Law* 151. See notably Case C-279/09 *DEB* [EU:C:2010:811].

90 Case C-327/10 *Hypotečni Banka* [EU:C:2011:745] paras. 49–54.

91 Case C-300/14 *Imtech Marine Belgium NV v. Radio Hellenic SA* [EU:C:2015:825]; Case C-119/13 *eco cosmetics* [EU:C:2014:2144]; C-341/04 *Eurofood* [EU:C:2006:281] para. 68; Case C-559/14 *Meroni* [EU:C:2016:349] paras. 45 and 55.

92 Case C-156/12 *GREP (order)* [EU:C:2012:342].

benchmark for procedural fairness as long as public policy clauses allow for scrutiny based on diverging domestic standards.

The crucial question for the purpose of seeing procedural rights assessed and developed by the ECJ in this context is whether national judges ask for a preliminary ruling under Article 267 TFEU. Are there enough incentives for doing so? In the past, the ECJ became notably involved in the context of enforcement challenges under the Brussels I Regulation. Recently, however, the conditions for refusal in the pertinent hypotheses of ineffective service and procedural public policy have converged insofar as the ECJ now also requires in the public policy context (Article 45(1)(a) Brussels Ia) that the individuals concerned must avail themselves of any available domestic remedy with a view to preventing a breach of public policy before it occurs.[93]

The requisite exhaustion of remedies[94] could further reduce the opportunities for the ECJ to exercise its control over the limits of public policy, thereby petrifying diverging standards of procedural fairness among the Member States.[95] This danger is also present within the scope of the automatic enforcement instruments, which provide for remedies almost exclusively in the Member State of origin. Granted, in contrast to the public policy clause in Article 45(1)(a) of Brussels Ia, most of these instruments lay down minimum requirements for service, safeguards and remedies. However, whether these requirements are fulfilled is a matter exclusively for the courts in the judgment state to determine, without there being sufficient incentives for involving the ECJ.

The ECJ's *Imtech Marine Belgium* judgment on the European Enforcement Order (EEO)[96] shows how dependent the fairness of an *exequatur*-free regime is on the alertness of judges and their willingness to make a preliminary ruling reference.[97] The case was referred by a Belgian court of appeal following a first instance refusal to certify a default judgment as an EEO due to the absence of appropriate domestic procedural legislation. In answering this reference, the ECJ found that, in order to certify such a judgment as an EEO, the court ruling on the application must satisfy itself that its national law effectively and without exception allows for a full review, in law and in fact, of the default judgment, and that periods for challenging a judgment on an uncontested claim should be extended where extraordinary circumstances beyond the

---

93 Case C-681/13 *Diageo Brands* [EU:C:2015:471] para. 64.

94 Case C-559/14 *Meroni* [EU:C:2016:349] para. 48. See in this connection already para. 78 of Case C-420/07 *Apostolides* [EU:C:2009:271].

95 See M. Safjan and D. Düsterhaus, "De l'encadrement de l'ordre public procédural des États membres à l'ordre procédural autonome de l'Union?" [Max Planck Institute, forthcoming].

96 Regulation (EC) No 805/2004 of the European Parliament and of the Council of 21 April 2004 creating a European Enforcement Order for uncontested claims (OJ 2004 L143, p. 15) (the "EEO Regulation").

97 Case C-300/14 *Imtech Marine* [EU:C:2015:825].

debtor's control prevented him from contesting the claim in question.[98] Most importantly, the ECJ insisted that the certification of a judgment as an EEO can be carried out only by a judge,[99] because of his status and qualifications and with a view to possibly triggering the preliminary ruling procedure. But how does the Court deal with its mission to apprise national judges of the EU standard of procedural rights?

4. THE COURT OF JUSTICE'S METHOD

It is submitted that the Court's constructive use of precedent[100] allows the incremental creation of horizontal procedural guarantees and principles by way of de-contextualising initially case-specific considerations. This may be illustrated with two contrasting aspects of EU procedural law, i.e. mutual trust and fair trial rights.

4.1. MUTUAL TRUST

Whilst not concerning a specific right, a highly topical example of the Court's method is the recent consecration[101] of the constitutional principle[102] of mutual trust. It has become a leitmotif of EU law on transnational civil litigation ever since it appeared in recital 16 of Brussels I, which solemnly declares that mutual trust in the administration of justice in the Community justifies judgments given in a Member State being recognised automatically without the need for any procedure except in cases of dispute.

Its origins lie nevertheless elsewhere. Indeed, 40 years ago, the Court of Justice started referring to mutual trust as being characteristic of the relationship between the Member States (as opposed to third states),[103] before famously making mutual recognition a catalyst for the free movement

---

98 Ibid, para. 42.

99 Ibid, para. 50.

100 D. Düsterhaus, "Eppur Si Muove! The Past, Present, and (possible) Future of Temporal Limitations in the Preliminary Ruling Procedure" (2018) 36 *Yearbook of European Law* 1.

101 See the Court's Opinion 2/13 on the draft ECHR accession treaty [2014] EU:C:2014:2454.

102 D. Düsterhaus, "In the Court(s) We Trust – A Procedural Solution to the Mutual Trust Dilemma", Freedom, Security and Justice: (2017) *European Legal Studies* 26–44; F. Meyer, "Der Grundsatz gegenseitigen Vertrauens – Konzeptualisierung und Zukunftsperspektiven eines neuen Verfassungsprinzips", *Europarecht Zeitschrift* (EuR) 2017, 163–186.

103 Case 138/77 *Ludwig v. Hamburg* [EU:C:1978:151], concerning veterinary and public health inspections upon importation. One should also stress that the term mutual trust itself was first used, in *Opinion 1/75* [EU:C:1975:145], in a sense similar to that of the duty of sincere cooperation now enshrined in Article 4(3) TEU. Ever since, "mutual trust" has been used in a number of internal market cases.

of goods.[104] The overall success of this approach, which combined negative with incidental harmonisation, seemed to make it a viable blueprint also for the new chapter of EU integration which is now the Area of Freedom, Security and Justice (AFSJ).[105] Assuming that "enhanced mutual recognition of judicial decisions and judgments and the necessary approximation of legislation would facilitate cooperation between authorities and the judicial protection of individual rights", the European Council meeting in Tampere on 15 and 16 October 1999 agreed that the principle of mutual recognition should become the cornerstone of judicial cooperation in both civil and criminal matters within the Union.[106] It should oblige the Member States to accept judicial decisions handed down in another Member State and to attach to these foreign decisions the same legal effects as similar national decisions.[107]

In the field of international civil procedure, the Court first referred to this principle in *Gasser* where it opined that already the Brussels Convention was based on the trust which the Member States accord to each other's legal systems and judicial institutions.

> It is that mutual trust which has enabled a compulsory system of jurisdiction to be established, which all the courts within the purview of the Convention are required to respect, and as a corollary the waiver by those States of the right to apply their internal rules on recognition and enforcement of foreign judgments in favor of a simplified mechanism for the recognition and enforcement of judgments. It is also common ground that the Convention thereby seeks to ensure legal certainty by allowing individuals to foresee with sufficient certainty which court will have jurisdiction.[108]

However, neither the Treaties nor secondary law define the principle of mutual trust, which may be described as "the confidence that Member States should have in each other's legal system and courts in the application of EU law, which results in the prohibition on reviewing what other states and their judiciaries are doing."[109] *Opinion 2/13* characterises mutual trust as requiring the EU

104 Case 120/78 *Rewe-Zentral* [EU:C:1978:151].

105 See in detail L. Leboeuf, *Le droit européen de l'asile au défi de la confiance mutuelle* (Limal, 2016), pp. 23–26; C. Janssens, *The Principle of Mutual Recognition in EU Law* (Oxford OUP, 2013).

106 Draft programme of measures for implementation of the principle of mutual recognition of decisions in civil and commercial matters, of 15 January 2001, OJ C 12, p. 1.

107 J. Ouwerkerk in Meijers Committee, *The Principle of Mutual* Trust in European Asylum, Migration, and Criminal *law – Reconciling Trust and Fundamental Rights* (Forum, Institute for Multicultural Affairs, Utrecht, 2011) 39.

108 Case C-116/02 *Gasser* [EU:C:2003:657], para. 72.

109 X.E. Kramer, "Cross-Border Enforcement and the Brussels I-bis Regulation: Towards a New Balance between Mutual Trust and National Control over Fundamental Rights" (2013) 60(3) *Netherlands International Law Review* 343, 364.

Member States to consider, save in exceptional circumstances, one another to be complying with EU law and in particular with the fundamental rights recognised by EU law.[110]

Spurred not least by its normative malleability, the idea of mutual trust has come to pervade the Court's interpretation not only in the AFSJ,[111] but also with regard to transnational procedures in other fields of law[112] and underpins the allocation of competence for fundamental rights protection. What about the different fair trial requirements?

4.2. FAIR TRIAL RIGHTS

Also with regard to the specific requirements of fair trial the Court's transversal application of precedent results in considerations made in one legal, factual and procedural context being transposed to other contexts, with a reference to a paragraph of the judgment rendered in one context justifying the validity of an argument in the other as well, if only by analogy.[113] In retrospect, apparent differences in purpose and scope may turn out to be negligible[114] and judgments on EU procedural law, domestic or transnational civil, criminal or administrative procedure all impart the EU standard of fair trial for Article 47 CFR as their common point of reference.[115] Notably national procedural standards and principles may eventually be taken on board, once their compliance with EU law has been ascertained by the Court. This incorporation of national standards through the case law is still indispensable due to the piecemeal state of written EU procedural law.[116]

Pertinent examples of a (possible) horizontal use of precedent under the umbrella of Article 47 CFR thus spring from a variety of fields and contexts and relate, beyond the institutional guarantees of judicial independence[117]

---

110 *Opinion 2/13*, para. 191.

111 See D. Düsterhaus, "In the Court(s) We Trust – A Procedural Solution to the Mutual Trust Dilemma", Freedom, Security and Justice: (2017) 1 *European Legal Studies* 26–44.

112 Case C-34/17 *Donnellan* [EU:C:2018:282].

113 For example, after having established in Case C-69/10 *Samba Diouf* [EU:C:2011:524] paragraph 69, that neither the pertinent secondary law, nor Article 47 of the Charter require there to be two levels of judicial decision, the Court has made this a transversal standard, see Case C-169/14 *Sánchez Morcillo and Abril Garcia* [EU:2014:2099].

114 D. Düsterhaus (n. 100 above).

115 M. Safjan and D. Düsterhaus (n. 40 above).

116 See in detail *M. Tulibacka*, "Europeanization of Civil Procedures: In Search of a Coherent Approach" (2009) 46 *C.M.L. Rev.* 1527–1565.

117 Case C-506/04 *Wilson* [EU:C:2006:587], Case C-393/10 *O'Brien* [EU:C:2012:110] paras. 47–49, Case C-199/11 *Otis* [EU:C:2012:684], Case C-58/13 *Torresi* [EU:C:2014:2088], Case C-222/13 TDC [EU:C:2014:2265], Case C-203/14 *Consorci Sanitari del Maresme* [EU:C:2015:664], Case C-64/16 *ASJP* [EU:C:2018:117], Case C-216/18 PPU *LM* [EU:C:2018:586].

and impartiality,[118] to the requirement of a prior settlement procedure,[119] the reasonableness of costs and fees,[120] legal representation[121] and legal aid,[122] regularity and means of service,[123] the right to be heard[124] and proceedings *in absentia*[125] burden[126] and standard[127] of proof, time limits,[128] unlimited

118 Case C-175/11 *H.I.D.* [EU:C:2013:45], Case C-199/11 *Otis* [EU:C:2012:684], Case C-300/14 *Imtech Marine Belgium* [EU:C:2015:825] para. 47.

119 Case C-63/01 *Evans* [EU:C:2003:650], Joined Cases C-317/08 to C-320/08 *Alassini and Others* [EU:C:2010:146], Case C-73/16 *Puškár* [EU:C:2017:725], Case C-300/17 *Hochtief* [EU:C:2018:635].

120 Case C-260/11 *Edwards*, Case C-61/14 *Orizzonte Salute* [EU:C:2015:655], Case C-495/14 *Tita* [EU:C:2016:230], Case C-205/15 *Toma* [EU:C:2016:499], Case C-439/14 *Star Storage* [EU:C:2016:688].

121 Case C-63/01 *Evans* [EU:C:2003:650], Case C-112/13 *A* [EU:C:2014:2195], Case C-52/15 P *Lambauer* (order) [EU:C:2015:549], C-464/16 P *PITEE* (order) [EU:C:2017:291], Case C-543/14 *Ordre des barreaux* [EU:C:2016:605], C-314/13 *Peftief* [EU:C:2014:1645], Case C-535/12 P *Faet Oltra* [EU:C:2013:373] para. 19, C-532/15 *Eurosaneamientos* [EU:C:2016:932].

122 Case C-279/09 *DEB* [EU:C:2010:811], Case C-156/12 *GREP* (order) [EU:C:2012:342], Case C-258/13 *Sociedade Agrícola e Imobiliária da Quinta de S. Paio, Lda v. Instituto da Segurança Social, IP* [EU:C:2013:810].

123 Case C-102/13 P *Germany v. Commission* (order) [EU:C:2014:2054] paras. 31 and 32, Case C-501/13 P *Page Protective Services Ltd.* (order) [EU:C:2014:2259] para. 30, Case C-325/11 *Alder* [EU:C:2012:824], Case C-519/13 *Alpha Bank Cyprus* [EU:C:2015:603], Case C-384/14 *Alta Realitat* (order) [EU:C:2016:316], Case C-354/15 *Henderson* [EU:C:2017:157], Case C-34/17 *Donnellan* [EU:C:2018:282], Case C-119/13 *eco cosmetics* [EU:C:2014:2144] paras. 37–41, Case C-300/14 *Imtech Marine Belgium* [EU:C:2015:825] para. 42.

124 Case C-682/13 P *Andechser Molkerei Scheitz v. Commission* [EU:C:2015:356], Case C-607/15 P *Magyar Bencés Kongregáció Pannonhalmi Főapátság* (order) [EU:C:2016:329], Case C-348/16 *Moussa Sacko* [EU:C:2017:591].

125 Case C-292/10 *G* [EU:C:2012:142], C-327/10 *Hypoteční Banka* [EU:C:2011:745], C-396/11 *Radu* [EU:C:2013:39], Case C-399/11 *Melloni* [EU:C:2013:107], Case C-619/10 *Trade Agency* [EU:C:2012:531], Case C-112/13 *A* [EU:C:2014:2195] para. 60.

126 Case C-72/12 *Gemeinde Altrip and Others* [EU:C:2013:712], Case C-479/12 *Gautzsch Großhandel* [EU:C:2014:75], Case C-35/09 *Speranza* [EU:C:2010:393] para. 48, Case C-3/17 *Sporting Odds* [EU:C:2018:130].

127 Case C-74/14 *Eturas* [EU:C:2016:42].

128 Case C-406/08 *Uniplex* [EU:C:2010:45], Case C-418/11 *Texdata* [EU:C:2013:588] para. 80–81, Case C-69/10 *Samba Diouf* [EU:C:2011:524], Case C-625/11 P *PPG* [EU:C:2013:594], Case C-334/12 RX-II *Arango Jaramillo* [EU:C:2013:134], Case C-73/10 P *IFG Weichert* (order) [EU:C:2010:684] paras. 41 and 49, Case C-426/10 P *Bell & Ross v. OHIM* [EU:C:2011:612] para. 43, Case C-603/10 *Pelati* [EU:C:2012:639] para. 30, Case C-478/11 P *Gbagbo* [EU:C:2013:258] para. 71, Case C-19/13 *Fastweb SpA* [EU:C:2014:2194] para. 58, Case C-161/13 *Idrodinamica Spurgo Velox* [EU:C:2014:307], Case C-501/13 P *Page Protective Services Ltd.* (order) [EU:C:2014:2259] para. 37, Case C-69/12 P *Noscira v. OHIM* (order) [EU:C:2012:589], Case C-35/15 P(R) *Commission v. Vanbreda* (order) [EU:C:2015:275] paras. 37–38, 47–48, Case C-70/15, *Lebek* [EU:C:2016:524] para. 55, Case C-326/16 P *LL* [EU:C:2018:83], Case C-411/16 P *Holistic Innovation Institute* (order) [EU:C:2017:445], Case C-325/18 PPU *CE* [EU:C:2018:739], Case C-452/09 *Iaia* [EU:C:2011:323], Case C-542/08 *Barth* [EU:C:2010:193], Case C-63/08 *Pontin* [EU:C:2009:666].

jurisdiction,[129] the adversarial principle,[130] equality of arms,[131] and a reasoned judgment[132] within a reasonable time.[133]

What the ECJ says in these cases, only few of which actually concern civil procedure, may not be novel or surprising. Only occasionally does it go beyond the floor level set by ECtHR case law.[134] Nevertheless, by relying on horizontal precedents in order to establish transversal principles, the ECJ establishes a coherent standard of procedural fairness across all fields of EU law.

5. CONCLUSION

This chapter has explored whether the European Court of Justice may, by construing rules of (civil) procedure in the light of Article 47 CFR, ultimately spur their harmonisation. The answer is affirmative, even though this outcome is neither intended, nor achieved in a straightforward manner. While it is certainly within the Court's mandate to assess the compliance of both EU and domestic procedural rules with the fundamental rights which these rules implement or, as the case may be, curtail, a constitutional reasoning involving

---

129 Case C-199/11 *Otis* [EU:C:2012:684], Case C-272/09 P *KME* [EU:C:2011:810], Case C-386/10 P *Chalkor* [EU:C:2011:815], Case C-389/10 P *KME* [EU:C:2011:816], Case C-501/11 P *Schindler* [EU:C:2013:522], C-122/16 P *British Airways* [EU:C:2017:861], Case C-430/93 *Schijndel* [EU:C:1995:441], para. 22, Case C-506/04 *Wilson*, para. 62, Case C-199/11 *Otis* [EU:C:2012:684], Case C-60/12 *Baláž* [EU:C:2013:733], para. 47, Case C-146/14 PPU *Ali Mahdi* [EU:C:2014:1320] para. 64, Case C-300/17 *Hochtief* [EU:C:2018:635], Case C-71/14 *East Sussex County Council* [EU:C:2015:656] paras 52–58.

130 Case C-530/12 *P OHIM v. National Lottery Commission* [EU:C:2014:186] paras. 53–54, Case C-507/10 *X* [EU:C:2011:873], Case C-491/10 PPU *Aguirre Zarraga* [EU:C:2010:828], Case C-277/11 *M.M.* [EU:C:2012:744] paras. 77–94, Case C-472/11 *Banif Plus Bank* [EU:C:2013:88], Case C-418/11 *Texdata* [EU:C:2013:588] paras. 83, 85, Case C-129/13 *Kamino International* [EU:C:2014:2041] paras. 67 and 72, Case C-276/01 *Steffensen* [EU:C:2003:228], Case C-278/15 P *Royal County of Berkshire Polo Club Ltd.* (order) [EU:C:2016:20] para. 52, Case C-239/12 *Abdulrahim v. Council* [EU:C:2013:331], Case C-89/09 P *Commission v. Ireland* [EU:C:2010:772] paras. 55–56, Case C-607/15 P *Magyar Bencés Kongregáció Pannonhalmi Főapátság* (order) [EU:C:2016:329] para. 21.

131 C-580/12 P *Guardian Industries* [EU:C:2014:2363] paras. 31–35, Case C-199/11 *Otis* [EU:C:2012:684] paras. 71–72, Case C-169/14 *Sánchez Morcillo and Abril Garcia* [EU:2014:2099] para. 48, Case C-205/15 *Toma* [EU:C:2016:499] para. 54, Case C-73/16 *Puškár* [EU:C:2017:725] paras. 97 and 98, Case C-543/14 *Ordre des barreaux* [EU:C:2016:605].

132 Case C-283/05 *ASML* [EU:C:2006:787] para. 28, Case C-619/10 *Trade Agency* [EU:C:2012:531] para. 60.

133 Joined Cases C-322, C-327, C-338/07 P *August Koehler* [EU:C:2009:500], Case C-385/07 P *Der Grüne Punkt* [EU:C:2009:456], Case C-578/11 P *Deltafina* [EU:C:2014:1742] paras. 86–90, Case C-40/12 P *Gascogne* [EU:C:2013:768], Case C-295/12 P *Telefónica de España* [EU:C:2014:2062] para. 66, Case C-467/13 P *ICF* [EU:C:2014:2274] paras. 56–63, Case C-500/10, *Belvedere Costruzioni* [EU:C:2012:186], Case C-612/15 *Kolev* [EU:C:2018:392], Case C-319/15 *Overseas Financial Limited* (order) [EU:C:2016:268].

134 As recalled above in section 2.1.

case-specific fundamental rights considerations in response to a preliminary ruling reference does not, as such, establish an EU-wide standard of procedural fairness, nor can it serve as a blue-print for new procedural legislation.

Nevertheless, the Court's interpretation of procedural (fundamental) rights, both within and beyond the field of civil judicial cooperation, naturally constitutes a source of inspiration for procedural harmonisation. As it appears, the EU law of civil procedure is, and will be, moulded in the image of domestic rules in the field, which are compared, discarded or, eventually, adopted as common rules. A judgment confirming the compliance of a domestic procedural provision or practice with EU law, including the Charter, will be an important argument in this connection. The same goes for EU law provisions in other fields, whose fundamental-right-compliant interpretation may eventually be transplanted to the field of civil procedure.

In this connection, the Court's specific use of precedent,[135] which involves more or less de-contextualised references to previous rulings, can foster the establishment and implementation of transversal principles. This is why, in my opinion, any interpretation of Article 47 CFR, even outside the realm of civil procedure, adds to the emerging EU standard of procedural rights. To this extent, the ongoing constitutionalisation of procedural law is a useful starting point for legislative harmonisation.

---

135 D. Düsterhaus, "Eppur Si Muove! The Past, Present, and (possible) Future of Temporal Limitations in the Preliminary Ruling Procedure" (2018) 36 *Yearbook of European Law* 1.

PART II

THE CURRENT SITUATION

Vertical and Horizontal Harmonisation

HAVE THE EU REGULATIONS ON JUDICIAL COOPERATION FOSTERED HARMONISATION OF NATIONAL PROCEDURES?

Fernando Gascón Inchausti

1. NATIONAL DIVERSITY, MUTUAL RECOGNITION AND HORIZONTAL HARMONISATION

Any general study on the future of civil procedure – and more specifically on harmonisation – in the European Union should start by analysing the current situation. How close to each other are national regulations of civil procedure within the EU Member States really? The answer is not easy, since it depends on where we put the focus and what we are comparing. The systems of civil procedure of the Scandinavian countries, for instance, are quite close to one another and, therefore, one could say that they are sufficiently harmonised. Similar conclusions could be reached if we compared England and Ireland, or France and Luxembourg. But if one looks at the general picture, the results are quite the opposite: national procedural systems are still very different from each other, as can be deduced from a broad study commissioned by the European Commission and performed under the lead of the Max Planck Institute Luxembourg for Procedural Law (the so-called "Luxembourg Study on European Procedural Law").[1]

The differences may not affect the basic and structural principles of civil procedure, such as access to courts, fairness of proceedings and equality of arms. But even the conception of overriding principles, such as the principles of party autonomy and party disposition may vary from one country to another. And, of course, differences grow bigger the more one scrutinises procedural technicalities, i.e., the precise way national legislators have considered it suitable to set the balance between the rights of plaintiffs and defendants or the roles of parties, lawyers and judges. Who serves the documents instituting the proceedings and how; who enforces a judgment or equivalent enforceable document and how; how strict are the rules on preclusion and timely production of documents; the need to be represented by a lawyer or not; the duty to pay upfront court fees, and of what amount; those, and many others, are issues that national legislation addresses in very heterogeneous manners.[2] As a result,

> a citizen or a resident of an EU Member State wishing to commence litigation in another EU Member State will not be able to expect to approach courts and authorities in any Member State as easily as in their own.[3]

The reasons for these differences are embedded in different legal histories, legal cultures and, of course, different approaches and views on the role of civil procedure in each society (which includes, of course, the role of judges and of lawyers).

In addition, we must start from the premise that the notion of harmonisation is quite ambiguous and imprecise, because it defines a result that admits of many gradations and nuances. This idea of harmonisation being a result also explains the different paths that can lead to it, at least in the scope of

---

1 B. Hess et al., *An evaluation study of national procedural laws and practices in terms of their impact on the free circulation of judgments and on the equivalence and effectiveness of the procedural protection of consumers under EU consumer law. Strand 1: mutual trust and free circulation of judgments* (2017): https://publications.europa.eu/en/publication-detail/-/publication/531ef49a-9768-11e7-b92d-01aa75ed71a1/language-en.

2 F. Gascón Inchausti/M. Requejo Isidro, "A Classic Cross-border Case: the Usual Situation in the First Instance" in *An evaluation study of national procedural laws and practices in terms of their impact on the free circulation of judgments and on the equivalence and effectiveness of the procedural protection of consumers under EU consumer law. Strand 1: mutual trust and free circulation of judgments* (above, n. 1) 44–167, 45–46.

3 M. Tulibacka/M. Sanz/R. Blomeyer, *Common minimum standards of civil procedure*, European Parliamentary Research Service, European Added Value. Assessment. Annex I, PE 581.385 (2016), 51.

civil procedure.[4] There is, of course, a possible "spontaneous" harmonisation, as a result of converging legal traditions, probably because the common solution is the best one (the most efficient and productive, maybe): this may explain, for instance, why all legal systems use the "loser pays" rule as the basic criterion for allocation of costs; but, of course, the details on how this rule applies and, moreover, quantitative limitations are still different and could be the basis of unsatisfied expectations.

Our focus, however, is policy driven harmonisation, i.e., harmonisation as a result intended, promoted or at least expectable by means of lawmaking decisions. Within the EU it has become frequent to distinguish between horizontal or general harmonisation, on the one hand, and vertical or sectorial harmonisation, on the other hand.[5] This paper will focus on the first one, that is, on the harmonising impact of the general regulations enacted by the EU in the field of judicial cooperation in civil and commercial matters. As we all know, there is a remarkable number of regulations and directives in this field, starting from the original version of the 1968 Brussels Convention. They have altogether served as the basis for the current *acquis communautaire* or, maybe more specifically, of a *corpus iuris processualis europaeum*, i.e., a European set of procedural rules.[6]

The list of directives and regulations enacted in less than 20 years is long and well known to all of us. The topics and approaches of those European rules are also different. Despite the differences, however, there is a common element: all those rules have been enacted on the basis of current Article 81 TFEU (former Article 65 TEC), that enables the Union to develop judicial cooperation in civil matters having cross-border implications. This shows, in turn, that the notion of "judicial cooperation" is quite broad and really far-reaching: for the European law-maker, judicial cooperation encompasses all the tools aimed at enabling smoother cross-border litigation, i.e. diminishing the impact of (political and legal) borders in order to achieve a common European Area of Justice. Some of the pieces of the *corpus iuris processualis europaeum* deal with judicial cooperation in a very strict sense, like the regulations on service and on the taking of evidence. Others address cooperation from the point of

4 C.H. van Rhee, "Harmonisation of Civil Procedure: An Historical and Comparative Perspective" in X.E. Kramer/C.H. van Rhee (eds.), *Civil Litigation in a Globalising World*, Asser Press, The Hague, 2012, 39–63.

5 G. Wagner, "Harmonisation of Civil Procedure: Policy Perspectives" in *Civil Litigation in a Globalising World* (above, n. 4), 93–119.

6 E. Storskrubb, *Civil Procedure and EU Law. A Policy Area Uncovered*, OUP, 2008; Z. Vernadaki, "Civil Procedure Harmonization in the EU: Unravelling the Policy Considerations" (2013) 19(2) *Journal of Contemporary European Research*; M. Weller/C. Althammer (eds.), *Mindeststandards im europäischen Zivilprozessrecht*, Mohr Siebeck, Tübingen, 2015; B. Hess/M. Bergstrom/E. Storskrubb (eds.), *EU Civil Justice. Current Issues and Future Outlook*, OUP, 2016.

view of the recognition and enforcement of foreign decisions, usually linked to the unification of the rules on jurisdiction and, sometimes, on conflict of laws. On some occasions, the EU legislator has created optional instruments; that is, European procedures offered as an alternative to litigants in specific cross-border situations. What remains stable, however, is the cross-border relevance, which appears sometimes quite shocking, as happens with the directives on legal aid and on mediation.

It is also very well known that, since the famous Tampere summit of 1999,[7] mutual recognition has been considered the *cornerstone* of judicial cooperation, at the service of the judicial protection of individual rights; the Conclusions of the Council in Tampere also acknowledged that "the necessary approximation of legislation" would also serve this purpose; but it was the notion of mutual recognition which was enthroned as the main principle underpinning the whole architecture of all subsequent legal developments that have led to build the current *corpus iuris processualis europaeum*.

To what extent have these directives and regulations contributed to harmonising national civil procedures? One might think that such an impressive body of rules should necessarily have had an impact on domestic legislation, in the direction of generating similarities. However, it does not have necessarily to be like this. Indeed, the political decision to build the European Area of Justice and, more specifically, judicial cooperation in civil matters, on the basis of the principle of mutual recognition may represent, in practice, a waiver to harmonise civil proceedings at a national and domestic level. As stated, among others, by Hess, "[f]rom the perspective of the Member States, the less invasive regulatory choice of European law-making is to simply coordinate national procedures without harmonizing them".[8] In theory, mutual recognition and harmonisation are not necessarily mutually exclusive, since they operate in partially different spaces. It is possible to activate a system of judicial cooperation on the basis of mutual recognition because there exists an underlying trust between those expected to cooperate among them. Trust, in turn, can of course be sustained on the harmonisation or approximation of the legal systems called to interact; but it can also rely on different grounds. Mutual trust is indeed a complex notion, encompassing many factors, some of them "softer" than others (like judicial education and judicial training

7 "33. Enhanced mutual recognition of judicial decisions and judgements and the necessary approximation of legislation would facilitate co-operation between authorities and the judicial protection of individual rights. The European Council therefore endorses the principle of mutual recognition which, in its view, should become the cornerstone of judicial co-operation in both civil and criminal matters within the Union. The principle should apply both to judgements and to other decisions of judicial authorities".

8 B. Hess, *Harmonized Rules and Minimum Standards in the European Law of Civil Procedure*, European Parliamentary Research Service, In-Depth Analysis, PE 556.971 (2016) 7.

in cross-border cooperation).[9] But, at the end of the day, "mutual trust presupposes, at a very fundamental level, that national judiciaries in the Union perceive each other's procedural arrangements (on both the level of law-on-the-books and of law-in-action) as guaranteeing fair civil proceedings".[10]

Traditionally, it seems that European law-makers – and maybe also EU Member States – have preferred to understand that the mutual trust needed to justify mutual recognition was that which derived from common EU membership – having in mind that the EU has mechanisms to ensure full respect of the rule of law by the MS,[11] and, more specifically, the confidence associated with the membership of the ECHR and with the ECtHR[12] – although, paradoxically, the Union's accession to the Convention has become a problematic taboo.[13] The entry into force of the CFREU also contributes to sustaining this diffuse idea that mutual trust should be somewhat "self-evident" and inherent to EU membership: Article 47 CFREU might appear to be restricted to the judicial protection of rights enshrined by EU law, but it has indeed a full scope of application when it comes to judicial cooperation, precisely due to the European origin of the rules.

This "self-evident" approach to mutual trust explains why the development of most legal instruments within the field of judicial cooperation in civil matters has been achieved without any previous or subsequent harmonisation. Harmonisation, of course, could be an excellent starting point for mutual recognition. But it is not "cheap", especially from a political point of view; and, more interestingly, it does not seem to be the only way to sustain mutual trust. This might explain the European law-maker's rush after Tampere into mutual recognition, without any previous harmonisation of civil proceedings.

A very good example of this "mutual recognition without harmonisation" paradigm is offered by the regulations that are more directly linked to

---

9 E. Storskrubb, "Mutual Trust and the Dark Horse of Civil Justice" (2018) 20 *Cambridge Yearbook of European Legal Studies* 179–201.

10 R. Mańko, *Europeanisation of civil procedure. Towards common minimum standards?*, European Parliamentary Research Service, In-Depth Analysis, PE 559.499 (2015) 26.

11 As the current situation with Poland shows, precisely in one of the fundamentals of the rule of law more directly linked to judicial cooperation, which is the independence of the Judiciary (*European Commission v. Republic of Poland*, Case C-619/18, action under Article 258 TFEU for failure to fulfil obligations, brought on 2 October 2018; more specifically, the Order of Court of 17 December 2018 granting interim measures, ECLI:EU:C:2018:1021).

12 But this does not mean that harmonisation has been achieved [R. Mańko (above, n. 10) 7], not even at the minimum level of guarantees: "The fact that Article 47 of the Charter is now binding, and pending the EU's accession to the ECHR, Article 6, in the guise of general principles, is part of the Union's legal order, does not necessarily mean that the level of protection of the right to a fair trial, and in particular the delicate balance between the claimant's right of access to justice and the defendant's rights of the defence, is harmonised across the EU".

13 *Opinion 2/13 of the Court* (Full Court), of 18 December 2014, ECLI:EU:C:2014:2454.

the classical notion of cooperation: those on service and on the taking of evidence. None of them has resulted in much harmonisation. The differences among EU Member States in the way service is performed are still very relevant and lead in practice to some difficulties when it comes to cross-border enforcement, namely in the case of default judgments that have been preceded by fictitious methods of service.[14] As far as the Evidence Regulation is concerned, two main issues should be highlighted: on the one hand, the system has been acknowledged by the ECJ to be optional (*Lippens*,[15] *ProRail*[16]) – at least if coercive measures are not required – with the consequence that no real interaction happens; on the other hand, the Regulation opens the doors to the taking of evidence abroad following the specifications of the *lex fori* (i.e., of the requesting authority), which renders harmonisation unnecessary – except for situations of infringement of the public policy of the executing Member State.[17] A similar failure to harmonise is attributable to the successive "Brussels Regulations": no real harmonisation of declaratory proceedings is required to allow the free circulation of judgments; in addition, the Regulations have not had any harmonising impact on national enforcement proceedings. There has been, of course, a legal unification, regarding the rules established by each Regulation; but much space is left to domestic procedural legislation. The latest formula to advance along the path of judicial cooperation, that of using "optional instruments", has also been considered as an alternative to harmonisation:[18] the EOP, the ESCP and the EAPO are genuine European procedures, created by the European legislator as – presumably better – alternatives to national procedures, although they all need to rely on national procedural legislation for everything that is not directly foreseen by the European standard. The principles of equivalence and of effectiveness of EU law may require some internal adaptations of national legislation, in order to ensure that these EU alternative procedures fit within the national systems; but the means to perform this implementation may differ from one Member State to another.

A possible explanation – or an additional factor – for this lack of harmonising impact of the current *acquis* can be found in the fact that the *corpus iuris*

---

14 F. Gascón Inchausti/M. Requejo Isidro (above, n. 2) 64–83.

15 Judgment of the Court, 6 September 2012, C-170/11, *Maurice Robert Josse Marie Ghislain Lippens and Others v. Hendrikus Cornelis Kortekaas and Others* ECLI:EU:C:2012:540.

16 Judgment of the Court, 21 February 2013, C-332/11, *ProRail BV v. Xpedys NV and Others*, ECLI:EU:C:2013:87.

17 In this vein, it has been emphasised that the Evidence Regulation's missed objective has been that of taking advantage of judicial cooperation as a vehicle for harmonisation (N. Trocker, "From ALI-Unidroit Principles to common European rules on access to information and evidence? A preliminary outlook and some suggestions" (2014) 19 *Uniform Law Review* 239–291, 267–269).

18 R. Mańko (above, n. 10) 16.

processualis europaeum covers only a limited corner of civil procedure, that of cross-border litigation – which, moreover, has been interpreted in a restrictive manner by EU law-makers.[19] Judicial statistics do not always enable determination of the percentage of cases having "cross-border implications", but they are still few in comparison to the whole picture of civil litigation. Cross-border litigation is therefore reduced and it is not always duly taken into account by national law-makers as a possible source of inspiration when it comes to reforming domestic litigation. It is obvious that not any policy decision which contributes to a better functioning of cross-border litigation is suitable for transplantation into purely domestic cases. However, European directives and regulations offer sensible solutions to common procedural problems, many times on the basis of a "better law approach" and one might have expected a higher degree of cross-fertilisation than that which has really taken place.

It is also worth noting that the EU law-maker has not – or at least not yet – followed in civil matters an equivalent path to the one taken in the field of criminal proceedings,[20] where the production of a relevant number of framework decisions and directives on judicial cooperation in criminal matters has been accompanied – or rather followed – by the establishment of minimum standards regarding the rights of suspects and accused persons.[21] Mutual recognition – also the cornerstone of the system in criminal matters – seemed to need in this field enhanced mutual trust, beyond the "self-evident approach" prevailing in civil cooperation. And this "upgrade" is being achieved

19 Even if sometimes the EU lawmaker wants to flexibilise the notion of "cross-border implication", the limitation still exists and this, in turn, also explains the limited practical impact of the *corpus iuris processualis europaeum*: see G. Wagner (above, n. 5) 98–99.

20 M. Requejo Isidro, "Do We Need Harmonisation to Achieve Harmonious Cooperation? Judicial Cooperation in Criminal Matters as a Testing Field" in B. Hess/X.E. Kramer (eds.), *From common rules to best practices in European Civil Procedure*, Nomos, Baden-Baden, 2017, 77–118.

21 Directive 2010/64/EU of the European Parliament and of the Council of 20 October 2010 on the right to interpretation and translation in criminal proceedings (OJ L 280, 26.10.2010); Directive 2012/13/EU of the European Parliament and of the Council of 22 May 2012 on the right to information in criminal proceedings (OJ L 142, 1.6.2012); Directive 2013/48/EU of the European Parliament and the Council of 22 October 2013 on the right of access to a lawyer in criminal proceedings and European arrest warrant proceedings and on the right to have a third party informed upon deprivation of liberty, and to communicate with third persons and with consular authorities (OJ L 294, 6.11.2013); Directive (EU) 2016/343 of the European Parliament and of the Council of 9 March 2016 on the strengthening of certain aspects of the presumption of innocence and of the right to be present at the trial in criminal proceedings (OJ L 65, 11.3.2016); Directive (EU) 2016/800 of the European Parliament and of the Council of 11 May 2016 on procedural safeguards for children who are suspects or accused persons in criminal proceedings (OJ L 132, 21.5.2016); and Directive (EU) 2016/1919 of the European Parliament and of the Council of 26 October 2016 on legal aid for suspects and accused persons in criminal proceedings and for requested persons in European arrest warrant proceedings (OJ L 297, 4.11.2016).

by means of harmonisation; not, of course, a full harmonisation of criminal proceedings, but at least the harmonisation resulting from setting minimum standards regarding the safeguards of suspects and accused persons. A first reading of the titles of the directives could convey the impression that those standards are too obvious to be necessary or useful, at least from the perspective of some legal systems with a long democratic tradition; the truth, on the contrary, is that all EU Member States have needed to make legal reforms in order to implement the directives, which shows the real impact on domestic procedural rules and, moreover, that some safeguards were not as unnecessary as it might have initially appeared.

In civil matters, at least until very recent developments,[22] setting minimum standards was not a real concern. Maybe the EU law-makers considered that the unification of the rules on conflict of laws and the harmonisation of different sectors of substantive law could make it unnecessary. The fact, nevertheless, is that some procedural safeguards are being understood and respected differently and this, in turn, may be a source of trouble when the systems have to cooperate, namely in the enforcement phase: the *ordre public* clause has been used in cases where the infringement was not due to a pathological situation in the Member States of origin, but rather attributable to its legal system itself (as in *Gambazzi*,[23] *Alder*[24] or similar cases where fictitious methods of service, enabled by domestic legislation, had been put into practice);[25] the field of the enforcement of decisions on wrongfully removed or retained children under the Brussels II bis Regulation offers also several examples of mutual distrust.[26]

Distrust, indeed, remains, despite the grandiloquent proclamations of mutual trust and despite the firm commitment to mutual recognition, "without anaesthesia", that apparently transpires from the EU regulatory activity in the field of judicial cooperation in civil matters. The public policy clause has remained as a ground to refuse enforcement in the Brussels I bis Regulation, showing that abolition of exequatur is in fact just the abolition of exequatur proceedings, but not of exequatur as a filter or control, even if performed *ex post*, once enforcement has begun. The new Article 54 of the Brussels I bis Regulation may also be regarded as an unconscious proof

---

22 I refer, of course, to the 2017 Directive Proposal on common minimum standards of civil procedures, which will be dealt with in two other chapters of this book.

23 Judgment of the Court (First Chamber) of 2 April 2009, C-394/2007, *Marco Gambazzi v. DaimlerChrysler Canada Inc. and CIBC Mellon Trust Company*, ECLI:EU:C:2009:219.

24 Judgment of the Court, 19 December 2012, C-325/11, *Krystyna Alder and Ewald Alder v. Sabina Orlowska and Czeslaw Orlowski*, ECLI:EU:C:2012:824.

25 F. Gascón Inchausti, "Service of proceedings on the defendant as a safeguard of fairness in civil proceedings: in search of minimum standards from EU legislation and European case-law" (2017) 13(3) *Journal of Private International Law* 475–518.

26 E. Storskrubb (above, n. 9) 192–193.

of the EU law-maker's "bipolar" state of mind: it is intended to remind national judicial authorities that differences, by themselves, do not necessarily amount to public policy infringements. The EU pushes mutual recognition further and further, although it is aware that there is a latent lack of trust between legal systems, probably founded on the perception that they are not similar when it comes to minimum standards on the fairness of proceedings.

In short, the adoption of such a broad set of civil procedural rules does not compel the conclusion that a true procedural harmonisation has been achieved thanks to them or that, at least, an approximation has been produced between the national legislation greater than that which would exist without this *corpus iuris processualis europaeum*. However, this is not in itself a failure, unless that had been the objective pursued by the European legislator. In other words, if there has been some harmonisation, it will be good news, because it means that it was achieved even if it was not the initial purpose. In any case, it would be a little naive, at least to some extent, to think that the European law-maker does not have in mind the possibility that its regulations and directives on judicial cooperation in civil matters can or should end up displaying harmonising effects beyond the boundaries of cross-border litigation. Even if it is not addressed explicitly, the European law-maker is always aware of the expansive force of its regulatory actions, once they are implemented at the national level: sometimes, however, the internal repercussions do not run along the paths discreetly sought by the European legislator;[27] occasionally, in fact, it can be considered that the European law-maker hinders internal legal developments, imposing devices that might not work well or limiting pre-existing possibilities that were performing well.[28]

2. EUROPEAN JUDICIAL COOPERATION RULES WITH (A POSSIBLE) HARMONISING IMPACT

What has been described so far was not meant to offer a negative, disappointed or pessimistic view of things. In fact and in this author's opinion also fortunately, it is not a complete picture of the situation. It is true that the European legislator has built civil judicial cooperation without being forced to harmonise civil procedural legislation, and without even establishing minimum standards in relation to the fairness of proceedings. But there are also elements that allow us to see a half-full glass. In fact, it is possible to

---

27 As reminded by M. Tulibacka, "Europeanization of civil procedures: in search of a coherent approach" (2009) 46(5) *Common Market Law Review* 1527–1565, at 1545.

28 See on this M. Tulibacka (above, n. 27) 1559–1561, explaining the negative impact in the Netherlands patent litigation of the provisions of the 2004 IP Directive in the field of costs.

deduce from the regulations on civil judicial cooperation and from the case law of the CJEU that has interpreted them some minimum standards that could be later reflected in future European statutes aimed at harmonising civil proceedings. And, regardless of what the European legislator decides to do in the future, the rules themselves and the case law of the Court of Justice also give rise to legislative policy options that are considered as "good practices", which have had or may have regulatory repercussions on national processes, which, in turn, may end up generating a practical harmonisation, perhaps more spontaneous than deliberate.

2.1. PROVISIONS WITH EXPANSIVE FORCE AND POTENTIAL HARMONISING IMPACT

As has been pointed out before, many of the rules that make up the *corpus iuris processualis europaeum* have been the result of a careful analysis in search of the best solution to problems common to cross-border litigation: the European legislator has tried to offer the best answer, regardless of the peculiarities of national procedural systems. The regulations that establish alternative European procedures are undoubtedly the best example of the above: although they make references to national procedural legislation, they contain important legislative policy decisions about the best way to face certain procedural difficulties and how to distribute benefits and burdens between the parties to the process. It is clear that some of these rules only make sense in cross-border matters; but sometimes they are "exportable" to purely national litigation and, consequently, they become suitable models for internal procedural reforms. In other words, the European law-maker can take advantage of the rules of the *corpus iuris processualis europaeum* to offer national legislators better models and solutions than those existing in their internal systems: if national legislators decided to adapt their systems to these "peculiar" recommendations, they would end up producing a procedural harmonisation.[29]

The European law-maker, in short, can use the European provisions on international judicial cooperation to offer indications, recommendations or guidance on questions that are not only useful for cross-border litigation; and, above all, not only with regard to issues that affect the main procedural principles, but also to more detailed aspects, in which different solutions are

29 S. Huber, *Entwicklung transnationaler Modellregeln für Zivilverfahren – am Beispiel der Dokumentenvorlage*, Mohr Siebeck, Tübingen, 2008; A. Nylund/B. Krans, *The European Union and National Civil Procedure*, Intersentia, Cambridge, 2016; J.T. Nowak, "Considerations on the Impact of EU Law on National Civil Procedure: Recent Examples from Belgium" in V. Lazic/S. Stuij (eds.), *International Dispute Resolution*, Asser-Springer, The Hague, 2018, 1–41.

theoretically imaginable and in which the best possible solution is offered. Thus, it is possible that a European standard, designed to apply in cross-border settings, runs also to internal situations: the national lawmaker can be induced to reform the internal rules to adapt them to those for cross-border scenarios, either by simply imitating or by truly adopting the European solution in the belief that they are better quality standards, in order to avoid placing litigants in cross-border cases in a better position than in purely internal settings.

The following may be considered as examples of this phenomenon:

- A preference for self-representation in small claims cases, as established in the ESCP Regulation,[30] as a way to diminish costs, which entails in turn the need for the court to assume a more active role in determining the facts and selecting the applicable legal rule. If the EU law-maker considers this the best solution for cross-border small claims, where language and distance difficulties could in principle support mandatory representation by a lawyer, it goes without saying that the standard should apply more easily in purely domestic settings. This trend is maintained, indeed, in the more complex setting of provisional measures, with Article 41 of the EAPO Regulation ("Representation by a lawyer or other legal professional shall not be mandatory in proceedings to obtain a Preservation Order").
- A preference for the provisional enforceability of first instance judgments, notwithstanding the pendency of appellate proceedings. Already in 1968 the Brussels Convention had admitted the possibility of provisional cross-border enforcement of judgments, an option maintained with the Brussels I and the Brussels I bis Regulations: but this option was based on the premise that the decision was provisionally enforceable according to the legislation of the state of origin. The relevant issue is that, in at least two instances, the European legislator has made it clear that provisional enforcement must or should be mandatory in cross-border situations: on the one hand, for small claims, according to Article 15.1 ESCP-Regulation ["The judgment shall be enforceable notwithstanding any possible appeal. The provision of a security shall not be required"]; and on the other hand, in maintenance cases, according to Article 39 of the Maintenance Regulation ["The court of origin may declare the decision provisionally enforceable, notwithstanding any appeal, even if national law does not provide for enforceability by operation of law"]. It is clear that those are cases where the interest of speedy recovery may prevail over legal certainty.

30 This kind of "reflective and expansive" effectiveness of EU legislation became clearly visible in the Spanish legal system in 2011, when the minimum threshold for the mandatory intervention of a lawyer was raised from 900 euros – the amount initially established by the Code of Civil Procedure – to 2000 euros, foreseen at that time by the ESCP Regulation, in order to align national proceedings with the European small claims procedure (see Law 4/2011 of March 24).

But, even assuming this caveat, if provisional enforceability is established by EU law as mandatory in cross-border situations, it is difficult for national law-makers to explain to "domestic" litigants that it is not so in internal cases.

- The minimum items to be covered by any legal aid system.[31] According to the 2003 Legal Aid Directive, legal aid in cross-border situations should encompass the costs associated with some activities; if those items were not previously covered for purely domestic situations, the pressure to harmonise would certainly be strong.[32] It is worth noting, however, that the Directive has not harmonised the criteria on which the granting of legal aid depends.[33]

On a more general level, European legislation on international cooperation shows the convenience of incorporating parameters of efficiency and proportionality into national procedural systems: in current times of austerity and recurrent lack of public resources, the EU law-makers show the need to find a balance between access to justice and the right to an effective judicial remedy, on the one hand, and the reality of the administration of justice systems, on the other. This trend explains, at least partially, the EU interest in promoting mediation and ADR schemes. But it is also visible within judicial solutions, and from different points of view.

- On the one hand, it is worth mentioning the new Article 15a.1 of the ESCP Regulation, requiring that the court fees charged for the European Small Claims Procedure must not be disproportionate (and also that they shall not be higher than the court fees charged for national simplified court procedures). In a similar vein, Article 42 of the EAPO Regulation also calls for proportionality between court fees in proceedings to obtain a Preservation Order or a remedy against an Order and fees for obtaining an equivalent national order or a remedy against such a national order.
- On the other hand, there are also some European provisions that show the choice for the least expensive method to carry on proceedings, at least when the amount of the claim is reduced. Therefore, Article 5.1 of the ESCP Regulation shows a preference for the conduction of proceedings in writing and Article 5.1a establishes that oral hearings shall only be

---

31 R. Mańko (above, n. 10) 22.

32 In this vein, see M. Tulibacka (above, n. 27) 1543–1544, explains how Article 3(2)(a) of the Directive, establishing the requirement to cover pre-litigation advice led to an extension of legal aid to out-of-court advice and assistance, in general terms (although the author also explains that the Directive did not help harmonising the criteria to grant legal aid in each Member State).

33 F. Gascón Inchausti /M. Requejo Isidro (above, n. 2) 83–94.

held if the court considers that it is not possible to give the judgment on the basis of the written evidence or if a party so requests, although such a request may be refused by the court if it considers that, with regard to the circumstances of the case, an oral hearing is not necessary for the fair conduct of the proceedings.

- The option for efficiency is probably also underpinning the trend of the EU law-maker to foster the use of e-Justice devices, again traceable from the wording of the ESCP Regulation after its 2015 amendment: according to Article 13, service of documents should be performed by electronic means, especially once the proceedings have been instituted; and, according to Article 8, oral hearings – where considered necessary – shall be held by making use of any appropriate distance communication technology, such as videoconference or teleconference, available to the court or tribunal, unless the use of such technology, on account of the particular circumstances of the case, is not appropriate for the fair conduct of the proceedings.

2.2. COMMON STANDARDS DEDUCED FROM THE *CORPUS IURIS PROCESSUALIS EUROPAEUM* AND INTERPRETATIVE CJEU CASE LAW

What has been described so far are legal policy options that the European law-maker considers reasonable, which have been incorporated into certain regulations and directives that make up the *corpus iuris processualis europaeum* and which, for the reasons mentioned above, have the potential to be transplanted from cross-border settings to the domestic sphere. But it seems to this author, in addition, that certain common procedural standards can also be extracted from some of the rules within the *corpus iuris processualis europaeum* and from the case law of the CJEU that interprets them; that is, it is possible to deduce from them the European conception of certain procedural safeguards, applicable in general to any procedural scope (not only cross-border and, of course, not only international cooperation). Indeed, the application of the CFREU by the Court of Justice – namely of Article 47[34] – is causing the Court of Justice to progressively establish – sometimes perhaps only to detect[35] – minimum standards in various areas of civil proceedings: it

34 On the interplay between Article 47 CFREU and the development of European Civil Procedure, M. Hazelhorst, *Free Movement of Civil Judgments in the European Union and Right to a Fair Trial*, Asser-Springer, The Hague, 2017, 123 and following.

35 As pointed out by M. Tulibacka et al. (above, n. 3) 28, "While some procedural standards now accepted as part of the EU procedural system were ascertained in the CJEU jurisprudence, the contribution of the Court should ultimately be seen as standard-interpreting rather than

can be spoken, also in this field, of the progressive construction of a sort of "Praetorian Law" and, at the same time, of a phenomenon of progressive constitutionalisation of European civil procedural law.[36]

In particular, it seems to this author that these standards mostly refer to the defendant's legal position and are related to his/her right of defence, at least in two major moments.

1. The first moment – and, without a doubt, of the maximum relevance – is when the defendant is informed of the existence of the procedure. At this point, European rules establish certain minimum standards, which the case law of the Court of Justice has helped to identify, especially in recent years, when the Court has tended to link the rules of the *corpus iuris processualis europaeum* with Article 47 CFREU. Synthetically, these standards, which – this author insists – are general for all civil proceedings and not only for cross-border litigation, deal especially with service methods and with language, and include at least the following:
   a) The duty of Member States to use service methods ensuring reception by the recipient, which can be retrieved from the EEO, the EOP and the ESCP Regulations. These European procedures, indeed, tend to "create a common EU standard, which, presumably, should increase mutual trust in judgments rendered under these procedures".[37] These minimum requirements for service allow deduction of what the European legislator considers essential in order to ensure the right of the defendant to a fair trial. More precisely, service procedures must be designed using a scaled system, such that:
      (i) precedence is given to personal service, whether electronic or not, which can provide acknowledgement of receipt or an equivalent proof of success;
      (ii) the use of "less secure" methods – that is, without acknowledgement of receipt, but with a reasonable probability of success – is subsidiary; and
      (iii) fictitious service methods are absolutely subsidiary and exceptional, and any type of automation in their use must be avoided. The starting point in CJEU case law is that resorting to fictitious service of process on the defendant is not per se

---

standard-building. The manner in which the Court deals with the procedural principles and standards should be narrowed down to the context of the specific case, and drawing more general conclusions from its jurisprudence may be problematic." In practice, however, both scholars and national courts tend to operate in the opposite sense, attributing to the Court's case law a value far beyond the specific case that was decided.

36 Cfr. B. Hess, "Procedural Harmonisation in a European Context" in *Civil Litigation in a Globalising World* (above, n. 4) 159–173, at 169–171.

37 R. Mańko (above, n. 10) 27.

incompatible with the Brussels I bis Regulation system or with Article 47 CFREU, provided that all pertinent inquiries were made and that maximum diligence was employed – albeit unsuccessfully – in order to avoid using these methods.[38] The key, then, should not be the fact itself that service of process was fictitious, but whether said fictitious service was truly justified and not "premature", i.e., whether before resorting to this method, the "investigations required by the principles of diligence and good faith have been undertaken to trace the defendant".[39]

(b) The right to understand from the very beginning the scope of the proceedings. The content of the first notice and the language in which the document initiating proceedings and any basic attachments are written must allow the addressee to identify the basic elements that define the claim and to be in a position to adequately defend himself (Article 8 Service Regulation; Article 49 EAPO; Article 7 Legal Aid Directive). The standards set by the EU legal provisions and traced by the ECJ case law seem focused on the issue of language – the most sensitive in cross-border settings – but beneath this lies the real relevant safeguard; that of being able to understand what the whole case is about.[40]

(c) When serving proceedings on the defendant, and, in particular, when choosing the method that should be followed, when performing service, and when defining its content and language, maximum diligence must be demanded of national authorities; it is reasonable, furthermore, for national authorities to be in a position to offer proof or accreditation of their use of maximum diligence when attempting to ensure that the defendant was served notice under the best terms.[41]

---

38 Judgment of the Court of 17 November 2011, C-327/10, *Hypoteční banka a.s. v Udo Mike Lindner*, ECLI:EU:C:2011:745 (§§52–54); Judgment of the Court of 15 March 2012, C-292/10, *G v. Cornelius de Visser*, ECLI:EU:C:2012:142 (§§56–58); Judgment of the Court of 11 September 2014, C-112/13, *A v. B*, ECLI:EU:C:2014:2195 (§60). See also Articles 28 of the Brussels I bis Regulation and 19(2) of the Service Regulation.

39 Judgment of the Court in *Hypoteční banka a.s. v Udo Mike Lindner* (above, n. 38) §52; Judgment of the Court in *G v. de Visser* (above, n. 38) §59.

40 The scope of the defendant's right to a translation of the documents accompanying the claim was explained by the Judgment of the Court of 8 May 2008, C-14/07, *Ingenieurbüro Michael Weiss und Partner GbR v. Industrie- und Handelskammer Berlin*, ECLI:EU:C:2008:264: it covers, naturally, the document instituting the proceedings or equivalent document, but not those attachments which are of a merely evidentiary nature and are not necessary for understanding the purpose or cause of the claim. This, in turn, shows how the relevant element is this notion of «understanding the purpose or cause of the claim».

41 C. Crifò, "Europeanization, Harmonization and Unspoken Premises: The Case of Service Rules in the Regulation on a European Small Claims Procedure (Reg. 861/2007)" (2001) 30 *Civil Justice Quarterly* 283 and following.

2. The second relevant moment is when judgment is rendered and concerns not only the defendant, but any party to the proceedings. Parties have the right to be served with the judgment and, more specifically, to understand it, in order to arrange properly their reaction to it. Service of the judgment on the defendant is required by the Brussels I bis Regulation as a prerequisite to enforcement; and, since January 2015, the requirement has been added that the judgment is, where appropriate, translated into a language that the defendant understands – or is deemed to understand (Article 43.2). All the rules belonging to the *corpus iuris processualis europaeum* establish, additionally, the right to challenge final judgments rendered against defaulting defendants, in case of serious infringement of procedural rights: although, here again, the "written" standard seems to apply only in cross-border settings, it reflects indeed a minimum standard of fairness applicable to any judicial proceedings. In this vein, the current *acquis* shows that procedural regulations must provide sufficient remedies to correct dysfunctions in effecting service that have weakened or voided the defendant's right to defence through no fault of his own. This requirement is the necessary counterpoint to the admissibility of service methods without the defendant's acknowledgement of receipt and, in any event, must be provided for to deal with exceptional situations. It could be said, therefore, that Article 47 CFREU requires all Member States to set a balance between legal certainty – linked to the notion of *res judicata* – and procedural fairness.

2.3. THE "EU-FRIENDLINESS TESTS" PERFORMED BY THE CJEU AND THEIR POTENTIAL HARMONISING IMPACT

From a completely different angle, it should also be pointed out how the role of the Court of Justice as a negative legislator – also in civil procedural matters – has given rise to a new functionality, which we could perhaps call "preventive comparison". When the Court responds to preliminary questions that require it to decide on the compatibility with EU law of a certain national provision – for now, a procedural rule – it is obvious that only that specific rule is subject to scrutiny. And yet, the rest of the Member States must be aware of the outcome of the preliminary ruling procedure, especially when they find that their own rules are equivalent to those in question or when they plan to introduce a standard equivalent to that. A positive response can reassure them or even encourage them to follow the neighbour's example and that is probably why it is common for them to be actively involved in the proceedings before the Court of Justice.

For example, the Court's judgments in the *Alassini* case,[42] in the *Menini and Rampanelli* case[43] or in the *Peter Puškár* case,[44] allowed Member States to follow the Italian model and to introduce the mandatory attempt at mediation or conciliation as a prerequisite to the taking of legal action, provided, of course, that the limits set by the Court itself are respected, in order to consider that this does not disproportionately affect the right to effective judicial protection enshrined in Article 47 CFREU. Consequently the prior exhaustion of those remedies must not lead to a substantial delay in bringing a legal action; it must involve the suspension of the limitation period of the rights concerned; it must not involve excessive costs; consumers must not be compelled to be assisted by a lawyer and they shall be able to withdraw from a mediation procedure without the need to demonstrate the existence of a valid reason in support of that decision; electronic means must not be the only means by which the settlement procedure may be accessed; and interim measures must be possible in exceptional cases where the urgency of the situation so requires. It is obvious that the ECJ case law has set here clear minimum standards, which should be common to all national regulations: in order to reach the level of "comfort" referred to above, it will be essential to compare the national procedural system – or the one projected at the national level – and the one that was judged by the Court of Justice and, where appropriate, adapt it to the Court's case law.

And, conversely, a judgment of the Court that establishes the incompatibility with Union law of a specific national rule may end up having effects beyond the national legislation concerned, if a comparison with the forecasts of another or other Member States allows the conclusion to be reached that they also concur in the same defect: the domestic legislator or, where appropriate, the courts of that other state could use the judgment of the CJEU to, starting from a comparative analysis, repeal or cease to apply the national standard in question. Thus, to give an example again, the *Hubbard* judgment[45] served to put an end to the *cautio judicatum solvi* in respect of all persons domiciled in the Union, even though the Court had only examined the German legislation; the same thing happened after the *Mund & Fester* ruling[46] with the preventive

---

42 Judgment of the Court of 18 March 2010, Joined Cases C-317/08, *Rosalba Alassini v Telecom Italia SpA*, C-318/08 *Filomena Califano v Wind SpA*, C-319/08 *Lucia Anna Giorgia Iacono v Telecom Italia SpA*, and C-320/08 *Multiservice Srl v Telecom Italia SpA*, ECLI:EU:C:2010:146.

43 Judgment of the Court of 14 June 2017, C-75/16, *Menini and Rampanelli v. Banco Popolare – Società Cooperativa*, ECLI:EU:C:2017:457.

44 Judgment of the Court of 27 September 2017, C-73/16, *Peter Puškár v. Finančné riaditeľstvo Slovenskej republiky and Kriminálny úrad finančnej správy*, ECLI:EU:C:2017:725.

45 Judgment of the Court of 1 July 1993, C-20/92, *Anthony Hubbard (Testamentvollstrecker) v. Peter Hamburger*, ECLI:EU:C:1993:280.

46 Judgment of the Court of 10 February 1994, C-398/92, *Mund & Fester v. Hatrex Internationaal Transport*, ECLI:EU:C:1994:52.

seizure of the property of foreign defendants due to the fact of their being so; and, as has just been seen, it will also happen, under the protection again of the *Menini and Rampanelli* judgment, with those legal systems that have established the mandatory intervention of a lawyer in a mediation that affects a consumer.

What is most interesting about these "preventive comparisons" is that they take place between the systems of different Member States, using as a *tertium comparationis* compatibility or not with the European legal order, a *tertium* that, in turn, is offered – or rather, imposed – by the Court of Justice. The aim of such a comparison is not exclusively functional, but primarily constitutional: the ultimate purpose is not to seek a more effective solution to a common problem in a foreign law, but to avoid maintaining or introducing a regulation contrary to EU law, which gives, in turn, harmonising impact to the standards detected by the CJEU scrutinising EU provisions, including also those which make up the *corpus iuris processualis europaeum*.

3. CONCLUSIONS

In any case, after watching the part of the glass that is half-full, the overall feeling is still bittersweet, because there is a lot of voluntarism when it comes to assessing the harmonising impact of the *corpus iuris processualis europaeum*: in the abstract, the potential is great; but in practice, the fruits have been scarce. In fact, the aforementioned Luxembourg Study on European Civil Procedure made it possible to reach certain conclusions, which can serve as a basis for reflection:

1. Judicial cooperation in civil matters governed by the rules of the *corpus iuris processualis europaeum* is increasingly common and intense, although the national procedural regulations are still very different and also although, as a rule, there is still a high level of "mutual lack of knowledge".
2. Divergences and mutual lack of knowledge remain despite the apparently intense regulation of cross-border civil proceedings by European provisions. And this, in turn, can create difficulties for the better functioning of cross-border litigation, which is – we should always bear in mind – the aim pursued by the *corpus iuris processualis europaeum*.

   Many of the difficulties faced by cross-border litigation in the European Union do not come from the procedural rules adopted by the European Union itself, or approved in the Member States as a direct result of them, but rather stem from the national procedural rules themselves; i.e. how national law-makers address the regulation of civil proceedings with a cross-border element. It cannot be forgotten that cross-border proceedings are still national proceedings, whose regulation has been influenced by European legislation in a limited way: European provisions usually establish the broad bases and the nuclear elements of a regulation that aspires to be uniform, but they always refer for the development of proceedings and for technicalities to the national procedural regulation of each Member State, which can be very different. At this point, there are two main sources of dissatisfaction:

- In the first place, it is not uncommon for national legislators to neglect the regulation of cross-border proceedings, provoking situations in which due process guarantees may suffer.[47]
- In other cases, the diversity between national procedural laws, regardless of any consideration of cross-border issues, can in itself cause difficulties for the recognition and enforcement of judgments in another Member State.[48]

For instance, the infringement of public policy has been used to reject the enforcement of decisions that showed serious divergences between the procedural systems of the state of origin and the state of enforcement. In this vein, the Greek courts have on occasion denied the enforcement of costs awards granted abroad that were considered excessive according to their own parameters.[49] And the courts of several Member States have also regarded as against their public policy the recognition and/or enforcement of non-reasoned judgments issued in other countries, although in those countries, in certain cases, these types of decisions are admissible[50] (as in the case of Ireland with judgments issued by the Circuit judges).

3. If divergences are a source of difficulties for the proper functioning of cross-border litigation, then perhaps we are finding arguments to justify the need for closer approximation of laws. If it is concluded that there is a lack of basic "tuning" in some relevant aspects of civil procedure that the EU regulations on judicial cooperation – i.e., the *corpus iuris processualis europaeum* as a whole – have not corrected (probably also because they could not do it either), then it makes more sense to study the convenience

---

47 F. Gascón Inchausti/M. Requejo Isidro (above, n. 2) 45–46.

48 F. Gascón Inchausti/M. Requejo Isidro (above, n. 2) 138–167.

49 According to the Greek legal system, indeed, the amount of the costs cannot exceed the value of the procedure. Hence, the Court of Appeal of Corfu refused the exequatur to an English costs award on the ground that a Greek court could have never imposed such an amount (more than £80,000, where the value at stake in the proceedings was £17,000). With more detail, see F. Gascón Inchausti/M. Requejo Isidro (above, n. 2) 136.

50 The problem has arisen in several Member States, although with results that are not always the same [see, with more detail, F. Gascón Inchausti/M. Requejo Isidro (above, n. 2) 130–133, with examples from Germany, the Netherlands, France or Spain].

of taking one more step, that of a greater approximation of national procedural legislation in the strict sense. Indeed, from a European logic, the difficulties generated by diversity would be reduced if the rules were more harmonised. In short, if the problems do not come from European legislation, but from national procedural legislation, the solution to the problems, from the point of view of the European Union, involves influencing national procedural rights and, ultimately, harmonisation.[51]

[51] B. Hess, "Ein einheitliches Prozessrecht?" (2016) 6(1) *International Journal of Procedural Law* 55–85.

HARMONISATION OF THE RULES ON PROTECTIVE MEASURES?

The European Account Preservation Order

María Luisa VILLAMARÍN LÓPEZ*

Music creates order out of chaos: for rhythm imposes unanimity upon the divergent, melody imposes continuity upon the disjointed, and harmony imposes compatibility upon the incongruous.

Yehudi Menuhin

I take the liberty of starting this chapter with a quote from Yehudi Menuhin, known as the Einstein of the violin, whose words about music can, in this author's opinion, be extrapolated to the world of European Law to approach the phenomenon of harmonisation.

In the field of law, harmonisation implies the approximation of laws to eliminate their disparities by establishing common minimum standards that affect the harmonised states operating "with equivalent rules of the game".[1]

---

* This work is the result of research undertaken within the frame of a Research Project called "The harmonization of the civil procedure within the European Union" (DER2015-64756-P), funded by the Spanish Ministry of Science and led by Prof. Gascón Inchausti. It was partially the content of a lecture given at the Max Planck Institute of Procedural Law in Luxembourg on 19 July 2018.

1 Cf. F. Gascón Inchausti, *Derecho Europeo y legislación procesal civil nacional: entre autonomía y armonización*, Marcial Pons, 2018, p. 59.

Before answering the question about whether the European Account Preservation Order has contributed to the harmonisation of precautionary measures in the Union, it is necessary, in this author's view, to answer two preceding questions. First: are precautionary measures relevant at a cross-border level? The answer is clearly positive: in these transnational procedures it is necessary to guarantee the success of a subsequent enforcement procedure, even, if possible, with greater intensity than at the national level since they normally last longer, among other things, due to the difficulty in the practice of notifications and evidence. Bearing this in mind, the second question arises: are these measures working well within the European Union?

For years, it has been pointed out that the securing of debtors' funds in cross-border transactions did not sound properly and that this jeopardised the beneficial end of the enforcement of European judicial judgments.[2] It is well known that the Brussels Regulation (in its different versions) has already dealt with cross-border protective measures in general. In fact, via articles 35 and 36, defendants' accounts can be frozen; in particular, it was calculated in 2011 that an average of 34,000 to 36,000 cross-border account preservation orders were issued annually across Member States. But, as is well-known, for years now, after the *Denilauler* case, this kind of measure could only be taken after having notified the debtor.[3] Given the special volatility of the assets affected by account preservation orders, in particular since, with online bank transfers, assets can disappear very quickly and easily with just one click of the debtor, the lack of the so-called "surprise effect" in the Brussels Regulation very often frustrated the effectiveness of these measures. This requirement of previous notification to the debtor could have been simply eliminated from the Brussels Regulation but the European legislator understood that, even if this obstacle were overcome, another great difficulty was apparent: all the Member States provided for freezing orders in their procedural rules, and each one did so in a different way and with a diverse scope. In fact, experts advised of the danger of forum shopping for provisional measures in these cases, given the great disparities between the national legislation.[4] Some of the main questions on which significant discrepancies can be seen can be briefly pointed out: (a) adoption of the measures

---

2 To analyse these difficulties in detail, see the Study No. JAI/A3/2002/02, on making more efficient the enforcement of judicial decisions within the European Union, produced by B. Hess in 2004. Available at: http://ec.europa.eu/civiljustice/publications/docs/enforcement_judicial_decisions_180204_en.pdf.

3 The CJEU limited the application of these measures in the *Denilauler* case justifying the prohibition of *ex parte* proceedings to avoid the drastic effects of those measures, to better protect the debtor and to avoid its effect in their parties (C-125/79 *Denilauler v. S.N.C. Couchet Freres* [1980] ECR 1553 (ECLI:EU:C:1980:130)).

4 Cf. B. Hess, Study No. JAI/A3/2002/02, on making more efficient the enforcement of judicial decisions within the European Union, 2004, p. 16. See also pp. 60 and ff.

without giving an initial hearing to the debtor. For example, this possibility in four of the Member States is only foreseen in exceptional situations; (b) no uniform criterion as to who should adopt and when the measures should be adopted; (c) different standards regarding their pre-requisites; (d) appeal system; (e) need of lawyer assistance; and (f) court fees.

This situation, together with other added difficulties of a linguistic nature, may discourage more than one creditor from going to court, and, in any case, it is an enormous effort for those who decide to start down this slow and expensive path. Each legal system has such a different rhythm that it made this melody not only very expensive, but also difficult to sound good at European level.

After several years of works,[5] Regulation 655/2014 of 15 May 2014, establishing a European Account Preservation Order (EAPO) Procedure,[6] was passed with the intention of improving accessibility and effectiveness and granting creditors better protection of their right of access to the courts.

We can wonder at this point: has a melody been achieved that harmoniously combines the different European sounds in terms of account preservation orders?

The European legislator faced the challenge of establishing a new, comprehensive account preservation order procedure, totally independent of national rules, or of opting for the technique of legislative harmonisation, setting minimum common standards. Selecting only the first model would have implied that all the many aspects that are concerned when adopting a protective measure of this nature would have to be regulated in detail. It would probably not have been possible to reach a consensus on all the issues affected and, if it had been done, it would have been against the principle of subsidiarity by which European legislation obliges us. What was preferable, therefore, in this case? A model which combines both options, as was done by Regulation 655/2014.

Let us, therefore, try to distinguish which areas of the preservation order procedure have been subject to standardisation and which areas to harmonisation, in order to have thereafter the possibility to examine whether the combination was good enough to assure the success and efficiency of the Regulation.

---

5 In particular, various studies held by the European Commission (especially the Study No. JAI/A3/2002/02, on making more efficient the enforcement of judicial decisions within the European Union, 2004, n. 1 above, and the *Study for an impact assessment on a Draft legislative proposal on the Attachment of Bank Account*, Final Report, European Commission, 5 January 2011), the Green Paper on improving the efficiency of the enforcement of judgments in the European Union: the attachment of bank accounts (24 October 2006), the Stockholm Programme of December 2009 and finally the Proposal for a Regulation Creating an Account Preservation Order to facilitate cross-border debt recover in civil and commercial matters, of July 2011.

6 Available at: https://eur-lex.europa.eu/legal-content/EN/TXT/?uri=CELEX%3A32014R0655.

1. UNIFORM STANDARDS IN THE EAPO REGULATION

The European legislator chose to standardise the skeleton of this particular procedure, most of its phases and the relevant issues it deals with.

The Regulation provides a pan-European *ex parte* procedure with the intention of ensuring "the surprise effect of the order" and "that it will be a useful tool for a creditor trying to recover debts from a debtor in cross border cases" (Recital 15). It provides an autonomous regulation of many aspects of the procedure. First, some terms are defined just for the purposes of the Regulation such as, for example: "cross border cases" in Article 3; "bank creditor" or "authentic instrument" in Article 4; or initiation of proceedings in Article 10.3. Second, specific jurisdictional rules are also provided (Article 6), with special attention to consumers, who are benefited by establishing in their favour the jurisdiction of their domicile. Third, very clear deadlines are set for each phase of the procedure, unifying and, as a general rule, shortening the time-limits established all around Europe (e.g. Article 18). Fourth, a unique treatment is given to the general course of the various phases of the procedure (that may only begin at the request of a party). This includes the application (Article 8), that may be lodged even before the initiation of the main proceedings, during them or even once they are finished; the initiation of the procedure and its effects (Article 10);[7] the court's decision on the application and the detailed content and form of the preservation order issued (Article 17); its recognition, which is done automatically (Article 22); its enforcement by the Member State of enforcement (Article 23) and its implementation by the banks – with a special regime of bank liability – (Articles 24 and ff.); the service on the debtor (Article 28); and, lastly, a detailed regime of remedies (Articles 33 and ff.). Finally, the Regulation also guarantees the homogenous application of two very important rules to eliminate barriers to accessing cross-border measures: firstly, the non-obligatory nature of legal representation during the course of the procedure – as foreseen in several Member States – except in the subsequent phase of appeals, for which the national rules should applied (Article 41); and, secondly, in accordance with the principle of equivalence, that the costs of the procedure (court fees, costs incurred by banks and amounts required by the intervening authorities) cannot be different from those imposed on equivalent national orders (Articles 42, 43 and 44).

It is also important to remark that to facilitate the application of the Regulation the procedure set is written and is simplified through the use of standardised forms, passed in October 2016 by the Commission, in a document that includes

---

7 On these two aspects see in detail C. Senés Motilla, *La orden europea de retención de cuentas*, Aranzadi, 2015, pp. 90 and ff.

detailed clarifying guidelines to help their users.[8] These forms are also available via the web in the different official languages of the Union.[9]

Given the general nature of these provisions, nothing would prevent them from being used as a basis for the construction of a general European procedure for the adoption of all types of protective measures.

2. THE HARMONISING RULES IN THE EAPO REGULATION

Together with the specific aspects that, with greater or lesser accuracy, can be established *ad hoc* in an autonomous European procedure of this type, a series of co-existent issues of great importance need a common treatment to guarantee the effectiveness of these orders throughout Europe, despite the difficulty of homogenising them given their diverse regulation in national civil proceedings. For this reason, the harmonisation was also necessary to establish common minimum parameters that allow the rules to be applied in a similar way wherever the order is requested or enforced, but leaving the details of its application to the national law.

Some issues should be analysed at this point: the first, whether the harmonisation could be deemed satisfactory enough; and, second, whether important pieces have not been dealt in the whole of the Regulation. And also, since all these legal provisions that we have been analysing have created a kind of "harmonising island" in relation to the preservation orders, whether it would be possible and appropriate to extrapolate them to a common European system of protective measures.

There are, in this author's opinion, three most intense areas of harmonisation in the Regulation: the provisions on the prerequisites for the adoption of protective measures, the regime of liability that is imposed on the creditor, and the procedure for obtaining information on the debtor.

2.1. PRE-CONDITIONS FOR THE ADOPTION OF A PRESERVATION ORDER

Although almost all Member States share a similar doctrine about the substantive requirements that must be fulfilled to adopt protective measures, their scope

8 Commission Implementing Regulation (EU) 2016/1823 of 10 October 2016 establishing the forms referred to in Regulation (EU) No. 655/2014. Available at: https://eur-lex.europa.eu/legal-content/EN/TXT/?uri=uriserv:OJ.L_.2016.283.01.0001.01.ENG.

9 https://e-justice.europa.eu/content_european_account_preservation_order_forms-378-en.do?clang=en.

is probably one of the issues on which there is more disparate regulation in the different Member States.[10] The EAPO Regulation echoes, in Articles 7 and 12, the three conditions in which the European systems tend to coincide: *fumus boni iuris* (Article 7.2), *periculum in mora* (Article 7.1) and security (Article 12).[11] The legislator has extracted in Article 7 the common points of the national procedural laws to define these requisites in such a generic way that its literal meaning could be applied to any other protective measure that may be adopted, regardless of its nature.

In respect to the *fumus boni iuris*, all the Member States agree to maintain a low standard of proof regarding the possibility of the claim succeeding, though using different terminologies. For example, in Belgium, only "sufficient evidence to establish that the claim exists" is required; in Spain, Malta or Denmark, *prima facie* evidence; in Germany, sufficient evidence; in Hungary, Slovenia or Sweden, probable evidence; in the UK, a good arguable case must be presented; and, as an exception, no formal evidence is required in Italy.[12] Article 7.2 of the Regulation attempts to reach a common point by the following definition: "The creditor shall submit sufficient evidence to satisfy the court that he is likely to succeed in the substance of his claim against the debtor." Neither the degree of sufficiency nor the required likelihood[13] is clarified by the text, so that the condition should be ultimately read according to the national requirements.[14]

The interpretation of the *periculum in mora* offers more disparity among Member States. Although in most European legal systems the recognition of the risk that an eventual judgment will not be satisfied is required, the content or the level of exigency is not consistent across Member States. As an example, Slovenia and Romania do not require proof of the risk and, as regards urgency, some jurisdictions (such as France, Belgium and Luxembourg) do not consider it as

---

10 The level of discretion of the court is also different in the different regimes because in some countries, like in the UK, even if the pre-conditions are fulfilled, the court may deny the order when it is not "just and convenient". The Regulation, by contrast, obliges the court to issue the Order once the pre-conditions are met. On this topic, see also N. Kyrikiades, "European Account Preservation Order: what does the common law tradition have to say?", in S. Francq and M. Gardeñes Santiago (eds.), *Boundaries of European Private International Law*, Bruylant, 2015, p. 193.

11 More detail on this issue can be found in I. Antón Juarez in A. Calvo Caravaca and J. Carrascosa González, *Litigación internacional en la Unión Europea III*, Aranzadi, 2018, pp. 70–75, Hilbig-Lugani, *Münchener Kommentar*, C.H. Beck, 2017, pp. 43–46, F. Mohr, *Die vorläufige Kontenpfändung*, Lexis Nexis, 2014, pp. 45–49.

12 A more complete analysis on these differences can be found in B. Hess, Study No. JAI/A3/2002/02, n. 1 above, p. 129.

13 Even though, it is suggested by Kyrikiades that when using the expression "likely" they are "satisfied even with a less than 50% chance", what could be detrimental for the debtor. Cf. N. Kyrikiades, "An economic analysis of the European Commission's Proposal for a European Account", (2013) 3(4) *Risk, governance and control: financial markets and institutions* 52.

14 In this sense also G. Cuniberti and S. Migliorini, *The European Account Preservation Order*, Cambridge University Press, 2018, p. 118.

a necessary condition and, those that do, interpret it in a very different way.[15] The Regulation echoes this European doctrine and chooses to incorporate the notions of risk and urgency in Article 7.1:

> The court shall issue the Preservation order when the creditor has submitted sufficient evidence to satisfy the court that there is an urgent need for a protective measure in the form of a preservation order because there is a real risk that, without such a measure, the subsequent enforcement of the creditor's claim against the debtor will be impeded or made substantially more difficult.

Some examples of the risk are given in the Preamble (Recital 14) such as the debtor's conduct in respect of the creditor's claim or the debtor's credit history. What remains unclear is if urgency and risk must concur simultaneously. It must be pointed out that, in the event they must coincide, the "availability of the preservation orders will be limited as urgency entails that evidence of immediate danger being provided", losing the relevance of facts as the debtor's credit history or the debtor's behaviour in previous disputes.[16] In any case, a broad interpretation of the nature of the risk has been accepted by the Regulation, which includes not only the danger that "the enforcement of the creditor's claim against the debtor will be impeded" but also that such enforcement is "made substantially more difficult".

The third condition is the security which is required in most of the Member States,[17] albeit with very different forms in accordance with the national law (for example, as mentioned in Recital 18, deposit, bank guarantee or mortgage[18]). As a general rule, it will be necessary to provide it, although it may be waived "if it is considered inappropriate given the circumstances of the case" (Article 12.1) such as the lack of means of the creditor or if the order could not cause any damage to the debtor (Recital 18). Even though the amount and the forms in which it is established are in accordance with the national laws, the Regulation establishes common rules with regard to the essence of the security. Thus, in fixing its amount, the court shall consider that the security fulfills a double purpose mentioned in Article 12.1: preventing the abuse of the procedure and ensuring compensation for any damage suffered by the debtor as a result of the order. Apart from that, this assessment would also include the consideration of

---

15 For more details of this comparative analysis, see B. Hess, Study No. JAI/A3/2002/02, n. 1 above, p. 129.

16 Cf. G. Cuniberti and S. Migliorini, *The European Account Preservation Order*, n. 13 above, pp. 114 and 115.

17 Except in seven Member States: Belgium, Czech Republic, Luxembourg, Slovakia, Slovenia and Scotland. Cf. *Study for an impact assessment on a Draft legislative proposal on the Attachment of Bank Account*, Final Report, European Commission, 5 January 2011, p. 78.

18 For example, a bailiff's deposit account in Latvia, a deposit at court in Denmark, undertakings as to damages provided to the court in England, Wales and Ireland, or the form provided by the court, as in Austria, Greece or France. Cf. *Study for an impact assessment*, n. 4 above, p. 78.

the requirement of proportionality set forth by the ECHR and CJEU in order not to limit the fundamental right to access to justice.

The way of proving these pre-conditions or any other data relevant to the procedure is also harmonised. In principle it will be done through documentary evidence, although, "provided that this is admitted by national law" and if it does not unduly delay the course of the procedure, "any suitable means of proof", such as the hearing of the creditor or of witnesses, even through "videoconferencing or other communication technology" (Article 9.1). And, interestingly, the judicial body is empowered, too, to authorise *ex officio* evidence if that possibility is provided by the national law (Article 9.2).

2.2. CREDITOR'S LIABILITY REGIME

To counteract the privileged position in which the creditor is placed in the Regulation, it was also essential to ensure that the creditor shall be answerable for possible damages caused to the debtor as a result of the agreed measure. The lack of sufficient counterbalances could place debtors in irreversible situations. Although the European legislator could have been more daring, imposing on the creditor the duty to take responsibility for all the consequences derived from his petition, it was decided to set a minimum standard of liability due to fault (Article 13.1), supplemented by certain special cases in which the creditor's fault is presumed, *iuris tantum* (Article 13.2).[19] There is, however, no autonomous definition of what should be understood by "fault" nor any special procedure to follow, so that national regulations must be applied, even though they are quite different.[20] From this minimum, Member States can establish a higher level of protection, both in their burden of proof rules and in the type of responsibility required, as is the German case, with a system of strict liability.[21]

Deserving of special mention is an additional obligation, imposed on the creditors, of stating the truth in their protection order requests (Article 8.6), subject to liability. Although this is a duty hitherto only foreseen directly or indirectly in a few European legal systems (for example, in Spain under the principle of procedural good faith), in this author's opinion, it is a great success that the European legislator has dared to impose a measure of this nature that reveals and punishes ill-intentioned creditors who would like to use these measures in a tortious manner.

---

19 On the debate on this issue in the preparatory works, Hess and Raffelsieper, "Die Europäische Kontenpfändungsverordnung: eine überfällige Reform zur Effektuierend grenzüberschreitender Vollstreckung im Europäischer Justizraum", *IPrax*, 2015, p. 7.

20 See different CJUE judgments where these differences are referred. Cf. G. Cuniberti and S. Migliorini, *The European Account Preservation Order*, n. 13 above, p. 170, fn. 287.

21 See also more in detail on the regime of responsibility and in particular on its application in Austria in F. Mohr, *Die Vorläufige Kontenpfändung*, Lexis Nexis, 2014, pp. 158 and ff.

Summing up, despite the reluctance of the United Kingdom on the regime of conditions and liability, which they considered so low that they could undermine companies (especially those with financial difficulties) and make insolvency more likely, in this author's view the harmonisation of these requirements as analysed above seems to have been successful. And, in fact, this Regulation is so generic, that could be applicable to all kinds of measures, both conservative and anticipatory.

2.3. REGIME FOR OBTAINING INFORMATION ON THE DEBTOR'S ACCOUNT

Finally, let us commentate on the regime for obtaining information on the debtor's accounts, specifically provided for this particular kind of measure. Without its harmonisation, it would have been impossible to put European retention orders in place, since some states do not rule these to be sensitive issues and did not allow other states to ask their banks for information on their clients at all, or did it insufficiently.

The Regulation gives the creditor the possibility to lodge an application for post-judgment preservation orders[22] even if he does not know in which bank the debtor holds an account, establishing mechanisms in Article 14 for obtaining the information required and identifying the debtor's accounts. The system is based on a fundamental requirement: these searches cannot be done for the sole purpose of investigating where the debtor has bank accounts, as fishing expeditions, but only when the creditor justifies its need. The creditor must hold a title and should demonstrate

> why he believes that the debtor holds one or more accounts with a bank in the specific Member State and shall provide all relevant information available to him about the debtor and the account or accounts to be preserved [Article 14.2].

But, undoubtedly, the most important and controversial aspect of the harmonisation refers to the methods of obtaining such information. There was a project to pass a European Assets Declaration that generalised the debtor's obligation to disclose their assets throughout the European Judicial Area, setting minimum standards regarding the content, conditions and sanctions derived

---

22 In Recital 20, it is explained that, as a rule, this possibility is limited to enforceable titles "given the particular nature of such intervention by public authorities and of such access to private data" although in Art. 14.1 second paragraph it is exceptionally provided the possibility of submitting these requests even if the title is not yet enforceable "when the amount to be preserved is substantial", the circumstances are relevant and the "creditor has submitted sufficient evidence to satisfy the court" of the "urgent need for account information".

from these measures, guaranteeing an "equal access to information about assets within the European Judicial Area".[23] But at the time this Regulation was passed, that instrument was not ready, so that the Regulation 655/2014 had to refer to the methods for obtaining information "whether temporarily or permanently". Three specific methods and a final open clause have been included in Article 14.5, leaving to the Member States the task to introduce in their legal systems "at least" one of them.[24] The three first methods mentioned are the following: first, the bank obligation to disclose the debtor's data (paragraph (a)); second, the access by the information authority to the relevant data when "held by public authorities or administrations in registers or otherwise" (paragraph (b)); and, third, the possibility to the courts to oblige the debtor to disclose his bank information related to the petition (paragraph (c)). In this author's view, what is hardly admissible is to accept the last clause that allows any other method "effective and efficient in order to obtain the relevant information, provided it is not disproportionate in its cost or duration" (paragraph (d)). Far from harmonising, this rule leaves absolute freedom to Member States, so that the defendant's private life could be easily intruded upon.[25] In any case, it is to be consider very positive to have managed to unify these criteria, since it was one of the issues on which the Member States showed greatest reluctance.

3. WHAT WAS NOT HARMONISED BY THE EAPO REGULATION?

At this point, we still have to consider whether it would have been appropriate to go further in the harmonisation of the account preservation orders so that the Regulation could have worked better.

There are three areas in which, in this author's opinion, the Regulation could have gone a little further: the methods for obtaining information, to which we have already referred; the scope of the seizure of bank accounts, in particular the exemption regime;[26] and, finally, the rankings among different creditors.

---

23 New instrument for some Member States, such as Belgium, Italy, France, Luxembourg, Netherlands and Scotland. More information about the pros of this Declaration could be found in B. Hess, Study, n. 1 above, p. 148.

24 The national information on this issue and other aspects that must be concrete by each Member State is available via web at: https://e-justice.europa.eu/content_european_account_preservation_order-379-en.do.

25 In this sense, Cuniberti remarks that "the freedom of Member States under Art. 14.5.d seems unlimited". Cf. G. Cuniberti and S. Migliorini, *The European Account Preservation Order*, n. 13 above, p. 186.

26 For detail and a comparative analysis on shared accounts see N. Ritz, *Vorläufige Kontenpfändung in Europa*, Peter Lang Verlag, 2019, pp. 106 and ff.

As regards the scope of these measures, the different Member States provide various effects when freezing assets. In most of the European legal systems this kind of measure produces effects *in rem*, which content may vary between affecting all the debtor's assets (such as in France or in the Netherlands) or freezing only the amount that corresponds to the debt discussed (for example, in Spain). In contrast, in other countries they may even have *in personam* injunctions with very different consequences (as a general rule, when not complying with the order, the debtor could be sanctioned by the court, which could impose fines or even imprisonment), as occurs in Ireland and Cyprus. Although during the preparatory works on the Regulation it was considered better to introduce only measures *in rem*, this proposal was left out and, as clarified in Recital 28, the "*in personam* orders" should be considered included in the reference to "equivalent national orders" provided in the Regulation. Therefore, this decision of the European legislator entails that European preservation orders may display any of these effects, producing marked inequalities between debtors whose accounts are in different Member States. The danger that this can involve for legal traffic in general (and, especially for certain companies in situations of weakness) could not be hidden, especially when preservation orders are requested simultaneously in several countries, especially if all the debtor´s assets could be frozen in some or all of them. In this sense, some authors regret that this issue has not been harmonised in the Regulation to improve the "functionality and fairness of the instrument".[27]

Regarding exemptions from seizure and rankings, the Regulation opted again for a wide solution. Instead of harmonising these issues, Articles 31 and 32 referred to the national regimes of the Member State of enforcement, despite the great divergences foreseen in European national laws on these two important questions. Two main problems could be derived from these provisions. The first, that it deprives the debtor of the protection of the rules of the place of his domicile, which normally would protect him better. And, second, that it could encourage a sort of forum shopping, in the sense that debtors may decide to open their bank accounts depending on the country where their balances are most protected against these measures.[28] All these questions can be detrimental to the effectiveness of preservation orders and, of course, it has been a lost opportunity to reach a consensus on a minimum common standard that could be applied to any other type of European cross-border protective measure.

---

27 Cf. N. Kyrikiades, "European Account Preservation Order", n. 10 above, p. 193.

28 Cf. G. Cuniberti and S. Migliorini, *The European Account Preservation Order*, n. 13 above, p. 272 and also Hilbig-Lugani, n. 11 above, pp. 92 and ff.

4. CONCLUSION

Despite these shortcomings, Regulation 655/2014 deserves our praise as it has gone beyond its initial goal. In addition to establishing a fairly complete regime for account preservation orders, a very important breakthrough has been made in the path of the construction of a common system of protective measures that can be applied throughout the territory of the Union. Plenty of the requirements on which the regulation of any of these measures is based have been agreed so that they can serve as a worthy starting point for future common regulations at a European level. Therefore, to finish in a musical key, as I started, I consider that Regulation 655/2014 has accomplished a quite harmonious melody that hopefully may be reflected in the next years in wonderful symphonies on protective measures like Beethoven's Ninth that unifies all our hearts within Europe.

HARMONISING ACCESS TO INFORMATION AND EVIDENCE

The Directives on Intellectual Property and Competition Damages

Enrique VALLINES GARCÍA*

* This chapter has been made possible with the support of the Spanish Ministry for Economy and Competitiveness, in the context of the Research Project "La armonización del proceso civil en la Unión Europea" (DER2015-64756-P) and the Thematic Network "Justicia civil: análisis y prospectiva" (DER2016-81752-REDT).

1. INTRODUCTION

This chapter deals with the harmonisation of the procedural rules governing access to information and access to evidence in civil cases within the EU, sometimes known as the rules on "discovery" or "disclosure".

These rules come into play whenever some information about the facts of the case or some pieces of evidence relevant to the case are not within the reach of the party needing that information or that evidence for building up his or her claims or defences. In other words, the rules on access to information and evidence are applicable whenever (i) a party to a civil dispute needs to obtain relevant information or evidence for his or her case, (ii) that information or evidence is under someone else's control and, ultimately, (iii) that someone is not willing to hand it over.

Indeed, in order to present a civil case, the parties to a dispute need information and evidence. Information about the facts of the case, so that they can put forward all the relevant details concerning their pleadings; and sufficient evidence to support the factual information that is to be submitted to the court.

In the United States of America, the parties usually enjoy the opportunity for broad discovery of information and evidence kept by the opponent or even by third parties. On a general basis, the American Federal Rules of Civil Procedure follow a system of "notice pleading", whereby plaintiffs may start civil proceedings by way of a very simple brief, which needs only to contain a short and plain statement of the claim showing that the pleader is plausibly entitled to relief; and, once that brief has been filed, the rules on discovery make it relatively easy – although expensive – for the parties to have access to all kinds of information and evidence about the case which is under someone else's control.[1]

Conversely, generally speaking, none of the EU Member States – not even the UK[2] – has rules of broad discovery like the ones applicable to civil litigation

1 Rule 8, rules 26 to 37 and rule 45 of the Federal Rules of Civil Procedure.

2 See N. Trocker, "From ALI-UNIDROIT Principles to common European rules on access to information and evidence? A preliminary outlook and some suggestions" (2014) 19 *Uniform Law Review* 239–291, at 251–252; also M. Taruffo, "Rethinking the standards of proof" (2003)

in the US federal courts. European countries usually prefer a system of "fact pleading", where the initial pleading standard is stricter, so that the parties are required to go into the details of the case in their initial briefs and, normally, to submit or, at least, to describe the relevant evidence from the very beginning.[3] Within the context of such a system, the parties are expected to endeavour to obtain the relevant information or evidence on their own – without bothering the court, the opponent or any other person – and, only when it is impossible or very difficult for a party to get that information or that evidence, might a limited set of legal provisions on disclosure apply.

Hence, there appears to be a close relationship between the initial pleading standard and the scope of disclosure. Indeed, where the pleading standard is lax, after the claimant has filed his or her complaint containing just a short and plain statement (a "notice") of the cause of action, the detailed facts of the case are still to be discovered and introduced in the proceedings, what then amounts to broad powers of discovery. On the contrary, where, in the context of a "fact pleading" system, the parties are required to investigate on their own and to exhaust the details of the case in their initial briefs, that investigation and

---

51(3) *American Journal of Comparative Law* 659–678, at 675. However, UK rules on disclosure are still much more open than those of other EU Member States. In fact, when dealing with the transposition of Directive 2004/48/EC ("IPRED"), the UK argued "no action required" in regard to the implementation of the rules on disclosure foreseen in the Directive. See N. Coulson, C. Muyl and R. Schlötter, "The impact of the European Enforcement Directive: A new regime for gathering and preserving evidence?", (Fall/Winter 2007) *IP Perspectives – Jones Day* 24–29, at 27–28 (available at: https://www.jonesday.com/files/Publication/f8ed5432-67e0-42c9-aa02-2eb90839f958/Presentation/PublicationAttachment/8b0e3b31-653e-4512-829e-40d6a84149d8/IP_Perspectives_Winter_07.pdf).

3 On the distinction between "fact pleading" and "notice pleading", see L.J. Priestley, "Fact pleading v. Notice pleading: Its significance in the development of evidence" (2001) 6(4) *Uniform Law Review* 841–855; American Law Institute (ALI)/International Institute for the Unification of Private Law (UNIDROIT), *Principles of transnational civil procedure* (Cambridge University Press, New York, 2006), at 7–8; and Trocker, above n. 2, at 244–248. It has been argued that, in view of the construction of rule 8 of the Federal Rules of Civil Procedure set forth by the US Supreme Court in *Bell Atlantic Corp. v. Twombly* (2007) and *Ashcroft v. Iqbal* (2009), "the United States appears to be shifting away from the notice-based exceptionalism toward a fact-based model more akin to the pleading standards in the rest of the world" (S. Dodson and J.M. Klebba, "Global Civil Procedure Trends in the Twenty-First Century" (2011) 4(1) *Boston College International and Comparative Law Review* 1–26, at 8; available at: http://lawdigitalcommons.bc.edu/iclr/vol34/iss1/2). However, on the one hand, when interpreting rule 8, these two cases have not taken into consideration any hypothetical need of convergence with the fact-pleading standard applicable in other countries (Dodson/Klebba, above n. 3, at 22). And, on the other hand, subsequent cases, such as *Matrixx Initiatives, Inc. v. Siracusano* (2011) and *Skinner v. Switzer* (2011), appear to have been decided upon the traditional notice pleading standard (S. Dodson and C. Starger, "Mapping Supreme Court Doctrine: Civil Pleading" (2014) 7(1) *The Federal Courts Law Review* 275–284, at 283–284; available at: http://ssrn.com/abstract=2422160; also on video: http://vimeo.com/89845875).

that exhaustive pleading usually result in a much more restricted disclosure. Shortly put, the stricter the pleading standard is, the narrower the scope of discovery tends to be.[4] This relationship might certainly be one of the reasons why EU Member States are not willing to import the US approach to discovery: since EU Member States usually follow a strict pleading standard, Europeans seem to be well off with a system of limited disclosure.

Furthermore, it might be argued that, apart from legal tradition and the link between pleading standard and discovery, the preoccupation of European authorities with the protection of privacy and business secrets also plays an important role in keeping things different. Indeed, sometimes the application of the American rules on broad discovery has brought about "fishing expeditions", it has created risks to privacy and business secrets and, in extreme cases, it is said to have even facilitated blackmail and extortion.[5] European law-makers do not seem eager to accept these risks, so that when balancing the need for information and evidence, on the one hand, and the need to protect privacy and business secrets, on the other, they appear to be willing to stress that they are much more concerned with the latter than their US colleagues are. And these concerns would probably explain why the use of the term "discovery" – greatly resembling the American rules – has been avoided in European Law and why "broad discovery is regarded with horror by most European lawyers, judges, and government officials".[6]

Thus, in the Member States of the EU, the procedural rules on access to information and evidence – the rules on disclosure – are much more limited than their counterpart rules in the US.[7] Yet, despite this common feature, every Member State has its own particular rules, which differ significantly

---

4 As explained in the Introduction to the ALI/UNIDROIT *Principles of Transnational Civil Procedure*: "The pleading rule requiring specific allegations of fact reduces the potential scope of discovery, because it provides for tightly framed claims and defences from the very beginning of the proceeding" (ALI/UNIDROIT, above n. 3, at 8). Similarly, see M.H. Reddish, "Pleading, Discovery, and the Federal Rules: Exploring the Foundation of Modern Procedure" (2012) 64(4) *Florida Law Review* 845–883, at 870–871 (available at: http://scholarship.law.ufl.edu/flr/vol64/iss4/2); and N. Trocker, above n. 2, at 247–248. Accordingly, Dodson argues that "new pleading, new discovery", i.e., that any changes in the pleading standard shall also bring about changes in the scope of discovery (S. Dodson, "New pleading, new discovery" (2010) 109(1) *Michigan Law Review* 53–89; available at: http://repository.law.umich.edu/mlr/vol109/iss1/2).

5 See Reddish, above n. 4, at 871–872.

6 G.H. Hazard Jr., "Civil Procedure Rules for European Courts" (2016) 100(2) *Judicature* 58–64, at 59 and 62; available at: https://repository.uchastings.edu/cgi/viewcontent.cgi?article=2322&context=faculty_scholarship.

7 See N. Mosunova, "Disclosure of Evidence in Cartel Litigations in the EU: Is Balance of Victims' Rights and Public Interests Possible?" (2015) II(1) *BRICS Law Journal*, 125–155, at 135; available at: https://www.bricslawjournal.com/jour/article/view/27.

from one country to another.[8] This diversity raised the issue of a certain need for harmonisation,[9] which, for the moment, has only taken place "vertically" via two Directives applying to two specific fields of civil litigation, namely intellectual property and competition damages.

2. ACCESS TO INFORMATION AND EVIDENCE IN THE INTELLECTUAL PROPERTY RIGHTS ENFORCEMENT DIRECTIVE AND THE COMPETITION DAMAGES DIRECTIVE

2.1. THE IPRED AND THE CDD AS INSTRUMENTS OF "VERTICAL" HARMONISATION

As Wagner explains, whereas "horizontal" harmonisation of procedural law in the EU is carried out on the basis of Article 81 TFEU by way of EU legislation applicable to cross-border disputes only, "vertical" harmonisation consists of introducing EU procedural rules applicable to both cross-border and domestic cases "on specific subject-matter areas in which the EU has a competence other than that granted by Article 81 TFEU".[10]

There are two Directives vertically harmonising rules on access to information and evidence: Directive 2004/48/EC, of 29 April 2004, on the enforcement of intellectual property rights, a.k.a. "Intellectual Property Rights Enforcement Directive" ("IPRED");[11] and Directive 2014/104/EU, of 26 November 2014, on certain rules governing actions for damages under national law for infringements of the competition law provisions of the Member States of the European Union, a.k.a. "Competition Damages Directive" ("CDD").[12]

The specific subject-matters of the two Directives just mentioned – the IPRED and the CDD – are, as said, intellectual property and competition damages; and

---

8 See B. Hess, "Preservation and taking of evidence in cross-border proceedings – Comparative remarks in the context of IP litigation", in A. Nuyts (ed.), *International Litigation in Intellectual Property and Information Technology* (Wolters Kluwer, The Netherlands, 2008), 289–301, at 291.

9 See Hess, above n. 8, at 293.

10 G. Wagner, "Harmonization of Civil Procedure – Policy Perspectives" in X.E. Kramer and C.H. Rhee (eds.), *Civil litigation in a globalising world* (TMC Asser press, The Hague, 2012), 93–119, at 101, available at: https://ssrn.com/abstract=1777233 or http://dx.doi.org/10.2139/ssrn.1777233. See also F. Gascón Inchausti, *Derecho europeo y legislación procesal civil nacional: entre autonomía y armonización* (Marcial Pons, Madrid, 2018), at 37 and 64–68.

11 OJ L 195, 2.6.2004, p. 16.

12 OJ L 349, 5.12.2014, p. 1.

both Directives were passed under the competence attributed by Article 114 TFEU to the EU as to the approximation of legal instruments aiming at ensuring the proper functioning of the internal market.[13]

2.2. OVERVIEW OF THE IPRED RULES

In regard to access to information and evidence in intellectual property cases, the IPRED contains three provisions:[14]

- Article 6 IPRED allows the parties to ask the court for an order for the *disclosure of evidence*, including – should the infringement of an intellectual property right have been committed "on a commercial scale"[15] – the disclosure of banking, financial or commercial documents.
- Article 7 IPRED gives the parties the opportunity to obtain an order for the *preservation of evidence* by way of any "effective provisional measures", such as the description or the seizure of the infringing goods, of the materials and implements used in the production and/or distribution of these goods and of the documents relating thereto.[16]
- Finally, Article 8 IPRED permits the parties to apply for an order for the *disclosure of information* about the origin and the distribution networks

13 See Recitals (1), (3), (8), (9) and (10) IPRED; and Recitals (1), (6), (7), (8), (9), (10), (34) and (54), along with Article 1 CDD.

14 See European Union Intellectual Property Office – EUIPO, *Evidence and right to information in intellectual property rights* (2010), pdf 1–170, at 7–8, available at: https://euipo.europa.eu/ohimportal/documents/11370/80606/Evidence+and+right+of+information+in+Intellectual+Property+rights/9cce8f61-35a1-4e66-b9a4-3e730c09307c.

15 Recital (14) IPRED states: "The measures provided for in Articles 6(2), 8(1) and 9(2) need to be applied only in respect of acts carried out on a commercial scale ... Acts carried out on a commercial scale are those carried out for direct or indirect economic or commercial advantage; this would normally exclude acts carried out by end consumers acting in good faith". In spite of Recital (14), Member States have taken different approaches when defining the meaning of "commercial scale". In this respect, see V. Peter (coordinator), *Support study for the ex-post evaluation and ex-ante impact analysis of the IPR enforcement Directive (IPRED)*, 2017, 1–345, at 53 (available at: https://publications.europa.eu/en/publication-detail/-/publication/29df5fb0-d0cc-11e7-a7df-01aa75ed71a1/language-en/format-PDF/source-search); and EUIPO (2010), above n. 14, at pdf 9, 22–23 and 133–145.

16 It has been argued that coercive entry and search of premises for the purposes of collecting evidence to be preserved are included among the "effective provisional measures" that can be obtained, similarly to the types of measures that may be afforded by the *Anton Piller* orders at common law or the French "counterfeiting seizure" (*saisie-contrefaçon*). See, in this regard Coulson/Muyl/Schlötter, above n. 2, at 28–29; and Trocker, above n. 2, at 280 (fn. 152). However, national implementing provisions may vary significantly, since, "in several Member States there is a distinction drawn between a search order (which allows entry into premises and the recording of information) and a seizure order (which allows seizure of items and documents), and in many cases it is easier to obtain a search order than a seizure order" (EUIPO (2010), above n. 14, at pdf 9).

of the goods or services that infringe an intellectual property right "on a commercial scale".[17] As appropriate, such an order may require the disclosure of "the names and addresses of the producers, manufacturers, distributors, suppliers and other previous holders of the goods or services, as well as the intended wholesalers and retailers"; and it may also require the disclosure of "information on the quantities produced, manufactured, delivered, received or ordered, as well as the price obtained for the goods or services in question".[18]

These provisions appear to be directly inspired by Articles 43, 47 and 50 of the Agreement on trade-related aspects of intellectual property ("TRIPS agreement"), concluded in 1994 in the framework of the World Trade Organisation and approved, as part of the multilateral negotiations of the Uruguay Round, by Council Decision 94/800/EC.[19]

And, recently, Articles 6, 7 and 8 IPRED themselves seem to have inspired the corresponding provisions on access to information and evidence that will likely apply to cases before the Unified Patent Court ("UPC"), namely Articles 59, 60 and 67 of the Agreement establishing the UPC[20] and Articles 190 to 199 of the Draft Rules of Procedure of the UPC.[21]

2.3. OVERVIEW OF THE CDD RULES

For competition damages cases, the CDD includes four articles[22] dealing with access to information and evidence:

- Article 5 CDD contains a similar provision to that of Article 6 IPRED, enabling the parties to get a court order for the *disclosure of evidence* that is relevant to a claim for damages based on an infringement of competition law.
- Articles 6 and 7 CDD lay out a set of *special rules for the disclosure of evidence included in a competition authority's file*. Taking into consideration the need

17 As to the meaning of "on a commercial scale", see n. 15, above.

18 These types of orders for the disclosure of information in intellectual property cases are similar to the so-called *Norwich Pharmacal* orders of the common law. In this respect, see Coulson/Muyl/Schlötter, above n. 2, at 27; and Trocker, above n. 2, at 280–281.

19 OJ L 336, 23.12.1994, p. 1.

20 OJ C 175, 20.6.2013, p. 1.

21 https://www.unified-patent-court.org/news/draft-rules-procedure-updated-march-2017.

22 Which appear to have been built on the system of the IPRED (A. Galič, "Disclosure of Documents in Private Antitrust Enforcement Litigation" (2015) 8(12) *Yearbook of Antitrust and Regulatory Studies* 99–126, at 104, available at: http://www.yars.wz.uw.edu.pl/yars2015_8_12/99.pdf).

to safeguard the effectiveness of the public enforcement of competition law,[23] these two provisions limit the litigants' access to the file:

(i) internal documents of the competition authorities, correspondence between competition authorities, leniency statements[24] and settlement submissions[25] are always excluded from disclosure – Recitals (21) and (26), and Articles 6(3), 6(6) and 7(1);[26]

(ii) other evidence that has been specifically created for the competition authority's file may be subject to an order for disclosure only after the competition authority has closed its proceedings and if no party or third party is reasonably able to provide the evidence in question – Recitals (25) and (29), and Articles 6(5), 6(10) and 7(2); and

(iii) pre-existing evidence (i.e., evidence that, although appearing in the file, exists irrespective of the proceedings before the competition authority)[27]

---

23 Which it may be seen as a need arising out of the principle of effectiveness of EU law (A.D. Chirita, "The Disclosure of Evidence under the 'Antitrust Damages' Directive 2014/104/EU" in V. Tomljenović, N. Bodiroga-Vukobrat, V. Butorac Malnar and I. Kunda (eds.), *EU Competition and State Aid Rules: Public and Private Enforcement* (Springer, Berlin/Heidelberg, 2017), 147–173, at 151–153, available at: https://papers.ssrn.com/sol3/papers.cfm?abstract_id=2800910). In any case, although Article 1.2 CCD states that the Directive purports to "coordinate" public and private enforcement of competition law, it appears that, when the two types of enforcement conflict, the CDD favours public enforcement (V. Butorak Malnar, "Access to Documents in Antitrust Litigation – EU and Croatian Perspective" (2015) 8(12) *Yearbook of Antitrust and Regulatory Studies* 127–160, at 142–149, available at http://www.yars.wz.uw.edu.pl/yars2015_8_12/127.pdf).

24 According to Article 2(16) CDD, "'leniency statement' means an oral or written presentation voluntarily provided by, or on behalf of, an undertaking or a natural person to a competition authority or a record thereof, describing the knowledge of that undertaking or natural person of a cartel and describing its role therein, which presentation was drawn up specifically for submission to the competition authority with a view to obtaining immunity or a reduction of fines under a leniency programme, not including pre-existing information".

25 Pursuant to Article 2(18) CDD, "'settlement submission' means a voluntary presentation by, or on behalf of, an undertaking to a competition authority describing the undertaking's acknowledgement of, or its renunciation to dispute, its participation in an infringement of competition law and its responsibility for that infringement of competition law, which was drawn up specifically to enable the competition authority to apply a simplified or expedited procedure".

26 It has been pointed out that European rules excluding specific materials from disclosure (such as Articles 6(6) and 7(1) CDD, as to the exclusion of leniency statements and settlement submissions) do not prevent plaintiffs from requesting these materials from defendants within discovery proceedings instituted in a jurisdiction outside the EU and under the procedural rules of that jurisdiction. Among these rules, it is worth mentioning Section 1782 of the US Code, which allows a person to request the US courts to order discovery of information or evidence *to be used in a proceeding, actual or contemplated, before a tribunal outside the US*. If such a request is lodged, according to the decision of the US Supreme Court in *Intel Corporation v. Advanced Micro Devices* 542 U.S. 241 (2004), US courts may grant discovery even though the evidence sought was not "discoverable" in the non-US country where the proceedings on the merits have been or are intended to be initiated. See, in this regard, Trocker, above n. 2, at 287–291; and Mosunova, above n. 7, at 144–149.

27 See Article 2(17) CDD.

may be subject to an order for disclosure at any time, again provided that no party or third party is reasonably able to provide the evidence in question – Recitals (28) and (29), and Articles 6(9) and 6(10).[28]

- Ultimately, Article 8 CDD deals with an important issue that was ignored by the IPRED, namely the need to establish *penalties* for those who do not comply with court orders related to the disclosure of evidence. These penalties shall be "effective, proportionate and dissuasive" and shall include "the possibility to draw adverse inferences, such as presuming the relevant issue to be proven or dismissing claims and defences in whole or in part, and the possibility to order payment of costs".

3. THE CORE OF THE IPRED AND THE CDD RULES

There are indeed differences between the IPRED rules and the CDD rules governing access to information and evidence. Nevertheless, in this author's understanding, there is a common thread, a common core, that guides them all. This thread refers to: (i) the type of technique that the Directives have chosen for allowing access to information and evidence; and (ii) the basic condition that must be met by a party to gain access, namely proportionality.

3.1. COURT-ORDER-BASED SYSTEM OF ACCESS

When regulating access to information and evidence, the law may establish different types of procedures. "Some of these procedures may be carried out between the parties without a court order or supervision; some may be enforced by court order in the event of dispute between the parties; some are available only by court order".[29]

---

[28] See M. Palma Rodríguez, "Disclosure of evidence under the Damages Directive: conflicts and compatibility between the ECJ's case-by-case analysis and the rules on protection of immunity recipients' information" (Europa-Kolleg Hamburg – *Institute for European Integration Study paper no. 01/2018*), 1–76, at 29–35 (available at: https://europa-kolleg-hamburg.de/wp-content/uploads/2018/03/SP-01-18.pdf); L. Domínguez Ruiz, "La exhibición de pruebas en la Directiva 2014/104/UE, sobre reclamación de daños por infracciones del derecho de la competencia, y su transposición al ordenamiento español" (2017) 41 *Revista General de Derecho Procesal (Iustel)* 1–46, 16–23 (III.2) (available at: https://www.researchgate.net/publication/323737485_La_exhibicion_de_pruebas_en_la_Directiva_2014104UE_sobre_reclamacion_de_danos_por_infracciones_del_derecho_de_la_competencia_y_su_transposicion_al_ordenamiento_espanol); P. Yanes Yanes, "Confidencialidad y clemencia en la 'Directiva de daños': una aproximación" in *Estudios sobre el futuro Código Mercantil: libro homenaje al profesor Rafael Illescas Ortiz* (Universidad Carlos III de Madrid, 2015), 1140–1162, at 1147–1154 (available at: http://hdl.handle.net/10016/21046); and Mosunova, above n. 7, at 132.

[29] Priestley, above n. 3, at 846. Also, Trocker, above n. 2, at 248.

The latter technique – access is made available only by court order – is the one followed by both Directives: any access to information or evidence that is based on the IPRED or on the CDD requires a party's application to the court and a subsequent decision of the court, either granting or denying the application. In short, the Directives establish a court-order-based system of accessing information and evidence.[30]

3.2. PROPORTIONALITY

3.2.1. References to Proportionality in the Texts of the Directives

In order to decide whether access to information or evidence shall be granted, both the IPRED and the CDD require the court to apply the proportionality test. If the request for access appears to be proportionate, the court shall grant access; if not, the court shall reject the petition.

Establishing proportionality as the main condition to be satisfied to gain access to information or evidence is probably the most important part of the common core of the IPRED and the CDD rules.

In the IPRED, the references to proportionality are mostly implicit in the wording of its Articles 6, 7 and 8:

- When dealing with the disclosure of evidence, Article 6 IPRED, on the one hand, requires the applicant (i) to show a *prima facie* case (i.e., to present "reasonably available evidence sufficient to support his/her claims") and (ii) to specify the evidence that he or she wishes to have access to; and, on the other hand, Article 6 IPRED ends up stating that any court decision on the application shall be "subject to the protection of confidential information". In this author's view, the idea of proportionality is here implicitly formulated, since the court is to balance the interests of the applicant (in terms of how relevant the requested evidence might be for his or her case) and the interests of the respondent (in terms, at least, of how harmful disclosure will be for him or her if confidential information is unveiled).
- A similar implicit reference to proportionality may be seen in Article 7 IPRED in regard to applications for the preservation of evidence. Again, the court appears to be needing to assess, on the one hand, how important the specific evidence to be preserved is for the case of the applicant: the applicant must submit "reasonably available evidence to support his/her claims" and the court may take account of whether "any delay is likely to

30 In this regard, Recital (16) CDD remarks that "national courts should be able, under their strict control … to order disclosure".

cause irreparable harm to the rightholder" or if there is a "risk of evidence being destroyed". And, on the other hand, the interests of the respondent are also to be considered by the court, since any decision must be "subject to the protection of confidential information" and compensation for the potential "prejudice suffered by the defendant" must be ensured.

- Finally, when regulating disclosure of information, a more explicit mention of proportionality is contained in Article 8 IPRED, which requires the application for disclosure to be "justified and *proportionate*". In this regard, there are a number of decisions of the ECJ, all dealing with the interpretation of Article 8 IPRED, that stress the need to ensure a "fair balance between the various fundamental rights involved" (*Promusicae*,[31] *LSG*,[32] *Coty Germany*[33]) or, in other words, the need to "weigh the conflicting interests involved" (*Bonnier Audio*[34]).[35]

For its part, the CDD, that was passed some ten years after the IPRED, has clearly referred to the proportionality test:

- As to applications for disclosure of evidence in general, paragraphs (1) and (2) of Article 5 CDD – similarly to Article 6 IPRED – require the applicant to show a *prima facie case* and to specify the evidence in which he or she is interested. Then, paragraph (3) provides:

  > Member States shall ensure that national courts limit the disclosure of evidence to that which is *proportionate*. In determining whether any disclosure requested by a party is *proportionate*, national courts shall *consider the legitimate interests of all parties and third parties concerned*. They shall, in particular, consider:
  >
  > (a) the extent to which the claim or defence is supported by available facts and evidence justifying the request to disclose evidence;
  > (b) the scope and cost of disclosure, especially for any third parties concerned, including preventing non-specific searches for information which is unlikely to be of relevance for the parties in the procedure;

---

31 Judgment of 29 January 2008, *Productores de Música de España (Promusicae) v. Telefónica de España SAU*, C-275/06, EU:C:2008:54, §§65 and 70.

32 Order of 19 February 2009, *LSG-Gesellschaft zur Wahrnehmung von Leistungsschutzrechten GmbH v. Tele2 Telecommunication GmbH*, C-557/07, EU:C:2009:107, §§28–29.

33 Judgment of 16 July 2015, *Coty Germany GmbH v. Stadtsparkasse Magdeburg*, C-580/13, EU:C:2015:485, §§29, 33 and 36–38.

34 Judgment of 19 April 2012, *Bonnier Audio AB and others v. Perfect Communication Sweden AB*, C-461/10, EU:C:2012:219, §§59–61.

35 Containing an interesting report on the case law dealing with Article 8 IPRED, see European Union Intellectual Property Office – EUIPO, *IP Enforcement case-law collection on the balance between the right of information and fundamental rights in the European Union* (2018), 1–32, available at: https://euipo.europa.eu/tunnel-web/secure/webdav/guest/document_library/observatory/documents/reports/Case_Law_Report/Case_law_report_EN.pdf.

(c) whether the evidence the disclosure of which is sought contains confidential information, especially concerning any third parties, and what arrangements are in place for protecting such confidential information. (emphasis added)

– When it comes to regulating access to the competition authorities' files, the CDD takes account of public interest, privacy and commercial interests as potential grounds to refuse disclosure, since Recital (20) and Article 6(2) CDD refer to the "rules and practices" of Article 4 of Regulation (EC) 1049/2001, of 30 May 2001, regarding public access to European Parliament, Council and Commission documents.[36] And, furthermore, Article 6(4) CDD sets forth some special rules on proportionality, basically aiming to protect public enforcement of competition law from unjustified interferences. Specifically, Article 6(4) says:

When assessing, in accordance with Article 5(3), the *proportionality* of an order to disclose information, national courts shall, *in addition*, consider the following:

(a) whether the request has been formulated specifically with regard to the nature, subject matter or contents of documents submitted to a competition authority or held in the file thereof, rather than by a non-specific application concerning documents submitted to a competition authority;
(b) whether the party requesting disclosure is doing so in relation to an action for damages before a national court; and
(c) in relation to paragraphs (5)[37] and (10),[38] or upon request of a competition authority pursuant to paragraph (11),[39] *the need to safeguard the effectiveness of the public enforcement of competition law*. (emphasis added)

3.2.2. *The Different Aspects to be Considered in the Proportionality Test*

In view of all these provisions, the main idea about proportionality is clear: when deciding upon an application based on Articles 6, 7 or 8 IPRED or on Articles 5 or 6 CDD, the court must make sure that the application is proportionate, having balanced "the legitimate interests of all parties and third parties concerned" – Article 5(3) CDD.

In particular, in figuring out proportionality, the court shall consider four elements or aspects that might be at stake, namely the legitimate interests of the

36 OJ L 145, 31.5.2001, p. 43.

37 Paragraph (5) of Article 6 CDD states that disclosure of documents that have been specially created for the proceedings carried out before the competition authority shall only be granted after those proceedings have been closed.

38 Paragraph (10) of Article 6 CDD says that disclosure of evidence from a competition authority shall be the last possible resort, so that it will only be granted when "no party or third party is reasonably able to provide that evidence".

39 According to paragraph (11) of Article 6 CDD: "To the extent that a competition authority is willing to state its views on the proportionality of disclosure requests, it may, acting on its own initiative, submit observations to the national court before which a disclosure order is sought".

applicant, the legitimate interests of the respondent, the legitimate interests of third parties and the public interest.

3.2.2.1. Legitimate Interests of the Applicant

Strength of the applicant's case

Both Directives require the applicant to show a *prima facie* case, i.e, – quoting Article 5(1) CDD – that the applicant has "presented a reasoned justification containing reasonably available facts and evidence sufficient to support the plausibility of his or her claim". Hence, the degree of strength or weakness of the applicant's case[40] is one of the key issues that the court must weigh when deciding if the proportionality test has been met; or, using the words of Article 5(3)(a) CDD, the court shall consider "the extent to which the claim or defence is supported by available facts and evidence justifying the request to disclose evidence".

Relevance of the requested evidence or information to the applicant's case

The law urges the applicant to *specify* the evidence or information that he or she wishes to have access to, as well as to show its *relevance* to the applicant's case. Under the IPRED rules, the applicant needs to have "*specified* evidence" "*in substantiating his or her claims*" – Article 6(1); or show that measures are necessary "to preserve *relevant* evidence" – Article 7(1); or demonstrate that there is a need for accessing "information on the origin and distribution networks of the goods or services *which infringe an intellectual property right*" – Article 8(1). The CDD, for its part, requires that the application for disclosure shall refer to "*relevant* evidence" – Article 5(1) – and, in particular, to "specified items of evidence or *relevant* categories of evidence ... on the basis of reasonably available facts in the reasoned justification" – Article 5(2) – so that, when figuring out proportionality, the court must look at the "the scope of disclosure" and discard disclosure of evidence that "is unlikely to be of *relevance* for the parties in the procedure" – Article 5(3)(b) (emphasis added).

The applicant's right to an effective judicial remedy and the applicant's substantive rights whose protection is sought

The two prior aspects of the proportionality test – strength of the applicant's case and relevance of the information or evidence to that case – must not be considered in isolation. They shall also be assessed jointly and, then, be put in relation to a

[40] The "verisimilitude" of the case, in the words of Yanes Yanes, above n. 28, at 1144.

third – and much broader – aspect, namely the effectiveness of the applicant's fundamental rights to an effective judicial remedy and to a fair trial (Articles 47 CFREU and 6 ECHR),[41] along with the effectiveness of the substantive rights whose judicial protection is being claimed by the applicant.[42] The greater the strength of the applicant's case and the higher the relevance of the evidence or information requested by the applicant for that case, the greater the justification for facilitating access in order to ensure the fulfilment of the right of the applicant to an effective remedy/fair trial and the enforcement of the substantive rights that might be at stake.

This relationship has been pointed out by the ECJ in the cases concerning the application of Article 8 IPRED just mentioned above. In this regard, special emphasis shall be put on the case of *Coty Germany*, where the ECJ found that a national provision establishing bank secrecy as an unlimited ground to refuse an application for the disclosure of information in relation to an infringement of an intellectual property right "is liable to frustrate the right to information recognised in Article 8(1) of Directive 2004/48 and is therefore ... such as to infringe the fundamental right to an effective remedy and the fundamental right to intellectual property".[43]

Furthermore, in respect of the effectiveness of the substantive rights of the applicant, Article 7(1) IPRED suggests that potential "irreparable harm to the rightholder" is one of the issues to be considered by the court examining an application for the preservation of evidence.

3.2.2.2. Legitimate Interests of the Respondent

Protection against an intolerable degree of intrusiveness: the prohibition of "fishing expeditions"

When both Directives require the applicant to be specific on the information or evidence that he or she wishes to have access to, they don't merely purport to help the Court measure the degree of relevance – as it has just been explained. They also seek to protect the legitimate interests of the respondent, by entailing

[41] The connection between the right to a fair trial and effective access to evidence has been stressed by the ECtHR. See, in this regard, ECtHR Judgment of 28 April 2009, *K.H. and others v. Slovakia*, App. 32881/04, §§59–69; and ECtHR Judgment of 9 June 1998, *McGinley and Egan v. United Kingdom*, App. 10/1997/794/995-996, §§86 and 90.

[42] See Trocker, above n. 2, at 264, who, in turn, cites A. Zuckerman, *Zuckerman on Civil Procedure: Principles of Practice* (Sweet and Maxell, London, 2006), at 127: "A system that leaves witnesses free to refuse to testify and allows litigants to withhold relevant documents from their opponents would fail to provide citizens with an effective and meaningful procedure for vindicating their rights".

[43] Judgment of 16 July 2015, *Coty Germany*, C-580/13, EU:C:2015:485, §§29, 33 and 36–38.

the prohibition of orders granting indiscriminate and unlimited access to all the information or evidence that might lie under someone else's control.

In this respect, Article 5(3)(b) CDD – and, similarly, Article 6(4)(a) CDD, after referring to the need to control the "scope of disclosure" – make clear that "non-specific searches" are to be averted. This means, borrowing the words of Recital (23) CDD, that the court assessing proportionality has the duty to prevent "'fishing expeditions', i.e. non-specific or overly broad searches for information", and that, hence, "disclosure requests should not be deemed proportionate where they refer to the generic disclosure" of completely unidentified information or evidence.[44]

The need to protect confidential information

The Directives appear to be somewhat obsessed with the need for the court to guarantee the protection of confidential information when deciding upon an application based on Articles 6–8 IPRED or on Articles 5–6 CDD. Articles 6(1), 6(2) and 7(1) IPRED provide that any court order on the disclosure or preservation of evidence shall be "subject to the protection of confidential information"; Article 8(3)(e) IPRED states that any order on the disclosure of information shall be issued "without prejudice to other statutory provisions which … govern the protection of confidentiality of information sources or the processing of personal data"; and Article 5(3)(c) CDD prescribes that, when assessing the proportionality of an application for disclosure, the court shall consider "whether the evidence the disclosure of which is sought contains confidential information".

In this author's understanding, these provisions may well amount to the denial of the application for disclosure or preservation. Within the context of the proportionality test, if the risks arising out of a potential disclosure of confidential information outweigh the interests of the applicant, the application shall be denied. And, in particular, if the application refers to confidential information protected by legal professional privilege, the court appears to have no choice but to reject the application, according to Article 5(6) CDD: "Member States shall ensure that national courts give *full effect* to applicable legal professional privilege under Union or national law when ordering the disclosure of evidence" (emphasis added).

44 Fishing expeditions are also to be averted in the context of *public* enforcement of legal provisions. Hence, any inspection carried out by a competition authority shall be based on specific evidence or indications showing that an infringement of competition law has been committed; purely speculative searches are then prohibited. In this regard, see M. Michalek, "Fishing expeditions and subsequent electronic searches in the light of the principle of proportionality of inspections in competition law cases in Europe" (2014) 7(10) *Yearbook of Antitrust and Regulatory Studies* 129–157, at 135–144 (available at: http://www.yars.wz.uw.edu.pl/yars2014_7_10/129.pdf).

Nevertheless, both the IPRED and the CDD seem to discard this solution – rejection of the application on the grounds of the need to protect confidential information – *as the general rule*. On the contrary, as long as the proportionality test is met, the Directives appear to be giving the courts leave to grant orders for the disclosure of information or evidence or orders for the preservation of evidence, even though there is some risk of disclosing confidential information, provided that the court issues the order *subject to additional measures* aimed at preserving the confidential information from being openly disclosed.

The expressions used in Articles 6, 7 and 8 IPRED ("subject to the protection of confidential information"; "without prejudice to other statutory provisions which … govern the protection of confidentiality of information sources or the processing of personal data") allow this interpretation, as the ECJ has confirmed in the case of *Coty Germany*.[45] Accordingly, when dealing with the interpretation of Article 8 IPRED, the European Commission concludes that the disclosed information "can include personal data, where such disclosure occurs in compliance with the applicable legislation on the protection of personal data and provided safeguards exist to ensure a fair balance between the various fundamental rights at issue".[46] And, more generally, the Commission states that access to information or evidence may be granted under the IPRED provided that "appropriate means" are put in place to protect confidential information. These means might consist of, for example, the presentation of the confidential information "only to the competent judicial authorities or to an independent and impartial third party which is appointed to assist in the proceedings or inspections with a view to description or seizure and which is subject to appropriate confidentiality obligations".[47]

Much more explicit about the possibility of granting access with additional measures to protect confidential information is the CDD:

- Recital (18) CDD stresses that the protection of confidential information cannot be an insurmountable obstacle preventing the applicant from exercising his or her rights: "Measures protecting business secrets and other confidential information should … not impede the exercise of the right to compensation".
- Article 5(3)(c) CDD encourages the court deciding on an application for disclosure to look at "what arrangements are in place for protecting such

[45] Judgment of 16 July 2015, *Coty Germany GmbH v. Stadtsparkasse Magdeburg*, C-580/13, EU:C:2015:485, §§29, 33 and 36–38.

[46] European Commission, *Guidance on certain aspects of Directive 2004/48/EC of the European Parliament and of the Council on the enforcement of intellectual property rights* (Communication of 29/11/2017 from the Commission to the European Parliament, the Council and the European Economic and Social Committee), 1–32, at 12 (available at: https://ec.europa.eu/docsroom/documents/26582/attachments/1/translations/en/renditions/native).

[47] European Commission (2017) (Guidance), above n. 46, at 14.

confidential information". In this regard, Article 5(4) CDD provides that the court shall "have the power to order the disclosure of evidence containing confidential information where they consider it relevant to the action for damages [i.e., proportionate]", using "any effective measures to protect such information". And Recital (18) CDD provides examples of "effective measures to protect confidential information": "redacting sensitive passages in documents, conducting hearings in camera, restricting the persons allowed to see the evidence, and instructing experts to produce summaries of the information in an aggregated or otherwise non-confidential form".[48]

- Eventually, Article 8(1)(c) CDD calls for the imposition of "penalties on parties, third parties and their legal representatives in the event of … their failure or refusal to comply with the obligations imposed by a national court order protecting confidential information".

Costs of disclosure

Article 5(3)(b) CDD specifically refers to the importance of assessing the "cost of disclosure" when figuring out proportionality.

In this author's opinion, it seems clear that, according to this provision, if the costs of disclosure or preservation appear to be intolerable for the person who would be disclosing or preserving the information or the evidence, the proportionality test may lead to a denial of the order sought by the applicant.

But, similarly to what has been said in regard to the protection of confidential information, high costs cannot turn into an excuse for refusing disclosure right away. Again, courts have powers to grant disclosure or preservation together with additional measures alleviating the expenses of the persons called to disclose or preserve.

In this respect, Article 7(4) IPRED foresees that these persons might be entitled to "appropriate compensation for any injury caused by those measures"; and, consistently, Article 7(2) IPRED allows the court the power to grant an order for the preservation of evidence "subject to the lodging by the applicant of adequate security or an equivalent assurance intended to ensure compensation for any prejudice suffered by the defendant".

Protection of the rights of the respondent: in particular, the right to privacy and the freedom to conduct a business

The three aspects that have just been mentioned – prohibition of fishing expeditions, protection of confidential information, and costs – must be

[48] On these provisions, Chirita, above n. 23, at 157–161.

evaluated together when determining the legitimate interests of the person against whom the application for disclosure or preservation has been filed. But the court shall look even further in determining those interests, since it is to assess the full extent to which the rights of that person will be affected, should the application be granted.

This obviously includes the need to care about property rights, as seems clear from the need to take costs into consideration. And, most significantly, it includes the need to look cautiously at the *fundamental right to privacy* – Articles 7 and 8 CFREU[49] – and the *freedom to conduct a business* – Article 16 CFREU[50] – which appear to be the grounds for the rules prohibiting fishing expeditions and emphasising the protection of confidential information.

Indeed, the persons' rights to run their lives and businesses without undue interferences from the state entail the prohibition on the state of conducting investigations which are not based on the existence of some kind of indication against the investigated person; consequently, searches without such indications – i.e., "fishing expeditions" – are to be excluded. In our field – the IPRED and the CDD – the indications justifying access to information or evidence consist of the *prima facie* case shown by the applicant, together with the "specified items" of evidence or information or, at most, the "categories" of evidence or information – see Article 5(2) CDD – that appear to be relevant to substantiate that case; where an applicant fails to show these indications, his or her application may be deemed non-specific and, therefore, it may be refused.

Moreover, the right to privacy and the freedom to conduct a business is the underlying rationale governing any statutory provisions on the protection of confidential information: where legislation protects specific types of information (such as personal data or business secrets) compliance with the fundamental European values of privacy and business freedom is always at stake. And, indeed, these very same values have been explicitly foreseen as one of the bases upon which disclosure of documents may be refused by competition authorities, according to the reference in Article 6(2) CDD to Article 4 Regulation 1049/2001.[51]

Hence, where Articles 6–8 IPRED and Articles 5–6 CDD establish the prohibition of fishing expeditions and the need to protect confidential information as an important part of the proportionality test, in truth, they are

49 It must be recalled that, according to the ECtHR, the fundamental right to privacy is not limited to natural persons, since it may also apply to *legal* persons. In this regard see, Judgment of 16 April 2002, *Société Colas Est and others v. France*, App. 37971/97, §§49–50; and Judgment of 16 December 1992, *Niemietz v. Germany*, App. 13710/88, §31.

50 See European Commission (2017) (Guidance), above n. 46, at 11.

51 Article 4 of Regulation 1049/2001 provides that disclosure shall be refused, among other grounds, when it would undermine the protection of "privacy and the integrity of the individual, in particular in accordance with Community legislation regarding the protection of personal data" or the "commercial interests of a natural or legal person, including intellectual property".

telling the court to appraise the degree of harm that the measures sought by the applicant will cause to the privacy and business freedom of the respondent and, once that appraisal has been carried out, to use the result for the proportionality test. This is also, in the view of this author, the overall conclusion that might be extracted from the ECJ cases mentioned above (*Promusicae*,[52] *LSG*,[53] *Coty Germany*[54] and *Bonnier Audio*[55]).

3.2.2.3. Legitimate Interests of Third Parties

Article 5(3) CDD stresses the need to protect "third parties" against disproportionate applications for the disclosure of evidence. To be specific, this provision urges the courts to also "consider the legitimate interests of all … *third parties* concerned"; to carefully look at "the scope and cost of disclosure, *especially for any third parties concerned*"; and, finally, to assess "whether the evidence the disclosure of which is sought contains confidential information, *especially concerning any third parties*" (emphasis added).

The expression "third party" is sometimes used in the CDD to refer to the person against whom an application for disclosure has been lodged when he or she is not a party to the dispute arising out of an infringement of competition law. This is, in this author's opinion, the meaning of the expression in Articles 5(1), 6(6) and 8(1) CDD, as to the possibility of filing an application for disclosure against a "third party" and of imposing penalties on "third parties" if they fail to comply with a disclosure order. Obviously, in these types of situations – where the application is lodged against someone who is neither the claimant nor the defendant – the "third party" is the *respondent* in the incidental proceedings regarding disclosure and, therefore, his or her legitimate interests shall be considered by the court in the terms that have just been explained above.

In Article 5(3) CDD, though, it is this author's belief that the expression "third party" has a broader meaning, including not only third-party respondents, but also third-party *non*-respondents. In other words, that Article 5(3) CDD requires that, when evaluating proportionality, the court shall not only look at the legitimate interests of the respondent, but also at the legitimate interests of other persons – of "third parties" – that might be affected if disclosure were eventually granted.

---

52 Judgment of 29 January 2008, *Promusicae*, C-275/06, EU:C:2008:54, §§65 and 70.

53 Order of 19 February 2009, *LSG-Gesellschaft zur Wahrnehmung von Leistungsschutzrechten GmbH v. Tele2 Telecommunication GmbH*, C-557/07, EU:C:2009:107, §§28–29.

54 Judgment of 16 July 2015, *Coty Germany GmbH v. Stadtsparkasse Magdeburg* C-580/13, EU:C:2015:485, §§29, 33 and 36–38.

55 Judgment of 19 April 2012, *Bonnier Audio AB and others v. Perfect Communication Sweden AB*, C-461/10, EU:C:2012:219, §§59–61.

The legitimate interests of these third-party *non*-respondents shall consist of the equivalent interests of the respondent, so that the court shall assess:

- whether disclosure may entail unlimited and indiscriminate access to the third party's sphere – i.e., a fishing expedition in regard to the third party;
- the need to protect confidential information in regard to the third party;
- the costs that disclosure may bring about for the third party; and
- the overall harm that disclosure may cause to the rights of the third party.

All these aspects shall be "*especially*" evaluated – see subparagraphs (b) and (c) of Article 5(3) – which, in this author's view, refers to the obligation of the court to carefully analyse the allegations of the applicant and of the respondent, in order to find out whether the rights of any third party are also concerned. And, should this be the case, that third party shall be given an opportunity to be heard prior to the decision of the court.

3.2.2.4. Protection of the Public Interest

Finally, there is a fourth relevant aspect of the proportionality test, namely the need to protect the public interest.

This aspect has been explicitly mentioned in Article 6 CDD, when dealing with applications for the disclosure of evidence contained in a competition authority's file.

In this regard, the existence of specific types of evidence contained in the competition authority's file which are excluded from disclosure – Recitals (21) and (26), and Articles 6(3), 6(6) and 7(1) – along with the prohibition on accessing other types of evidence while proceedings before the competition authority are still pending – Recitals (25) and (29), and Articles 6(5), 6(10) and 7(2) – shows how the public interest in the application of competition law will override the private interests of claimants seeking damages based on the private enforcement of the same area of the law.[56]

In any case, it should also be recalled that, when dealing with proportionality, Article 6(4)(c) CDD stresses "the need to safeguard the effectiveness of the public enforcement of competition law", so that, as Recital (23) CDD puts it,

> the requirement of proportionality should be carefully assessed when disclosure risks unravelling the investigation strategy of a competition authority … or risks having

---

[56] Indeed, although Article 1.2 CCD states that the Directive purports to "coordinate" public and private enforcement of competition law, it appears that, when both types of enforcement conflict, the CDD favours public enforcement (Butorak Malnar, above n. 23, at 142–149).

a negative effect on the way in which undertakings cooperate with competition authorities.

In addition, from a more general perspective, Recital (20) and Article 6(2) CDD refer to the applicability of Article 4 Regulation 1049/2001, which, in its turn, foresees that disclosure shall be refused on the basis of the need to protect "the public interest as regards public security, defence and military matters, international relations, and the financial, monetary or economic policy of the [Union] or a Member State", as well as to protect "court proceedings and legal advice" and "the purposes of inspections, investigations and audits".

Consequently, from these rules of the CDD a general conclusion may be drawn: the protection of the public interest shall also be taken into consideration when figuring out the proportionality of an application for access to information or evidence. Obviously, this aspect will be more significant whenever the respondent is a public body (like a competition authority). Yet, it may also be relevant when the application is filed against a private individual or a company and the information or evidence sought refers to matters of public interest.

3.2.3. The Proportionality Test Itself

After going through the different aspects that are to be considered within the proportionality test, it is time to briefly refer to the test itself.

On the one hand, the court is to weigh all the interests of the applicant, in terms of strength of his or her case, relevance of the requested information or evidence and, generally speaking, the effectiveness of his or her rights.

On the other hand, the court must weigh the interests of the respondent and of the third parties, by way of making sure that the applicant is not pursuing a fishing expedition, of determining the extent to which confidential information may be compromised, of looking at costs and of establishing the overall harm that the upholding of the application may cause to the rights of the respondent or third parties. Eventually, together with the interests of the respondent and third parties, the court shall also assess the extent to which the granting of the application may undermine the public interest.

Ultimately, where the interests of the applicant outweigh those of the respondent and third parties, as well as the need to protect the public interest, the application shall be granted, with or without additional measures to protect confidential information or to prevent excessive costs, as appropriate. Conversely, if the interests of the respondent or third parties and/or the need to safeguard the public interest are greater than the interests of the applicant, the court shall reject the petition.

4. PARTICULAR ISSUES ABOUT THE IPRED AND CDD RULES

The very essence of the IPRED and CDD rules on access to information and evidence is, as explained, a court-order-based system that pivots on the proportionality test.

The rules also raise some issues in relation to specific points that, at least at first sight, seem to be different in each Directive. The following pages will be devoted to analysing some of these issues and, eventually, to determining whether the particular rules of the IPRED and the CDD differ as much as one may think in the first place.

4.1. TYPES OF ORDERS FOR ACCESS TO INFORMATION AND EVIDENCE

As noted above, for intellectual property cases, the IPRED allows the parties to ask for three different types of court orders: orders for the *disclosure of evidence* (Article 6), *orders for the preservation of evidence* (Article 7), and *orders for the disclosure of information* (Article 8).

For its part, in the context of competition damages cases, the CDD apparently just deals with the possibility of one single type of order, namely that for the *disclosure of evidence*. In this regard, the headings of Chapter II CDD and of Article 5 and 6 CDD read: "Disclosure of evidence".

As may be seen, Articles 5 and 6 CDD seem to embrace a similar provision to that of Article 6 IPRED, allowing orders for the disclosure of evidence. However, no equivalent provisions to Articles 7 and 8 IPRED – about orders for the preservation of evidence and for the disclosure of information – appear to be found in the CDD. Does this mean that orders for the preservation of evidence and orders for the disclosure of information are not permitted in competition damages cases?

In this author's understanding, currently, no orders for the *preservation* of evidence can be granted on the basis of the CDD rules; the EU law-maker has only regulated these types of orders in Article 7 IPRED, but not in the text of the CDD.

Things are different, though, regarding orders for the disclosure of *information*, since the actual wording of CDD – not just the headings of Chapter II and of Articles 5 and 6 – makes the type of orders foreseen in Article 8 IPRED (orders for disclosure of *information*) also available in the field of competition damages. In this regard:

- Recital (15) CDD acknowledges that the rules on the "disclosure of evidence" are introduced to counterbalance the "*information* asymmetry" which typically characterises competition law litigation, which suggests that applications for disclosure may cover any evidence or *information* needed to overcome the said "asymmetry".

- The whole emphasis of the CDD on the protection of confidential *information* – see Recital (18), and Articles 5(3)(c), 5(4) and 8(1)(c), already commented on above – reveals that the orders for the "disclosure of evidence" foreseen in Articles 5 and 6 may be used to obtain information.
- When dealing with the prohibition of fishing expeditions, Recital (23) and Article 5(3)(b) CDD refer to the veto on "non-specific searches for *information*", which shows that specific searches for *information* are allowed.
- Recital (25) CDD talks about "*information*" that is "disclosable".
- Recital (30) CDD refers to the applications set forth in Articles 5 and 6 using the expression "requests for the disclosure of *information*".
- The order that can be obtained under Articles 5 and 6 CDD is called "order to disclose *information*" by Article 6(4).
- Article 6(5)(a) and (b) CDD refer to the potential disclosure of "*information*" (emphasis added).

Nevertheless, it may be argued that there might be two important differences between the IPRED and the CDD as to orders for the disclosure of *information*. The first difference relates to the actual information to which the order may refer. If the order is based on Article 8 IPRED, the information requested must stick to what the legal provision allows the applicant to ask for, namely information on the origin and distribution of the goods or services infringing an intellectual property right on a commercial scale, including information about names, addresses, quantities and prices. However, there are no similar limitations in the CDD and, hence, it may be concluded that the applicant is allowed to ask for *any* information that is relevant to his or her case.

The second difference affects the *form* in which *information* may be disclosed. Since Article 8 IPRED does not specify the form in which the *information* shall be provided ("competent judicial authorities may order that information … be provided"), it appears that the court may require the respondent not only to hand over documents with the relevant information, but also to appear in person before the court to testify.

In the CDD this latter conclusion – the possibility of an order to give testimony – is not that clear. Despite its references to the disclosure of *information*, it cannot be denied that Articles 5 and 6 CDD mostly refer to the disclosure of "evidence"; and, according to the definition set forth in Article 2(13), "'evidence' means all types of means of proof admissible before the national court seised, in particular documents and all other objects containing information, irrespective of the medium on which the information is stored". Hence, a reading of Articles 5 and 6 CDD in conjunction with Article 2(13) seems to lead to the conclusion that any application for the disclosure of information based on the CDD must be channelled through an application to disclose a "means of admissible proof" and "in particular" a "document" or any "other object" containing information. If one simply looks at the first part of the CDD's definition of "evidence" ("means of admissible proof"), one may conclude that testimony is not excluded, since it is a common "means of admissible proof". However, the second part of the definition ("in particular documents and all other objects containing information") suggests that the CDD is just thinking about *inanimate* tangible pieces of evidence containing information ("documents" and "objects"), but not about *persons* capable of giving testimony.

Then, if this second interpretation were to prevail, we will be forced to conclude that a court order for the disclosure of information based on Article 5 or on Article 6 CDD just amounts to a direction to hand over a *document or affidavit* containing the required information – no matter whether the document already existed prior to the moment when the application for disclosure was filed or, on the contrary, it was prepared afterwards by the person who knew the information in question to duly comply with the court order. In other words, whereas in intellectual property cases the IPRED gives the court the power to summon someone to testify, in competition damages cases the CDD appears to just allow the court to request information in writing from the person with knowledge of the relevant information.

4.2. PERSONS WHO MAY APPLY FOR AN ORDER

Some additional differences may be seen in the IPRED and the CDD as to who is entitled to apply for access to information and evidence and, therefore, to be granted an order thereto.

The references in Articles 6 and 7 IPRED to the "claims" of the "party" applying for an order for the disclosure or for the preservation of evidence suggest that only claimants – but not defendants – are given the opportunity to obtain such an order. Indeed, both provisions require that such orders shall only be granted "on application by a party who has presented reasonably available evidence to support his/her *claims*"; and, when dealing with the need to specify the evidence to be disclosed, Article 6 goes on to say that the applicant shall have specified evidence "substantiating those *claims*" (emphasis added).

It should be noted, though, that, when referring to the applicant, Articles 6 and 7 IPRED have not used the word "claimant" but a neutral word: "party" ("on application by a party"). There is no doubt that that "party" will normally be the claimant; i.e., the one asserting a "claim" consisting of the infringement of his or her intellectual property rights. Yet, in this author's opinion, the principle of equality of arms requires that defendants shall also be entitled to apply for the disclosure or the preservation of relevant evidence that might support their defences. At the end of the day, defendants are also "parties" and, broadly speaking, they will also be asserting a "claim" (for the dismissal of the case) before the court.[57]

Things are different with applications for the disclosure of information, as regulated in Article 8 IPRED. This provision openly states that such application is to be filed by the "claimant", so excluding defendants. In principle, the exclusion of defendants from the scope of Article 8 appears to be justified, in light of the fact that the only and specific types of information to which access may be applied for seem to be relevant just for the claimant, i.e., information on the origin and distribution networks of the goods or services that infringe an intellectual property right on a commercial scale, including names and addresses, quantities and prices involved in the infringement. However, the possibility of a defendant needing this type of information to support a defence cannot be completely ruled out – imagine a defendant that was mistakenly sued and wants to show the court that she had no participation in the infringement whatsoever. Thus, again, the principle of equality of arms will require that "a party" be read where Article 8(1) now says "the claimant".

Ultimately, when it comes to competition damages cases, the rules on who is entitled to apply for an order to disclose evidence are clean and clear: under Article 5(1) CDD, such orders may be granted "upon request of a claimant" or "upon request of the defendant", "in order to ensure equality of arms" – Recital (15) CDD.

4.3. PERSONS AGAINST WHOM THE ORDERS MAY BE ISSUED

Further differences between the IPRED and the CDD are to be found in regard to whom an application for access to information or evidence may be filed against and, hence, in regard to whom the orders granting access may be issued against.

The key question here is whether such application may only be filed against the opposing party to the dispute or whether it may also be filed against third parties.

Articles 7 and 8 IPRED allow the filing of applications against both parties and third parties. Regarding applications for the preservation of evidence, Article 7 IPRED allows the court to order "prompt and effective provisional measures to preserve relevant evidence in respect of the alleged infringement", without specifying against whom – opposing party, third party or any of those – the application for such an order may be made. And, in respect of applications for the disclosure of information, Article 8 IPRED clearly states that the court

57 Also in this regard, J.J. Forner Delaygua, "The impact of the Enforcement Directive on the Brussels I regime" in A. Nuyts (ed.), *International Litigation in Intellectual Property and Information Technology* (Wolters Kluwer, the Netherlands, 2008), 257–288, at 263.

may order that information be provided by the opposing party ("the infringer") or by the third party knowing the information in question, namely

> any other person who
>
> (a) was found in possession of the infringing goods on a commercial scale;
> (b) was found to be using the infringing services on a commercial scale;
> (c) was found to be providing on a commercial scale services used in infringing activities; or
> (d) was indicated by the person referred to in point (a), (b) or (c) as being involved in the production, manufacture or distribution of the goods or the provision of the services.

However, when dealing with applications for the disclosure of evidence, Article 6 IPRED just states that they are to be filed against someone who is the "opposing party" to the dispute in question ("[where the applicant has] specified evidence that lies in the control of the *opposing party*, the competent judicial authorities may order that such evidence be presented *by the opposing party*"(emphasis added)), which may lead to the conclusion that these applications are excluded where third parties are concerned. The consequences of this conclusion do not seem very reasonable: under the IPRED rules, in intellectual property cases, the evidence that is under the control of a third party would be unreachable, unless a need for the preservation of that evidence arose as foreseen in Article 7, or unless the evidence contained the information referred to in Article 8. The unreasonableness of the conclusion must lead, in this author's opinion, to the interpretation that the "opposing party" in Article 6 IPRED is any person who is in control of the relevant evidence to be disclosed and, hence, is the opponent in the incidental proceedings thereto.

Probably aware of this interpretation problem, some ten years after the IPRED was passed, for competition damages cases, Article 5 CDD has clarified the issue by unequivocally stating that, upon request of a claimant, "national courts are able to order the defendant *or a third party* to disclose relevant evidence"; and that, upon request of the defendant, they are also able "to order the claimant *or a third party* to disclose relevant evidence" (emphasis added).

4.4. THE NOTION OF "CONTROL"

Article 6 IPRED and Article 5 CDD require that the person against whom an application for access is filed – either the opposing party to the dispute or a third party – shall enjoy "control" over the evidence that the applicant wishes to have access to ("evidence which lies in the *control*"; "documents under the *control*"; "evidence which lies in their *control*").

In some Member States, "uncertainties have arisen as to whether the term 'control' should only refer to possession of evidence, or whether it should be understood more broadly, and extend even to require the opposing party to undertake a reasonable search".[58]

In this author's understanding, the use of the word "control" amounts to a broad interpretation, by virtue of which applications might be made (and orders might be granted) against anyone capable of making the requested evidence pass from someone's hands to the court and, at the end of the day, to the applicant. This means that a person might be subject to an order for the disclosure of evidence not only when he or she has actual possession of the evidence in question, but also when he or she has the legal or factual power to find the evidence and hand it over. Specifically, using the European Commission's words, a legal person or a business shall be deemed to be "in control" of the requested information or evidence when it is able "to carry out a diligent search for the evidence within its organisation (including separate legal entities which it controls)".[59]

However, the right of the applicant to a diligent search by the respondent cannot entail a right for the creation of new information or new evidence – i.e., the creation of currently non-existing information or evidence. Indeed, in any case, in both the IPRED and the CDD, it appears clear that the *information* or the *evidence* that the application for access refers to *must have existed prior to the filing of the application*; or, in other words, that the information or evidence to be disclosed or preserved must already be known or controlled by the respondent by the time the applicant lodges his or her application. Hence, applications aiming at the respondent generating *new* information or evidence will be denied.[60]

4.5. THE NEED TO SPECIFY THE REQUESTED INFORMATION OR EVIDENCE

As has been discussed above, both the IPRED and the CDD require the applicant to *specify the information or the evidence that he or she wishes to have access to*, since such specification is necessary to determine different aspects of the proportionality test, such as relevance for the applicant's rights, or degree of intrusion into privacy and/or the respondent's freedom to conduct a business.

58 European Commission (2017) (Guidance), above n. 46, at 13.

59 Ibid.

60 Thus, for example, an application for a report that still needs to be generated (and that, therefore, does not exist) shall not be admissible; however, by contrast, an application to access the actual information or evidence that might be used to generate that as yet non-existing report may indeed be allowed.

In the IPRED, the need to be specific is stated in Article 6(1), where the applicant is to have "*specified* evidence". And, in this author's view, that need is also implicit in Article 7(1) (where only "relevant" evidence is to be preserved) and in Article 8 (according to which the application shall refer to specific types of information).

For its part, the CDD devotes Article 5(2) to that same need, providing that disclosure shall be "of specified items of evidence" or "relevant categories of evidence circumscribed as precisely and as narrowly as possible" – circumscription that, according to Recital (16) CDD, may be carried out "by references to common features of its constitutive elements such as the nature, object or content of the documents the disclosure of which is requested, the time during which they were drawn up, or other criteria". And, further on, when dealing with access to the file of a competition authority, Article 6(4)(a) insists on the application having "been formulated specifically with regard to the nature, subject matter or contents of documents".

As may be seen, there seem to be differences between the IPRED and the CDD when they come to regulate the specificity requirement for accessing information or evidence. Probably, the most important one is that, whereas the CDD explicitly allows the applicant to ask for "categories of evidence", the IPRED simply refers to "evidence". This dissimilarity might be interpreted as though the IPRED does not allow disclosure of "categories of evidence" in intellectual property cases.

However, this author is of the belief that the difference is merely apparent and, hence, "categories of evidence" may also be disclosed under the IPRED. In this regard, it is worth noticing that the "specified *items* of evidence" and "relevant *categories* of evidence" referred to in Article 5(2) CDD when dealing with the specificity requirement are, in truth, able to fall within the concept of the "evidence" that an applicant should have "specified" under Article 6(1) IPRED. In other words, since both an "item" and a "category" of evidence are, at the end of the day, "evidence", items and categories of evidence may be disclosed not only in competition damages cases – as expressly stated in Article 5(2) CDD – but also in intellectual property cases – under Article 6(1) IPRED. There certainly is a contrast between the very few words used by the IPRED in 2004 as to the specificity requirement and the much richer wording of the CDD on the same matter ten years later. Yet, in this author's understanding, this contrast simply reveals that the EU law-maker wanted to *clarify* – not change – the rules in the new legal instrument.[61]

Finally, regarding the need to specify the information or evidence requested (either an "item" or a "category"), it should be added that courts should not follow a very restrictive approach, since requiring applicants to be exhaustive

61 This is also the view of the European Commission (2017) (Guidance), above n. 46, at 12–13.

when giving the details of the information or evidence sought may compromise the system of access as a whole. Indeed, although specification is needed to determine a number of aspects of the proportionality test, as explained, it does not seem reasonable to call on applicants to specify the exact character, the precise location, the actual reference number, the concrete page numbers or even the particular contents of the information or evidence requested. Getting to know these details might be extremely difficult, if not impossible, for an applicant who might have never seen that information or evidence. Hence, requiring from the applicant such a high degree of specification calls into question the effectiveness of the measures of access to information or evidence provided for in the IPRED and the CDD.[62]

4.6. THE PROCEDURE FOR GRANTING ACCESS

About the proceedings that should follow up an application for access to information or evidence, nothing is said in Articles 6 (disclosure of evidence) or 8 (disclosure of information) IPRED. However, regarding applications for the preservation of evidence, Article 7 does contain rules on procedure, which read:

> Those measures [i.e., measures to preserve relevant evidence] shall be taken, if necessary, without the other party having been heard, in particular where any delay is likely to cause irreparable harm to the rightholder or where there is a demonstrable risk of evidence being destroyed.
>
> Where measures to preserve evidence are adopted without the other party having been heard, the parties affected shall be given notice, without delay after the execution of the measures at the latest. A review, including a right to be heard, shall take place upon request of the parties affected with a view to deciding, within a reasonable period after the notification of the measures, whether the measures shall be modified, revoked or confirmed.

Upon the rules established in this provision, a conclusion may be drawn for intellectual property cases:

- The general rule is that, once the application for access to information or evidence has been filed, the court is to give "the other party" (i.e., the person that is expected to disclose the information or the evidence or to preserve the evidence) an opportunity to be heard. Only after that opportunity has been used or has elapsed, will the court be deciding upon the application, either granting or denying it.

62 See European Commission (2017) (Guidance), above n. 46, at 12.

- The exception is that, when it comes to an application for the preservation of evidence, proceedings may be conducted *ex parte* (i.e., "without the other party having been heard") "if necessary" and "in particular where any delay is likely to cause irreparable harm to the rightholder or where there is a demonstrable risk of evidence being destroyed". Therefore, in such circumstances, the court will decide upon the application right after it has been filed; and, if an order for the preservation of evidence is eventually granted, the court may also conduct enforcement proceedings *ex parte*, as appropriate. In any case, "the parties affected shall be given notice, without delay after the execution of the measures at the latest", so that they will then be given an opportunity to challenge the order and get "a review" from the court.

For competition damages cases, the CDD sets forth two basic rules on procedure. On the one hand, it shall be ensured "that those from whom disclosure is sought are provided with an opportunity to be heard before a national court orders disclosure" – Article 5(7). And, on the other hand, "to the extent that a competition authority is willing to state its views on the proportionality of disclosure requests, it may, acting on its own initiative, submit observations to the national court before which a disclosure order is sought" – Article 6(11) – "in light of the impact that such disclosure would have on the effectiveness of the public enforcement of competition law" – Recital (30).

As may be seen, the CDD simply imports the general rule that is to be extracted from Article 7 IPRED (no order shall be granted without the other party enjoying a prior opportunity to be heard) and takes into account the peculiarities of competition law by way of allowing the public authorities to intervene in any case. However, the CDD makes no mention of potential *ex parte* proceedings.[63] This appears to be consistent after all, since the IPRED just foresees *ex parte* proceedings for applications for the preservation of evidence and the CDD excluded this type of application from its realm, as explained above.

Ultimately, putting aside the provision allowing competition authorities to intervene, none of the Directives refers to the possibility of hearing third-party *non*-respondents, i.e., persons other than the applicant and the respondent. However, in this author's opinion, since the court is to "especially" care for the interests of these persons – Article 5(3)(b) and (c) – there is little doubt that they must also be granted an opportunity to state their views prior to the decision of the court on the application for disclosure.[64]

---

63 "Without prejudice to national law providing for *ex parte* proceedings", as reminded by Recital (30) CDD.

64 See 3.2.2.3 above.

4.7. ACCESS TO INFORMATION AND EVIDENCE PRIOR TO THE FILING OF THE COMPLAINT

One of the most important issues that, in this author's opinion, requires clarification in both the IPRED and the CDD is that of whether or not these Directives allow the parties to apply for access to information and evidence *prior to the filing of the complaint* instituting the main proceedings.

There is no doubt about the parties' right to apply for access to information and evidence at the very moment they lodge their initial briefs on merits of the case, or even subsequent to that moment, provided that the main proceedings are still pending and a supervening need for access arises. *Actual* claimants and *actual* defendants are always entitled to apply for access to information or evidence under the IPRED and the CDD. However, the Directives are not clear about whether a *prospective* claimant or a *prospective* defendant also enjoys that same right of access, with a view to substantiating future complaints or injunctions, to substantiating future defences on the merits or protective letters, or eventually to assessing any alternatives to litigation.

Within the field of intellectual property litigation, a strict interpretation of Articles 6, 7 and 8 IPRED may lead to the conclusion that only applications for the *preservation* of evidence – Article 7 – will be allowed prior to the commencement of the proceedings on the merits of the case. Therefore, any application for the *disclosure* of evidence or information – Articles 6 and 8 – will necessarily need to be filed together with the initial briefs in respect of those proceedings, or afterwards as long as they have not ended yet.

In this regard, it should be noted that only Article 7 explicitly states that applications for the preservation of evidence may be lodged "even before the commencement of proceedings on the merits of the case", whereas Articles 6 and 8 do not entail such an assertion within the rules governing applications for the disclosure of evidence or information. Hence, under the interpretation rule *inclusio unius est exclusio alterius*, it would not seem unreasonable to conclude that these latter applications are only permitted once the main proceedings are initiated.

Moreover, this conclusion – that applications under Articles 6 and 8 IPRED are only permitted once the main proceedings are initiated – might be backed by the actual wording of Articles 6 and 8 IPRED. Article 6 seems to assume that, by the time an application for the disclosure of evidence is filed, the applicant's "claims" on the merits of the case will have already been "substantiated" and have already been submitted to the court ("on application by a *party* which has presented reasonably available evidence sufficient to support its *claims* and has, *in substantiating those claims*, specified evidence" (emphasis added)). Similarly, Article 8 appears to make the same assumption, since applications for the disclosure of information are to be filed "*in the context of proceedings* concerning an infringement of an intellectual property right and in response to a justified and proportionate request of *the claimant*" (emphasis added).

However, in this author's opinion, a much broader interpretation of Articles 6, 7 and 8 IPRED must be made, whereby the filing of all types of applications for access to information or evidence – not only of those based on Article 7 IPRED, but also of those grounded upon Article 6 or Article 8 IPRED – shall always be permitted prior to the commencement of the main proceedings on the merits of the case.[65]

As Trocker remarks,

> in many situations, for parties wishing to pursue their rights in court it is extremely important to have access to information and evidence in the pre-action phase in order to determine whether there are sufficient elements for a realistic claim to be made or to decide against whom a suit can be brought.

Additionally, "access to information and evidence in the pre-action phase may also be important to enable a party to decide whether to look for an extrajudicial settlement of the dispute or initiate litigation in court".[66]

And, above all, it is clear that, in procedural systems of 'fact pleading' – such as the European ones,[67] – it is very important for *prospective* claimants to have access to the relevant information and the relevant evidence, so that that information and that evidence may be deployed in the complaint initiating the main proceedings, as appropriate.[68] Indeed, with a 'fact pleading' standard, the claimant's fundamental rights to an effective remedy and to a fair trial cannot be duly satisfied if he or she is forced to start a civil case 'half-blind', i.e., by way of a complaint that omits to state paramount facts or fails to refer to key pieces of evidence, simply because the law did not enable the possibility of accessing those facts or that evidence prior to the filing of the complaint.[69]

Thus, there is a strong rationale – the need of prospective claimants to be able to prepare their future complaints pursuant to the 'fact pleading' standard, which clearly connects with their fundamental rights to an effective remedy and to a fair trial – for allowing applications for the disclosure of information or evidence prior to the commencement of proceedings on the merits of the case

---

65 This is also the interpretation followed by the implementing provisions of Articles 6 and 7 IPRED in most Member States. See Peter, above n. 15, at 54 and 179–185; and EUIPO (2010), above n. 14, at pdf 12 and 26–31.

66 Trocker, above n. 2, at 274.

67 See the introduction to this chapter in 1 above.

68 See Trocker, above n. 2, at 275–276.

69 In this regard, in Judgment of 28 April 2009, *K.H. and others v. Slovakia*, App. 32881/04, the ECtHR found that the denial of photocopies of medical records needed for substantiating a *future* civil claim amounted to a violation not only of Art. 8 of the Convention (privacy) (§§37–58), but also to a violation of Art. 6 (fair trial) (§§59–69).

and, hence, for ruling out the maxim *inclusio unius est exclusio alterius* when interpreting Articles 6, 7 and 8 IPRED.

Furthermore, the fact that Article 6 IPRED refers to the "substantiated claims" of the applicant does not necessarily amount to the parties being excluded from applying for disclosure of evidence before the main proceedings have started. In fact, Article 7 IPRED itself, after making explicit that applications for the preservation of evidence are allowed "even before the commencement of proceedings of the merits of the case", goes on to say that, in order for such applications to be granted, the applicant should have presented "reasonably available evidence to support his/her *claims*". This provision can only mean that, when applying under Article 7, the applicant has to show what his or her claim arising out of an infringement of an intellectual property right *is* – should the proper complaint have already been filed – or what it *will be* – in the cases where the application is filed before proceedings have commenced; in other words, to show a *prima facie* case,[70] either actually or potentially pending. Thus, if a reference to the "claims" of the applicant in Article 7 IPRED does not impede the application being filed prior to the initiation of the main proceedings, the same conclusion must be reached as to the references to the "claims" of the applicant in Article 6 IPRED.

Finally, in this author's understanding, the fact that Article 8 IPRED indicates that an application for the disclosure of information shall come from "the claimant" and "in the context of proceedings concerning an infringement" is not sufficient to interpret that a *prospective* claimant is to be barred from making such application. On the one hand, broadly speaking, "the claimant" may be interpreted as the person claiming against another, not necessarily having brought his or her case to court yet; and, on the other hand, since the word "context" refers to what precedes and what follows something, there should not be any problem in understanding that any search for information prior to the initiation of civil proceedings is something that precedes those proceedings and, therefore, that occur in the "context" of those proceedings. In fact, it might be argued that, in the case of *New Wave CZ*, the ECJ appears to have reached a similar conclusion, since it found that from Article 8(1) IPRED "it does not follow … that the applicant must assert the right to information laid down in that article in the selfsame proceedings in which a finding is sought of an infringement of an intellectual property right".[71]

[70] See 3.2.2 above.

[71] Judgment of 18 January 2017, *New Wave CZ a.s. v. ALLTOYS, spol. s.r.o.*, C-427/15, EU:C:2017:18, §21. However, it should be noted that the issue raised in the case of *New Wave CZ* was not exactly whether an application under Article 8(1) IPRED is allowed prior to the commencement of the main proceedings, but, rather, whether such application is permitted subsequent to the termination of the main proceedings, with a view to institute new proceedings in regard to the same infringement. In the case of *New Wave*, a purely declaratory

Similar comments may be made in regard to applications for the disclosure of evidence concerning competition damages cases. If the wording of Article 5(1) CDD were to be interpreted narrowly, such applications could only be filed together with the complaint initiating the main proceedings, or subsequent to the filing of that complaint. In this regard, Article 5(1) CDD states that the courts will be able to grant disclosure "*in proceedings* relating to an action for damages" – which suggests that main proceedings must be pending by the time disclosure is requested; that disclosure shall be granted "upon request of *a claimant*" or of "the *defendant*" – which seems to be barring prospective claimants or prospective defendants from making such requests; and that, where the applicant happens to be a claimant, he or she is to present "a reasoned justification containing reasonably available facts and evidence sufficient to support the plausibility of its *claim* for damages" – which might interpreted as a need for the "claim" having already been filed when disclosure is requested (emphasis added).

Yet, in this author's opinion, the strong rationale mentioned above – the need of prospective claimants to be able to prepare their future complaints pursuant to the 'fact pleading' standard, which clearly connects with their fundamental rights to an effective remedy and to a fair trial – shall lead to a broad interpretation of Article 5(1) CDD, allowing applications for the disclosure of evidence both *prior* and *subsequent* to the commencement of the main proceedings on the merits of the case. Indeed, in this author's understanding, there should not be great difficulties in giving the expression "in proceedings relating to an action" of Article 5(1) CDD the same meaning as "in the context of proceedings concerning an infringement" of Article 8(1) IPRED. Nor there should be great difficulties in interpreting the use of the expressions "claim", "claimant" and "defendant" as generic, i.e., that "claim" is simply the right asserted by someone against another person – not only in court but also out of court – that the "claimant" is that "someone" and that the "defendant" is that "another person".

judgment stating that Alltoys had infringed one of New Wave's intellectual property rights had already been granted. Now, New Wave wanted to file a new complaint against Alltoys seeking compensation for the same infringement and, to this end, New Wave had filed an application for the disclosure of information under Article 8 IPRED and the corresponding national provision. A Czech court rejected the application on the basis that "a claim to a right of information could not be brought by an application submitted independently" and that "the action concerning infringement of a right had already been terminated by the final judgment given in the first action". The ECJ rejected these arguments and responded that, indeed, applications under Article 8 were allowed in those types of situations, the reasons for that finding being: the meaning of the word "context"; the analysis of the different language versions of the Article 8(1); the possibility to file the application against a third party, i.e., against "persons [who] are not necessarily parties to the proceedings in which a finding is sought of an infringement of an intellectual property right", which would confirm "that the wording of Article 8(1) of Directive 2004/48 cannot be interpreted as being applicable only in such proceedings"; the objective of the IPRED to ensure a high level of protection of intellectual property rights; and, finally, the fundamental right to an effective remedy guaranteed in Article 47 CFREU (§§20–27).

4.8. PENALTIES

Ultimately, one of the most significant differences between the rules on access to information and evidence included in the IPRED and those in the CDD is that, whereas the CDD has tackled the issue of the need to establish negative consequences ("penalties") for those refusing to abide by a court order regarding disclosure – see Article 8 CDD – the IPRED contains no provision whatsoever on the matter.

That the law prescribes – and the courts apply – these negative consequences is, in this author's view, an absolute must for the proper compliance with and enforcement of the rules governing access to information and evidence, no matter the field of litigation we might be dealing with.[72]

5. CONCLUSION: THE IPRED AND CDD RULES AS AN INSPIRATION FOR NEW RULES APPLICABLE TO ALL CIVIL CASES

The rules contained in the IPRED and in the CDD on access to information and evidence in the fields of intellectual property and competition damages may well inspire future rules on the matter applicable to *all civil cases*. Indeed, if the peculiarities dealing with intellectual property and competition damages were put aside, those rules will be valid for any field of civil litigation.

Paraphrasing Wagner, if the language derived from the intellectual property world and the competition world were eliminated and replaced by the general concepts of applicant and respondent, the IPRED and the CDD rules on access to information and evidence would fit in well within any decent code of civil procedure; in other words, the procedural provisions of the IPRED and the CDD may be controversial at one point or another, but all in all they seem well-balanced and thus suitable for generalisation.[73]

Since under Article 81 TFEU the EU does not seem to have competence to horizontally harmonise the national rules of procedure applicable to domestic cases, for the time being, the inspiration provided by the IPRED and the CDD

---

72 See, also in this regard, Trocker, above n. 2, at 260; European Commission, *Evaluation accompanying the document Guidance on certain aspects of Directive 2004/48/EC of the European Parliament and of the Council on the enforcement of intellectual property rights* (Commission staff working document of 29.11.2017), 1–72, at 23 (available at: https://eur-lex.europa.eu/legal-content/EN/TXT/PDF/?uri=CELEX:52017SC0431&from=en); and EUIPO (2010), above n. 14, pdf 7, 10 and 11.

73 Wagner, above n. 10, at 104 and 110 (11 and 17). Of the same opinion are Trocker, above n. 2, at 282, and Gascón Inchausti (2018), above n. 10, at 133–134.

as to access to information and evidence is to be taken into account by national law-makers as an opportunity with a view to future legal reforms of national procedural law.[74]

Obviously, national law-makers would have to preserve the common core of the IPRED and the CDD rules, namely, the court-order-based system of access, along with the central role of proportionality and the need to balance all the legitimate interests of the persons concerned and the public interest.

And, then, national legislators may seize the occasion given by a legal reform to harmonise differences and to clarify issues arising out of the current text of Articles 6, 7 and 8 IPRED and Articles 5, 6, 7 and 8 CDD. In this author's view, according to what has been discussed above, this task of harmonisation and clarification must entail that in the context of any civil dispute:

- The parties are allowed to apply for the three types of orders foreseen in the IPRED, namely orders for the disclosure of information, for the disclosure of evidence and for the preservation of evidence.
- The orders are available not only to claimants and defendants, but also to prospective claimants and prospective defendants.
- The orders may be granted against anyone having control of the relevant information or evidence, including third parties.
- Someone is deemed to have "control" of pieces of information or evidence not only when he or she has "possession" of those pieces, but also when he or she has the legal or factual power to find the evidence and hand it over. In particular, as far of legal persons and businesses are concerned, they will be regarded as "in control" of the requested information or evidence whenever they are able to carry out a diligent search for the evidence within their organisation (including separate legal entities which they control).
- The orders may refer to either "items" or "categories" of information or evidence, as long as the items or categories have been sufficiently specified by the applicant, so that proportionality can be duly assessed by the court; however, when specifying those items or categories, the applicant shall never be required to give details that, in light of the circumstances of the case, he or she is unable to provide.
- As a general rule, no order shall be granted without the other party having been previously heard; exceptionally, *ex parte* proceedings might be allowed where any delay is likely to cause irreparable harm to the applicant or where there is a demonstrable risk of evidence being destroyed. In any case, public authorities involved in the public enforcement of the applicable law will always be entitled to intervene and state their views in the proceedings

[74] The idea of "Europe as an opportunity" for national legislators to make better procedural rules has been stressed by Gascón Inchausti (2018), above n. 10, at 131–134.

following an application for access to information or evidence. Eventually, should there be third parties concerned, they will be given an opportunity to be heard prior to the decision of the court.

- Any application for access to information or evidence may be filed even before the main proceedings have started, so that prospective claimants and prospective defendants can duly prepare their future pleadings.
- Negative consequences are established in order to guarantee full respect to the content of the court orders granting access to information or evidence.

It should be added that, up until now, at least two proposals have been presented in this regard. At a national level, a proposal was drafted in 2016 by the Spanish General Commission for Codification (*Comisión General de Codificación*) amending the Civil Procedure Act (*Ley de Enjuiciamiento Civil*) and introducing general rules on "Access to sources of evidence" that were intended to be applicable to all civil cases; the proposal was not finally passed into law.[75] And, at a multi-national level, the European Law Institute (ELI) and the International Institute for the Unification of Private Law (UNIDROIT) have formulated a set of draft model rules on "Access to evidence", which, in this author's view, are likely to be a very relevant and useful tool for national law-makers willing to face future legal reforms of civil procedure.[76]

75 The text of the Spanish proposal is available at: http://www.mjusticia.gob.es/cs/Satellite/Portal/1292427769696?blobheader=application%2Fpdf&blobheadername1=Content-Disposition&blobheadername2=Grupo&blobheadervalue1=attachment%3B+filename%3DPropuesta_de_Ley_de_la_Seccion_Especial_para_la_Trasposicion_de_la_Directiva_2014_104_UE__del_Parla.PDF&blobheadervalue2=Docs_CGC_Secciones+especializadas. For comments on the proposal, C. Herrero Suárez and M.L. Escalada López, "La transposición de la Directiva de daños antitrust. Reflexiones a raíz de la publicación de la propuesta de ley de transposición de la Directiva" (2016) 8(1) *Cuadernos de Derecho Transnacional*, 150–183, at 157–165 (available at: https://e-revistas.uc3m.es/index.php/CDT/article/view/3024/1730); F. Gascón Inchausti, "Aspectos procesales de las acciones de daños derivados de infracciones de las normas sobre defensa de la competencia: apuntes a la luz de la Directiva 2014/104 y de la Propuesta de Ley de transposición" (2017) 9(1) *Cuadernos de Derecho Transnacional*, 125–152, at 139–146 (available at https://doi.org/10.20318/cdt.2017.3616); and Domínguez Ruiz, above n. 28, at 26–42 (IV).

76 The ELI/UNIDROIT rules were drafted in the context of their joint project "From Transnational Principles to European Rules of Civil Procedure". They may be found at: http://www.europarl.europa.eu/RegData/etudes/IDAN/2017/556972/IPOL_IDA(2017)556972_EN.pdf.

HARMONISATION OF CONFIDENTIAL INFORMATION PROTECTION IN LEGAL PROCEEDINGS

The Trade Secrets Directive

Patricia LLOPIS NADAL*

* The participation as a speaker in the conference "Harmonization of civil procedure in the European Union: How far can we go?", as well as the drafting of this chapter, resulted from a two-month research stay at the Max Planck Institute Luxembourg for International, European and Regulatory Procedural Law, funded by a research grant from the "Fundación Privada Manuel Serra Domínguez" in order to promote the study of procedural law.

1. INTRODUCTION

The Directive 2016/943[1] ("the Trade Secrets Directive"), has recently contributed to the vertical harmonisation regarding civil procedure in the European Union. This sectoral Directive, aimed at protecting undisclosed know-how and business information against unlawful acquisition, use and disclosure, contains some provisions whose implementation will have an impact on national civil procedures. Amongst these provisions of the Trade Secrets Directive, its Article 9 should be highlighted, as it harmonises the protection of confidential information in the course of legal proceedings.[2] Nevertheless, the vertical nature of this EU rule determines that the measures envisaged for preserving confidentiality will only be applied, in theory, when the protection of a Trade Secret is at stake.

In that sense, it is convenient to respect the following structure in this chapter. First, the concept of *trade secrets*, for the purposes of the European Union Directive, should be briefly explained. Then, the core of the exposition will be focused on the need for preserving confidential information in the course of trade secrets proceedings, as well as the confidentiality measures required under Article 9 of this Directive – by distinguishing between the measures addressed to those who do not participate in the civil procedure and the measures provided for those who take part in legal proceedings. To conclude, some final remarks concerning the utilisation, the implementation and the application by analogy of these confidentiality measures will be outlined.

2. THE TRADE SECRETS DEFINITION ACCORDING TO THE EU DIRECTIVE

When it comes to explain the concept of *trade secrets*, it is easier to offer some examples than trying to set a definition – one of the reasons for this being the lack of a generally accepted definition.[3] For instance, the *Coca Cola* recipe or *Google Search* algorithm are amongst the best kept secrets in the world and the most valuable ones. These ideas help us to define *trade secrets* as any kind of confidential information, which provides its holder with an advantage

---

[1] Directive (EU) 2016/943 of the European Parliament and of the Council of 8 June 2016 on the protection of undisclosed know-how and business information (trade secrets) against their unlawful acquisition, use and disclosure, OJ, 15 June 2016, L 157, pp. 1–18.

[2] F. Gascón Inchausti, *Derecho europeo y legislación procesal civil nacional: entre autonomía y armonización*, Marcial Pons, 2018, p. 30.

[3] J. Pila and P. Torremans, *European Intellectual Property Law*, Oxford University Press, 2016, p. 535.

over their competitors in the marketplace – recipes, algorithms, inventions, processes, etc.[4]

Nowadays, trade secrets have become a very popular way of protecting intangible assets.[5] On the one hand, this is due to the fact that Intellectual Property rights (especially patents and copyrights) have a limited duration, while a trade secret, if correctly kept, could last forever.[6] On the other hand, this is a result of the fact that some valuable information cannot be protected as an exclusive right (e.g., know-how, business methods, marketing strategies ...) according to most of the European legal systems.[7]

Despite trade secrets importance, and their relevance in the internal market,[8] Member States had shown differences regarding their legal nature and their level of protection.[9] It was not until the 2016 Directive, that the European Union triggered the subsidiarity principle in order to harmonise the trade secrets regulation.[10] As the starting point of this harmonisation, the legislator has stated a legal definition for *trade secrets*: information that is secret, has commercial value and has been kept undisclosed fulfils the necessary requirements to be considered a *trade secret* for the purposes of this European Union Directive.

The above-mentioned requirements are defined under Article 2 of the Trade Secrets Directive. The information will be secret if it is not generally known or readily accessible to those who are part of the business sector where this knowledge could be used. The commercial value of this information should result from its secret nature, could be either an actual or a potential value and shall be considered in a broad sense.[11] Furthermore, the person lawfully

4 About the notion of trade secrets and a list of the different types including the most popular ones, see the entry in the blog of *Vethan Law Firm* https://info.vethanlaw.com/blog/trade-secrets-10-of-the-most-famous-examples.

5 T. Farkas and P. Koch, "The disclosure – fair trial dilemma when enforcing trade secrets in civil court proceedings" (2016) 11(12) *Journal of Intellectual Property Law & Practice* 902; G. Grassie, "Trade Secrets: the new EU enforcement regime" (2014) 11(8) *Journal of Intellectual Property Law & Practice* 678.

6 R. Niebel, L. De Martinis and B. Clark, "The EU Trade Secrets Directive: all change for trade secret protection in Europe?" (2018) 13(6) *Journal of Intellectual Property Law & Practice* 447.

7 G. Grassie, "Trade Secrets: the new EU enforcement regime", n. 5 above, p. 677; P. Torremans, "The road towards the harmonisation of Trade Secrets Law in the European Union" (Julio-Diciembre 2015) 20 Revista la Propiedad Inmaterial 27 and 28.

8 Trade Secrets Directive, recital (3).

9 Trade Secrets Directive, recital (6). P. Torremans, "The road towards the harmonisation of Trade Secrets Law in the European Union", n. 7 above, p. 28, refers to the different national approaches concerning the legal nature and the protection of trade secrets. Furthermore, J. Pila and P. Torremans, *European Intellectual Property Law*, n. 3 above, pp. 535 and 536 offer a detailed explanation concerning the traditional approaches.

10 R. Niebel, L. De Martinis and B. Clark, "The EU Trade Secrets Directive ...", n. 6 above, p. 446.

11 "Such know-how or information should be considered to have a commercial value, for example, where its unlawful acquisition, use or disclosure is likely to harm the interests of

in control of the information must have taken the reasonable steps, under the concurring circumstances, in order to keep it secret.

Nevertheless, even if the EU legislator has introduced a common definition for trade secrets, it should be pointed out that their legal nature in each Member State has been respected – subject to the requirement of implementing properly the basis provided for in the Directive to obtain their protection before the courts.[12] In that sense, it could be maintained that with reference to substantive law, trade secrets have been subject to minimal harmonisation – which includes their definition as well as the infringing activities – whereas the procedural aspects concerning their legal protection have been the main focus of the Trade Secrets Directive; namely, measures, procedures and remedies in order to obtain an effective civil redress. This procedural harmonisation will guarantee, irrespective of the Member State in which legal proceedings are instituted, a minimum protection through these common aspects.

3. PROTECTION OF CONFIDENTIAL INFORMATION IN THE COURSE OF TRADE SECRETS PROCEEDINGS

Concerning how far we can go in the harmonisation of civil procedure in the European Union, the preservation of confidentiality in the course of legal proceedings constitutes the main new element in relation to prior vertical rules with procedural consequences, as well as the most remarkable step further taken by the EU legislator with its Trade Secrets Directive – just as it was one of the most controversial issues during the law-making process.[13] As it has happened previously with other sectoral Directives – e.g., the Damages Directive[14] – the indicated *forward move* serves to introduce in national legal systems new

the person lawfully controlling it, in that it undermines that person's scientific and technical potential, business or financial interests, strategic positions or ability to compete" [Trade Secrets Directive, recital (14)].

12 T. Aplin, "A critical evaluation of the proposed EU Trade Secrets Directive", *King's College London Law School Research Paper No. 2014-25*, 18 July 2014, p. 8.

13 A. Benetó Santa Cruz and L. Cachón Marinel·lo, "El proyecto de Directiva Comunitaria relativa a la protección del saber hacer y la información empresarial no divulgada (secretos comerciales), contra su obtención, utilización y divulgación ilícita" (Enero-Abril 2016) 77 *Comunicaciones en propiedad industrial y derecho de la competencia* 194.

14 Directive (EU) 2014/104 of the European Parliament and of the Council of 26 November 2014 on certain rules governing actions for damages under national law for infringements of the competition law provisions of the Member States and of the European Union, O.J., 5 December 2014, L 349, pp. 1–19. Regarding the main procedural implications of the Damages Directive, with particular reference to the Spanish implementation, see F. Gascón Inchausti, "Aspectos procesales de las acciones de daños derivados de infracciones de las normas sobre defensa de la competencia: apuntes a la luz de la Directiva 2014/104 y de la propuesta de ley de transposición" (2017) 9(1) *Cuadernos de derecho transnacional*, in particular, p. 141, para. 44.

regulations that will have an impact on procedural aspects, in this case, with regard to access to evidence and hearings, publication of the judicial decisions and the duty of confidentiality in relation to the litigated information.[15]

3.1. THE NEED FOR PRESERVING CONFIDENTIAL INFORMATION

Trade secrets are based on confidentiality – their commercial value being a direct consequence of their secret nature – therefore, confidentiality should also be the basis for the civil procedure aimed at obtaining their protection. Before the adoption of this Directive, most Member States showed a poor protection of confidentiality in their legal proceedings.[16] As a result, trade secrets holders were deterred from litigating: they were afraid of losing the secret character of their valuable information.[17] In other words, the lack of measures to protect trade secrets in legal proceedings was hindering their holders' access to justice. This obstacle was due to an evident paradox: to protect their *secret* information they had to *disclose it* in court and to *make it public.*[18]

The solution has come through the *preservation of confidentiality* guaranteed by means of two kinds of specific measures provided for in Article 9 of the Trade Secrets Directive – depending on whether a person is part of the proceedings or not. This regulation is reinforced with sanctions in case of non-compliance – that is, if those bound by the confidentiality measures fail or refuse to respect them. For that purpose, Article 16 obliges Member States to ensure that the competent

---

15 Concerning the Spanish Civil Procedure Act, this will have direct implications on the existing norms on *public oral proceedings* (Article 138) as well as *information of procedures* (Article 140) because, as a result of implementing the Directive, the preservation of confidentiality in the course of trade secrets proceedings will constitute a new ground for derogating the general rule of publicity [Ley 1/2000 de Enjuiciamiento Civil, *B.O.E.*, No. 7, 8 January 2000].

16 As *Baker & McKenzie Final Study on Trade Secrets* prepared for the European Commission summarises "The right for a party to request that the entire proceeding or a part thereof be heard in private to preserve confidentiality of the trade secrets exists only in a few jurisdictions (Bulgaria, Estonia, Hungary, Germany, the Netherlands, Poland, Romania, Slovakia, Slovenia). But even where this possibility theoretically exists, it is seldom applied in practice and no case law is reported on this point. Only Hungary (through *in camera* proceedings), Germany (through the so-called 'Düsseldorf procedure') and the UK (by means of specific agreement between the parties limiting the duty of disclosure) seem to have in place effective procedural measures to prevent disclosure of trade secrets in the course of civil proceedings" [*Final Study on Trade Secrets and Confidential Business Information in the Internal Market*, April 2013, prepared by Baker & McKenzie for the European Commission (Contract number: MARKT/20117128/D), p. 7].

17 Trade Secrets Directive, recitals (7) and (14).

18 T. Farkas and P. Koch, "The disclosure – fair trial dilemma ...", n. 5 above, p. 902; R. Montagnon, "The Trade Secrets Directive – consistency of approach required, with or without Brexit" (2016) 11(9) *Journal of Intellectual Property Law & Practice* 643.

judicial authorities are enabled to impose these sanctions. However, neither their nature nor their level is defined by the Directive, leaving this decision to national legislators – therefore, allowing for new fragmented regulations with regard to the non-observance of the confidentiality measures.

The following analysis of these measures brings to light that the EU legislator has considered the existing case law of the European Court of Justice concerning trade secrets and the confidentiality requirement. In the *Varec* case, having maintained that the right to the protection of confidential information is *in essence* a substantive right whose exercise can have procedural consequences,[19] the ECJ states that confidentiality in proceedings should be preserved respecting the requirements of effective legal protection, the rights of defence of the parties and the right to a fair trial.[20]

3.2. THE CONFIDENTIALITY MEASURES ADOPTED AND THEIR IMPACT ON NATIONAL PROCEDURES

3.2.1. *The Measures to Protect Confidential Information from Third Parties*

In the course of legal proceedings *per se*, the Trade Secrets Directive tries to protect confidential information from those who do not take part in the proceedings. To this effect, the EU legislator has introduced a *non-exclusive* list of measures, which could be enlarged by Member States while implementing the Directive in their legal systems. Nevertheless, national laws aimed at protecting trade secrets *shall at least include* the three confidentiality measures explicitly provided for in Article 9.2 of the Directive.

The first confidentiality measure concerns the possibility of restricting access to any document – or to evidence, in a broad sense, as set out in the recitals – containing trade secrets, whereas the second confidentiality measure refers to restricting access to hearings – as well as to their record or transcript – where trade secrets could be disclosed. In both cases, a number of persons should be excluded from these access restrictions in order to respect the right to an effective remedy and to a fair trial. This will be decided by Member States when implementing the Directive, but shall include, at least: a natural person from each party, the respective lawyers or other qualified representatives to the proceedings according to national procedural law – for instance, in Spain the *representative ad litem* has been included.[21] However, as it will be explained later,

[19] ECJ, Case C-450/06 (ECLI:EU:C:2008:91), *Varec SA v. État belge*, 14 February 2008, paragraph 28.
[20] ECJ, Case C-450/06 (ECLI:EU:C:2008:91), *Varec SA v. État belge*, 14 February 2008, paragraph 52.
[21] Article 15.2 *in fine* of the Draft Act [Proyecto de Ley de Secretos Empresariales, *Boletín Oficial de las Cortes Generales – Congreso de los Diputados, XII Legislatura*, No. 23-1, 1 June 2018].

the referred persons are also subject to a particular confidentiality requirement that shall remain in force after trade secret proceedings have ended.

The third measure provided for in Article 9.2 consists in making available to the public a non-confidential version of *any* judicial decision by eliminating the parts containing trade secrets. This should be respected regardless of who publishes the decision – and even if the publication is imposed at the expenses of the infringer. Nevertheless, the limited number of persons with full access to documents and hearings – it is, those excluded from the restrictions contained in the first and second confidentiality measures –, should also have access to any judicial decision in its entirety. As a result of this full access, even the infringer according to the judgment on the merits – after being awarded relief the trade secret holder – will obtain a complete court ruling where the information concerning the trade secret has not been removed – however, as it is explained below, the party shall respect the obligation not to use or disclose this secret information.

With regard to these measures aimed at protecting confidential information from those who do not participate in legal proceedings, it should be highlighted that, according to the Directive, its adoption shall be requested by the interested party on a *duly reasoned application*. Thus, when implementing this EU rule, all Member States must recognise the possibility to request them to the plaintiff and to the defendant. However, concerning the adoption of confidentiality measures *ex officio*, the Directive does not set an obligation to enable the judge to take them on its own initiative – conversely, it states that Member States *may also* allow the competent judicial authorities to adopt these measures on their own – and as a result, there could be differences between the national legal systems.[22]

In addition, it should be pointed out that the requirement of confidentiality does not extend to the whole proceedings, but only to those procedural acts involving the disclosure of trade secrets. It is important because the fundamental right *to a fair and public hearing* could be at stake – and, in that sense, it is true that Article 9 of the Directive has been respectful with this right enshrined in Article 47.2 of the Charter of Fundamental Rights of the European Union.[23] This is the reason why both, first, the national legislator when implementing the

---

22 The Directive Proposal limited the adoption of confidentiality measures to the application by a party [European Commission, Proposal for a Directive of the European Parliament and of the Council on the protection of undisclosed know-how and business information (trade secrets) against their unlawful acquisition, use and disclosure, 28 November 2013, COM(2013) 813 final]. However, the Directive finally approved has also introduced the possibility of taking confidentiality measures addressed to those who do not participate in legal proceedings *ex officio*. This enlargement carried out in the final version was a result from the revision made by the Council in its *general approach* to the Trade Secrets Directive Proposal [Council of the European Union, General Approach, 19 May 2014, 9870/14, based on the previous Presidency compromise].

23 R. Knaak, A. Kur and R.M. Hilty, "Comments of the Max Planck Institute for Innovation and Competition on the Proposal for a Directive on the protection of undisclosed know-how

Directive and, then, the judge when deciding on these measures should only derogate the principle of publicity to the extent strictly necessary: if there is a document (evidence), a hearing (as well as its record or transcript) or a judicial decision with secret information.

Concerning the national legislators, although they could go further when implementing these measures, the Directive provision turns out to be *a minimum and a maximum rule*. The reason is that Article 47 of the Charter[24] – in accordance with its Article 52[25] – are acting as a straightjacket to any movement of the Member States in order to provide further protection to confidential information, because the Trade Secrets Directive has already gone far enough while limiting these fundamental rights.[26] This probably explains why the implementations carried out to date have mainly been using *the copy-paste technique*,[27] without adding new measures to those explicitly envisaged under Article 9.2 of the Directive and ensuring the same procedural guarantees to trade secrets in all Member States – the *minimal* provided for the EU regulation.

Concerning the judge, Article 9 of the Directive already provides the aspects that shall be considered when deciding on these measures and assessing their proportionality. The disposition refers explicitly to the legitimate interests of the parties – or third parties – and to any potential harm that could be caused by his decision – granting or rejecting the confidentiality measure. It also states that the competent judicial authority shall take into account the need to ensure the right to an effective remedy, as well as the right to a fair trial, while analysing the opportunity of awarding the measure and the suitability of its extent.

3.2.2. The Measures to Protect Confidential Information from Parties to Legal Proceedings

The second kind of measure is addressed to those who, somehow, take part in legal proceedings. This should include, *at least*, the court officials, the parties and

---

and business information (trade secrets) against their unlawful acquisition, use and disclosure" (2014) 45(8) *IIC – International Review of Intellectual Property and Competition Law* 964.

24 Concerning the right to an effective remedy and to a fair trial, being particularly important its second paragraph on the entitlement to a fair and public hearing.

25 On the requirements that should be met in order to limit the exercise of the fundamental rights recognised in the Charter.

26 It is with good reason that, as Benetó Santa Cruz and Cachón Marinel·lo note, Article 9.2 has *possibly* been the most amended provision of the Trade Secrets Directive during its law-making process ["El proyecto de Directiva Comunitaria relativa a la protección del saber hacer y la información empresarial no divulgada …", n. 13 above, p. 194].

27 Even though, as was the Spanish case, some of these implementations were still drafts or proposals when this chapter was completed. A study of the current situation of the implementation in the different Member States could be performed through EUR-Lex website: https://eur-lex.europa.eu/legal-content/EN/NIM/?uri=CELEX:32016L0943.

their lawyers or representatives and any witnesses or experts. The confidentiality measure consists of *an obligation* not to use or disclose any secret information of which they have become aware due to their participation in legal proceedings. Nevertheless, this measure will only be applied if the judicial authority has *previously* identified the litigated information as confidential.

It means that, according to the Directive, the above-mentioned people are not under the obligation to preserve confidentiality *by the mere fact of participating* in a case involving trade secrets; on the contrary, to have this obligation a prior court order should be issued. As with the measures concerning those who do not participate in legal proceedings, the court order stating the secret nature of the contentious information shall be requested by the interested party – based on a duly reasoned application. Furthermore, if the national legislator has expressly implemented it, the competent judge can act *ex officio* and, as a consequence, those who take part in legal proceedings will be bound by confidentiality.

The obligation of confidentiality provided for in Article 9.1 of the Trade Secrets Directive shall be applied in the course of legal proceedings. Additionally, the duty of preserving confidentiality shall remain in force after proceedings have ended, unless there are reasons to maintain that the information concerned does not meet the requirements to be considered a trade secret – as a result of a judgment on the merits or due to its spreading within the circles that use this information.

Regarding the measures aimed at protecting confidential information from those who participate in legal proceedings, there are some ideas that should be highlighted. First, we could discuss if there was really a need to introduce this provision, as people who participate in legal proceedings as professionals – hence, the parties and witnesses excluded – are subject to deontological rules. In that sense, the express declaration of confidentiality by the judge would help to increase their secrecy character and, for sure, would justify the imposition of special sanctions under the EU trade secrets regulations.

Second, it should be pointed out that Member States are respecting this measure in their implementation – mostly copy-pasting the wording of the Trade Secrets Directive. This protection could have been enlarged, for instance, by considering that the obligation of confidentiality exists since the lawsuit is aimed at protecting an alleged trade secret – that is, without the need for a previous court order stating the secret nature of the information.[28] However, due to the need for respecting the fundamental right to a fair and public hearing[29] – and the above-mentioned exceptions under Article 9.2 – national legislators are

28 The Trade Secrets Directive Proposal automatically required this obligation to those who participated in legal proceedings, but the final version has subjected this duty to the prior existence of a statement of confidentiality made by the competent court, either on its own initiative or in response to an application submitted by the interested party.

29 T. Farkas and P. Koch, "The disclosure – fair trial dilemma ...", n. 5 above, p. 902.

not able to provide further protection to confidential information by restricting access to documents, hearings and the completed judicial decisions to the alleged – or already found – trade secret infringer. In that sense, it seems clear that the EU legislator has decided not to derogate from the adversarial principle by excluding the defendant from the evidence, the observations and those parts of the judgment involving the disclosure of a trade secret.

Nevertheless, in order to guarantee the effectiveness of this confidentiality measure, the national legislators should also implement properly the general obligation under Article 6 of the Directive, which states the need to avoid unreasonable time-limits or unwarranted delays with regard to the measures, procedures and remedies aimed at protecting trade secrets. This is because, from the moment the applicant institutes legal proceedings, until the judge decides on its confidential character, other people different from the trade secret holder will have gained access to the secret information. A possible option in order to protect the information is to grant the confidentiality measure together with the acceptance of the lawsuit: namely, in the same (and initial) court order and without hearing the defendant – notwithstanding the defendant's entitlement to appeal against these measures, particularly once a final judgment is obtained.

3.3. THE PREVIOUS NATIONAL AND SUPRANATIONAL REGULATIONS TO PRESERVE CONFIDENTIALITY

Concerning the *national systems*, some of them already had legal mechanisms to preserve confidentiality, these national instruments could have been applied to protect trade secrets in the course of legal proceedings.[30] In that sense, we should refer to the *in-camera* hearings – that is, when the hearing takes place behind closed doors – in Member States such as the Netherlands or Hungary. The *Düsseldorf procedure*, developed in Germany for patent law – a procedure where the court orders independent proceedings to preserve evidence.[31] As well as the so-called *confidentiality clubs* in the United Kingdom – based on an agreement between the parties to limit the disclosure of information.[32] Furthermore, in some Member States it was even possible to exclude the public from the trade

---

30 For a detailed exposition with regard to the protection of confidentiality in the course of legal proceedings, see European Commission Staff, *Working Document Impact Assessment accompanying the document proposal for a Directive on the protection of undisclosed know-how and business information (trade secrets) against their unlawful acquisition, use and disclosure*, 28 November 2013, SWD(2013) 471 final, Annex 15, pages 216–224.

31 T. Farkas and P. Koch, "The disclosure – fair trial dilemma ...", n. 5 above, pp. 907 and 908.

32 R. Montagnon, "The Trade Secrets Directive – consistency of approach required ...", n. 18 above, p. 643, the author considers that the EU regulation will make available to the rest of the Member States the *confidentiality clubs* already existing in the United Kingdom.

secrets hearings – as was the case of legal systems such as the Bulgarian, the Finnish or the Polish – although, as pointed out by *Baker & McKenzie Final Study on Trade Secrets*, that possibility was infrequently used.[33] Nevertheless, the measures regulated in the Trade Secrets Directive differ from the mentioned national instruments.

Within the *EU legal system*, the Damages Directive already introduced an embryonic idea in 2014. Under its Article 5, the EU legislator obliged Member States to provide their courts with effective measures to protect evidence containing confidential information. However, the guidelines were only set in the recitals (recital (18)), where measures such as in-camera hearings, access restrictions or non-confidential versions were suggested. One might say that this was even a subtler technique to harmonise the civil procedure in the European Union, because when implementing the Directive, some legislators included this non-exclusive list of measures – provided for in the recitals – as part of the binding provisions in their national regulations.[34] As it has been shown in this chapter, with the Trade Secrets Directive the harmonisation of confidentiality in the course of legal proceedings has gone further.

4. FINAL REMARKS

4.1. THE USE OF LEGAL PROCEEDINGS TO PROTECT TRADE SECRETS

In the recent past, legal proceedings aimed at protecting trade secrets were unusual, specially, due to the outlined paradox: the need for disclosing the secret in order to obtain its protection. It is true that this situation is changing in all Member States by means of the harmonisation of confidentiality in the course of trade secrets proceedings. However, the described measures remain something new, therefore, we still need time to verify whether this improves the right to an effective remedy in these particular cases and, as a consequence, it increases the use of trade secrets proceedings in order to obtain civil redress.

---

33 *Final Study on Trade Secrets and Confidential Business Information in the Internal Market*, April 2013, prepared by Baker & McKenzie for the European Commission (Contract number: MARKT/20117128/D), pp. 34 and 35.

34 For instance, by means of the Royal Decree-law 9/2017, the Spanish legislator has introduced the guidelines provided for in the recitals of the Damages Directive in Article 283.*bis*.(b).5 of the Spanish Civil Procedure Act – it is, between the binding provisions – [Real Decreto-ley 9/2017 por el que se transponen directivas de la Unión Europea en los ámbitos financiero, mercantil y sanitario, y sobre el desplazamiento de los trabajadores, *B.O.E.*, No. 126, 27 May 2017, article 4].

4.2. THE IMPLEMENTATION OF CONFIDENTIALITY MEASURES

The deadline for implementing the Trade Secrets Directive was 9 June 2018. At that time, only a few Member States had implemented it – while most of the implementations were still drafts or proposals. For national legislators, to implement the preservation of confidentiality is not an easy task, because they have to introduce new procedural rules – or modify the existing ones – trying to fit them in their legal systems. The study of the implementation carried out so far – including drafts or proposals – shows that most Member States are mainly copy-pasting the confidentiality provisions. As a result, it seems that, more than "a harmonisation" – which is to be expected when the EU instrument is a Directive – we are faced with a "standardisation" concerning these confidentiality measures.

4.3. THE APPLICATION (BY ANALOGY) OF THE CONFIDENTIALITY MEASURES

These confidentiality measures will only be applied in the course of trade secrets proceedings. However, once introduced in a legal system, we cannot exclude its application by analogy in other areas of private law – for instance, they could be notably helpful in evidence for damages, patent litigation or privacy protection. This extension by analogy could be done by the competent judicial authority – when facing the need for preserving confidentiality in a particular case. Furthermore, the national legislator could introduce these confidentiality rules in areas where there is no regulation, or even replace the existing ones. In both cases, this would mean a step further in harmonising national civil procedures, but not only limited to trade secrets proceedings, which was the original Directive's aim.

PROCEDURAL HARMONISATION AND PRIVATE ENFORCEMENT IN THE GDPR

Marta Requejo Isidro*

* This contribution is up to date as of July 2019.

1. INTRODUCTION

Article 8 of the Charter of Fundamental Rights of the European Union, embedded in Chapter II ("Freedoms"), recognises the right to data protection as an independent right:

> 1. Everyone has the right to the protection of personal data concerning him or her.
> 2. Such data must be processed fairly for specified purposes and on the basis of the consent of the person concerned or some other legitimate basis laid down by law. Everyone has the right of access to data which has been collected concerning him or her, and the right to have it rectified.
> 3. Compliance with these rules shall be subject to control by an independent authority.

The right exists as well in the Treaties: according to Article 16.1 TFUE,[1]

> 1. Everyone has the right to the protection of personal data concerning them.

In the secondary legislation, already in the 1990s some pieces had been enacted in relation to natural persons' data, with the double objective of harmonising the protection of the right in respect of processing activities and ensuring the free flow of data between the Member States. The most relevant pieces of legislation in this regard were Directive 95/46/EC on the protection of individuals with regard to the processing of personal data and on the free movement of such data;[2] and Directive 97/66/EC on the processing of personal data and the protection of privacy in the telecommunications sector.[3] The latter was repealed in 2002 by Directive 2002/58/EC, on privacy and electronic communications ("the 'cookies' Directive"),[4] amended in turn in 2009 by Directive 2009/136/EC.[5] The former was repealed by Regulation (EU) 2016/679 on the protection of natural persons

1 Former Article 286 TEC: the contents of the new provision are nevertheless notably different.

2 Directive 95/46/EC of the European Parliament and of the Council of 24 October 1995 on the protection of individuals with regard to the processing of personal data and on the free movement of such data, OJ L 281, 23.11.1995.

3 Directive 97/66/EC of the European Parliament and of the Council of 15 December 1997, on the processing of personal data and the protection of privacy in the telecommunications sector, OJ L 24, 30.1.1998.

4 OJ L 201, 31.7.2002.

5 OJ L 337, 18.12.2009. The Directive is still in force; see nonetheless the Proposal for a Regulation of the European Parliament and of the Council concerning the respect for private life and the protection of personal data in electronic communications and repealing Directive 2002/58/EC (Regulation on Privacy and Electronic Communications), COM/2017/010 final – 2017/03.

with regard to the processing of personal data and on the free movement of such data (GDPR), which entered into force in 2016 and is fully applicable since 25 May 2018.[6]

The Preamble to the GDPR acknowledges that the principles underlying Directive 95/46/CE remain sound. This notwithstanding, the need was felt to repeal the Directive and enact new rules for two reasons. First of all, rapid technological developments and globalisation had brought new challenges for the protection of personal data. Second of all, the Directive did not prevent fragmentation in the implementation of data protection across the Union, and

> differences in the level of protection of the rights and freedoms of natural persons, in particular the right to the protection of personal data, with regard to the processing of personal data in the Member States may prevent the free flow of personal data throughout the Union.[7]

As a reaction, the GDPR sets out in detail and reinforces the rights of data subjects; it emphasises the obligations of controllers and processors, and provides for equivalent powers to ensure compliance with the rules and sanctions for infringements, in all Member States.

The "provision for powers" just mentioned is not only addressed to the public authorities; it benefits the data subject too. To be sure, the GDPR privileges public enforcement, but provides as well for a right of the data subject to an effective judicial remedy, where he or she considers that his or her rights under the Regulation have been infringed as a result of the processing of his or her personal data in non-compliance with it (Article 79). Scholars claim the GDPR strengthens the right to an effective judicial remedy and facilitates private enforcement actions.[8] At a first glance, in view of provisions such

---

6 Regulation (EU) 2016/679 of the European Parliament and of the Council of 27 April 2016 on the protection of natural persons with regard to the processing of personal data and on the free movement of such data, and repealing Directive 95/46/EC, OJ L 119 4.5.2016. Further instruments address the protection of personal data in specific domains: see the Directive (EU) 2016/680 of the European Parliament and of the Council, of 27 April 2016, on the protection of natural persons with regard to the processing of personal data by competent authorities for the purposes of the prevention, investigation, detection or prosecution of criminal offences or the execution of criminal penalties, and on the free movement of such data, and repealing Council Framework Decision 2008/977/JHA, OJ L 119, 4.5.2016). Not personal data. Regarding non-personal data see the recent Regulation (EU) 2018/1807 of the European Parliament and of the Council of 14 November 2018 on a framework for the free flow of non-personal data in the European Union, OJ L 303, 28.11.2018.

7 The EU focus regarding personal data has always combined the concern to facilitate the free flow and trade of data (in light of its direct impact in other economy sectors, such as the purchase of services and goods on line) with the fundamental right approach.

8 Recently L. Lundstedt, "International Jurisdiction over Cross-Border Private enforcement Actions under the GDPR", *Stockholm Faculty of Law, Research Paper Series no. 57*, at 214.

as Article 79 just mentioned, or in Article 80 on representative actions, this opinion can be shared. Furthermore, it could be added that by offering to the individual procedural tools to support the defence of his/her right in court, the GDPR contributes to the harmonisation of civil procedural law within the EU. On a second look, however, it appears that the impact of the GDPR may not be so significant, either in relation to private enforcement or to procedural harmonisation. In what follows we will present the pertinent GDPR rules in context; at a second stage we will assess them from the perspective of their relevance both to private enforcement and to the harmonisation of procedural rules in the EU.

2. SETTING THE SCENE

2.1. COMMON DATA PROTECTION VIOLATIONS

In 2014, the European Union Agency for Fundamental Rights (FRA) conducted a survey of 16 Member States on the access to data protection remedies in EU Member States.[9] Among other issues, interviewees were asked about the type of data protection violations faced in the previous three years. The answers provided can be accepted as still holding true:[10] already by then the most commonly reported violations related to internet-based activities – social media, online shopping, hacking of email accounts, security breaches and misuse of personal data by global internet companies, involving some kind data processing, i.e. collection, storage, disclosure, dissemination.[11] Illustrative examples were the unjustified transfer of personal data from data controllers to third parties (for instance, from credit institutions to debt collection companies); improper and excessive collection and storage of personal data by supermarket chains, without legitimate purpose and guarantees of security; manipulation of data stored and processed legally; unlawful disclosure of personal data to unauthorised persons; publication of personal data in the media or on the internet; refusal to correct, delete and block information in personal data files. Video surveillance at the work place or in the public spaces, direct marketing and commercial prospecting without the consent of the recipient, as well as selling personal data to third parties, were also mentioned.[12]

---

9 https://fra.europa.eu/en/publication/2014/access-data-protection-remedies-eu-member-states (last visited 14.02.2019).

10 Cf. Recital 85 GDPR.

11 FRA Study (n. 9 above) under para. 3.1, at 25.

12 Ibid., at 26.

2.2. THE LEGAL BACKGROUND PRIOR TO 25 MAY 2018

For the purposes of this chapter it should be noted that under Article 22 Directive 95/46/EC (Remedies), Member States were obliged to make a judicial remedy available for any breach of the rights guaranteed by the national law applicable to the data processing. Article 23 of the Directive (Liability) addressed the right to compensation from the controller in case of damage having been suffered as a result of an unlawful processing operation, or of any act incompatible with the national provisions adopted pursuant to the Directive. In spite of these possibilities private enforcement was very seldom used to support data protection: scholars' writings,[13] as well as the 2014 Survey mentioned above, show that very few victims of data protection violations filed for an injunction or for compensation – to the point that some of the interviewees could not recall one single civil case on the subject matter during their careers.[14] At the theoretical level this may be explained by a conceptual hesitation in the Directive: entitled "(Directive) on the protection of individuals with regard to the processing of personal data and on the free movement of such data", its recitals refer to the protection of "fundamental rights and freedoms", adding "notably the right to privacy" (Recitals 2, 7, 10, 11, 68; see as well Article 1). However, data protection and privacy are different rights; a violation of the former may perfectly well take place without touching upon the latter.[15] Data protection can actually be described as a "hybrid". On the one hand it works as a guarantee for other fundamental rights, particularly the right to privacy; combined, the protection of privacy and of personal data underpin the right to a private life and the individual's dignity. On the other hand, data protection is an independent right: in the face of the threats derived from new technologies, personal data protection is needed to further the scope of protection provided by traditional rights, but also to ensure personal freedom. Here, the fundamental right to personal data protection goes beyond the boundaries of privacy and is not any longer instrumental to it;[16] it involves the empowerment of the individual to control the access to, and the

---

13 See D. Korff, "New Challenges to Data Protection Study – Comparative Chart: Divergences between Data Protection Laws in the EU" (February 15, 2010), European Commission DG Justice, Freedom and Security Report. Available at SSRN: https://ssrn.com/abstract=1638951 or http://dx.doi.org/10.2139/ssrn.1638951 (last visited 14.02.2019). L. Bygrave, *Data Privacy Law*, Oxford University Press, 2014, at 178.

14 FRA Study (n. 9 above), at 32, referring to Finland. L. Bygrave (n. 13 above): national courts are increasingly generating data privacy jurisprudence, but the development is slow.

15 See O. Lynskey, *The Foundations of EU Data Protection Law*, Oxford University Press, 2015, in particular Part I, Chapter 4, on the relationship between data protection and privacy.

16 In this sense already in the 1990s, the decision of the Spanish Constitutional Court 254/1993, 20.07.1993, *BOE* No. 197, 18.08.1993, para. 6 of the legal grounds.

availability of, personal information, and can thus be referred to as the "right to informational self-determination".[17] This dual dimension[18] of the protection of personal data was not clear under Directive 95/46/EC. The ambiguity probably accounts for the difficulties in identifying the violations and associated harms in the domain of data protection as legally actionable *per se*.[19]

In practice, in their path to the civil courts data subjects faced multiple obstacles, both legal and factual. On the factual side it is worth mentioning that data protection breaches are often "hidden": the data subject only becomes aware as a result of further problems experienced in his/her daily life, or at work.[20] Moreover, data protection breaches do not necessarily result in a financial loss; actually, the commonest harms of data processing are intangible – "a feeling of helplessness and unease", due to the information asymmetries between the controllers and processors and the individuals whose data are processed; a "chilling effect on individual behaviour", consequent to the impression of being monitored and under surveillance; the "erosion of the ability of the individual to self-present" in a manner they are comfortable with; the apprehension of future harm.[21] The very nature of the damage may work as a barrier to claiming redress: individuals may not identify the harm as actionable; they may prefer to forget the situation for fear of worsening it, and/or have concerns about anonymity and confidentiality. Often, the perception that the controller or processor are too powerful, and that the offence is too common to be socially considered as a real violation, deters the data subject from going to court.[22] Particularly in some Member States the amount of damages awarded for data protection violations actually supported this conviction of unworthiness: for instance, before 2014 the greatest award for distress in an English reported case was £750, with a nominal £1 for financial loss (*Halliday v. Creation Consumer Finance*).[23]

---

17 The identicality of the translation to different languages ("Recht auf informationelle Selbstbestimmung"; "derecho a la autodeterminación informativa"; "droit à l'autonomie informationnelle") cannot be taken for granted.

18 For a third theoretical approach to data and data protection in support of regulating data as property see O. Lynskey (n. 15 above), Part II, Chapter 7; J. Ritter, A. Mayer, "Regulating Data as Property: A New Construct for Moving Forward" (2018) 16 *Duke Law & Technology Review* 220.

19 According to the FRA Study mentioned above (n. 9 above, p. 26), often the data protection violations were only identified after a violation of privacy had taken place.

20 Ibid., p. 27. O. Lynskey (n. 15 above), at 212.

21 *Halliday v. Creation Consumer Finance* O. Lynskey (n. 15 above), Chapter 6, under E. See as well FRA Study (n. 9 above), under 3.2. Reported financial damages are usually of minor importance; they relate to refusal of access to credit, financial losses due to identity theft, and costs incurred on telephone calls, postage and having records accessed and amended.

22 FRA Study (n. 9 above), at 30–31.

23 See S. Atkinson, "Privacy and data protection cases: quantifying damages for distress", 23.02.2017: https://www.brownejacobson.com/training-and-resources/resources/legal-updates/2017/02/privacy-and-data-protection-cases-quantifying-damages-for-distress (last visited 13.02.2019). The author continues: "Contrast this with awards in privacy cases, such as

In addition to the factual obstacles, procedural hindrances played a role as well in the decision not to sue or to claim for compensation: common factors accounting for self-restraint were the duration of the civil proceedings (compared with those for administrative redress); the costs, to be borne, at least initially, by the claimant and unforeseeable, but presumably high, especially due to the need to hire a lawyer familiar with a complex subject matter; and the difficulties related to the gathering of evidence and to the burden of proof – in particular regarding internet-based activities.[24] It is interesting to note that in some legal systems a private law action for data protection infringements is of recent origin – or does not even exist; the same goes for the type of actionable damage.[25]

3. THE GDPR AND PRIVATE ENFORCEMENT

3.1. "PUTTING INDIVIDUALS IN CONTROL OF THEIR PERSONAL DATA"

In its Communication to the European Parliament, the Council, the European Economic and Social Committee and the Committee of the Regions, entitled "Safeguarding Privacy in a Connected World. A European Data Protection Framework for the 21st Century", of 2012,[26] the Commission acknowledged that individuals

> ... feel they are not in control of their data. They are not properly informed of what happens to their personal information, to whom it is transmitted and for what purposes. Often, they do not know how to exercise their rights online.

As a consequence, new legislative acts were needed "to strengthen rights, to give people efficient and operational means to make sure they are fully informed about what happens to their personal data and to enable them to exercise their rights more effectively." Administrative and judicial remedies had to be enhanced for the case of breach of data protection rights; the Commission mentioned expressly "qualified associations" being able to bring actions to court on behalf of the individual.[27]

---

in the leading case of *Gulati & Ors v MGN Limited* (confirmed by the Court of Appeal in *Representative Claimants v MGN Limited*), where the court awarded various celebrities who were victims of phone hacking between £72,500 and £260,250 to compensate for the distress they had suffered."

24 FRA Study (n. 9 above), under para. 4.1.

25 D. Svantesson, "Enforcing Privacy Across Different Jurisdictions" in D. Wright, P. de Hert (eds.), *Enforcing Privacy. Regulatory, Legal and Technological Approaches*, Springer, 2016, pp. 195–222, at 211, 214.

26 COM(2012) 9 final, 21.01.2012.

27 Ibid., at 6.

The GDPR takes up and gives legislative shape to the "individual's control over personal data" principle. At the substantive level, it strengthens existing subjective rights and provides for more in Chapter III: the right of access, the rights to rectification and erasure, the right to obtain from the controller restriction of processing, right to data portability, right to object to the processing of personal data, and not to be subject to a decision based solely on automated processing, including profiling. Both the right to obtain restriction of processing – Article 18 – and to data portability – Article 20 – are new. The obligations of controller and processor, grouped largely under Chapter IV, are increased and refined. Of the utmost relevance are the rules on information – what it encompasses and how it shall be communicated – enabling the data subject to exercise his/her rights. Regarding the minimum information that data controllers must convey about the collection and processing of data received from the data subject, or from third parties, by explicit mandate of Article 12[28] the controller must take appropriate measures to provide it in a concise, transparent, intelligible and easily accessible form, using clear and plain language, in particular when the information is addressed specifically to a child. The right of access of the data subject under Article 15[29] is fine-tuned relative to Directive 95/46/EC: data subjects are entitled to information such as the envisaged period for which the personal data will be stored (or the criteria used to determine that period), or the source of the data when they have not been collected from the data subject. In addition, according to Article 15 the controller must provide for free a copy of the personal data undergoing processing. Article 17[30] sets out the circumstances for the exercise of the right to erasure, and as a complement, Article 19[31] imposes on the controller the obligation to communicate any rectification or erasure of personal data, or restriction of processing, to each recipient to whom the personal data have been disclosed.

Further provisions secure the position of the data subject *vis-à-vis* the controller, but also the processor. For our purposes one of the most relevant rules in this regard relates to the right of compensation and liability: according to Article 82,[32] any person who has suffered material or non-material damage as a result of an infringement of the Regulation shall have the right to receive compensation from the controller or processor for the damage suffered.

In order to ensure obedience to the rules the GDPR provides as well for enforcement mechanisms under Chapter VIII, including a private prong. Pursuant

---

28 Entitled "Transparent information, communication and modalities for the exercise of the rights of the data subject". Often the obligations to inform are nuanced, or conditional upon elements such as the proportionality of the effort on the side of the controller.

29 "Right of access by the data subject".

30 "Right to erasure" ("right to be forgotten").

31 "Notification obligation regarding rectification or erasure of personal data or restriction of processing."

32 "Right to compensation and liability."

to Article 79,[33] the data subject has a right to an effective judicial remedy against a controller or processor; the right to compensation for damages, as well as rules on liability, is set up by Article 82 as indicated. Both provisions find an immediate precedent in the Directive 95/46/EC: the former corresponds to Article 22, the latter to Article 23. The scope of the current rules, in particular of Article 82, is nevertheless much broader. Moreover, the GDP Regulation backs private claims with procedural tools which were not foreseen under the Directive (see below, under section 3.2). From a practical viewpoint the support to private enforcement can be explained by reference to the weaknesses of the Data Protection Authorities – currently "supervisory authorities", involving both factual and legal issues: lack of financial and human resources, lack of independence and/or transparency.[34] In cross-border settings, this weakness gets more severe due to the typical unwillingness of states to recognise and enforce foreign decisions given in the domain of administrative, public and criminal law: private law judgements do not face a similar *a priori* rejection.[35] Conceptually, enhanced private enforcement represents another step towards the empowerment of individuals, in line with the very essence of the fundamental right to personal data protection.

3.2. TOOLS PERTAINING TO PROCEDURE

Throughout the GDPR several rules pertaining to (civil) procedure can be identified, and grouped as follows.

3.2.1. *Rules on International Jurisdiction and Parallel Pending Proceedings*

The rise of the internet has resulted in the exponential growth of situations of a cross-border nature. Directive 95/46/EC pre-dated these developments: this may explain why it did not include any rule on international jurisdiction.[36] The grounds for jurisdiction were to be found in other EU Regulations – in particular, in Regulation (EU) No. 1215/2012, of the European Parliament and of the Council,[37] or the instruments preceding it – when applicable; otherwise,

---

33 "Right to an effective judicial remedy against a controller or processor."

34 FRA Study (n. 9 above), under 4.2. Cf. Chapter VI of the GDPR.

35 D. Svantesson (n. 25 above), at 211.

36 In terms of applicable law, Article 4 addressed the delimitation – territorial scope – of the EU national provisions adopted pursuant to the Directive. It could therefore be understood as a conflict of law rule (incomplete, though: for instance, the case of a controller established in several Member States was not solved).

37 Regulation (EU) No. 1215/2012 of the European Parliament and of the Council of 12 December 2012 on jurisdiction and the recognition and enforcement of judgments in civil and commercial matters, OJ L 351, 20.12.2012.

in the legal systems of the Member States. By contrast, the GDPR includes rules on international jurisdiction: according to Article 79.2,

> Proceedings against a controller or a processor shall be brought before the courts of the Member State where the controller or processor has an establishment. Alternatively, such proceedings may be brought before the courts of the Member State where the data subject has his or her habitual residence ....

Recital 145 makes it clear that the choice is given to the plaintiff. Recital 147 explains that general jurisdiction rules such as those of Regulation (EU) No. 1215/2012 should not prejudice the application of the GDPR specific rules.

Additionally, the GDPR anticipates in Article 81 a situation of parallel proceedings pending before competent courts in different Member States. Courts are instructed to get in contact to confirm that this is the situation; should this be the case, any court other than the one first seised may suspend the proceedings; if the proceedings are pending in the first instance, the court may decline jurisdiction if the court first seised has jurisdiction over the actions in question and its law permits the consolidation thereof. The wording of the provision is all inclusive: at least at first sight it could be equally applied to judicial proceedings for a remedy against a decision of a supervisory authority, or to a civil remedy between private parties.

3.2.2. Rules on Standing

Pursuant to Article 80 GDPR,[38] not-for-profit bodies, organisations or associations satisfying specific requirements are entitled to exercise the right to lodge a complaint with a supervisory authority, and the right to a judicial remedy (against a supervisory authority, or against a controller or processor) of the data subject on his/her behalf. Where provided for by Member State law and subject to the mandate from the holder of the right, the above-listed bodies may also exercise the right to receive compensation.

3.2.3. Rules on Evidence

Although with varying intensity, several provisions of the GDPR can be read as relating to evidence and proof.

Article 5 GDPR, on the principles relating to processing of personal data, lays down the principle of "proactive responsibility", which encompasses both actual compliance with data protection principles and obligations, and – more relevant for the purposes of this chapter – the ability to prove it: "The controller

[38] See also Recital 142.

shall be responsible for, and be able to demonstrate compliance with, paragraph 1". Further provisions in the operative text of the Regulation tune up the obligations of controller and processor, stressing anew the need to be able to demonstrate compliance. Moreover, the Regulation lists features which may be used as elements in that demonstration. In particular, adherence to approved codes of conduct (in the sense of Article 40, "Codes of conduct") or approved certification mechanisms (in the sense of Article 42, "Certification") may be used as an element by which to demonstrate compliance with the obligations: see Articles 24.3, 25.3, 28.5, 32.3, and 35.8. The same idea appears in the Recitals: when the processing is to be carried out by the processor on behalf of the controller, the adherence of the processor to an approved code of conduct or an approved certification mechanism may be used as a means to demonstrate compliance with the obligations of the controller and/or processor (Recital 81).

Pursuant to Article 6 the lawfulness of data processing is conditional upon several requirements, one of them being the consent of the data subject. Should processing be based on consent, the controller must be able to demonstrate that the data subject has consented to the processing of his or her personal data (Article 7, Recital 42). Moreover, consent must be freely given; it will be presumed not to be freely given if it does not allow separate consent to be given to different personal data processing operations despite it being appropriate in the individual case, or if the performance of a contract, including the provision of a service, is made dependent on the consent despite such consent not being necessary for such performance (Article 7, Recital 43).

As a rule, a controller cannot refuse to act on the request of the data subject for exercising his or her rights under Articles 15 to 22 even in cases where processing does not require identification of the data subject for the purposes of complying with the Regulation; however, the controller will be exempted if it demonstrates that it is not itself in a position to identify the data subject (Article 12.2). Where requests from a data subject are manifestly unfounded or excessive, in particular because of their repetitive character, the controller may charge a fee or refuse to act on the request; it must bear the burden of demonstrating the manifestly unfounded or excessive character of the request (Article 12.5).

Article 21 GDPR establishes the right of the data subject to object. In case of objection the controller must no longer process the personal data unless it demonstrates compelling legitimate grounds for the processing which override the interests, rights and freedoms of the data subject or for the establishment, exercise or defence of legal claims.[39]

[39] See as well Recital 69: "It should be for the controller to demonstrate that its compelling legitimate interest overrides the interests or the fundamental rights and freedoms of the data subject."

According to Article 82, on the right to compensation and liability, a controller or processor shall be exempt from liability for the damage caused by processing which infringes the Regulation (the controller), or where it has not complied with obligations of the Regulation specifically directed to processors, or where it has acted outside or contrary to lawful instructions of the controller (the processor), if it proves that it is not in any way responsible for the event giving rise to the damage.

3.2.4. *Rules on Remedies*

Data subjects have the right to lodge a complaint before the competent courts of the Member States in accordance with Article 79, and to obtain redress and compensation under Article 82. Pursuant to the latter, the claim for compensation may be lodged against the controller and/or the processor, by any person who has suffered material or non-material damage as a result of an infringement of the Regulation. As stated above, it is not impossible to be exempted from liability, but the standard of proof is high: a controller or processor must prove that it is not *in any way* responsible for the event giving rise to the damage (emphasis added).

On the scope of the remedy, according to Recital 146 the concept of damage should be broadly interpreted in the light of the case law of the Court of Justice, in a manner which fully reflects the objectives of the Regulation.

3.2.5. *Out of Court Proceedings, ADR*

Private enforcement refers typically to litigation in the courts; however, other alternative mechanisms are available and may get to the desired outcome in a quicker and less expensive manner, such as *ombuds* systems.[40] The GDPR is quite succinct in this respect: out-of-court procedures are just mentioned as a possible content of codes of conduct to be prepared by associations and other bodies representing categories of controllers or processors for the purpose of specifying the application of the Regulation; they shall not prejudice the rights of data subjects pursuant to Articles 77 and 79 (Article 40.2(k) GDPR).

4. ASSESSMENT

The analysis of the procedural elements offered by the GDPR to support private enforcement leads to the following conclusions in terms of harmonisation (4.1 below), and *vis-à-vis* the purported effort to enhance private enforcement (4.2 below).

---

40 Briefly, C. Hodges, "Delivering Data Protection: Trust and Ethical Culture" (2018) 4 *European Data Protection Law Review* 65, 78.

4.1. HARMONISATION

To some extent the GDPR is a Regulation worded as a Directive. It expressly grants a margin of manoeuvre for Member States to specify – even to restrict – its rules in relation to particular areas of data processing (see for instance Recital 10, Recital 129).[41] Divergence at the level of the implementation of the Regulation is to be expected as a consequence of open-ended or incomplete provisions which – for the purposes of the judicial application of the rules – open the door to the procedural autonomy of the Member States. Uniform interpretation may prove to be difficult too.

4.1.1. Rules on International Jurisdiction and Parallel Proceedings

Article 79.2 GDPR is a clear provision only on the surface. Its wording actually casts doubts on how it relates to other grounds of international jurisdiction (particularly those of the Regulation (EU) No. 1215/2012), and whether they remain available only as ancillary rules. An example would be a dispute involving a data subject without residence in the EU but who is in the EU, and a controller without an establishment in any EU Member State; the processing of the data of the former may still fall under the scope of the GDPR pursuant to Article 3.2,[42] but none of the grounds of Article 79.2 are given.[43] Interpretative doubts arise as well about the meaning of "establishment" – scholars claim that the Regulation, by using in Recital 22 the same wording as Directive 45/96/EC, takes up the case law of the CJEU on the latter,[44] – and of "habitual residence" of the

41 That is why Member States may, as far as necessary for coherence and for making the national provisions comprehensible to the persons to whom they apply, incorporate elements of the Regulation into their national law (Recital 8).

42 "This Regulation applies to the processing of personal data of data subjects who are in the Union by a controller or processor not established in the Union, where the processing activities are related to: (a) the offering of goods or services, irrespective of whether a payment of the data subject is required, to such data subjects in the Union; or (b) the monitoring of their behaviour as far as their behaviour takes place within the Union."

43 Cf. M. Requejo Isidro, "La aplicación privada del derecho para la protección de las personas físicas en materia de tratamiento de datos personales en el reglamento (UE) 2016/679" (2017) 42 *La Ley Mercantil* 1, para. IV.2.a; and the different view of A. Pato, "The Collective Private Enforcement of Data Protection Rights in the EU" in L. Cadiet/B. Hess/M. Requejo (eds.), *Privatizing Dispute Resolution and Its Limits*, Nomos, 2019, text to fn. 47, with further references.

44 M. Gömman, "The New Territorial Scope of EU Data Protection Law: Deconstructing a Revolutionary Achievement" (2017) 54 *Common Market Law Review* 567, 570–574; P. de Miguel Asensio, "Aspectos internacionales de la protección de datos: las sentencias Shrems y Weltimmo del Tribunal de Justicia" (2015) 31 *La Ley Unión Europea* 1–10; P. de Miguel Asensio, "Competencia y Derecho aplicable en el Reglamento General sobre Protección de Datos de la Unión Europea" (2017) 69 *Revista española de Derecho internacional* 75, para. 12.

data subject.[45] Moreover, in light of the ECJ case law on the interpretation of the grounds for jurisdiction set up for the protection of weak parties in cross-border litigation, whether a representative action in the sense of Article 80 GDPR can be brought before the court of the habitual residence of one or several of the represented data subjects is disputable.[46]

Moving to the rule on parallel pending proceedings in Article 81, in light of the wording the provision could apply both to judicial proceedings for a remedy against a decision of a supervisory authority, or to those for a civil remedy between private parties. Recital 144 points to a different understanding, though: literally it restraints the scope of the rule to a situation

> ... where a court seised of proceedings against a decision by a supervisory authority has reason to believe that proceedings concerning the same processing, such as the same subject matter as regards processing by the same controller or processor, or the same cause of action, are brought before a competent court in another Member State.

4.1.2. Rules on Standing (and on the Identification of the Defendant)

On the side of the claimant, Article 80, on representative actions, is a GDPR example of an open provision implemented (or to be implemented) in the Member States in different ways.[47] A comparative analysis of several EU systems concludes that, as expected,[48] the conditions regarding standing of the interested not-for-profit body, organisation or association to bring proceedings, differ. In addition, today some Member States offer broader advantages than the GDPR – e.g., the Spanish model allows representative entities to bring actions for compensation without having been mandated by the data subject; standing to sue benefits a number of actors not referred to by the Regulation, such as groups of individuals gathered *ad hoc*, just for the purposes of bringing a claim;[49] in the UK a representative claim may be filed by an individual on behalf of a class.[50]

---

45 At the EU level there is no single definition of "habitual residence", but one which may vary depending on the legal context (family law, child abduction, social security law) where it is used.

46 See Case C-498/16, EU:C:2018:37; M. Requejo Isidro, "Max Schrems Against Facebook. CJEU, case C-498/16", *MPI Working Paper series*, 2018 (4), at 10.

47 It is worth noting that the Proposal for a Regulation of the European Parliament and of the Council concerning the respect for private life and the protection of personal data in electronic communications and repealing Directive 2002/58/EC does not provide for representative actions. Pursuant to the Explanatory Memorandum "All matters concerning the processing of personal data not specifically addressed by the proposal are covered by the GDPR". It is legitimate to ask whether this is one of those matters.

48 See already M. Requejo Isidro (n. 43 above), under para. III.2.a.

49 M. Requejo Isidro, n. 43 above; A. Pato (n. 43 above), under para, 2.2.

50 Although after *Lloyd v. Google LLC* [2018] EWHC 2599 (QB) the conditions of availability will certainly not be easy to meet.

On the side of the defendant, difficulties and divergence are predictable, having in mind the vagueness of the category – in particular that of "controller" – still in the process of determination. Indeed, a definition has been provided in the Regulation, Article 4.7 (for the controller) and 8 (for the processor). However, as we will see below, the real problem does not lie with the lack of a legal concept, but rather with the identification of those falling under its scope.

4.1.3. Rules on Evidence

The exact implications of the requirement that controllers must "be able to demonstrate compliance", which appears all through the GDPR, are unclear. To start with, the Regulation does not state whether the obligation exists *vis-à-vis* the data subject or the supervisory authorities, or both.[51] As a consequence, to the question whether the duty is tantamount to a reversed burden of proof, scholars hesitate: "On peut se demander si cette répartition de la charge de la prevue n'est pas modifié du fait de l'existence d'un nouveau principe introduit par le RGPD."[52] Conclusions differ from the assertion

> Since pursuant to para.1 [Article 7] the controller bears the *burden of proof* for the issuance of consent and its scope,[53] (emphasis added)

to

> [the obligation to demonstrate compliance] does not result in a shifting of the burden of proof ... [Since] accountability is not a right of the data subject ... the ability to demonstrate compliance is not a legal obligation but may help to fulfil the burden of proof;[54]
>
> At the very least, the argument can be made that the provisions of the GDPR regarding accountability ... reinforce the notion that the controller is in fact 'best placed' to proffer evidence of the measures it has taken to ensure compliance.

---

51 *A priori*, its violation could be sanctioned with a fine pursuant to Article 83 (see nonetheless A. Ingold, "Article 7" in Sydow (ed.), *Europaïsche Datenschutzgrundverordnung*, 2nd edn., Nomos, 2018, p. 445, para. 53, claiming it may be a disproportionate reaction). Additionally, Article 30.4 and Recital 82 could be read as limiting the duty to the relationship with the supervisory authorities.

52 K. Rosier, A. Delforge, "Le régime de la responsabilité civile du responsable du traitement et du sous-traitant dans le RGPD" in C. de Terwangne/K. Rosier (eds.), Le Règlement Général sur la protection des Données (RGPD), Larcier, 2018, 665, 682.

53 L. Feiler, N. Forgó, M. Weigl, *The EU General Data Protection Regulation* (GDPR): *A Commentary*, GLP, 2018, p. 87 (bold in original). In the same lines, A. Bensoussan, *Tèglement Européen sur la Protection des données*, 2nd edn., Bruylant, 2018, 105.

54 L. Feiler, N. Forgó, M. Weigl (n. 53 above), at 76.

> Even if the legal burden of proof is still borne by the data subject, the evidential burden of proof should de facto shift to the controller as soon as the data subject has offered prima facie evidence of an unlawful processing activity.[55]

4.1.4. Rules on Remedies

The GDPR is silent regarding relevant aspects of civil remedies; different interpretations are thus to be expected. For instance, no reference is made to preventive measures: literally they are not admissible under the GDPR,[56] for, according to Article 79,

> ... each data subject shall have the right to an effective judicial remedy where he or she considers that his or her rights under this Regulation *have been infringed* as a result of [a] processing ... in non-compliance with this Regulation. (emphasis added)

Regarding injunctions, doubts are likely to arise regarding the territorial scope of the obligation to erase or to rectify personal data. They have been left to be decided by the courts, or by the CJEU.[57]

Moving to compensation – Article 82 – there is no mention in the GDPR to treble or punitive damages awards, either to include or to forbid them. Recital 146 could be read as pointing to their exclusion – "Data subjects should receive full and effective compensation for the damage they have suffered" – but a different understanding could be supported by another sentence of the text – "The concept of damage should be broadly interpreted in the light of the case-law of the Court of Justice in a manner which fully reflects the objectives of this Regulation". Indeed, the assertion might only relate to the concept of damages encompassing material and non-material ones (as expressly stated under Article 82), in order to avoid doubts about the latter: it is worth recalling that awards of moral damages in the field are a recent development in some Member States.[58]

---

55 B. Van Alsenoy, "Liability under EU Data Protection Law: From Directive 95/46 to the General Data Protection Regulation" (2016) 7(3) *Journal of Intellectual Property, Information Technology and E-Commerce Law (JIPITEC)* 271, under 3.1.3.

56 Preventive measures are addressed in Recital 137, Article 62.7, Article 66, in the context of joint operations of supervisory authorities and the consistency mechanism.

57 See the conclusions of AG Szpunar to Case C-136/17, *G.C., A.F., B.H., E.D. v. Commission nationale de l'informatique et des libertés (CNIL)*, EU:C:2019:14, and Case C-505/17, *Groupe Léa Nature v. EUIPO*, EU:C:2019:15, both of 10 January 2019. See also his conclusions to Case C-18/18, *Glawischnig-Piesczek*, EU:C:2019:458, of 04 June 2019.

58 The typical example is the UK, see *Google Inc. v. Vidal Hall*, [2016] QB 1003, [2015] EWCA Civ 311.

Still on compensation, the wording of Article 82 is unclear as to whether the mere violation of data protection rules, without any additional harm, could be a ground for a claim for compensation.[59] Furthermore, the provision does not address the calculation of damages, in spite of the very different practices in the Member States (in some of them the calculation methods are established by the law-maker; in others they are left to the courts), especially in relation to moral damages.[60]

Lastly, the difference in the wording of Article 79 on the right to an effective remedy, which benefits the data subject, and of Article 82 on the right to compensation, where the entitlement is general ("Any person"), is not explained in the text and may result, as well, in a divergent application of the provisions in the Member States.

4.1.5. Out of Court Proceedings, ADR

While the GDPR contemplates the enforcement of the rights of the data subject by means of ADR, it does not provide for a framework where relevant questions could be answered uniformly. For instance, on the relation between out-of-court proceedings and the rest of the remedies, Article 40 requires indeed that they do not prejudice the rights of data subjects pursuant to Articles 77 and 79, but what the actual margin of flexibility is remains open.

The Regulation is vague as well about the implementation procedures of the right to rectification (Article 16) or the right to erasure (Article 17), which are certainly acknowledged, but not coupled with a common procedure for having them enforced; as a consequence controllers choose their own ways to comply. The Regulation does not even set up a deadline – the only time requirement pursuant to Articles 16 and 17 is that rectification and erasure shall be obtained

---

59 In favour, Center on Regulation in Europe (CERRE), *Consumer privacy in network industries – a CERRE policy report*, 25.01.2016, available at: http://www.cerre.eu/sites/cerre/files/160125_CERRE_Privacy_Final.pdf, p. 58. The recent UK decision *Lloyd v. Google* [2018] EWHC 2599 (QB), para. 55 ff. – still applying the Data Protection Act 1998 – would point to the contrary.

60 A. Galetta, P. de Hert, "The Proceduralisation of Data protection Remedies under EU Data Protection Law: Towards a More Effective and Data Subject-oriented Remedial System" (2015) 8(1) *Review of European Administrative Law* 125, 149, regret that the EU law-maker has neither fixed thresholds for compensation awards, nor established any other tailored form of compensation, along the lines of those existing for passengers' rights. Looking beyond the EU, other jurisdictions which have recently adopted rules on data protection provide for lists of relevant factors. See for instance the California Consumer Privacy Act of 2018 (approved June 28, 2018; into effect as of January 2020), s. 1798.150: "In assessing the amount of statutory damages, the court shall consider any one or more of the relevant circumstances presented by any of the parties to the case, including, but not limited to, the nature and seriousness of the misconduct, the number of violations, the persistence of the misconduct, the length of time over which the misconduct occurred, the wilfulness of the defendant's misconduct, and the defendant's assets, liabilities, and net worth."

"without an undue delay". Nor does it address the judicial follow up of a refusal to remove or to erase the data – something which indeed happens in practice.[61]

4.2. PRIVATE ENFORCEMENT

4.2.1. Tools for Private Enforcement: First Sight Evaluation

Private enforcement rests on the will and initiative of the individuals to go to court. Generally speaking, procedural tools supporting such will and promoting private enforcement can be grouped into three categories:

a. Regarding access: representative actions; rules on costs and on fees; funding opportunities; disclosure (for instance of the identity of the defendant).
b. Regarding incentives to engage in litigation (for parties and lawyers): rules on remedies (damages, particularly opening the door to punitive or treble damages; privacy-specific remedies, such as those to restore a reputational harm).
c. Regarding empowerment for litigation: they relate to evidence, means of proof, burden of proof, standard of proof, discovery; and also, to the interaction between private/public enforcement (follow-on actions, the evidentiary value of administrative decisions in civil procedures).

Having in mind those elements, and particularly if compared to the legal framework under Directive 95/46/EC, the GDPR may be regarded as a step forward. The rules on disclosure and information, representative actions, international jurisdiction, or evidence, place the data subject in a much better position to defend his/her rights than before. Suffice it to recall a case like *Richardson v. Facebook*, where the claimant applied for permission to appeal against a master's rejection of her claims for damages for libel and breach of her right to respect for her private life, and for a question to be referred to the European Court of Justice for a preliminary ruling.[62] She had brought actions after a profile and a blog, which purported to have been created by her but which she maintained were fakes, were published on two websites; under this profile personal information had been posted relating to the claimant, and various

---

61 Cf. Google *Transparency Report* from May 2014 to February 2019, https://transparencyreport.google.com/eu-privacy/overview, showing that more than 50% of the requests for de-listing are denied. At this stage the decision lies solely with Google.

62 [2015] EWHC 3154 (QB). Both applications were refused. On the difficulties in identifying the defendant, see A. Mills, "Suing Facebook: Vertical Private International Law Issues in Online Social Media", presentation at the Max Planck Institute Luxembourg, 16.10.2017, pending publication; K. Takahashi, "Unmasking Anonymous Online Infringers of Personality Rights" (2015–16) 17 *Yearbook of Private International Law* 181.

allegations were made concerning her private life. The master rejected her claim regarding the profile on the first website because the corporate entity which she had named as the defendant did not exist and when she later named one which did exist, without having applied for it to be substituted as defendant, she named the website owner's UK subsidiary, which was not responsible for hosting the site or for controlling what was published thereon. The master struck out her claim regarding the blog on the second website because she had also brought it against the website owner's UK subsidiary, which again was not responsible for hosting the site or for controlling what was published thereon. In the face of cases such as this one, the obligation the GDPR imposes on the controller to disclose its identity and contact details (Article 13, Article 14) may turn out to be of particular interest.

4.2.2. *A Second Glance*

In spite of the foregoing, it is here submitted that from the perspective of enhanced private enforcement the GDPR falls short of expectations. In other words, it does not provide for important elements in terms of access to the court, opportunities to litigate and/or incentives to do it:

a. *Cause of action*. To start with, the Regulation does not arrange for a specific civil action regarding data protection; nor does it impose on the Member States the obligation to create one.[63] In this regard the situation has not changed in comparison to the Directive, and this may have consequences in terms of obstacles to litigate. The well-known case *Google Inc. v. Vidal Hall*[64] is worth recalling here: the claimants had applied for permission to serve out of the jurisdiction in respect of the claims for misuse of private information and for breach of confidence; the cause of action for misuse of private information is a tort for the purposes of the rules providing for service of proceedings out of the jurisdiction, thus service out of the jurisdiction is allowed; breach of confidence is not, therefore service is not allowed.
b. *Limitation periods*. A further omission relates to the limitation periods for claiming compensation, which are neither harmonised nor regulated in the GDPR. The only reference thereto appears in Recital 65 and has no correspondence in the operative text: regarding the right to be forgotten,

> ... where the data subject has given his or her consent as a child and is not fully aware of the risks involved by the processing, and later wants to remove

---

63 To be sure, in order to comply with EU law it may be sufficient for each Member State to try to accommodate the already existing legal framework – although this is certainly not the best solution in terms of uniformity.

64 Above n. 58.

such personal data, especially on the internet. The data subject should be able to exercise that right notwithstanding the fact that he or she is no longer a child.

c. *Identification of the defendant*. It has just been said that the GDPR rules on the controller's duty to disclose its identity and contact details will certainly help the data subject to identify the person to be sued. However, nothing is said about the processor.[65] Moreover, the category of controller is still under construction and the case law very hesitant. In the aftermath of the CJEU preliminary ruling in *Google Spain*,[66] the Spanish Supreme Court rendered two decisions: one by the civil senate (5 April 2016), the other by the administrative senate (13 June 2016); according to the latter, Google Spain does not determine the purposes and means of the processing of personal data and therefore is *not* a controller; it *is*, though, according to the former. In the claim of Maximilian Schrems against Facebook Ireland Ltd. before the Handelsgericht Wien – which ended up with the well-known decision of the CJEU in Case C-498/16 – M. Schrems asked the court to have his own role, and Facebook's role, determined in this regard, and was willing to accept that he was sometimes acting as data subject and sometimes as a controller.[67] Case C-210/16 of the CJEU (*Unabhängiges Landeszentrum für Datenschutz Schleswig-Holstein v. Wirtschaftsakademie Schleswig-Holstein GmbH.*),[68] is worth being recalled as well along the same lines. In addition, data protection breaches may perfectly easily be provoked by an anonymous infringer;[69] multi-party processing operations on the internet are also likely to raise complex issues related to the identification of the defendant.[70]
d. *Specific procedural track*. Already before the GDPR some Member States, such as Belgium or Greece, contributed to private enforcement offering easier access to court in the form of a special procedure. Scholars regret that the GDPR has not been taken as an occasion to fix summary proceedings before national courts for data protection violations.[71] It is worth noticing that the GDPR suggests means to facilitate the submission of complaints to the supervisory authority – e.g., providing a complaint submission form

---

65 According to Articles 13 and 14 GDPR the controller must give the contact details of its representative to the subject, but (at least literally) not of those of the processor. Whether Article 27.4 would allow for suing the representative in the EU in addition to or instead of the controller or processor is disputable.

66 C-131/12, EU:C:2014:317.

67 *Maximilian Schrems v. Facebook Ireland Ltd.*, 31 July 2014, Handelsgericht Wien, available in English: http://www.europe-v-facebook.org/sk/sk_en.pdf.

68 EU:C:2018:388. See as well the recent decision in Case C-40/17, *Fashion ID GmbH & Co. KG*, EU:C:2019:629, 29 July 2019.

69 Cf. K. Takahashi (n. 62 above), on the legal bases for disclosure under Japanese, French, US and English approaches.

70 Cf. T. Wisman, "Case Notes – Introduction: Privacy and Data Protection – Fundamentally Complex" (2018) 4 *European Data Protection Law Review* 118, 119.

71 See A. Galetta, P. de Hert (n. 60 above), 148.

which can also be completed electronically (Article 57, Recital 141) – but not *vis-à-vis* civil actions.

e. *Evidence.* Regarding evidence, as explained above, the opinion on a reversed burden of proof resulting from the "accountability principle" is not unanimous. Moreover, the Regulation has not set a presumption of damage once the violation has been established: both the damage and the causality need to be proved. In addition, there is no rule on the relation between public enforcement and private follow-on actions which would allow using evidence or admissions in a prior administrative proceeding as (at least) *prima facie* evidence in a civil claim.[72]

f. *Remedies.* It would have been useful to have a provision on injunctions and their scope: the replication in practice of the (broad) scope of application of the GDPR according to Article 3 may simply lead to a refusal of the recognition and enforcement of the injunction in the affected foreign countries, for want of international jurisdiction.

g. *Costs, funding.* There is nothing in the GDPR on the costs of the proceedings – in contrast to other Regulations such as Regulation (EC) No. 861/2007 establishing a European Small Claims Procedure,[73] Article 16 – or regarding legal aid – like in Article 44, 45 Council Regulation (EC) No. 4/2009 of 18 December 2008 on jurisdiction, applicable law, recognition and enforcement of decisions and cooperation in matters relating to maintenance obligations.[74] It may indeed be claimed that the Regulations are not comparable: the Small Claims Regulations is only about procedure in cross-border cases; the scope of the maintenance Regulation is restricted to cross-border situations. However, the same international nature is to be expected in many of the constellations falling under the scope of the GDPR; besides, nothing prevented the law-maker from adopting a rule limited to cross-border cases.

h. *Enforcement.* Difficulties may arise linked to enforcement of a decision. On the one hand, in practice it might not be easy to make sure whether an injunction has really been complied with – in other words, to assess whether the data at stake have been removed from all possible places where they could be stored. On the other hand, the cross-border enforcement of decisions on personal data protection may be problematic, even among the EU Member States. The Proposal of the Commission included a rule on the compulsory enforcement of decisions given as a consequence of a

72 But not only: see as well Recital 82, "In order to demonstrate compliance with this Regulation, the controller or processor should maintain records of processing activities under its responsibility."

73 Regulation (EC) No. 861/2007 of the European Parliament and of the Council of 11 July 2007 establishing a European Small Claims Procedure, OJ L 199, 31.7.2007.

74 OJ L 7, 10.1.2009.

claim *inter privatos* in intra-EU cross-border cases, without differentiating between injunctive or compensatory relief;[75] but it did not make its way into the final text. Regarding third countries, it is worth mentioning that the decisions on defamation and privacy are excluded from the Convention of 2 July 2019 on the Recognition and Enforcement of Foreign Judgments in Civil or Commercial Matters. Although claims related to personal data protection are not expressly mentioned as excluded, one could legitimately assume that this is the case.[76]

i. *Assistance, information*. The EU has clearly opted for a strong policy of data protection. In spite of this, it is fair to say that the culture of personal data protection is still underdeveloped; the idea of taking the defence of one's right in hand is alien to the EU citizens. In fields such as consumer protection the EU law-maker has taken a proactive role, in that it imposes obligations on the Member states to provide information to the general public and professional circles about specific possibilities to go to court.[77] The occasion to do the same has been missed in the GDPR.

5. CONCLUSION

Directive 95/46/EC could not prevent legal fragmentation in the implementation of personal data protection across the Union. Its outcome in terms of private enforcement was equally poor: individuals did not find arguments persuasive enough to engage in civil judicial litigation to remedy data protection violations in the Member States.

The analysis presented earlier allows the conclusion that the GDPR is also a humble instrument from the point of view of private enforcement: it "envisages and permits" both private and public enforcement,[78] but strongly privileges the second. The same holds true for the harmonisation of the rules of civil procedure in the EU – insofar as private enforcement does not play a big role, the need for harmonisation is limited. In this regard the field of personal data protection remains far away from other areas like damages in competition law or IP rights.[79]

---

75 Proposal for a regulation of the European Parliament and of the Council on the protection of individuals with regard to the processing of personal data and on the free movement of such data (General Data Protection Regulation), COM(2012) 11 final, Article 75.4: "The Member States shall enforce final decisions by the courts referred to in this Article."

76 Cf. C. Mariottini, "The Exclusion of Defamation and Privacy from the Scope of The Hague Draft Convention on Judgments" (2017/2018) 19 *Yearbook of Private International Law* 475, 486, on an alternative to the wording placed in square brackets at the time the article was written, with a specific mention to claims arising from the processing of personal data.

77 Cf. Article 24 Small Claims regulation (n. 73 above).

78 C. Hodges (n. 40 above), 66.

79 Cf. E. Vallines García, "Harmonising Access to Information and Evidence: The Directives on Intellectual Property and Competition Damages", Chapter 6 in this volume.

Individual control over data can play an instrumental role in rendering data protection more effective. In fact, the GDPR endorses this belief; by according the data subjects the rights of access, rectification, erasure, etc. it helps build up the empowerment feeling. In addition it offers the individual possibilities to manage his/her data and to keep the control; not, however, by way of civil proceedings.

In point of truth, whether personal data protection is an area for private enforcement to work as a regulatory tool may be disputed. The reasons may be harm-related: the right to data protection can be violated without harm; when it occurs, it often pertains to the category of intangible harm as opposed to physical damage. It is unlikely that the individual will react without harm, or an easily identifiable harm. In addition, there is a widely shared conviction in the sense that data protection violations not only affect the data subject but also the general public (the "social fabric"), and (at least in Europe) an equally widespread perception of court procedures not being about the "social fabric" but rather victim-focused.[80] This notwithstanding, to the extent that the choice of the type of enforcement is a political one, we belief that relegating private enforcement to a discrete second place sends out the wrong signal at a crucial moment in the process of building up a culture of personal data and compliance. Cases of personal data violations before the courts, particularly against powerful controllers and processors, are widely covered by the media; in this way they contribute to raise awareness among data subjects about the right to "informational self-determination" and its scope. And still, under the GDPR civil court procedures remain largely unavailable. To be sure, the GDPR has opened a door to representative actions where arguments can be raised based on data protection law against the big companies in the internet business, such as Facebook or Google.[81] Scepticism should be allowed, though, regarding this single and, above all, incomplete provision; in particular in light of cases such as the recent *Lloyd v. Google LLC*.[82]

---

80 A. Galetta, de Hert (n. 60 above), p. 139.

81 So far collective claims have usually been filed by consumer associations, based on consumer and competition law: see the cases reported by C. Etterldorf, "Consumer Association Succeeds in First Round of Dispute Concerning Facebook's Terms of Service and Privacy Setting" (2018) 4 *European Data Protection Law Review* 114. See as well P. Rott, "Data protection law as consumer law – How consumer organizations can contribute to the enforcement of data protection law" (2017) 6(3) *Journal of European & Consumer Market Law* (EuCML) 113.

82 Above n.50 above, para. 82 ff. Google was sued for its role in the collection, collation, and use of data obtained via the *Safari Workaround*, and for breach of duty. The claim was brought in reliance on CPR 19.6, which is headed "Representative Parties with the Same Interest". The Court analysed on its own motion whether the parties had the same interest and concluded they had not. In addition, it appreciated insuperable practical difficulties in ascertaining whether any given individual is a member of the Class; further and alternatively, the Court's discretion would in any event be exercised against the continuation of the action as a representative action. For an on-going class action complaint in the US for security breach, see: *Echavarria et al. v. Facebook Inc*, Case3:18-cv-05982, available at: https://www.pacermonitor.com/public/case/25776427/ECHAVARRIA_et_al_v_Facebook,_Inc (last visited 16.02.2019).

PART III

CURRENT INITIATIVES FOR FURTHER HARMONISATION

The ELI/UNIDROIT Project

THE ELI/UNIDROIT PROJECT

A General Introduction

Elisabetta Silvestri

More or less, readers will know what the ELI/Unidroit project is about, and therefore this introduction should be somewhat brief. The project was inaugurated in 2013 in Vienna and is still ongoing, with a view to being completed in May 2019 (at least, this is the completion date that appears on the ELI website). The official title of the project is "From Transnational Principles to European Rules of Civil Procedure", and the reference to transnational principles makes it clear that the basis of the project, meaning the canvass on which the different working groups that have been established are supposed to work (although not exclusively), rests on the Transnational Principles and Rules of Civil Procedure that were the product of a joint venture between the ALI (American Law Institute) and Unidroit at the end of the last century and the first years of the present one.[1] The ALI/Unidroit project was intensely discussed in academic circles all around the world; it was translated into a variety of languages, and it gave rise to a huge amount of scholarly writing.[2] Unfortunately though, it never

1 The original text of the Principles and the Rules jointly drafted by the two institutions, and proudly qualified as "a major new instrument in the field of private law harmonization", can be read (in English and in French) in a special issue of the *Uniform Law Review* (volume IX, 2004-4), which includes a few commentaries authored by academics and legal practitioners representing different legal traditions.

2 The literature on the project is extensive, and it seems excessive to try to list all the contributions published on this subject. Here are a few essays that can provide the reader with an understanding of the basics of the project and its main purpose: M. Taruffo, "Harmonization in a Global Context: The ALI/UNIDROIT Principles" in X.E. Kramer and C.H. van Rhee (eds.), *Civil Litigation in a Globalizing World* (Springer, 2012); R. Stürner, "The Principles of Transnational Civil Procedure. An Introduction to Their Basic Conception"

went beyond the stage of an intellectual endeavour and a remarkable exercise in the study of comparative civil procedure, considering that the aim of the project was to combine the best and most efficient aspects of litigation according to both the civil law and common law traditions in a set of rules that – if adopted – would help parties litigate in other national jurisdictions with the peace of mind provided by a system of rules and principles that were uniform throughout the whole world. The project was certainly ambitious, maybe too ambitious at that time, and therefore it was never taken into account by any institutions, either national ones or international ones.

Maybe now the time is ripe for a new attempt at devising common procedural principles, on a smaller scale, meaning at the European Union level. In fact, the European institutions, originally involved in the ELI/Unidroit project simply as observers, in the last couple of years have shown a deeper interest in the project, producing a variety of documents in which aspects of the project are under scrutiny. The latest document (issued in June 2017) is the EU Parliament Resolution with recommendations to the Commission for the adoption of a directive on common minimum standards of civil procedure.[3] Personally, this author finds the document very interesting, but here and now is not the right time to analyse it. However, one should emphasise one feature of the Resolution, which is the reference to "common minimum procedural standards". This approach seems particularly welcome and, if the ELI/Unidroit project goes on in this direction (meaning in the direction of designing a set of basic procedural standards) it will have good chances of success. It is argued that the idea of a code of civil procedure for the whole European Union is a utopia that will never become real for a variety of reasons, one of which is the fact that harmonisation of procedural rules (a positive aspect) is often perceived as a push towards homologation (something quite negative). As the Resolution clarifies:

> The proposed directive is not aimed at substituting national civil procedure systems in their entirety. While respecting national specificities and the fundamental right to an effective remedy and to a fair trial, which ensures effective and efficient access to justice, it is aimed at establishing common minimum standards regarding the function and conduct of Member States' civil proceedings in relation to all matters

(2005) 69 *Rabels Zeitschrift für ausländisches und internationales Privatrecht* [*RabelsZ*] 201; G.C. Hazard, Jr., M. Taruffo, R. Stürner, A. Gidi, "Introduction to the Principles and Rules of Transnational Civil Procedure" (2000) 33 *New York University Journal of International Law & Policy* 769; G.B. Born, "Critical Observations on the Draft Transnational Rules of Civil Procedure" (1998) 33 *Texas International Law Journal* 387.

3 Common minimum standards of civil procedure – European Parliament resolution of 4 July 2017 with recommendations to the Commission on common minimum standards of civil procedure in the European Union (2015/2084(INL)), available at: http://www.europarl.europa.eu/sides/getDoc.do?pubRef=-//EP//NONSGML+TA+P8-TA-2017-0282+0+DOC+PDF+V0//EN.

falling within the scope of Union law. It is also aimed at providing a basis for the gradual deepening of the approximation of civil procedure systems of Member States.[4]

There would be a lot to say about the optimal instrument for the adoption of common minimum standards, since both a directive and a regulation have pros and cons, but it is not possible to expand on this issue just now. Personally, this author would prefer a directive, since the transposition of a directive leaves national legislators a certain measure of leeway, which is likely to make the standards to be implemented more palatable, so to speak, most of all when the transposition is supposed to imply significant changes to the statutes and regulations in force.

1. THE ELI/UNIDROIT PROJECT: THE CHALLENGES AHEAD

The ELI/Unidroit project is being developed by several working groups in charge of different aspects of civil procedure: a complete list of the different working groups and their members, together with the names of the members of both the advisory committee and the consultative committee can be found on the website of the European Law Institute, where a few institutions classified as "observers" are listed as well.[5] The rules prepared by each group will be arranged in a comprehensive text by the so-called "Structure Group" that is called upon to prepare a cohesive and coherent set of rules. And here at least two challenges can be foreseen.

First, as a member of the Working Group on Obligations of Parties, Lawyers and Judges,[6] this author can say that, due to the fact that all the members come from different legal cultures and traditions, it was not easy to reach an agreement on some of the rules. It seems that the hurdles are even higher when the rules of the various working groups will have to be arranged in a single text, which inevitably will likely reflect the background and the personal preferences of the members of the "Structure Group".

---

4 See Common minimum standards of civil procedure, above n. 3, Annex to the resolution: recommendations for a directive of the European parliament and of the council on common minimum standards of civil procedure in the EU, A. Principles and aims of the proposal requested, no. 7.

5 The ELI website can be reached at https://www.europeanlawinstitute.eu/projects-publications/current-projects-feasibility-studies-and-other-activities/current-projects/civil-procedure/.

6 Alan Uzelac and Remco van Rhee act as reporters for this Working Group; the other members are Emmanuel Jeuland, Bartosz Karolczyk, Walter Rechberger, John Sorabji and Magne Strandberg.

The second challenge is the language. The rules or common principles are drafted in English (sometimes in French, too), but that can bring about other challenges. The challenges are of different natures. One challenge is that in the legal language of each Member State there are some terms that cannot be rendered into English without losing their specific meaning. An example is the English word "settlement" which is a sort of umbrella term, whereas Italian, French, Spanish and German have different words for different types of agreement reached in court or out of court with a view to ending a dispute.[7] Another challenge stems from a linguistic approach to the endeavour that each working group is supposed to carry out. Some readers probably are familiar with the so-called Eurolect, which is the peculiar language that the EU translation services have developed in the translation of legal terms.[8] These translation solutions, in their turn, influence the national legal terminology. I think that the members of the "Structure Group" should be familiar with the legal *corpora*, and be aware of a dimension to their work that is not strictly legal. In my opinion, the "Structure Group" would benefit from the expertise of linguists.

2. "OBLIGATIONS OF PARTIES, LAWYERS AND JUDGES": THE ACHIEVEMENTS OF THE WORKING GROUP

Now, a few words about the working group to which this author belongs and the results of an intense exchange of ideas among its members. No detailed description of the rules agreed upon will be given here. The goal is simply to present the reader with the trends that inspired he group.[9]

First and foremost, in the view of the working group, adjudication (meaning the procedure before the courts of first instance) must be the focus of the whole process. That is an important feature; most of all a noteworthy change in those legal systems that have a different concept, and think that the true judgment is

7 On the problems arising in the translation of terms concerning civil procedure, see extensively E. Jeuland, S. Lalani (sous la direction de), *Recherche lexicografique en procédure civile – Lexicographical research in civil procedure* (IRJS Éditions, 2017).

8 On the Eurolect, see in general L. Mori (ed.), *Observing Eurolects: Corpus Analysis of Linguistic Variation in EU Law* (John Benjamin Publishing Co., 2018); S. Marino, L. Biel, M. Bajčić, V. Soson (eds.), *Language and Law. The Role of Language and Translation in EU Competition Law* (Springer, 2018); L. Biel, *Lost in the Eurofog: The Textual Fit of Translated Law* (Peter Lang, 2014).

9 An extensive analysis of the rules drafted by the Working Group can be found in A. Uzelac, "Towards European Rules of Civil Procedure: Rethinking Procedural Obligations" (2017) 58 *Hungarian Journal of Legal Studies* 3.

the judgment issued on appeal. In our view, adjudication must not be seen as a "warm-up game" in the resolution of disputes.

How can adjudication be made the heart of litigation? The strategy pursued by the working group includes a variety of measures. First of all, it appears to be necessary to increase the duties and obligations placed on the parties as well as on their lawyers. Therefore, for the parties a duty of loyal cooperation is foreseen; a similar duty is envisioned for their lawyers, according to the rules governing their professional conduct. Of course, any abuses of process imply sanctions, essentially sanctions in the allocation of costs.

The duty of loyal cooperation means that claims and defences must be put forward as soon as possible, so as to allow a swift identification of the *thema decidendum* and the *thema probandum*. In this regard, a rule of paramount importance is the one providing the following:

> Parties and their lawyers have a duty to identify the matter in dispute *as early as possible*, taking into consideration the views of the other party if these have become known to them.
>
> Parties and their lawyers are *under the duty to present relevant facts and identify evidence in a diligent and complete way*, ordinarily in *their earliest statements of case*. Later presentation of facts and evidence has to be justified (emphasis added).

In addition, the working group is persuaded that it is essential to strengthen the managerial powers of the court, through the provision of a general management duty placed upon the court, and a set of rules that specify the different means of case management. The principles of party presentation and party prosecution are guaranteed, but the court may take evidence on its own motion, if it thinks that this is necessary for the proper adjudication of the case.

Furthermore, the principle of proportionality applied to the allocation of judicial resources to each case must be one of the primary canons followed by legislators in designing the path of a civil case. Ideally, proportional procedures tailored to the needs of the particular case should be devised, so as to reach a reasonable balance between the right of the parties to have their case decided in a just way, through a fair procedure, and the constraints of the limited budgetary resources allocated to the administration of justice. After all, the rule, according to which the time and expenses devoted to proceedings ought to be proportionate to what is at stake, is a simple but always valuable expression of common sense.

Reference to case management and the principle of proportionality might lead someone to think that the working group has relied too much on the solutions devised by the English Civil Procedure Rules. In reality, however, an efficient preparation of the case, based on constant cooperation between the parties and between the parties and the court, and strengthened by the proper exercise of the case management powers bestowed on the court, is a feature of a variety of civil procedural models (e.g. Germany, Austria and Spain), and is consistent with the trends followed by legislators in their most recent projects of reform (this being the case in France, for instance, as far as the prospective reform of the *mise en état* is concerned).

Finally, the members of the working group believe that the parties to a dispute must be persuaded to turn to ADR methods. The shared opinion is nevertheless that it is better to persuade the parties, and not to oblige them, to resort to ADR instruments. This concept is incorporated in the rule according to which, "Parties must co-operate in actively seeking to resolve their dispute consensually, both before and after proceedings are initiated." A system of incentives and sanctions is intended to help the parties avoid, if possible, adjudication: the sanctions, though, are not very harsh, which is necessary so as to prevent any hinderances to the right of access to the courts.

3. CONCLUSIONS

"Civil procedure rules are difficult to harmonize"[10] not only in light of the very nature of these rules, deeply embedded in the specific legal culture and societal features of a given legal systems, but also because the ideal of a European Union where everything, and not only legal rules, is harmonised nowadays more than ever seems to be a sheer Utopia or, in the words of the late Professor Marcel Storme, "a cathedral builders' dream".[11] In spite of that, with an exercise in optimism, it seems possible to believe that if common basic standards for a fairer and more efficient adjudication of disputes are adopted by the Union, this is likely to have positive effects for European citizens, and maybe that would persuade them to look upon the European institutions more charitably.

---

10 See M. Tulibacka, M. Sanz, R. Blomeyer, *Common minimum standards of civil procedure* (European Added Value assessment Annex I, Research Paper requested by the European Parliament's Committee on Legal Affairs, April 2016), available at: http://www.europarl.europa.eu/studies, at p. 23.

11 M. Storme, "A Single Civil Procedure for Europe: A Cathedral Builders' Dream" (2005) 22 *Ritsumeikan Law Review* 87.

THE ELI/UNIDROIT EUROPEAN RULES OF CIVIL PROCEDURE

Access to Information and Evidence

Michael STÜRNER

1. BACKGROUND AND PURPOSE

The general topic of this conference as such – the future harmonisation of civil procedure in the European Union – has a rather neutral underpinning. However, the organisers have endowed it with a somewhat ambiguous subtitle: "How far can we go?" Depending on the general attitude one has towards harmonisation, it leaves scope for positive and negative connotations alike. Some commentators might fear the impact further harmonisation will have on the national procedural systems and their traditions. Others will hail the advent of new initiatives as a more than welcome thrust of modernisation for old and somewhat rusty civil procedural laws. In that sense, the following chapter does not take a stand. However, it presents something which, in this author's view, sets out a possible way forward.[1] The model rules on access to information and evidence described

[1] In doing that, this chapter draws in part on Fernando Gascón Inchausti and Michael Stürner, "Access to Information and Evidence in the ELI/UNIDROIT European Rules of Civil Procedure: Some fundamental Aspects" in Adrian Simons, Aluisio Gonçalves de Castro Mendes, Álvaro Pérez Ragone, Paulo Henrique dos Santos Lucon (eds.), *Estudos em Homenagem a Ada Pellegrini Grinover e José Carlos Barbosa Moreira*, São Paulo 2019, pp. 567–585.

herein offer no less than a full set of harmonised rules, and yet they do not impose themselves like an act of secondary EU legislation would do: they can be seen as a piece of comparative academic scholarship which tries to bring together different perspectives in a coherent and intelligible manner without neglecting the cultural settings in which procedural systems are embedded.[2] In theory, the model rules are ready to be used in any given civil proceedings without major adaptation. At the same time, they may also serve as a source of inspiration for national and supranational legislators alike.

The background is by now well-known: since 2013, the European Law Institute (ELI) and the International Institute for the Unification of Private Law (UNIDROIT) jointly host a research project entitled "From Transnational Principles to European Rules of Civil Procedure."[3] It builds on the Principles of Transnational Civil Procedure adopted in 2004 by the American Law Institute (ALI) and UNIDROIT[4] and aims at a regional development of those Principles, which were designed to reduce uncertainty for parties litigating in unfamiliar surroundings and promote fairness in judicial proceedings through the development of a model universal civil procedural code. The first three Working Groups (Service and Due Notice of Proceedings; Provisional and Protective Measures; and Access to Information and Evidence) were constituted in 2014. Close-to-final drafts have already been discussed in the official bodies of both the ELI and UNIDROIT.[5] Other Working Groups have also finalised their work. Currently the Structure Group is concerned with issues of coherence and completeness of the drafts.

---

2 Cf. Rolf Stürner, "Der europäische Zivilprozeß – Einheit oder Vielfalt?" in Wolfgang Grunsky, Rolf Stürner, Gerhard Walter, Manfred Wolf (eds.), *Wege zu einem europäischen Zivilprozeßrecht*, Mohr Siebeck, 1992, pp. 1–24, at 9 (advocating a cautious approach towards harmonisation even when brought about on a comparative basis).

3 More detailed information on the project can be found on the ELI website at: http://www.europeanlawinstitute.eu/projects/current-projects/, and on the UNIDROIT website at: http://www.unidroit.org/work-in-progress-studies/current-studies/transnational-civil-procedure. Cf. also Rolf Stürner, "Principles of European civil procedure or a European model code? Some considerations on the joint ELI-Unidroit project" (2014) 19 *Uniform Law Review* 322; Nicolò Trocker, "From ALI-UNIDROIT Principles to common European rules on access to information and evidence? A preliminary outlook and some suggestions" (2014) 19 *Uniform Law Review* 239–291.

4 The English version of the Principles can be downloaded at: http://www.unidroit.org/english/principles/civilprocedure/ali-unidroitprinciples-e.pdf. For an analysis of the Principles written by the Co-Reporter of UNIDROIT, see Rolf Stürner, "The Principles of Transnational Civil Procedure. An Introduction to Their Basic Conceptions" (2005) 69 *Rabels Zeitschrift für ausländisches und internationals Privatrecht* 201–254. More recently cf. Michele Taruffo, "Harmonization in a Global Context: The ALI/UNIDROIT Principles" in Xandra E. Kramer, C.H. van Rhee (eds.), *Civil Litigation in a Globalizing World*, T.M.C. Asser, 2012, pp. 207–219.

5 For the "Final Version Draft Rules", which were discussed in the UNIDROIT Governing Council on 10–12 May 2017, see: http://www.unidroit.org/english/governments/councildocuments/2017session/cd-96-07-e.pdf.

The Working Group on Access to Information and Evidence[6] was entrusted with the task of identifying the common core of the law of evidence and drafting the most convenient rules, including those related to the management of evidence. While the ALI/UNIDROIT Principles of Transnational Civil Procedure – as the most succinct comparative account – have been used as a starting point, the Working Group also looked at recent legal instruments such as the 2010 IBA Rules on the Taking of Evidence in International Arbitration as well as European Union law, namely: the Directives on IP rights, competition damages claims and trade secrets; the Regulation on the European Small Claims Procedure; and the Rules of Procedure of the Unified Patent Court. Where appropriate, case law of both the European Court of Human Rights[7] and the Court of Justice of the European Union[8] was taken into account. No specific comparative research was carried out, as it goes without saying that the diversity of the legal backgrounds of the Working Group Members added to the comparative foundation of the rules.

The Draft Rules on Access to Information and Evidence ("the Draft Rules") apply to evidence and to access to information in civil and commercial matters. No specific rules have been devised for family cases or for consumer protection, although most of the proposed solutions might be suitable also for those proceedings. In their final version, the Draft Rules consist of four parts. The first part is entitled General Part, with sections on General Provisions on Evidence, on Presentation of Evidence, and on Management and Evaluation of Evidence. The second part deals with Access to Evidence Orders. The third part contains rules on types of evidence such as documents, oral testimony, examination of parties, expert evidence, and judicial inspection. The fourth and final part deals with cross-border issues.

The following chapter does not set out to give a complete picture of the Draft Rules on Access to Information and Evidence. It will try to shed some light on the principles underlying the set of rules (below, at section 2), on the use of modern technology (below, at section 3), on the standard of proof (below, at section 4), on illegally obtained evidence (below, at section 5) and on access to information (below, at section 6). Finally, the chapter will try to assess the possible impact of the rules (below, at section 7).

---

6 Co-Reporters of the Working group were: Neil Andrews (England, until September 2016), and Fernando Gascón Inchausti (Spain). Members were: Laura Ervo (Sweden and Finland), Frédérique Ferrand (France), Viktória Harsági (Hungary) and Michael Stürner (Germany).

7 E.g. with regard to the approach towards illegally obtained evidence, or pertaining to the right of a party to ask questions directly to a witness.

8 E.g. with regard to the duty to give a reasoned decision, or generally case law pertaining to the Evidence Regulation.

2. GENERAL PRINCIPLES

Like any field of law, evidence rests on a number of general principles. First and foremost, there is a fundamental right to evidence which follows from the right of access to justice (Article 6 ECHR) and the right to an effective remedy before a tribunal (Article 47 CFREU).[9] Such right of access to evidence, however, cannot be seen as an absolute right. It has to be balanced with other pertinent rights. In a number of procedural systems, procedural economy has reached the status of an overriding principle. To take an example from a piece of European legislation, it is the goal of the Small Claims Procedure Regulation[10] to "simplify and speed up litigation concerning small claims in cross-border cases, whilst reducing costs" (Recital 8). However, this may not infringe upon the fundamental right of access to evidence. In that light, Recital 9 of the Small Claims Procedure Regulation reads:

> This Regulation seeks to promote fundamental rights and takes into account, in particular, the principles recognised by the Charter of Fundamental Rights of the European Union. The court or tribunal should respect the right to a fair trial and the principle of an adversarial process, in particular when deciding on the necessity of an oral hearing and on the means of taking evidence and the extent to which evidence is to be taken.[11]

What takes precedence in the individual case – access to evidence or procedural efficiency – is decided by the principle of proportionality. It serves as an underlying meta-principle that can be used to justify judicial decisions in controversial situations and/or to grant the parties' motions. Proportionality, for instance, could be used under certain circumstances to refuse the taking of evidence if this would be too costly or would cause excessive delay to the proceedings. In the current situation of economic difficulties and public resources austerity, it is necessary to link proportionality to the notion of efficiency: among the relevant criteria to assess the proportionality of a decision on evidence, the time and costs implications cannot be overlooked.

Rule 7 of the Draft Rules tries to strike a balance between fairness and efficiency by entrusting the court with the respect of two overriding objectives: First, the parties (including prospective parties) shall enjoy equal treatment and *reasonable opportunity* to gain access to, and to present, evidence. Secondly,

---

9 CJEU, 27 September 2017, C-73/16, *Peter Puškár Finančné riaditeľstvo Slovenskej republiky and Kriminálny úrad finančnej správy*, ECLI:EU:C:2017:725.

10 Regulation (EC) No. 861/2007 of the European Parliament and of the Council of 11 July 2007 establishing a European Small Claims Procedure, O.J. L 199, 31.7.2007, p. 1.

11 See Michael Stürner, "Europäisches Bagatellverfahren" in Stefan Leible, Jörg-Philipp Terhechte (eds.), *Enzyklopädie des Europarechts, Band 3: Europäisches Rechtsschutz- und Verfahrensrecht*, 2nd ed., Nomos, forthcoming 2020, §21 at fns. 19–21 and 51–51a.

the rules themselves shall operate in a manner which is proportionate to the importance and complexity of the issues at stake.

In short, the whole set of rules on access to information and evidence contained in the Draft Rules is based on a pragmatic and realistic approach to the constitutional right to evidence.

3. USE OF "MODERN" TECHNOLOGY

While the Small Claims Procedure Regulation sees orality merely as a factor increasing the cost of litigation,[12] the rules proposed by the Working Group rest firmly on the assumption that the principles of orality and immediacy should lie at the heart of any system of civil proceedings. Therefore, some improvements have been proposed in order to reinforce their role as basic principles when it comes to the taking of evidence. This is the case with rule 18(3) of the Draft Rules, according to which "[a]ny hearing where evidence is taken shall be video recorded, provided that the necessary technical equipment is available. The video recording must be kept under the court's direction." This is a reasonable way to give support to oral hearings, allowing the court to view the recording in order to have a more accurate recollection of the way things evolved. It may also be of help in case an appellate court has to review the decision on the facts taken by the court of first instance.

The use of technology in civil proceedings is by now no longer a new, or modern, issue, but rather a common situation in many procedural systems. Therefore, a modern set of rules on evidence needs to treat as normal the possibility of making use of electronic communication technologies. This is the purpose of rule 18(6) of the Draft Rules, pursuant to which "[t]he taking of evidence, in hearings or *in camera*, can involve, where appropriate, the use of technology, such as videoconferencing or similar distance communication technologies".

The rule is intended to be technologically neutral, so that any possible technological system, currently existent or to be created in the future, may fall within its scope. The use of technology for evidentiary purposes may consist, for instance, in displaying electronic programs before the court (in order to permit the court to know the contents of non-documentary electronically-stored information), or activating audio or video software, and of course, using electronic devices and systems (such as videoconference) to establish direct communication with a person (such as a witness or an expert) located in a different place. Many jurisdictions admit this last possibility.

12 Also on this point cf. Michael Stürner, "Europäisches Bagatellverfahren" in Stefan Leible, Jörg-Philipp Terhechte (eds.), *Enzyklopädie des Europarechts, Band 3: Europäisches Rechtsschutz- und Verfahrensrecht*, 2nd ed., Nomos, forthcoming 2020, §21 at fns. 49–50.

At the outset, this rule is based on the assumption that oral evidence is more credible if the witness or expert is physically present in the courtroom. By contrast, the Small Claims Procedure Regulation is more open to new technologies, especially after the amendments made in December 2015.[13] A general preference for distance communication technologies in this field of small claims may be justified by the relatively low value of the claim at stake. However, as travel costs will mostly be higher than the costs of a videoconference, a generalisation of such a practice for all claims might be expected, which may lead to the result that there would be no more direct oral hearings in court. This result would, in turn, be also disproportionate and unacceptable.[14]

4. STANDARD OF PROOF

From a comparative perspective, standard of proof is a notion that belongs more to academic discussion than to legislation. Addressing the standard of proof, therefore, will imply the introduction of a new legal notion that many legal systems do not have. Consequently, a decision must be made as to the content of such a rule; that is, to propose what standard of proof should be considered the best for civil procedures in Europe. In legal theory it is common to make reference to different possible standards of proof, requiring different levels of certainty from the judge, the acceptable minimum of which would be the balance of probabilities (the judge considering the existence of a fact to be more probable than the non-existence thereof).

At the outset, the Working Group decided to include the topic, as the academic debate is growingly intense, and is indeed starting to influence practice and case law in many European countries.[15] Standard of proof is of paramount importance and influences heavily not only the court's fact finding, but also the parties' strategies. Therefore, one could expect that a new set of common European rules on evidence would include a proposal for regulation on this issue.

From a comparative view, different standards of proof can be found.[16] The big decision was whether to assume the US approach of the "balance of

---

13 Regulation (EU) No. 2015/2421 of the European Parliament and of the Council of 16 December 2015 amending Regulation (EC) No. 861/2007 establishing a European Small Claims Procedure and Regulation (EC) No. 1896/2006 creating a European order for payment procedure, O.J. L 341, 24.12.2015, p. 1.

14 Cf. Michael Stürner, "Europäisches Bagatellverfahren" in Stefan Leible, Jörg-Philipp Terhechte (eds.), *Enzyklopädie des Europarechts, Band 3: Europäisches Rechtsschutz- und Verfahrensrecht*, 2nd ed., Nomos, forthcoming 2020, §21 at fn. 82a.

15 Cf. Michele Taruffo, "Rethinking the Standard of Proof" (2003) 51 *American Journal of Comparative Law* 675; Luboš Tichý (ed.), *Standard of Proof in Europe*, Mohr Siebeck, 2019.

16 For a comparative analysis see Luboš Tichý, "Die Wahrscheinlichkeit und das Beweismaß im Schadensersatzrecht" in Peter Mankowski, Wolfgang Wurmnest (eds.), *Festschrift für Ulrich Magnus*, Sellier, 2014, pp. 709–720.

probabilities" or to require a higher level of certainty. The ALI/UNIDROIT Principles departed from the comparative assessment, that, as the comments point out, "[t]he standard of 'reasonably convinced' is in substance that applied in most legal systems. The standard in the United States and some other countries is 'preponderance of the evidence' but functionally that is essentially the same."[17] Consequently, Principle 21.2 on Burden and Standard of Proof reads: "Facts are considered proven when the court is reasonably convinced of their truth." Along these lines, rule 3 of the Draft Rules stipulates that "[a] contested issue of fact is proven when the court is reasonably convinced of its truth".[18]

The proposed rule aims at setting a qualified high standard of proof in civil proceedings. Requiring any court in any case to show "full" certainty, nevertheless, would be as demanding as it is difficult to imagine in practice. Therefore, the term "reasonably" used in the wording of the rule should be understood as meaning "as closely to fully convinced as possible", assuming that fully convinced is probably only an ideal. The term "truth" in this context must be read free from any philosophical connotation. It is merely intended to describe the level or degree of confidence that is sufficient for the court to pronounce a decision on the facts. The term "convinced" must also be taken with caution and should be understood to be a synonym for "satisfied". It is, therefore, necessary to assume that, within the aim of establishing a high standard, there is certain flexibility and a need to adapt to the circumstances in order to decide when a court is "reasonably convinced".

It goes without saying that the court may only consider itself convinced or satisfied of the truth taking account of all relevant evidence or other valid methods, such as admission of facts, common knowledge or presumptions; private knowledge of the court must never be the basis for a decision on issues of fact.

5. ILLEGALLY OBTAINED EVIDENCE

Another issue which was the source of many discussions among the Working Group, and which gave rise to a rich and fruitful debate during the general presentation of the Draft Rules in Vienna in November 2016, was that of illegally obtained evidence. It is a topic that has been developed in a very exhaustive manner in the field of criminal proceedings, but it may also have an impact on civil proceedings, with many possible examples: producing as documentary

17 ALI/UNIDROIT Principles, Comment P-21B.

18 Cf. on this issue Michael Stürner, "Evaluation of Evidence and Standard of Proof in the ELI/UNIDROIT European Rules of Civil Procedure" in Luboš Tichý (ed.), *Standard of Proof in Europe*, Mohr Siebeck, 2019, pp. 273–283.

evidence a letter addressed to somebody that was opened without his/her consent; producing the audio file of a conversation that was recorded without knowledge of the speakers; producing the contents of personal files gathered by an employer accessing an employee's computer;[19] utilisation of images recorded by a so-called "dash cam" located behind the windscreen of a car. There are two main difficulties from a European perspective regarding the regulation of this issue.

The first consists in defining what is illegal. Possibly one could take a conflict-of-laws perspective, and leave it to the applicable substantive law to determine illegality of a certain behaviour. For instance the taking of a video recording with a dash cam while driving in public streets is considered to be lawful in some jurisdictions, while others see it as illegal. However, such an approach would require the court to determine the applicable law in the first place. Moreover, it could give an incentive for parties to look for evidence in countries where there is no illegality attached to a certain behaviour. This is why the Working Group decided for follow the traditional *lex fori* approach.

The proposed rule does not define illegality, but for one point: it refers to the way evidence was obtained, not to its contents or to the taking of it in court. Only critical cases should be considered here; that is, only cases where evidence was obtained infringing fundamental rights or other equivalent constitutional values.[20] In other words, illegal is not an equivalent of "unlawful", a term with rather ethical perspectives, rather than legal ones; but neither is it an equivalent of "wrongful", because not every legal infringement would entail the severe consequences associated with illegality.

The second difficulty consists in finding an appropriate sanction for illegally obtained evidence, since it does not receive similar treatment in all jurisdictions.[21] The proposed rule 6 of the Draft Rules, reads as follows:

> Illegally obtained evidence should be excluded from the proceedings. However, in exceptional cases, the court may admit such evidence if it is the only way to establish the facts, taking into account the behaviour of the other party or of non-parties and the seriousness of the infringement.

The general rule is exclusion, to highlight the prominent role that material fundamental rights must always have. Exclusion, in this sense, means that the evidence shall not be the basis of any decision, either principal, or ancillary. This radical approach is consistent with the decision to define "illegality" in a

---

19 Cf. ECtHR 5 September 2017, Application no. 61496/08, *Bărbulescu v. Romania*.

20 This is by no means linked to the idea of the direct horizontal effect of fundamental rights. Rather, the reference to fundamental values signifies the threshold to be surmounted before holding that some behaviour is illegal.

21 Cf. Nicolò Trocker, "From ALI-UNIDROIT Principles to common European rules on access to information and evidence? A preliminary outlook and some suggestions" (2014) 19 *Uniform Law Review* 239, 264–265.

very strict manner: the narrower the scope of illegality, the severer the reaction against it.

The rule, nevertheless, is softened with exceptions for critical cases: the court may admit such evidence if it is the only way to establish the facts, taking into account the behaviour of the other party or of non-parties and the seriousness of the infringement.

This second limb is based on the principle of proportionality and reflects the view taken on certain occasions by the European Court of Human Rights, which seems to have established an exception, arising from the "right to evidence": if the illegally obtained evidence is the only way to establish the facts and to win the trial, it should be admissible.[22] Likewise the CJEU seems to endorse a similar approach in the *Peter Puškár* case: the Court required that a proportionality test should be carried out in order to decide on the exclusion or not of a confidential document allegedly gathered by the claimant without the authorisation of the public entity that had created it and containing the personal data of hundreds of persons.

In considering whether or not to apply an exception to the general rule of exclusion, an equilibrium should be reached between the rules of access to evidence, fundamental rights protection – namely those rights connected to privacy – and good faith and fair play: for instance, if one of the parties did not disclose a document required by his or her opponent, should he or she be entitled to claim its exclusion if the document is eventually produced after having been – presumably – obtained through illegal behaviour? On the other hand, it seems important to stress that the admission of exceptions should not be understood as fostering the illegal gathering of evidence as a sort of "precautionary" strategy; on the contrary, the general rule aims to deter such, and similar, practices.

By the same token, in a recent decision the German Bundesgerichtshof has held that illegally obtained dash cam recordings may be used as evidence in civil proceedings provided that the interest of the claimant in using the recordings overrides the interest of the defendant as to the protection of his or her personality rights.[23]

The general rule, indeed, needs to be read in conjunction with the proposed system of orders to access information and evidence, as outlined below, which should be the tool for obtaining information in difficult situations. Very roughly, one could say that the easier the access to information in a lawful manner, the less the need to get hold of it in an unlawful way.

---

22 Cf. ECtHR 10 October 2006, Application no. 7508/02, *L.L. v. France*, and ECtHR 13 May 2008, Application no. 65097/01, *N.N. and T.A. v. Belgium*.

23 Bundesgerichtshof 15 May 2018, VI ZR 233/17, ECLI:DE:BGH:2018:150518UVIZR233.17.0. Case note by Michael Stürner and Adrian Hemler, "Les enregistrements d'une caméra embarquée pour voiture comme moyen de preuve devant les tribunaux civils allemands, Bundesgerichtshof, arrêt du 15 mai 2018, no. VI ZR 233/17" (2018) *Revue trimestrielle de droit civil* 967–970.

6. ACCESS TO INFORMATION AND EVIDENCE HELD BY THE OPPONENT OR A THIRD PARTY

As a general rule, the burden lies with each party's to obtain access to the relevant information and to the sources of evidence, since it is elementary to procedural strategy to found claims or defences only on facts that the parties can reasonably expect to establish as true. Difficulties arise in practice, however, when relevant sources of evidence are in the possession of the counterparty or of a third party: refusal to provide the other party with information or sources of evidence could amount to a limitation of the right to an effective remedy before a court.

One of the most difficult, but also innovative, aspects of the project in the field of evidence was to try to build a "European way to discovery", to surmount the difficulties in accessing sources of evidence in the possession of the counterparty or of third parties, while avoiding the risks of fishing expeditions and US-style litigation. At this point the rules and practices of domestic legislation are very different; the same applies to legal cultures when it comes to complying with court orders or parties' requests. The main purpose has been to create a specific set of fairly autonomous rules to deal with this issue. Reference may be made to the rules on access to sources of evidence as provided by the Directive on competition damages claims[24] or the Regulation on the European Account Preservation Order.[25] Therefore, the Draft Rules are based on the criteria of judicial control and strict proportionality in order to decide whether a party or a non-party should be compelled to produce information, documents or sources of evidence. At the same time they establish strict rules of confidentiality, as well as serious sanctions in case of breach of an order.

The core of the system is the creation of a common institution, the so-called "access to evidence orders" or "orders for access to evidence", which will be granted by the court, before or during the proceedings, compelling another person – party or non-party – to produce documents, information or other relevant sources of information. It is important to note that the order will give the applicant access to sources of evidence and to information, but it will not mean by itself that the evidence is introduced into the proceedings: on the contrary, the requesting party bears the burden of introducing the gathered information or materials, as evidence, into the proceedings.

---

24 Directive 2014/104/EU of the European Parliament and of the Council of 26 November 2014 on certain rules governing actions for damages under national law for infringements of the competition law provisions of the Member States and of the European Union, O.J. L 349, 5.12.2014, p. 1, especially Articles 5–7.

25 Regulation (EU) No. 655/2014 of the European Parliament and of the Council of 15 May 2014 establishing a European Account Preservation Order procedure to facilitate cross-border debt recovery in civil and commercial matters, O.J. L 189, 27.6.2014, p. 59.

It will not be easy to get one of these orders, but if it is granted it will not be easy either to avoid compliance, as a set of sanctions applies. The whole system is based on the principle of proportionality and will be very demanding for the parties and for the judges. Orders for access to evidence shall only be made upon request of a party, as a rule on an adversarial basis (rule 29 of the Draft Rules). When necessary, the court may order an adversarial hearing. *Ex parte* applications are granted only in situations of urgent necessity (rule 29(3) of the Draft Rules). In such cases, if the application is granted, any party or non-party affected by the order can ask the court to reconsider it.

Access to evidence orders will be available for claimants, defendants or prospective claimants. This, in turn, also means that they may be used before or during the proceedings. If an order has been made prior to the initiation of the proceedings, where appropriate, the successful applicant might also be required to initiate proceedings within a specified reasonable period of time. If the applicant fails to comply with this requirement it lies within the discretion of the court to adopt appropriate measures: for instance, it may require return of all documents, records, and objects. It may also ensure that the data and information collected by, or made available to, the applicant cannot be used in any other process by that person or any other person to whom the information has been disclosed. It is possible that the information gathered (or not gathered) by means of the order leads the applicant to abandon his or her intention to commence proceedings; no sanction should seem necessary, but return of documents, records, and objects should in any case be appropriate.

As to the threshold, rule 23(1) of the Draft Rules provides that

> [t]he party or prospective party seeking an order for access to evidence must satisfy the court: (a) that the requested evidence is necessary for the proof or proposed proof of issues in dispute in pending proceedings or in proceedings which are contemplated; and (b) that the applicant cannot otherwise gain access to this evidence without the court's assistance.

Moreover, rule 23(2) of the Draft Rules establishes that the applicant must produce *prima facie* evidence of the merits of the claim or defence. If the order is requested prior to the initiation of proceedings, the applicant must indicate with sufficient precision all elements which are necessary to allow the court to identify the claim which the applicant intends to make.

In order to avoid fishing expeditions, rule 24(1) of the Draft Rules requires the applicant to

> identify, as accurately as possible in the light of the circumstances of the case, the specific sources of evidence to which access is sought or, alternatively, closely defined categories of evidence by reference to its nature, content, or date. The court shall refuse in any case to make an order in respect of a request which involves a vague, speculative, or unjustifiably wide-ranging search for information.

Moreover, pursuant to rule 24(2) of the Draft Rules, "[t]he applicant must justify that the requested measures are proportionate and reasonable. For this purpose the court will take into account the legitimate interests of all parties and all interested non-parties".

To enable the court to assess whether the application is premature or unnecessarily broad, in cases where the main proceedings have not been yet initiated, the rule makes clear that the applicant should provide adequate details of the intended main claim. Sometimes, indeed, the order may be necessary to define who will be the defendant and what sort of relief ought to be sought from the court.

In the light of the interest of the addressee of an access to evidence order to be granted protection of his/her confidential information, the court has to strike a balance between the conflicting interests of the parties in the light of the circumstances of the case. First, pursuant to rule 21(a) of the Draft Rules, access may be granted only to non-privileged information. If in other cases disclosure is ordered, a broad range of measures is available to the court to maintain confidentiality, pursuant to rule 25(2) of the Draft Rules, e.g. by redacting sensitive passages in documents, conducting hearings *in camera* or restricting the persons allowed to gain access to, or inspect, the proposed evidence. In exceptional circumstances, it might even be ordered that confidential information (e.g. concerning paramount trade secrets) is only shown to the court, but not to the opponent, at least in order to decide whether the information is to be made available to the applicant.

In addition, very severe rules are established to punish any breach of confidentiality. Rule 26 of the Draft Rules proposes a wide range of possible consequences to be imposed on the aggrieved party, including dismissal of the claim of the party in breach, where the main proceedings are still pending, declaring the party in breach liable for damages and ordering payment of such compensation, ordering the party in breach to pay the costs of the proceedings conducted under these rules, whatever the outcome of it might be, or even imposing on the party in breach (and/or on his representatives) an appropriate fine. It goes without saying that especially the sanction of dismissing the claim of the party in breach needs to be administered by the court very carefully, and should only apply to very serious breaches. However, it is a necessary tool in situations where monetary sanctions would not have a sufficiently deterrent power.

In order to give effect to access to evidence orders issued by the court, rule 31 of the Draft Rules entrusts the court with the task of

> prescribing all necessary and practical steps to ensure that its order under these rules is effectively and fairly implemented, including issuing directions concerning the appropriate place and manner in which the order is carried out. In particular, the court can direct that the applicant may be assisted by an expert.

If a person who is subject to, and aware of, an order for access to sources of evidence, destroys or conceals the relevant evidence, or otherwise renders it impossible to carry out the order successfully, the court may, pursuant to rule 32 of the Draft Rules, declare as admitted the facts which form the subject-matter of the relevant order. Furthermore, it may treat the defendant, or prospective defendant, as having impliedly conceded the basis, or any relevant part, of the claim which has been made or which was proposed by the applicant. Finally, the court may impose on the relevant respondent to the order (and in accordance with the relevant court's established disciplinary powers) an appropriate financial penalty per day of delay in implementing the order.

As to costs, the main rule should be for the applicant to bear the financial burden of the implementation of the order (rule 30(1) of the Draft Rules); however, the court may decide differently in its decision on costs at the end of proceedings. In addition, the respondent may request that the applicant provide security for any predictable expense to be incurred in the implementation of an order. If security is ordered by the court, it will be necessary for the applicant to provide such security before seeking to implement the order. The court will decide on the request and, where appropriate, determine the amount of the security.

7. THE POSSIBLE IMPACT OF THE RULES

The Rules on Access to Information and Evidence were devised to serve as a self-standing instrument to be used in legal proceedings of any type provided that the parties agree to their application in the first place. That presupposes, of course, the openness of the pertinent legal system to such a degree of procedural party autonomy.[26] But the main task of the Working Group was certainly to deliver a building block towards a coherent set of European rules on civil procedure. It may happen, therefore, that some provisions of the Draft Rules as they now stand will be moved to a different part, or be deleted altogether. Regardless of that, even the part on access to information and evidence as such might be used as a blueprint for reform of the law of evidence by a national legislator or indeed in a wider framework by the EU legislator. It is easy to imagine that the ELI/UNIDROIT Rules will be no more than a starting point for a legislative process, and thus serve as a source of inspiration. In short, the rules on civil procedure can be seen – like any model rules – as a multifunctional instrument.[27]

---

26 A prime example being (international) arbitration, see the 2010 IBA Rules on the Taking of Evidence in international Arbitration.

27 An overview of the different ways to promote transnational approximation in civil procedural law is given by Stefan Huber, *Entwicklung transnationaler Modellregeln für Zivilverfahren*, Mohr Siebeck, 2008, pp. 49–80.

Already during the process of drafting, the ELI/UNIDROIT Project received considerable attention from institutional observers. Amongst these are institutions concerned with law-making, such as the Hague Conference on Private International Law, the JURI Committee of the European Parliament, and the European Commission, but also those representing important professional associations, such as the Association for International Arbitration, the Council of Bars and Law Societies of Europe, the Council of the Notariats of the European Union, the European Network of the Councils of the Judiciary, the International Bar Association, the Union Internationale des Avocats, and the International Union of Judicial Officers.

Expressly referring to the ELI/UNIDROIT initiative, on 4 July 2017 the European Parliament adopted a Resolution with recommendations to the Commission on common minimum standards of civil procedure in the European Union (2015/2084(INL).[28] The recommendations include a Proposal for a Directive on common minimum standards ("the Directive Proposal"). The Directive Proposal is not aimed at substituting national civil procedure systems in their entirety. It states that

> while respecting national specificities and the fundamental right to an effective remedy and to a fair trial, which ensures effective and efficient access to justice, it is aimed at establishing common minimum standards regarding the function and conduct of Member States' civil proceedings in relation to all matters falling within the scope of Union law.

Furthermore, pursuant to the Resolution,

> common minimum standards of civil procedure are deemed necessary to form a sound basis for the approximation and improvement of national laws, in view of the flexibility it gives to Member States in preparing new civil procedure laws while reflecting a general consensus on the principles of civil justice practice.

Shortly afterwards, on 12 July 2017, the European Parliament's Legal Affairs Committee held a public hearing on "The ELI-UNIDROIT Civil Procedure Project: State of Play and Next Steps".[29]

---

[28] See here: http://www.europarl.europa.eu/oeil/popups/ficheprocedure.do?lang=en&reference=2015/2084(INL)).

[29] The interest of the European Parliament in this topic is also visible in the many studies it has commissioned: see, among others, European Parliamentary Research Service, In-Depth Analysis (R. Mańko), *Europeanisation of civil procedure. Towards common minimum standards?* PE 559.499 (June 2015); European Parliamentary Research Service, Study (M. Tulibacka/M. Sanz/R. Blomeyer), *Common minimum standards of civil procedure (European Added Value. Assessment. Annex I)*, PE 581.385 (June 2016); European Parliamentary Research Service, In-Depth Analysis (B. Hess), *Harmonized Rules and Minimum Standards in the European Law of Civil Procedure*, PE 556.971 (June 2016).

It is not the right place here to discuss this Resolution in detail, or to address the more general question whether the approach taken by the Parliament is to be applauded, or is even consistent, as it claims to set mere minimum standards, while at least partly proposing model rules.[30] It seems important to note that Article 7(1) of the Directive Proposal, under the heading of "Procedural Efficiency", establishes that

> Member States' courts or tribunals shall respect the right to an effective remedy and a fair trial which ensures effective access to justice and the principle of an adversarial process, in particular when deciding on the necessity of an oral hearing *and on the means of taking evidence and the extent to which evidence is to be taken* (emphasis added).

On the other hand, Article 10 of the Directive Proposal, devoted to "Evidence Taking", also shows this need to reconcile the access to justice and fair trial requirements with the notions of proportionality and efficiency. Pursuant to this provision,

> Member States shall ensure that *effective means* of presenting, obtaining and preserving evidence are available having regard to the rights of defence and the need to protection of confidential information. In the context of the taking of evidence, Member States shall encourage the use of modern communication technology. *The court or tribunal seised shall use the simplest and least-costly method of taking evidence* (emphasis added).

Both rules, namely the sentences highlighted in italics, clearly concentrate this balanced approach to the right to evidence in that, they reflect the approach taken by the Working Group on Access to Information and Evidence as described above.

More recently, on 31 May 2018, the EU Commission adopted a Proposal for a Regulation amending Council Regulation (EC) No 1206/2001 of 28 May 2001 on cooperation between the courts of the Member States in the taking of evidence in civil or commercial matters.[31] While the Evidence Regulation deals exclusively with the cross-border taking of evidence, the ELI/UNIDROIT Rules relate to the main proceedings themselves, containing only a short reference to cross-border issues in Part IV. Consequently, the Rules cannot be said to have a direct impact on the legislative initiative. However, just like the Draft Rules, the Regulation Proposal takes up a recent trend to make increased use of "modern"

---

30 On the Draft Report of the Committee on Legal Affairs (Rapporteur: Emil Radev) see Astrid Stadler, "Harmonisierung des Europäischen Zivilprozessrechts – Mindeststandards oder Modellregeln?" (2017) *JuristenZeitung* 693–701.

31 COM(2018) 378 final.

technology when taking evidence. According to the Explanation of the Proposal, the major obstacles concerning the present Evidence Regulation relate to delays and costs caused by failure to exploit the potential of modern technologies for speedier communication and the direct taking of evidence. As the Proposal states,

> [t]he most striking examples are failure to use electronic communication in exchanges between Member States' courts and authorities, which are still predominantly paper-based, and the marginal use of electronic communication, in particular videoconferencing, for the direct taking of evidence. The Regulation does not currently require the uptake of modern technologies in the judiciary; the fact that this depends entirely on Member States' individual efforts and the overall move towards digitalisation has led to very slow progress, in absolute terms and also in comparison with the use of modern technologies in domestic settings.[32]

Consequently the proposed Article 17a(1) on direct taking of evidence by videoconference requires that,

> [w]here evidence is to be taken by hearing a person domiciled in another Member State as witness, party or expert and the court does not request the competent court of another Member State to take evidence in accordance with Article 1(1)(a), the court shall take evidence directly in accordance with Article 17 via videoconference, if available to the respective courts, where it deems the use of such technology appropriate on account of the specific circumstances of the case.

Pursuant to Article 17a(2) of the Proposal, in such a case the hearing shall be held in the premises of a court. Moreover, where evidence is taken by videoconference, paragraph (3) lays down that

> the central body or the competent authority ... in the requested Member State may assign a court to take part in the performance of the taking of evidence in order to ensure respect for the fundamental principles of the law of the requested Member State.

In contrast to that, the parallel Proposal of the European Commission of 31 May 2018 for a Regulation of the European Parliament and of the Council amending Regulation (EC) No. 1393/2007 of the European Parliament and of the Council on the service in the Member States of judicial and extrajudicial documents in civil or commercial matters (service of documents)[33] integrates some important features of the Draft Rules issued by the Working Group on

---

32 COM(2018) 378 final, at p. 4.
33 COM(2018) 379 final.

Service and Due Notice of Proceedings. Notably, in Article 15a, the proposal introduces the electronic service of documents as an additional alternative method of service under the Regulation. In fact, this provision treats this type of the service of documents as an equivalent to service by post. The provision legitimises the electronic sending of a document from the user account of the sender directly to the user account of the recipient as a valid method of service of documents under the Regulation, provided that one of the alternative conditions included in paragraphs (a) and (b) is met. This is the model proposed in Article 7 of the Draft Rules on service.[34]

Admittedly not always the best model rule makes its way to a legislative proposal. To a large extent the fate of a draft provision depends on coincidences, often connected with cross-fertilisation generated by personal knowledge and acquaintance. Academic model rules have to be known by, or indeed made known to, the legislator. In a pejorative sense this may be called legal marketing. On the other hand legal academia must make itself heard; otherwise professional interest groups will inevitably dominate the legislative machinery, national and supranational.

[34] See Michael Stürner, "Die elektronische Zustellung im Kontext des digitalen Zivilprozesses" in Matthias Weller, Matthias Wendland (eds.), *Digital Single Market: Bausteine für einen digitalen Binnenmarkt*, Mohr Siebeck, 2019, pp. 143–172.

HARMONISATION OF THE RULES ON JUDGMENTS AND APPEALS IN EUROPE

A Few Remarks from the Inside

Christoph A. Kern

1. INTRODUCTION

Historically, procedural law has often been at the forefront when businesses or legislatures called for harmonised or uniform rules.[1] However, our "modern" nation states have all enacted their own procedural codes,[2] developed their own doctrinal approaches in academia and jurisprudence[3] and, last but not least, brought about different practical habits of the legal profession. Moreover, when it comes to the realisation of substantive law in the courts, everything is interconnected.[4] As a result, harmonising procedural law in the twentieth and twenty-first century is – despite all the literature about harmonisation at least on a European level[5] or among Civil Law Countries[6] – a thorny issue if one tries to show respect for, and take inspiration from, what exists on a national level. This is also true for two areas which, at first glance, may seem less difficult: judgments and appeals. The following pages aim at providing a very rough and incomplete overview of issues which have proven sensitive in the Working Groups "Judgments" and "Appeals" of the ELI/UNIDROIT Project "From Transnational Principles to European Rules".[7]

2. TERMINOLOGY AND PRECONCEPTIONS

2.1. GENERAL REMARKS

Whoever drafts a rule must use words. The basic rule follows the structure "if A then B". A and B may be words pointing directly to something fixed in the tangible world: If the light is red, then you have to stop. This is an easy rule,

---

1 Examples are the proceedings at the medieval fairs for collecting bills of exchange and cheques, and the unification of procedural law long before substantive law in Germany after 1870 (1879: Code of Civil Procedure, 1900: Civil Code).

2 See, e.g., for France, the Code de Procédure Civile of 1807, for Italy Codice di Procedura Civile of 1942, for Germany Civilprocessordnung of 1879; and nowadays even England: Civil Procedure Rules of 1999.

3 Cf. Rolf Stürner, "Das Zivilrecht der Moderne und die Bedeutung der Rechtsdogmatik", *Juristenzeitung* [*JZ*] 2012, 10, 11 et seq. (distinguishing between everyday doctrine ["*Gebrauchsdogmatik*"] and scientific doctrine ["*Wissenschaftliche Dogmatik*"]).

4 Abbo Junker, "Rechtsvergleichung als Grundlagenfach", *JZ* 1994, 921, 924.

5 See, e.g., for an early collection, Wolfgang Grunsky (ed.), *Wege zu einem europäischen Zivilprozessrecht. Tübinger Symposium zum 80. Geburtstag von Fritz Baur*, Tübingen: Mohr 1992; for a brand-new collection, Burkhard Hess and Xandra E. Kramer (eds.), *From Common Rules to Best Practices in European Civil Procedure*, Baden-Baden: Nomos 2018, passim.

6 See, e.g., C.H. van Rhee, "Towards a Procedural Ius Commune?" in J. Smits and G. Lubbe (eds.), *Remedies in Zuid-Afrika en Europa*, Antwerpen: Intersentia 2003, pp. 217–232.

7 On this project and its background, see, e.g., Geoffrey C. Hazard Jr., "Civil Procedure Rules for European Courts" (2016) 100 *Judicature* 58.

as it refers directly to a visible condition and tells the addressee what to do. A and B may also be words which do not point to something fixed in the tangible world, but to a process: If the light *turns* red *when* you are so close that you cannot stop any more, you may pass. This rule points not to something fixed, but includes a movement or, in other words, a temporal aspect. A and B may also be words which do not point directly to something in the tangible world, but to a concept: If the light is red but there is an *emergency*, you need not stop. Here, the concept is the emergency. What an emergency is cannot be determined only by using one of the five senses.

With respect to procedural law, many rules are of the more complex types: Procedure is, as the name reveals, a process, and many words only exist and have a meaning in the non-tangible system of the law. Putting together the complexity of the rules with national differences makes drafting in the area of procedural law particularly difficult: The processes are often similar, but not identical, and the same is true for the concepts and the words behind which they hide. It may well be that two lawyers from different jurisdictions use the same words, but have something completely different in mind, as the proceedings they know run differently and the concepts behind the same words are different. A rule which aims at harmonising the law can for this reason fail or, even worse, end up doing the opposite, i.e., create confusion and legal uncertainty.

Of course, comparative lawyers are well aware of this phenomenon. The prevailing method, the functional method, preaches that the comparatist should first define in non-legal terms a problem and then look for all kinds of rules with which the problem is resolved in the legal systems she wants to compare. For this purpose, the proponents of the functional method ask the comparatist to create her own terminology. This terminology should avoid legal terms, as they could have a different meaning.[8]

At first glance, this approach seems to be fruitful also for drafting harmonised rules. However, court proceedings are a pure product of the law. It is therefore not easy to develop a new terminology without creating even more confusion. The following two examples may serve as an illustration.

2.2. DEFAULT JUDGMENTS

If court proceedings are a pure product of the law, this is even more true for those of their results which are not normal decisions on the merits, based on

8 See generally Konrad Zweigert and Hein Kötz, *Einführung in die Rechtsvergleichung auf dem Gebiet des Privatrechts*, Tübingen: Mohr Siebeck 1996, pp. 33 et seq.; Peter V. Kunz, "Einführung zur Rechtsvergleichung in der Schweiz", *recht* 2006, 37, 47 et seq.; Christian Starck, "Rechtsvergleichung im öffentlichen Recht", *JZ* 1997, 1021, 1027 et seq.

a full evaluation of the facts and the law by a Solomonic judge. One of these results is default judgments: They can only occur in the context of civil proceedings, and they are a consequence of a particular development in the course of the legal process. Using the most general words, the situation can be described as follows: One of the parties fails to do something she is expected to do at a certain moment in the proceedings,[9] and as a consequence, a particular form of judgment is handed down. Traditionally, this form of judgment is called the default judgment. It would, of course, be possible to use another word than default in order to avoid diverging preconceptions. However, the available alternatives are not very attractive: "omission judgment" or "failure judgment" not only sound strange, but also bring to mind something else than what is meant. Therefore, using another term than default judgment does not seem advisable.

Nevertheless, the term "default judgment" cannot be used in drafting harmonised rules without a definition of what default means and what the effects of the default judgment are. In some legal systems, default judgments can only be handed down if a party does not undertake the necessary steps to start the proceedings like registering in the court's roll or replying to the complaint. If, at a later stage of the proceedings, the defendant does not appear this cannot give rise to a default judgment.[10] In other systems, though, a default can take the form of not defending the case after the complaint has been filed and of not appearing at the first hearing, but also of not appearing at any later hearing.[11] With respect to the effects, a default judgment can range from a full and plain victory of the opposing party without any further judicial inquiry,[12] to a judicial inquiry of the conclusiveness of the other party's position[13] or even evidence-taking,[14] to a mere adjourning of the case[15] or a decision based on the file.[16] These effects can be combined with different kinds of recourse against the default judgment, ranging from a mere demand to set the judgment aside to the *iudex*

---

9 Cf., e.g., art. 147 Swiss Code of Civil Procedure (Schweizerische Zivilprozessordnung, ZPO).

10 This is the case, e.g., in Italy, see arts. 165, 166, 171 Codice di Procedura Civile.

11 This is the case, e.g., in Germany, see ss. 330, 331, 332 German Code of Civil Procedure (Zivilprozessordnung, ZPO).

12 In Germany for default judgments against the plaintiff, see s. 330 ZPO.

13 In Germany, for default judgments against the defendant, see s. 331 ZPO.

14 This is especially the case in jurisdictions where the defendant in default is considered to be tacitly contesting the claim (*ficta contestatio*), e.g. in Italy, see Michele Angelo Lupoi, *Civil Procedure in Italy*, 2nd edn., Alphen aan den Rijn: Kluwer Law International, 2014, mn. 234 et seq.

15 In Germany, if none of the parties makes an appearance and the case cannot be decided on the file, see s. 227 ZPO.

16 In Switzerland, see art. 234(1) ZPO, and in Germany, if none of the parties makes an appearance and the case can be decided on the file, see ss. 251a, 227 ZPO, or if the party who appeared makes an application for such a judgment (s. 331a ZPO) which is not a default judgment.

a quo without any reasons[17] or with reasons justifying the default,[18] to an appeal to the *iudex ad quem* with or without a full justification of the failure.[19]

The Working Group on Judgments uses the term "default judgment" but provides a comprehensive set of rules defining the prerequisites and the consequences of such judgments. This solution seemed preferable, as the user would have to acquaint herself with the particular rules anyway to understand the functioning of default judgments as "pure" products of procedural law.

2.3. APPEAL

Another difficult term is the term "appeal". Does it cover only regular means of recourse against first-instance judgments or all kinds of recourse including, in particular, the second appeal which in some jurisdictions[20] is no "regular" means of appeal, but an extraordinary recourse? Of course, it would be possible to use the word "recourse" instead of appeal, but this would not really make things clearer.

The Working Group on Appeals uses, as its name already exhibits, the term "appeal". However, the Working Group has also resorted to the "functional approach" insofar as it speaks of "first" and "second" appeals. The aim of this terminology is to avoid terminological confusion and describe the procedural situation as neutrally as possible. Speaking of "first" and "second" appeals makes it unnecessary to cast precise terms for what is the "first" appeal which typically allows for an – albeit often restricted[21] – review of factual determinations and the "second" appeal which in most systems is an appeal to correct errors of law or procedure, but not errors of facts.[22] Moreover, the terms "first" and "second"

---

17 In Germany, see s. 340(2) ZPO.

18 In Switzerland, see art. 148 ZPO with the interesting requirement that "the defaulting party shows credibly that he or she was not responsible for the default or was responsible only to a minor extent."

19 E.g. in France where in most cases of default (*défaut*), technically speaking, no default judgment (*jugement par défaut*) is rendered, but a contradictory judgment (*jugement contradictoire*) or a judgment held to be contradictory (*jugement réputé contradictoire*), involving the appeal to a higher court (*appel*) being the available type of recourse, cf. Jacques Héron & Thierry Le Bars, *Droit judiciaire privé*, 4th edn., Paris: Montchrestien 2010, mn. 1117 et seq.

20 E.g., in France, see for an early source P.-P.-N. Henrion de Pansey, *De l'autorité judiciaire en France*, 2nd edn., Paris: T. Barrois, 1818, p. 397; for an overview on the historic development, see Xavier Godin, "La procédure de cassation au XVIIIe siècle", *Histoire, Economie et Société* (2010/3), 19 et seq.

21 See, e.g., in Switzerland, art. 317 ZPO; in Germany, ss. 529, 531 ZPO.

22 See, e.g., for Austria ss. 502, 504(2) of the Austrian Code of Civil Procedure (Zivilprozessordnung, ZPO); for Germany s. 545(1) ZPO; Peter L. Murray & Rolf Stürner, *German Civil Justice*, Durham NC: Carolina Academic Press, 2004, pp. 390 et seq.; for France, Pierre Julien and Natalie Fricero, *Droit judiciaire privé*, 3rd edn., Paris: Presses Universitaires

appeal also avoid any link to the particular court which has jurisdiction to hear the respective appeals. In particular, it does not use the formulation "appeal to the Supreme Court" in order not to tackle court organisation and court competences. However, this solution has one downside: A "second" appeal seems to imply that there has always been a "first" appeal. However, some systems know what is called "leapfrog" appeals[23] or allow the extraordinary appeal also against first-instance judgments.[24] This shows how difficult it is to create a new, neutral terminology.

3. PROCEDURAL RULES AND COURT ORGANISATION

3.1. GENERAL REMARKS

Over the decades, the European Union has gathered a considerable amount of experience in harmonising or unifying rules in the area of substantive law,[25] but also in the area of procedural law.[26] What it does not have, is experience in transforming the institutional design of existing national authorities, let alone courts. This is so because authorities have a life of their own, and rules on transforming existing authorities would interfere deeply with the Member States' national budget, national traditions, autonomy in matters of personnel,

de France 2009, n. 756; in Switzerland, the Court may also correct "obvious" errors in the determination of the facts, see art. 320 ZPO and arts. 95, 97 Swiss Act on the Federal Court (Bundesgerichtsgesetz, BGG); as a matter of principle, the last instance court may not admit new claims, assertions of facts and means of evidence, art. 326 ZPO, however, the exact scope is unclear, cf. Laura Jacquemoud-Rossari, "Les voies de recours" in Bénédict Foex and Nicolas Jeandin, *Le Code de procédure civile, Aspects choisis*, Geneva et al.: Schulthess, 2011, p. 126; David Hofmann and Christian Lüscher, *Le Code de procédure civile*, Bern: Stämpfli, 2009, p. 201; Andreas Lienhard, *Die materielle Prozessleitung der Schweizerischen Zivilprozessordnung*, Zurich & St. Gall: Dike 2013, mn. 734 et seq.; Karl Spühler, "Eine Neuentwicklung von europäischer Bedeutung – Die Einheitsbeschwerde in Zivilsachen ans Schweizerische Bundesgericht", *Zeitchrift für Zivilprozess International* [*ZZPInt*] 6 (2001), 255, 260. But see Per Henrik Lindblom, "The Role of the Supreme Courts in Scandinavia" (2000) 39 *Scandinavian Studies in Law* 325, 328 [edited version of the regional report to the 1997 IAPL conference mentioned in the introduction]: In Scandinavian countries, Supreme Courts can try questions of law and questions of fact, but normally cannot hear new evidence.

23 See, e.g., for Germany (Sprungrevision), s. 566 ZPO.

24 This seems to be the case in Romania (the author is grateful to Alina Ontanu for this indication).

25 See only the Directive 1999/44/EC of 25 May 1999 on certain aspects of the sale of consumer goods and associated guarantees, OJ L 171 of 7 July 1999, pp. 12–16, which has brought about a fundamental change in the German law of obligations; see Gesetz zur Modernisierung des Schuldrechts of 26 november 2001, Bundesgesetzblatt [BGBl.] I p. 3138.

26 See, e.g., the European Court of Justice's jurisprudence on the withdrawal of decisions of public authorities which differs in certain respects from ss. 48, 49 of the German Act on Administrative Proceedings.

and balance of power of the whole institutional design. Courts as an authority staffed with judges who enjoy the guarantee of judicial independence[27] are even more difficult to transform. Therefore, harmonisation of court organisation has always been considered to be impossible, and it cannot come as a surprise that the ELI/UNIDROIT project, as well, does not cover court organisation at all. Rather, differences in court organisation are a reality the ELI/UNIDROIT project must be aware of.

However, it is not possible to draft procedural rules without at least touching on aspects of court organisation, and this is particularly true for rules on judgments and on appeals, as the following remarks shall show.

3.2. JUDGMENTS AND COURT ORGANISATION

The Working Group on Judgments experienced the close connection between its topic and court organisation when it comes to default judgments, and more specifically the recourse against such judgments. If recourse against default judgments does *not* depend on bringing forward grounds which excuse the default, the number of cases which continue after a default judgment could increase in countries which, to date, *do* apply such restrictions. Moreover, as already described above, in some countries, recourse against default judgments must be sought through, and is tried in, the courts of second instance; in other countries, the courts of first instance also deal with recourse against default judgments. If recourse against the default judgment engages the courts of second instance, this alleviates the dockets of the first-instance courts whenever a default occurs, but increases the dockets of the second-instance courts. This means that in those countries for which the harmonising rules bring about a change the first or second instance courts need more judges to accommodate the growing number of cases, at least if one expects the number of default judgments to be significant.

The Working Group on Judgments tries to strike a compromise: Recourse against default judgments is only possible if the recourse can be excused, so that its number is presumably lower, but remains with the courts of first instance.

3.3. ADMISSIBILITY OF SECOND APPEALS

The close connection between procedural rules and court organisation is obvious with respect to appeals: The lower the admissibility threshold to bring

27 See, e.g., art. 97 of the German Constitution (Grundgesetz).

an appeal, the higher the number of appellate courts and judges. This issue is especially relevant for the second appeal: In some countries, the second appeal is an appeal as of right, sometimes even guaranteed in the constitution.[28] Obviously, in these countries, there is a huge number of appeals, and the second appeals court must comprise a high number of judges to cope with the workload. In other countries, the second appeals court has discretion on which – and how many – cases it takes.[29] In these countries, the judges of the second appeals court can regulate their workload themselves. For this reason, there are countries in which the second appeals court only sits in one formation and consists only of a handful of judges.[30] It should have become clear by now that the rules on the admissibility of appeals directly influence court organisation.

The Working Group on Appeals is contemplating rather restrictive admissibility criteria without directly leaving the acceptance of an appeal to the discretion of the judges of the appellate courts. This, again, is a compromise – a compromise which, of course, might allow "hidden" discretion, as the appellate judges can interpret the admissibility criteria more or less strictly, but nevertheless could be a wise solution, taking into account the great variety in the court organisation within Europe.

4. STRUCTURE OF PROCEEDINGS AND PARTICULAR PROCEDURAL FORMS

4.1. GENERAL REMARKS

Not only court organisation, but also the structure of proceedings differs considerably throughout Europe. Comparative procedural law of the younger generation distinguishes three structural models: The trial model with a trial phase as the culminating phase of the proceedings, before which the judges do not deal with the case too intensively; the Italian-canonical model with a sequence of hearings, traditionally before an instructing judge; and the main hearing model in which the judge and the parties interact in the interim phase to allow for a concentrated main hearing.[31] These three structural models also have a bearing on the sense of certain procedural institutions.

---

28 See, e.g. art. 111 of the Italian constitution and the discussion below at 5.2.

29 See, e.g., the Scandinavian countries.

30 See again the Scandinavian countries.

31 See, e.g., Rolf Stürner and Christoph Kern, "Comparative Civil Procedure – Fundamentals and Recent Trends" in Osman B. Gürzumar et al. (eds.), *Halûk Konuralp Anısına Armağan/ Gedächtnisschrift für Halûk Konuralp*, vol. 1, Ankara: Yetkin Yayınları, 2009, pp. 997, 1001 et seq.; Nicole Bettinger, *Prozessmodelle im Zivilverfahrensrecht*, Tübingen: Mohr Siebeck, 2016, passim.

4.2. THE SUMMARY JUDGMENT EXAMPLE

A good example is the summary judgment. In the trial model, a judgment normally is handed down after trial. If, at an earlier stage of the proceedings, i.e., before trial, it has become apparent that the case can be decided (often, but not only, by a dismissal on procedural grounds), this decision can be made. It is, however, something special – a summary judgment. In legal systems which pertain to the Italian-canonical model or the main hearing model – models in which the involvement of the judge with the case from the very beginning is not the exception, but the rule – it is nothing special that the case be decided as soon as it is "ripe" for decision, regardless of whether a "final" hearing or "main" hearing has taken place. Thus, for these legal systems, there is no need to carve out the institution of a summary judgment.

As the structure of the proceedings in the ELI/UNIDROIT project seems to be that of the main hearing model, the Working Group on Judgments has, after a long debate, abandoned the idea of creating rules for summary judgments.

5. CONSTITUTIONAL LIMITS TO PROCEDURAL HARMONISATION

5.1. GENERAL REMARKS

Many modern constitutions contain a number of provisions which deal with court organisation and court proceedings. Obviously, a reform of procedural law must either respect the boundaries set by constitutions or convince the national legislature to not only reform the procedural law, but also the constitution. Reforms of the constitution are typically much more difficult than reforms of sub-constitutional law. This is due to higher majority thresholds, but also to a higher psychological resistance to changes in the constitution. Therefore, a project aiming at harmonising procedural rules should try to remain within the boundaries of the national constitution.

Many of the constitutional provisions dealing with aspects of court organisation and court proceedings are, upon a closer look, rather principles than rules: the right to a natural judge, the right to be heard, the right to some form of recourse against decisions of the executive. Respecting these principles is relatively straightforward for the drafter of procedural rules who wishes to create a framework based on human rights and best practices. However, there are constitutional provisions which are from the outset phrased as rules or have brought about such rules through interpretation. Two examples may suffice.

5.2. CONSTITUTIONALLY GUARANTEED ACCESS TO THE SUPREME COURT

Article 111 of the Italian constitution decrees that

> [a]ppeals to the Court of Cassation in cases of violations of the law are always allowed against sentences and against measures affecting personal freedom pronounced by ordinary and special courts. This rule can only be waived in cases of sentences by military tribunals in time of war.[32]

This provision puts an unequivocal limit on the drafter of procedural rules when dealing with access to the Supreme Court, which typically is the court of second appeal: It is, under such a constitutional rule, almost impossible to restrict access to the second appeals court by setting admissibility requirements. This in turn has an effect on court organisation, as the second appeals court must be equipped with a large number of judges and will hand down a large number of judgments which are difficult to "digest" consistently for the lower courts, the second appeals court itself and the legal system as a whole.[33] Therefore, at least in our times, any reasonable drafter would not support such unlimited access to the second appeals court.

However, it is hard to imagine that national constitutions would be modified for the sole purpose of allowing the implementation of a harmonisation proposal. This is even more true for a sensitive issue like access to the Supreme Court: Reforming this rule would be perceived by many voters as eroding their rights, because the counter-argument that such a rule is responsible for court congestion and inconsistency of judgments is hard to explain to non-comparatists. It is, therefore, an open question how rules harmonising the law of appeals can be drafted if unlimited access to the second appeals courts must be taken as given.

The Working Group on Appeals has considered this issue. Despite the risk that Italy would not be able to harmonise its law accordingly,[34] it has decided to propose relatively strict limits for the admissibility of the second appeal, as otherwise a number of countries, mainly in Scandinavia, would have similar objections because of their court organisation, and restrictions on the admissibility seem to be a "best practice".

---

32 Translation provided by the Senate of the Italian Republic, available at: https://www.senato.it/documenti/repository/istituzione/costituzione_inglese.pdf.

33 See Remo Caponi, "Der italienische Kassationsgerichtshof vor dem Hintergrund des deutschen Revisionsrechts", *Zeitschrift für Zivilprozess* [*ZZP*] 115 (2002), 225, 240. Cf. also Felix Maultzsch, *Streitentscheidung und Normbildung durch den Zivilprozess*, Tübingen: Mohr Siebeck, 2010, p. 335; Michal Bobek, "Quantity or Quality? Reassessing the Role of Supreme Jurisdictions in Central Europe" (2009) 57 *American Journal of Comparative Law* 33.

34 Cf. Caponi (n. 33 above), at 240–241.

5.3. CONSTITUTIONAL INTERPRETATION

Even constitutional provisions which are drafted as principles may have developed into immediately operable rules due to their interpretation by the courts. A well-known example from outside Europe is the jurisprudence of the U.S. Supreme Court on the due process clause in the 14th amendment. According to the U.S. Supreme Court, the due process clause requires minimum contacts for a court to assume jurisdiction.[35] This, in turn, is considered to exclude provisions on territorial and international jurisdiction which would determine that the court where the plaintiff has its residence is competent. Of course, territorial jurisdiction based on the plaintiff's residence is an exception in any legal system. However, in certain circumstances, *inter alia*, in the context of maintenance claims of minors or the spouse, European countries allow for jurisdiction of the court at the plaintiff's residence in order to protect the impecunious child or spouse from the need to sue the defendant abroad.[36] U.S. representatives in international organisations like the Hague Conference on Private International Law have taken the position that even in this situation, a provision allowing the plaintiff to sue in the courts of his or her residence would be considered unconstitutional by the U.S. Supreme Court. For this reason, the U.S. did not ratify the Inter-American Convention on Support Obligations, drafted under the auspices of the Organization of American States and signed in Montevideo on 15 July 1989.[37] The Hague Conference, when drafting the Convention on the International Recovery of Child Support and Other Forms of Family Maintenance, was very cautious and allowed for a reservation against the relevant provision on indirect jurisdiction.[38] This approach has proven successful, as the U.S. has finally ratified the convention on 7 September 2016 so that it could enter into force on 1 January 2017.[39]

It cannot come as a surprise that the Working Groups on Judgments and on Appeals do not deal with jurisdiction. What is more, it is interesting to note that the project as a whole does not propose a harmonisation of the rules on direct or indirect jurisdiction, and this even though within Europe concerns about the U.S. Supreme Court's interpretation of the due process clause cannot

---

35 *International Shoe Co. v. Washington*, 326 U.S. 310 (1945).

36 Art. 3(b) Regulation (EC) No. 4/2009 of 18 December 2008 on jurisdiction, applicable law, recognition and enforcement of decisions and cooperation in matters relating to maintenance obligations, OJ L 7 of 10 January 2009, pp. 1–79.

37 See the status table, available at: http://www.oas.org/juridico/english/sigs/b-54.html.

38 For more details, see, e.g., Christoph A. Kern, in Thomas Rauscher (ed.), *Europäisches Zivilprozess- und Kollisionsrecht EuZPR/EuIPR*, vol. IV, 4th edn., Cologne: Otto-Schmidt, 2014, HUntVerfÜbk Einleitung mn. 16.

39 See the status table, available at: https://www.hcch.net/en/instruments/conventions/status-table/?cid=131.

be relevant. However, there is a straightforward explanation for the project's reticence on jurisdiction: International jurisdiction is already harmonised or even unified through the EU regulations[40] and the Lugano Convention,[41] and territorial jurisdiction within the European countries is a matter which can be left to the different states without creating too much trouble to potential litigants. Nevertheless, it cannot be excluded that there are other constitutional provisions in some countries which might have been interpreted in a way turning them into rules, directly impinging on the proposals made by the Working Groups.

6. SIMPLIFICATION AND SOPHISTICATION

6.1. GENERAL REMARKS

Projects aiming at a harmonisation or unification of the law on an international scale have a natural tendency towards simplification. This is even more true when they are driven by academics who have a fascination for "pure" ideas. However, this is not necessarily bad. Almost any law reform is a simplification as compared to the current state of the law, with diverging court decisions, disputes in academic literature and uncertainty for litigants. Over the years, even the clearest and plainest words of the legislature are covered with thick layers of court decisions and doctrinal considerations which often help to clarify the meaning and application of the law and do justice to extraordinary situations, but at the same time make it difficult for outsiders to grasp the actual state of the law and the policy considerations behind it. As time is precious and the willingness to discuss everything in detail is limited, the larger the scope of a harmonisation project, the more of the complexity of their home systems drafters of harmonised rules typically will be ready to abandon in order to strike a compromise and come to a result.

However, simplification does not come at no cost. It is true that sometimes, legal rules are complex or sophisticated as a result of compromises during the law-making process which do not reflect the needs of the law but have political or even personal reasons, and that sometimes the complexity is the result of an overzealous drafter, combined with the ignorance and lack of attention of the

---

40 See, *inter alia*, Regulation (EU) No. 1215/2012 of the European Parliament and of the Council of 12 December 2012 on jurisdiction and the recognition and enforcement of judgments in civil and commercial matters, OJ L 351 of 20 December 2012, pp. 1–32; Council Regulation (EC) No. 2201/2003 of 27 November 2003 concerning jurisdiction and the recognition and enforcement of judgments in matrimonial matters and the matters of parental responsibility, repealing Regulation (EC) No. 1347/2000, OJ L 338 of 23 December 2003, pp. 1–29.

41 Convention on jurisdiction and the recognition and enforcement of judgments in civil and commercial matters, OJ L 147 of 10 June 2006, pp. 5–43.

legislature. Normally, though, the complexity of the law and the sophistication of legal texts are consequences of the complexity of the reality. A text which simplifies too much will either bring about solutions which, in a number of cases, will be considered "unjust" or must take its final shape by operation of legal practice, with courts and practitioners carving out exceptions and justifying extensions. Two examples shall serve as an illustration.

6.2. THE PRINCIPLE OF COOPERATION

Like clothing, legal theories are subject to trends. A trend in civil procedure is to interpret the proceedings and the procedural rules under the aspect of cooperation between the parties and the court.[42] Probably, this trend is a reaction to excessively formalistic or excessively adversarial proceedings in some parts of the world. It should also be noted that the exact meaning of cooperation is not the same among its proponents and in different legal environments.[43] As such, the focus on cooperation clearly has the merit to introduce a fresh look at the role of the parties, their lawyers and the judge. However, some scholars are fascinated by the "new" idea of cooperation to a degree that sometimes loses track of procedural realities.[44] Thus, the Working Group on Obligations has

42 Carlos Alberto Alvaro de Oliveira, *Do Formalismo no Processo Civil*, 2nd edn., São Paulo: Saraiva, 2003, passim; Alvaro de Oliveira, "Poderes do Juiz e Visão Cooperativa do Processo" 30(90) *Revista da AJURIS* 56 (2003); Lucio Grassi Gouvea, "Cognição Processual Civil: Atividade Dialética e Cooperação Intersubjetiva na Busca da Verdade Real" in Fredie Didier Jr. (ed.), *Leituras Complementares de Processo Civil*, 5th edn., Salvador: Jus Podivm, 2007, pp. 183 et seq.; Daniel Mitidiero, "Colaboração no Processo Civil: Presuppostos sociais, lógicos e éticos" in Luis Guilherme Marinoni and José Roberto dos Santos Bedaque (eds.), *Coleçao Temas Atuais de Direito Processual Civil*, vol. 14, São Paulo: Revisto dos Tribunais, 2009, pp. 102 et seq.; Ronaldo Kochem, "Introdução às raízes históricos do princípio da cooperação (Kooperationsmaxime)", Ano 41 No. 251 *Revista de Processo* [*RePro*] 75 (2016).

43 In Germany, Austria and Switzerland, for example, the "principle of cooperation" is typically understood as referring to the way the court determines the facts. The traditional alternatives are the determination of the facts *ex officio* ("*Untersuchungsmaxime*") – which, in Germany and Switzerland, is not the case in most civil matters, but in criminal and administrative matters – or only within the allegations of the parties ("*Verhandlungsmaxime*"). The principle of cooperation is considered to be a "third way" between the two other principles. See, e.g., Karl August Bettermann, "Hundert Jahre Zivilprozeßordnung – Das Schicksal einer liberalen Kodifikation", *ZZP* 91 (1978), 365, 391; Rudolf Wassermann, *Der soziale Zivilprozeß*, Neuwied: Luchterhand 1978, p. 109; Helmut Rüßmann, *Alternativkommentar zur Zivilprozeßordnung*, Neuwied: Luchterhand, 1987, vor §284 mn. 3; Bernhard Hahn, *Kooperationsmaxime im Zivilprozess?*, Köln: Carl Heymanns, 1983, passim; Marianne Heer, "Von der Verhandlungs- zur Kooperationsmaxime" in *Richter und Verfahrensrecht. Festgabe 150 Jahre Obergericht Luzern*, Bern: Stämpfli 1991, p. 153; Klaus F. Kugler, *Die Kooperationsmaxime*, Linz: Trauner Verlag, 2002.

44 For critical remarks, see, e.g., Nevhis Deren-Yıldırım, "Die Kooperationsmaxime und ihre ideologischen Aspekte" in Ludwig Bittner et al. (eds.), *Festschrift für Walter H. Rechberger zum 60. Geburtstag*, Wien: Springer, 2005, pp. 103 et seq.

argued with force that cooperation should be the only overarching principle for the whole project. In reality, it is rather difficult to imagine parties who are in dispute cooperating fraternally, and even more difficult is it to see the judge who, in the very end, may have to decide according to the law, participating in cooperation with the parties. Cooperation can be ordered to a certain degree, and mutual respect is important. But cooperation can, despite all academic thinking, hardly be the most important principle in a system designed for the resolution of disputes.

The Working Groups on Judgments and on Appeals deal with subjects in which cooperation is hard to put into practice. The different types of judgments are a command of efficiency; the rules on default judgments sanction non-cooperation to a certain degree, but also aim at alleviating court dockets and, last but not least, protecting parties from lazy lawyers. A party who files an appeal is not satisfied with a decision; it is, in a sense, not cooperating with the lower court. From the perspective of judgments and appeals, cooperation is certainly one aspect, but one among others and probably not the most important one.

6.3. LEAVE TO APPEAL

Whenever there are restrictions on appeals, the question arises who has jurisdiction to verify whether the prerequisites for an appeal are met: The court whose decision is appealed against or the court which has to decide on the appeal. At first glance, a clear-cut and simple solution would be to determine that either the lower or the higher court has exclusive jurisdiction to decide on the leave for appeal. Interestingly, though, the German system has, in ordinary cases, combined both solutions: The lower court has the power to grant leave for appeal,[45] which is then binding on the higher court.[46] But the higher court has the power to grant leave once the lower court has mistakenly disallowed it.[47] Is this overly sophisticated or are there good reasons for such an approach?

The answer must depart from the idea that appeals serve the parties, but also the legal system as a whole. On the one hand, if only the lower courts can allow an appeal, one might fear that only few appeals would be permitted, as no judge wants his or her judgment to be censured and lifted on appeal and, even worse, see the case sent back for reconsideration. On the other hand, if the higher courts decide on the appeals, they may pick only cases in which they are interested, thereby ignoring the need to preserve the uniformity of the system. Indeed, lower courts may wish to have the higher court decide a case in order

45 S. 543(1) no. 1 ZPO.
46 S. 543(2) 2nd sentence ZPO.
47 S. 543(1) no. 2 ZPO.

to have guidance for future decisions. If the higher court could decline to take the case, legal uncertainty could persist for quite a long time, a situation which can sometimes be observed in the U.S. when the U.S. Supreme Court declines to grant a writ of certiorari despite parties' petitioning for it in a number of cases. Moreover, if the lower courts can "oblige" the higher court to decide a matter, but at the same time the higher court can take cases which the lower courts would not have liked to see controlled by the higher courts, this creates mutual checks and balances. Both the judges of the lower courts and the higher courts may feel less inclined to develop arrogance, and arrogance is one of the worst qualities of a judge.

The preceding lines have shown that there might be good arguments for a sophisticated solution with respect to the power to grant leave to appeal. Nevertheless, the Working Group on Appeals did not opt for this solution. The majority within the group considered this model to be too complex, and the arguments in favour of it not sufficiently compelling. The Working Group has opted instead for an exclusive power of the higher court to decide on the leave for appeal. This is, no doubt, a defensible position. Nevertheless, if it is put into place, constitutional or human rights courts will probably carve out loopholes for situations of an unwilling higher court.

7. CONCLUSION

Despite promising historical examples, harmonising civil procedure in today's world is more difficult than one might imagine at first glance. This even holds true for the areas of judgments and appeals – areas which are perceived to be technical but involve important policy decisions. The Working Groups do their best in proposing harmonised rules. Whether these proposals will make it to the final project, whether the final draft will receive the approval of ELI and UNIDROIT, and, most importantly, whether the project will have any consequences in the real world, are questions only time will answer. However, already the attempt is worth the time and money invested, as it contributes to a better understanding of procedural law – and this, ultimately, is what paves the way for a not necessarily harmonised, but harmonious, future.

PART III

CURRENT INITIATIVES FOR FURTHER HARMONISATION

The 2017 Directive Proposal on Common Minimum Standards of Civil Procedure

THE 2017 DIRECTIVE PROPOSAL ON COMMON MINIMUM STANDARDS OF CIVIL PROCEDURE IN THE EUROPEAN UNION

Fernando Gascón Inchausti

1. ORIGINS AND SCOPE OF THE PROPOSAL

1.1. ORIGINS

Since the development of the well-known "Storme Project",[1] there have been several indications that the EU institutions do not disregard a possible harmonisation of (some aspects of) civil procedure. The Action Plan for the implementation of the Stockholm Programme,[2] approved in 2010, already contained the expectation that the Commission would prepare a green paper on minimum standards for civil proceedings (in 2013) and that it would formulate a legislative proposal to improve coherence of the existing legislation in the Union in the field of civil procedural law (in 2014); however, these objectives did not materialise in the foreseen terms. After the exhaustion of the Stockholm Programme, the "Strategic Guidelines for the Area of Freedom, Security and Justice", approved by the European Council of 26–27 June 2014,[3] returned to the field of generality, without direct mention of a possible approximation of civil procedural legislation (the document refers, for instance, to "simplifying access to justice" or "improving the mutual recognition of decisions and judgments in civil matters", but it does include further details).

However, the issue has remained very active in the agenda of the EU institutions: various projects sponsored by the Commission have been focused on exploring the possibilities of civil procedural harmonisation;[4] and there is an open work line in the European Parliament,[5] which has organised meetings[6] and commissioned studies.[7] This work line led eventually to the resolution of the

---

1 M. Storme (ed.), *Approximation of judiciary law in the European Union*, Kluwer, 1994.

2 Doc. COM(2010) 171 final: http://eur-lex.europa.eu/legal-content/EN/TXT/?uri=celex:52010DC0171.

3 http://register.consilium.europa.eu/doc/srv?f=ST+79+2014+INIT&l=en#page=2.

4 See, namely, the "Luxembourg Study on European Civil Procedure", developed under the leadership of the Max-Planck-Institute Luxembourg for Procedural Law: B. Hess et al., *An evaluation study of national procedural laws and practices in terms of their impact on the free circulation of judgments and on the equivalence and effectiveness of the procedural protection of consumers under EU consumer law.* Strand 1: mutual trust and free circulation of judgments (2017): https://publications.europa.eu/en/publication-detail/-/publication/531ef49a-9768-11e7-b92d-01aa75ed71a1/language-en.

5 The interest of the European Parliament in advancing along the path of harmonisation is already announced by R. Bray, "Common Rules and Best Practices From the Perspective of the European Parliament" in B. Hess/X.E. Kramer (eds.), *From common rules to best practices in European Civil Procedure*, Nomos, Baden-Baden, 2017, 35–42.

6 See, for instance, the workshop "Common minimums standards of civil procedure", held on 15 June 2016 (https://europa.eu/newsroom/events/workshop-common-minimum-standards-civil-procedure_en).

7 See, for instance, R. Mańko, *Europeanisation of civil procedure. Towards common minimum standards?*, European Parliamentary Research Service, In-Depth Analysis, PE 559.499 (2015); M. Tulibacka/M. Sanz/R. Blomeyer, *Common minimum standards of civil procedure, European Parliamentary Research Service, European Added Value. Assessment. Annex I,*

European Parliament of 4 July 2017 with recommendations to the Commission on common minimum standards of civil procedure in the European Union.[8] This document represents an outstanding initiative in terms of harmonisation, not only because of its "official" nature, but namely because it includes the draft text of the proposal for a Directive on common minimum standards of civil procedure in the European Union. The proposed text comprises indeed 28 articles, divided into three chapters: a first chapter on subject matter, scope and definitions (Articles 1 to 3); a second chapter establishing the minimum standards of civil procedure (Articles 4 to 24); and a third chapter with the final provisions on transposition, review and entry into force (Articles 25 to 28).

The presentation of this proposal constitutes, without a doubt, a qualitative leap. Since the parliamentary vote no further steps seem to have been taken; it is therefore uncertain whether the text will be finally enacted and, anyhow, one would always expect differences in the content of a possible final text. Nevertheless, it is worth taking it into consideration, since it has the potential to set the pace for the future.

1.2. SCOPE OF THE PROPOSAL

The aim of the proposal is "to approximate civil procedure systems", as a means to ensure full respect for the right to an effective remedy and to a fair trial, as recognised in Article 47 CFREU and in Article 6 ECHR; this approximation is promoted "by laying down minimum standards concerning the commencement, conduct and conclusion of civil proceedings before Member States' courts or tribunals" (Article 1).

This objective, which in itself is very broad, is nevertheless limited in its scope of application – at least in appearance. Indeed, the approval of the directive should be based on the regulatory competence conferred by Article 81.2 TFEU, so that its application should be restricted to litigation "with cross-border repercussions" in civil and commercial matters.[9] However, the determination of what is meant by "litigation with cross-border repercussions"

PE 581.385 (2016); B. Hess, *Harmonized Rules and Minimum Standards in the European Law of Civil Procedure, European Parliamentary Research Service, In-Depth Analysis* PE 556.971 (June 2016: http://www.europarl.europa.eu/RegData/etudes/IDAN/2016/556971/IPOL_IDA (2016)556971_EN.pdf).

8 (2015/2084(INL)) http://www.europarl.europa.eu/sides/getDoc.do?type=TA&reference=P8-TA-2017-0282&language=EN&ring=A8-2017-0210.

9 United Kingdom (assuming Brexit does not materialise before any Directive has been passed), Ireland and Denmark would be outside of its geographical scope of application (Article 2.2). And the determination of what is meant by civil and commercial matters would be done according to the usual parameters (excluding revenue, customs or administrative matters and the liability of the State for '*acta iure imperii*': Article 2.1).

is done in a fairly loose and generous manner (Article 3.1),[10] so that the provisions of the Directive would come into play when:

(a) at least one of the parties is domiciled or habitually resident in a Member State other than the Member State of the court or tribunal seised; or
(b) both parties are domiciled in the same Member State as that of the court or tribunal seised, provided that the place of performance of the contract, the place where the harmful event takes place or the place of enforcement of the judgment is situated in another Member State; or
(c) both parties are domiciled in the same Member State as that of the court or tribunal seised, provided that the disputed matter falls within the scope of Union law.

The expansive potential is tremendous, especially if one takes into account the large number of areas of private law in which Union law is applicable, the most paradigmatic example being, of course, consumer law.

2. CONTENT: THE PROPOSED MINIMUM STANDARDS

Against this background, the text proposes a grouping of the minimum standards into four thematic blocks, which make up each of the sections of the second chapter: fair and effective outcomes; efficiency of proceedings; access to courts and justice; and fairness of proceedings. As will be seen below, there is a certain arbitrariness when configuring these categories and when including – sometimes, rather "fitting in" – in them some safeguards.[11] Nevertheless, the issues addressed by the proposal are symptomatic of the matters in relation to which the European law-maker is considering it appropriate to advocate minimum standards.

2.1. MINIMUM STANDARDS ON FAIR AND EFFECTIVE OUTCOMES

Under the umbrella of fairness and effectiveness of the outcomes, the proposal believes that minimum standards should be ensured in relation to three different issues: the right to effective judicial protection; personal appearance in oral hearings; and provisional and protective relief.

---

10 On the possibility of enlarging the interpretation of what are to be considered "cross-border implications", see M. Tulibacka et al. (above, n. 7), 66–67.

11 The proposal follows the systematisation used by M. Tulibacka et al. (above, n. 7) 19–20.

2.1.1. *Effective Judicial Protection*

In the first place, Article 4 makes a general proclamation of the Member States' duty to provide judicial protection of the rights conferred by Union law in civil matters, by means of measures, procedures and remedies that "shall be fair and equitable, that shall not be unnecessarily complicated or costly, or entail unreasonable time limits or unwarranted delays".

The provision is a more than obvious transposition of Article 47 CFREU from its "constitutional position" to the level of what we could call "ordinary legality": nothing can be objected to that which is established in it, since it is ultimately a reflection of the principles of equivalence and full effectiveness to the level of the regulation of civil proceedings – something, indeed, very frequent in the recent case law of the Court of Justice.

2.1.2. *Personal Appearance in Oral Hearings*

Article 5, by contrast, deals with a more daily problem, especially in cross-border litigation: the difficulty for the parties to physically appear in oral hearings (due, e.g., to distance, cost and/or other obstacles). At this point, a general duty is established for Member States to facilitate the holding of hearings by making use of any appropriate distance communication technology, such as videoconferencing or teleconferencing, available to the court or tribunal. More precisely, if the person to be heard is domiciled or habitually resident in a different Member State, it is established that that person's attendance at an oral hearing by way of videoconference, teleconference or other appropriate distance communication technology shall be arranged by making use of the procedures provided for in Regulation (EC) No. 1206/2001 (Evidence Regulation):[12] this implies the involvement of the judicial authority of the state of domicile or habitual residence, as a way of giving proof of the examination, although it may also mean a limitation on the simplicity invocation that usually accompanies the proposals to substitute physical appearances by video or teleconferences. In practice, indeed, videoconferencing does not always function as expected, due mostly to technical problems and language issues.[13]

---

12 This rule is clearly based on Article 8.1 of the European Small Claims Procedure regulation, as amended in 2015 (Regulation (EC) No. 861/2007 of the European Parliament and of the Council of 11 July 2007 establishing a European Small Claims Procedure, OJ L 199 31.7.2007). In this vein, it is important to recall that on 31 May 2018 the European Commission published its Proposal for an amendment of the Evidence Regulation [COM(2018) 378 final] including, among others, an emphasis on the use of new technologies.

13 On the troubles that videoconferencing may entail in cross-border litigation, see F. Gascón Inchausti/M. Requejo Isidro, "A Classic Cross-border Case: the Usual Situation in the First Instance" in *An evaluation study of national procedural laws and practices in terms of their impact on the free circulation of judgments and on the equivalence and effectiveness of the procedural protection of consumers under EU consumer law. Strand 1: mutual trust and free circulation of judgments* (above, n. 4) 44–167, at 119 and 125.

2.1.3. *Provisional and Protective Measures*

The third element that is considered key to ensuring the fairness and the effectiveness of the outcomes of the procedure is provisional and protective measures. At this point, Article 6 of the proposal synthesises the minimum basic elements that should characterise any advanced regulation of this institution:

i) Litigants must have at their disposal measures of a protective nature (i.e., "measures for the preservation of a factual or legal situation so as to secure the full effectiveness of a later judgment on the substance of the matter", including measures for the preservation of assets and of evidence), but also measures for the prevention of any imminent infringement or for the immediate termination of an alleged infringement. Proportionality must be the general rule regarding the determination of their content in each specific case (taking into account the features and the seriousness of the situation against which the measures are requested, and allowing where appropriate the provision of guarantees for the costs and the harm caused to the defendant by unjustified requests).
ii) Provisional and protective measures shall be available prior to proceedings on the substance of the matter being initiated and at any stage during such proceedings.
iii) Provisional and protective measures shall be granted on the basis of a *fumus boni iuris* (sustained by *prima facie* evidence – "reasonably available evidence", in the terms of the proposal) and requiring the applicant to assume full responsibility, which allows the court to demand the provision of guarantees for the costs and the harm caused to the defendant by unjustified requests.
iv) In certain circumstances of specific or aggravated *periculum in mora*, it must be possible to take these measures without the defendant having been heard, although, of course, with a right of the defendant to request a full – and adversarial – review, which may lead to compensation for any damages suffered as a result of those measures.

At this point, therefore, the proposal does not innovate, but reflects the traditional scholarship on provisional and protective measures, long ago assumed by the Court of Justice itself, which defined what should be understood as "provisional and protective measures", using a functional approach, as those "intended to preserve a factual or legal situation so as to safeguard rights the recognition of which is sought ... from the court having jurisdiction as to the substance of the matter",[14] a broad notion which encompasses also those

[14] Judgment of the Court of 26 March 1992, C-261/90, *Reichert Kockler v Dresdner Bank AG*, ECLI:EU:C:1992:149, §34.

measures able to satisfy the plaintiff's interest, even if only provisionally.[15] Indeed, this commonly shared notion of provisional and protective measures underpins also the first "European" protective measure, the European Account Preservation Order.[16]

2.2. MINIMUM STANDARDS ON THE EFFICIENCY OF PROCEEDINGS

Under the label of efficiency, safeguards and harmonisation proposals are grouped which refer to very heterogeneous issues, including the motivation of judicial resolutions, a more active case management and evidence.

2.2.1. Efficiency as a General Principle

From the outset, Article 7 attributes to efficiency the value of a general principle and, thus, of a basic interpretative canon when making procedural decisions of all kinds, making it clear that celerity – and not only costs – is part of that notion. It gives as an example three situations: the need for an oral hearing; the means of taking evidence; and the extent to which evidence is to be taken. It should therefore be understood that, with respect to the general principles of civil procedure and especially the principle of an adversarial process, the court must opt for the solution it considers most efficient, which may be not to hold a hearing (if the proceedings would be delayed), not to admit a certain means of proof (if it is considered very costly or delaying and the evidence is substitutable by another means that is less costly or less time-consuming) or to limit, according to equivalent parameters, what should be the scope of the taking of evidence (e.g., reduce the scope of an expert report to diminish its costs and the time it would take to prepare it). These ideas, indeed, also transpire from existing European regulations on civil procedure: the European Account Preservation Order (EAPO) regulation, for instance, when it comes to the evidence necessary to sustain the application for an order, shows a clear preference for documents, although it allows the court to use another appropriate method "provided that this does not delay the proceedings unduly" (Article 9.2).

---

15 Judgments of the Court of 17 November 1998, C-391/95, *Van Uden Maritime BV, trading as Van Uden Africa Line v. Kommanditgesellschaft in Firma Deco-Line and Another*, ECLI:EU:C:1998:543 and of 27 April 1999, C-99/96, *Hans-Hermann Mietz v. Intership Yachting Sneek BV*, ECLI:EU:C:1999:202.

16 Regulation (EU) No 655/2014 of the European Parliament and of the Council of 15 May 2014 establishing a European Account Preservation Order procedure to facilitate cross-border debt recovery in civil and commercial matters (OJ L 189, 27.6.2014).

2.2.2. *Motivation of Judicial Decisions*

Much more specifically, Article 8 establishes a general duty to justify or give the reasons for judicial decisions: this justification must be "sufficiently detailed" and is linked to the possibility of effectively exercising the right to challenge them. Justification is, therefore, attributed a first-rank value, which is commonly recognised in most Member States[17] and in the CFREU itself.[18] What the rule does not require is that the reasons be given at the very moment at which the decision is announced to the parties: it would be possible, therefore, to give them at a different moment, provided that it is done within a reasonable time. This proposal would serve to put an end to the problems that, on some occasions, lack of reasoned justification can generate when seeking the enforcement of judicial decisions abroad.[19]

2.2.3. *Active Case Management*

Article 9 offers the vision of what the role of the court should be in relation to the direction of proceedings: it seems necessary for the courts to have sufficiently powerful tools for the "active management of the cases", in the service of a fair and efficient disposition of disputes, in terms of time and costs.[20] Of course, the proposal does not intend to replace the principle of party disposition: therefore, it is expressly stated that active management should not impair "the freedom of the parties to determine the subject-matter of, and the supporting evidence for, their case" and, in addition, it establishes the duty of the court, as far as possible, to manage the case in consultation with the parties.[21]

There are several examples of "active case management" that, according to the proposal, should be incorporated into national legislation so that they can be said to be efficient and, therefore, that they meet the minimum standards for

---

17 F. Gascón Inchausti/M. Requejo Isidro (above, n. 13) 130.

18 The Court of Justice has held that the observance of the right to a fair trial requires that all judgments be reasoned to enable the defendant to see why judgment has been pronounced against him and to bring an appropriate and effective appeal against it (see Judgments of 14 December 2006, C-283/05, *ASML Netherlands BV v. Semiconductor Industry Services GmbH (SEMIS)*, ECLI:EU:C:2006:787, §28, and of 6 September 2012, Case C-619/10, *Trade Agency Ltd v Seramico Investments Ltd.*, ECLI:EU:C:2012:531, §53.

19 F. Gascón Inchausti/M. Requejo Isidro (above n. 13) 132.

20 C.H. van Rhee, "The development of civil procedural law in twentieth-century Europe: from party autonomy to judicial case management and efficiency" (2011) 7–8 *Russian Yearbook on Civil Procedure & Arbitration* 82–95; A. Cabral, "New Trends and Perspectives on Case Management" (2018) 1 *International Journal of Procedural Law* 10–36.

21 On the need to harmonise the rules on case management, see A. Uzelac, "Towards European Rules of Civil Procedure: Rethinking Procedural Obligations" (2017) 58(1) *Hungarian Journal of Legal Studies* 3–18; C.H. van Rhee, "Case Management in Europe: A Modern Approach to Civil Litigation" (2018) 1 *International Journal of Procedural Law* 65–84.

dealing with cross-border litigation in accordance with European parameters: (a) encouraging the parties to co-operate with each other during the proceedings; (b) identifying the issues at an early stage; (c) deciding promptly which issues need full investigation and disposing summarily of other issues; (d) deciding the order in which issues are to be resolved; (e) helping the parties to settle the whole or part of the action; (f) fixing timetables to control the progress of the action; (g) dealing with as many aspects of the action as possible before the court on the same occasion; (h) dealing with the action without the parties needing to attend in person; and (i) making use of available technical means. At this point, the proposal may be more innovative, especially with regard to some national procedural models, which tend toward rigidity.

2.2.4. Evidence

Also included in the section on efficiency are the two single provisions that the proposal devotes to evidence.[22] In general terms, a sort of fundamental right to evidence is enshrined, which obliges Member States to ensure that effective means of presenting, obtaining and preserving evidence are available, with the explicit limit of the protection of confidential information (Article 10.1). The efficiency approach becomes visible when it comes to the taking of evidence itself: the court will have to opt for the simplest and least-costly method, encouraging the use of modern communication technologies (Article 10.2).

Among the different types of evidence, only court experts disserve the proposal's attention in Article 11. Without excluding party-appointed experts, the proposal considers it necessary that the court may at any time appoint experts "in order to provide expertise for specific aspects of the case", who shall be subject to the same requirements of independence and impartiality as judges, and whose reports are to be brought to the attention of the parties, who will have the right to comment on them. The wording is too ambiguous to conclude clearly whether it is forcing national legislators to allow in any case *ex officio* expertise – something that would clash with the vision of things in many legal systems – or if it is limited to demanding that Member States set up a system that allows the courts to find experts, when they must or may appoint them; that is, *ex officio* – if their legislation permits it – or at the request of a party. This second interpretation appears sustained by paragraph 3 of proposed Article 11, which obliges the Commission to draw up a European directory of experts by bringing

---

22 N. Trocker, "From ALI-Unidroit Principles to common European rules on access to information and evidence? A preliminary outlook and some suggestions" (2014) 19 *Uniform Law Review* 239–291.

together existing national lists of experts and which will be made available via the European e-justice portal.[23]

In the more specific domain of cross-border cases, Article 11.2 of the proposal seems to have enshrined the solution offered by the Court of Justice in its *ProRail* judgment:[24] the courts may appoint an expert and order him or her to carry out "investigations" – *rectius*, expert actions – in another Member State without having to resort to the formal channels of cooperation between courts of the Evidence Regulation, unless carrying out the expert investigations requires coercive measures or access to places restricted or prohibited to certain persons.

2.3. MINIMUM STANDARDS ON ACCESS TO COURTS AND JUSTICE

2.3.1. Settlement of Disputes

Section 3 of Chapter 2 of the proposal groups together minimum standards related to the economic dimension of procedure, with the exception of the first one, addressing the settlement of disputes. Article 12, consistently with the notion of "active case management" of the procedure, establishes the need to empower the court so that, at any stage of the proceedings, if it considers that the dispute is suitable for a settlement, it may propose to the parties recourse to mediation in order to settle or to explore the possibility of a settlement. In any case, and to avoid misunderstandings, the right of the parties to abandon mediation and resort to judicial proceedings or arbitration is explicitly recognised – in line with the decision of the Court of Justice in *Menini and Rampanelli*, where it was stated that the 2013 Directive on consumer ADR[25] precludes national legislation which provides that consumers may withdraw from a mediation procedure only if they demonstrate the existence of a valid reason in support of that decision.[26]

2.3.2. Court Fees

Court fees are the first of the economic aspects of proceedings in relation to which the implementation of minimum standards is considered necessary. Article 13

---

23 More specifically, the directory shall be drawn up by bringing together existing national lists of experts and shall be made available via the European e-justice portal.

24 Judgment of 21 February 2013, C-332/11, *ProRail BV v. Xpedys NV and Others*, ECLI:EU:C:2013:87.

25 Directive 2013/11/EU of the European Parliament and of the Council of 21 May 2013 on alternative dispute resolution for consumer disputes and amending Regulation (EC) No. 2006/2004 and Directive 2009/22/EC (OJ 2013 L 165).

26 Judgment of the Court of 14 June 2017, C-75/16, *Menini and Rampanelli v. Banco Popolare – Società Cooperativa*, ECLI:EU:C:2017:457.

assumes that they are possible – but not compulsory, of course – and insists that they must be proportionate to the value of the claim and they shall not discourage citizens from bringing a case before a court or hinder in any way access to justice: how to translate these rather indeterminate legal notions in practice can be a source of difficulties. With a clearer approach to cross-border litigation, it is considered imperative that court fees can be paid by means of distance payment methods, also from another Member State other than that in which the court has its seat, by bank transfer or by credit or debit card payment.[27] In addition, the information in this regard must be easily accessible (and understandable) through the Internet and, in particular, through the European e-Justice Portal.

2.3.3. *Orders for Costs*

The proposal has also had the courage to venture into much thornier terrain, the order for costs; and it has done so with the will to establish as a minimum standard – and therefore as a common standard – the *loser pays principle* (i.e., the unsuccessful party bears the costs of the proceedings). Although it is a rule common to the procedural systems of almost all Member States, there are significant differences when it comes to specifying its reach and its exceptions and modulations.[28] Article 14 makes the following proposals in relation to this:

(i) An order for costs shall include those resulting from the fact that the other party was represented by a lawyer or another legal professional – regardless if their intervention was legally mandatory or not. Having in mind the cross-border nature of the case, mention is also made to any costs arising from the service or translation of documents. Common requirement for the expenses to be included in the order for costs is that they are proportionate to the value of the claim and they were necessarily incurred.
(ii) An order for costs shall not include unnecessary costs, i.e., incurred either by raising unnecessary issues or by being otherwise unreasonably disputatious.
(iii) Where a party succeeds only in part or in exceptional circumstances, courts have a discretionary power to order an equitable apportion of costs or that the parties bear their own costs.
(iv) The court shall also have the power to adjust its award of costs to reflect – or rather, sanction – unreasonable failure to cooperate or bad-faith participation in settlement endeavours.

---

27 Here again, the proposal is clearly inspired in Article 15a of the ESCP Regulation, as amended in 2015.

28 F. Gascón Inchausti/M. Requejo Isidro (above n. 13) 133–138; A. Dori/V. Richard, "Litigation Costs and Procedural Cultures – New Avenues for Research in Procedural Law" in *From common rules to best practices in European Civil Procedure* (above, n. 5) 303–351.

2.3.4. *Legal Aid*

Article 15 focuses on the flip side of the coin, legal aid. Although at this point the European Union already has the minimum standards of Directive 2003/8,[29] it is intended to go one step further, proclaiming not only the duty of Member States to grant it, but specifying the elements that should be covered, in whole or in part, by legal aid: (a) court fees, through total or partial discounts or rescheduling; (b) costs of legal assistance and representation for pre-litigation advice with a view to reaching a settlement prior to commencing legal proceedings; (c) costs of legal assistance and representation for commencing and maintaining proceedings before the court; (d) all costs relating to proceedings including the application for legal aid; (e) costs of legal assistance and representation for enforcement of decisions; (f) other necessary costs related to the proceedings to be borne by a party, including costs of witnesses, experts, interpreters and translators and necessary travel, accommodation and subsistence costs of that party and his representative; and (g) the costs awarded to the successful party, in the event that the applicant loses the action.

With regard to natural persons, the proposal aims to offer a kind of general benefit to all Union nationals or legal residents in the Union, subject to three requirements which, in this way, also become minimum standards: (i) lack of economic capacity (which, however, is not defined with greater precision); (ii) a reasonable prospect of success of the action; and (iii) the claimant seeking legal aid shall be entitled to bring actions under the relevant national provisions.

The proposed text goes beyond the scope of Directive 2003/8 by addressing the possibility of granting legal aid to legal persons. At this point, it is considered that, at least, they should have the right to obtain as legal aid a dispensation from advance payment of the costs of proceedings and/or the assistance of a lawyer. And, as for the elements to be taken into consideration for granting them legal aid, certain elements or criteria are offered in an open manner: (1) the form of the legal person in question and whether it is profit-making or non-profit-making; (2) the financial capacity of the partners or shareholders; and (3) the ability of those partners or shareholders to obtain the necessary amounts to initiate legal proceedings.

In addition, the proposal establishes the duty to provide information to potential beneficiaries of legal aid about the right and, above all, the procedure to be followed to seek it.

---

29 Council Directive 2003/8/EC of 27 January 2003 to improve access to justice in cross-border disputes by establishing minimum common rules relating to legal aid for such disputes (OJ L 26, 31.1.2003).

2.3.5. *Litigation Funding*

Article 16, for its part, deals with the new phenomena related to the financing of litigation and, more specifically, to third-party funding. Rather than regulating them, the aim is to establish certain limits, stemming from what had already been recommended in 2013 for collective actions:[30] (1) the private third party shall not seek to influence the plaintiff's procedural decisions, including those relating to settlements; (2) a private third party must not be allowed to fund a class action that is directed against a defendant who is a competitor of the fund provider or on whom the fund provider is dependent; (3) the private third party must not charge "excessive" interest on the funds provided; and (4) the remuneration or interest that goes to the private third party should not be based on the amount set in the settlement reached or in the compensation granted, unless the funding agreement is regulated by a public authority guaranteeing the interests of the parties. This last requirement will undoubtedly be a source of controversy, if one takes into account the usual dynamics of these funding schemes, frequently "allergic" to public supervision.

2.4. MINIMUM STANDARDS ON FAIRNESS OF THE PROCEEDINGS

2.4.1. *Service of Proceedings*

The last block of minimum standards includes those aimed at guaranteeing the fairness of the proceedings. Perhaps for that reason, the first provision is dedicated to the service of documents and, in a special way, to the documents instituting the proceedings.

Article 17 condenses to a large extent the *acquis communautaire* on service, which can be deduced, in particular, from the Regulations on the European enforcement order,[31] the European order for payment procedure,[32] and the

30 Commission Recommendation of 11 June 2013 on common principles for injunctive and compensatory collective redress mechanisms in the Member States concerning violations of rights granted under Union Law (OJ L 201, 26.7.2013). See on this *Statement of the European Law Institute on Collective Redress and Competition Damages Claims* (2014) at: 31–35 and 56: https://www.europeanlawinstitute.eu/fileadmin/user_upload/p_eli/Publications/S-5-2014_Statement_on_Collective_Redress_and_Competition_Damages_Claims.pdf (last access 11.1.2019).

31 Regulation (EC) No 805/2004 of the European Parliament and of the Council of 21 April 2004 creating a European Enforcement Order for uncontested claims (OJ L 143, 30.4.2004).

32 Regulation (EC) No 1896/2006 of the European Parliament and of the Council of 12 December 2006 creating a European order for payment procedure (OJ L 399, 30.12.2006).

European small claims procedure, and from the case law of the Court of Justice and the European Court of Human Rights.[33]

Starting from the preference for service methods guaranteeing receipt of the served documents, the proposal places at the same level personal service, postal service and service by electronic means, such as fax or email (taking for granted, in relation to these, that appropriately high technical standards, guaranteeing the identity of the sender and the safe transmission of the served documents, shall be used). Service shall be attested by an acknowledgment of receipt including the date of receipt, which shall be signed by the addressee. In case of personal service, it may also be attested by a document signed by the competent person who effected it, stating that the addressee has received the documents or refused them without any legal justification, and the date of the service.

As subsidiary methods of service, but provided that the defendant's domicile is known with certainty, the following are considered acceptable – but not necessarily to be incorporated into national legislation: (a) in person at the defendant's personal address, on persons who are living in the same household as the defendant or are employed there; (b) in the case of a self-employed defendant or a legal person, personal service at the defendant's business premises, on persons who are employed by the defendant; (c) deposit of the documents in the defendant's mailbox; (d) deposit of the documents at a post office or with competent public authorities and the placing in the defendant's mailbox of written notification of that deposit, provided that the written notification clearly states the character of the documents as being court documents or the legal effect of the notification as effecting service and setting in motion the running of time for the purposes of time limits;[34] (e) postal service without proof of receipt where the defendant's address is in the Member State of origin; and (f) electronic means attested by an automatic advice of delivery, provided that the defendant has expressly accepted this method of service in advance.[35]

In all cases – i.e., with or without acknowledgement of receipt by the addressee – service may also be effected on the defendant's legal or authorised

---

33 Cfr. F. Gascón Inchausti, "Service of proceedings on the defendant as a safeguard of fairness in civil proceedings: in search of minimum standards from EU legislation and European case-law" (2017) 13(3) *Journal of Private International Law* 475–518.

34 In the first four mentioned situations, service shall be attested by a document signed by the competent person who effected the service, indicating all of the following: (i) the full name of the person who served the notification or communication; (ii) the method of service used; (iii) the date of service; (iv) where the served documents have been served on a person other than the defendant, the name of that person and his or her relationship to the defendant; and (v) other compulsory information to be provided under national law. As an alternative, but only for the first two mentioned situations, the proposal also admits an acknowledgement of receipt by the person served.

35 As mentioned above, this list of direct and subsidiary methods of service is not original, but based on the pre-existing provisions of Articles 13 and 14 of the EEO Regulation, 13 and 14 of the EOP Regulation, and 13 of the ESCP Regulation.

representative. And for cross-border service of documents, reference is made to the Service Regulation[36] or to the 1965 Hague Convention, depending on their scope of application.

The proposal, however, does not address one of the main problems generated by the need to make the plaintiff's access to justice compatible with the defendant's right to a fair trial: what to do when the defendant's domicile is unknown and/or how to operate when, despite the diligence and efforts of the court or of the plaintiff, it is not possible to obtain an acknowledgement of receipt attesting service. Most legal systems admit methods of fictitious service, which the proposal does not prohibit explicitly, since the general rule is that methods guaranteeing receipt of the served documents shall be used *as a matter of principle*. The silence of the proposal – understandable given the thorny nature of the issue – would have to mean, in practice, the need to deal, at least in cross-border situations, with the provisions: of the Service Regulation – regarding the possibility or not of pursuing the process (Article 19); of the Brussels I bis Regulation – on the refusal of recognition and enforcement in case of involuntary default (Article 45.1 (b);[37] and of the Regulations on the European enforcement order, the European order for payment procedure and the European small claims procedure – regarding the possibility of obtaining a review in case of ignorance of the existence of the proceedings.

2.4.2. Legal Representation

For obvious reasons, the proposal also links to the fairness of proceedings the need to guarantee the right to use a lawyer. In particular, Article 18 seeks to provide a balance between the different legal traditions regarding legal representation and the special needs of cross-border litigation. The general rule, of course, is the right of the parties to use a lawyer of their choice, which is associated with the confidentiality of communications of all kinds between the parties to a case and their lawyers (including meetings, correspondence and telephone conversations or other forms of communication). The special feature, for cross-border litigation, is the recognition of the right to the "double lawyer": the parties should have the right to a lawyer in their state of origin for preliminary advice and another in the host state to conduct the litigation. It would be coherent to understand that both lawyers are covered by the privilege of confidentiality and that requests for legal aid could be formulated in relation to both.

---

36 Bear in mind that on 31 May 2018 the European Commission published a Proposal for a Regulation amending the Service Regulation [COM(2018) 379 final].

37 See the Judgments of the Court of 17 November 2011, C-327/10, *Hypoteční banka a.s. v. Udo Mike Lindner*, ECLI:EU:C:2011:745; 15 March 2012, C-292/10, *G v. Cornelius de Visser*, ECLI:EU:C:2012:142; and 11 September 2014, C-112/13, *A v. B*, ECLI:EU:C:2014:2195 (§60).

As far as self-defence is concerned, it should be remembered that European procedural law favours exempting litigants from mandatory legal representation (e.g., European order for payment procedures, European small claims procedures or consumer ADR schemes). The situation is heterogeneous within the national systems,[38] something that the proposal is aware of. However, even assuming that there are Member States where the main rule is mandatory legal representation, the proposal establishes the right to waive it if two conditions and a safeguard are met. The conditions are: (1) parties must have been provided orally or in writing with clear and sufficient information in simple and understandable language about the possible consequences of the waiver; and (2) the waiver must be voluntary and unequivocal. And the safeguard is the revocability *ad libitum* of the waiver at any time (which includes the duty to inform the parties about that possibility).

Perhaps with a minor rank – although not at all negligible – Article 19 recognises the duty of Member States to provide citizens with transparent and easily available information regarding the commencement of various procedures, limitation or prescription periods, the competent courts to hear different disputes, and the necessary forms that need to be filled in for that purpose. It is, obviously, a complement to the self-defence powers that are recognised, but also an additional manifestation of the duty of the states to facilitate active citizenship and a better knowledge of the rights of each one, as a means to face the monopolies – *de iure* or *de facto* – of legal professions in many systems. The proposal clarifies, however, that the information to be provided on the basis of this safeguard must be general, not specific and related to a specific case ("legal assessment of a specific case"): this will only be required, where appropriate, under the rules on legal aid.

2.4.3. Translation and Interpretation

In close relationship to the right of the parties to understand the entire proceedings, Article 20 of the proposal includes the duty of Member States to ensure that interpretation and written translations of all *essential* documents are available in order to safeguard the fairness of proceedings.[39] This concern is directly linked to cross-border litigation and is aligned with the most

---

[38] For an overview, F. Gascón Inchausti/M. Requejo Isidro (above n. 13) 100–103.

[39] What documents are to be considered essential can only be assessed on a case-by-case basis. Nevertheless, the Court of Justice – when it comes to the scope of Article 8 of the Service Regulation – has established that this notion encompasses the document instituting the proceedings or equivalent document, but not those attachments which are of a merely evidentiary nature and are not necessary for understanding the purpose or cause of the claim (Judgment of the Court of 8 May 2008, C-14/07, *Ingenieurbüro Michael Weiss und Partner GbR v Industrie- und Handelskammer Berlin*, ECLI:EU:C:2008:264).

recent trend in EU legislation on civil procedure to reinforce the fairness of proceedings also from a linguistic point of view (Article 8 Service Regulation; Article 49 EAPO Regulation; Article 7 Legal Aid Directive; and, more recently, Article 43.2 of the Brussels I bis Regulation, requiring, where appropriate, translation of the judgment into a language that the defendant understands – or is deemed to understand).[40]

2.4.4. *Procedural Good Faith*

Article 21, on the other hand, deals with a question as controversial as it is old: procedural good faith. Under the somewhat ambiguous rubric of "obligations of the parties and their representatives", it establishes the duty of Member States to ensure that the parties and their representatives "conduct themselves in good faith and with respect" when interacting with the court and with other parties and do not "misrepresent cases or facts" either deliberately or recklessly. It should be noted that the direct addressees of the provision are Member States: for that reason, the transposition of a possible directive with such content would probably oblige them, even if it is not expressly stated, to establish a sanctions or consequences regime in case of infringement to the duty of procedural good faith; and a delicate issue would be to calibrate what would be the catalogue of consequences and, above all, their proportionality.[41]

2.4.5. *Public Proceedings and Confidentiality*

The general principle of public proceedings, which also belongs to the bundle of safeguards associated with the notion of fairness, is recognised in Article 22 of the proposal. Hearings must be open to the public, unless the court decides that they should take place behind closed doors in the interest of one of the parties, third parties, justice or public order. The publicity of written proceedings shall also be encompassed in the provision, enabling the court to keep "confidential" written parts of the judicial files. It might be advisable to link this rule with a regulation – absent in the proposal – of the protection of personal data contained in judicial files.[42]

---

40 An overview on how Members States deal with translation and interpretation issues can be found, again, in F. Gascón Inchausti/M. Requejo Isidro (above n. 13) 95–100 and 116.

41 See A. Uzelac (above n. 21) 12–13.

42 See, in this regard, the recent developments in France with the *Rapport "L'open data des décisions de justice"* (November 2017), drafted by a working group led by Prof. L. Cadiet, which analyses the necessary changes and arrangements to allow open accesss to any judicial decision while safeguarding the fundamental right to the protection of personal data (http://www.justice.gouv.fr/publication/open_data_rapport.pdf).

2.4.6. *Independence and Impartiality*

The catalogue of principles ensuring fairness of proceedings is completed by Article 23 with judicial independence and impartiality, which are defined in a simple and peacefully accepted manner: the absence of instructions, influences or pressures on judges in the performance of their duties; and a composition of courts and tribunals that excludes any reasonable doubt about their impartiality, with exemption of individuals displaying any personal prejudice or bias in any given case. Both requirements stem directly from Article 47 CFREU and have been considered by the Court of Justice[43] as prominent pillars to ensure smooth and lawful cooperation between Members States in civil and criminal matters – something that justifies their mention in a proposal directly linked with cross-border litigation.

2.4.7. *Training*

The last factor to be considered sufficiently prominent as to be included in the proposal for a directive is the training of judges and legal professions in Union law and procedures, covered by Article 24: these matters will have to be included in the training plans for them. The purpose is to force Member States to mitigate one of the biggest problems affecting European civil procedure legislation: its lack of knowledge or its deficient knowledge.[44] The proposal, moreover, is singularly detailed when specifying the scope and the methodological orientation of those "compulsory" training programmes: orientation to practice, linked to practitioners' everyday work, of short duration, the use of active and modern learning techniques, a combination of initial and continuing training possibilities or training in foreign languages, among others. The limits between the content of a directive and a recommendation are blurred here, although the concern underlying this proposal seems clear.

3. A GENERAL ASSESSMENT

The value – not only symbolic – of this proposal and the impact it will undoubtedly have on future developments are undeniable. A more exhaustive study will only become meaningful if the initiative moves forward, but in any case what has been analysed so far serves to verify, above all, that harmonisation of civil

---

43 Judgment of the Court of 27 February 2018, *Associação Sindical dos Juízes Portugueses v. Tribunal de Contas*, C-64/16, EU:C:2018:117; Judgment of the Court of 25 July 2018, *LM*, C-216/18 PPU, EU:C:2018:586; Order of the Court of 17 December 2018, *European Commission v. Republic of Poland*, C-619/18, ECLI:EU:C:2018:1021.

44 See on this the findings in F. Gascón Inchausti/M. Requejo Isidro (above n. 13) 49.

proceedings has not reached its ceiling and that it is starting to be considered necessary to achieve developments that should be at the same time direct and general: direct, in the sense that the European law-maker is not satisfied with the possible indirect impact that its rules on cross-border litigation may have on the level of internal litigation;[45] and general, that is to say, not limited only to the judicial relief regarding certain parts of substantive law, as has been happening to date with the genuine and directly harmonising provisions that have emanated from the European Union – the so-called horizontal harmonisation.

The proposal contains a conglomerate of provisions grouped under the label of "minimum standards", which combines proclamations of fundamental procedural safeguards – such as judicial independence, impartiality or public proceedings – that could be deduced directly from Article 47 CFREU or Article 6 ECHR (and which, to that extent, may be redundant), together with true "legal" provisions, addressing issues that support diverse legislative policy approaches and in which the final solution conforms to the will of the law-maker to choose the one it considers best – as occurs, e.g., with the promotion of mediation, with the "loser pays" rule in matters of costs, with the limits to the financing of litigation by third parties or with the extent of the case management.

This heterogeneity in the content of the proposal also affects the level of detail with which the matters and the minimum standards are treated – or left untreated. The detail when establishing minimum standards relating to active case management, service or legal aid, for instance, contrasts with the brevity when providing content to issues that are more directly linked to Article 81.2 TFEU, like the right to interpretation and translation, or the procedural expenses associated with the cross-border nature of the proceedings.

It is, possibly, one of the weakest flanks of the proposal. On the one hand, it may seem unnecessary to approve a directive that seeks only to "legalise" provisions that already have fundamental status. On the other hand, it may be considered an unnecessary omission in the battered procedural autonomy of Member States, since the European law-maker would be taking legal policy options regarding aspects of civil procedure with little or no impact on the "European dimension" of legal life in Member States – both in terms of cross-border litigation and the internal market.

Indeed, the formulation of the proposal does not seem to follow the same logic of the harmonisation of criminal proceedings, which has been focused on the safeguards of victims, suspects and accused persons, as a basis for legitimising intensive judicial cooperation. In civil and commercial matters cooperation has always been prior and the acceptance of mutual recognition – and of the mutual trust on which it is based – has been at the same time less controversial, possibly because the public policy clause has always been

---

45 See on this Chapter 4 of this book.

considered an appropriate piece to maintain the balance between mutual trust and the safeguard of national essential values. Good proof of the above are the discussions that, on the occasion of the recasting of the Brussels I Regulation in the Brussels I bis Regulation, raised the need to maintain or delete the public policy clause as a ground for refusal of recognition and enforcement,[46] and that culminated in its survival – a survival, in fact, that was re-emphasised shortly afterwards by the EAPO Regulation, the enforcement of which must also be rendered ineffective if it is manifestly contrary to the public order of the Member State of enforcement.[47] In short, we do not seem to be facing a harmonisation that is necessary to legitimise judicial cooperation in civil matters, nor to legitimise the so-called "European procedures", in that part in which their provisions refer to the national procedural rules of the Member States.

In a different way, the aim is rather to raise the quality standards of national procedural systems, so the impact would be different for each of them. And this seems to be due to the fact that such a way to proceed is considered positive – perhaps necessary? – for the better development of cross-border litigation, insofar as Article 81.2 TFEU is being invoked as its underpinning basis.

The relationship between the content of the proposal and cross-border litigation, however, can be quite voluntarist in some aspects. Many minimum standards are clearly and directly related to it, as happens with those regarding the holding of hearings, expert investigations abroad, distance payment of court fees, the reimbursable nature of procedural expenses associated with the cross-border nature, legal aid in this type of litigation, interpretation and translation, or the right to a "double lawyer".

On the other hand, many other minimum standards affect internal aspects of civil proceedings that do not have a direct impact on cross-border litigation: this

46 The possible suppression of the public policy clause gave rise to strong criticism and discussions. Among others, see P. Beaumont/E. Johnston, "Abolition of the Exequatur in Brussels I: Is a Public Policy Defence Necessary for the Protection of Human Rights?" *IPRax* 2/2010, 105–111; G. Hohloch, "Zur Bedeutung des Ordre public-Arguments im Vollstreckbarerklärungsverfahren" in D. Baetege/J. von Hein/M. von Hinden (eds.), *Die richtige Ordnung: Festschrift für Jan Kropholler zum 70. Geburtstag*, Mohr Siebeck, Tübingen, 2008, 809–818; F. Pocar, "Révision de Bruxelles I et ordre juridique international: Quelle approche uniforme?" *Rivista di diritto internazionale privato e processuale* (2011) 47(3), 591–600; T. Schilling, "Das Exequatur und die EMRK" *IPRax* 1/2011, 31–40; P.F. Schlosser, "The Abolition of Exequatur Proceedings – Including Public Policy Review?" *IPRax* 2/2010, 101–105; A. Stadler, "Das Europäische Zivilprozessrecht im Spannungsfeld zwischen Beschleunigung und Beklagtenschutz" in E.-M. Kieninger/O. Remien (eds.), *Europäische Kollisionsrechtsvereinheitlichung*, Nomos, Baden-Baden, 2012, 165–184. On the real impact of the public policy clause, see B. Hess/T. Pfeiffer, *Interpretation of the Public Policy Exception as referred to in EU Instruments of Private International and Procedural Law* (2011): http://www.europarl.europa.eu/RegData/etudes/etudes/join/2011/453189/IPOL-JURI_ET(2011)453189_EN.pdf.

47 See Article 34.2 of the EAPO-Regulation.

is the case, for example, with the Member States' duty to ensure the independence and impartiality of judges, the principle of procedural good faith, public proceedings and public hearings, provisional and protective relief, reasoned judicial decisions, the efficiency of proceedings, an active case management, encouragement of mediation, reasonable court fees, effective service of decisions and of the claim or equivalent document instituting proceedings, the "loser pays" principle as the main criterion to govern the decision on costs, the limits to litigation funding by third parties or, as a last example, the possibility to waive legal representation by a lawyer.

To the extent that they help in raising or clarifying standards, these "general" provisions can be very useful to reinforce a trust[48] which, in principle, was credited as already existent, as well as to eliminate certain obstacles for the circulation of judicial decisions – some of them already detected, like the absence of justification or the disproportionate amount of an order for costs. From this perspective, their legitimacy could be upheld under Article 81.2 TFEU: they foster a better effective access to justice [Article 81.2 (e) TFEU]; they also serve to eliminate obstacles to the proper functioning of civil proceedings and to promote the compatibility of the rules on civil procedure applicable in the various Member States [Article 81.2 (f) TFEU]; they also contribute to the development of alternative methods of dispute settlement [Article 81.2 (g) TFEU]; in addition, the minimum standards for training are anchored directly in Article 81.2 (h) TFEU, which empowers the Union to adopt measures to support the training of the judiciary and judicial staff. In a more global way, it must be noted that the existence of effective and reliable systems of judicial resolution of disputes is essential for the proper functioning of the internal market (Article 81.2 TFEU), thereby reinforcing the contents of the proposal with its alleged source of competence.

It should also be noted how the proposal has made an obvious use of the existing *corpus iuris processualis europaeum* and of the case law interpreting it.[49] The minimum standards on service are directly linked to what has already been established by some European Regulations (those that create the European enforcement order, the European order for payment procedure and the European small claims procedure); and the rules on financing of litigation by third parties find their precedent in the 2013 Commission Recommendation on collective proceedings.[50] The relationship between the minimum standards

---

48 See also E. Storskrubb, "Mutual Trust and the Dark Horse of Civil Justice" (2018) 20 *Cambridge Yearbook of European Legal Studies* 179 at 180.

49 See also E. Storskrubb (above n. 47) 22; in a very detailed manner, Tulibacka et al. (above n. 7) 33–51.

50 Recently followed by the Proposal for a Directive of the European Parliament and of the Council on representative actions for the protection of the collective interests of consumers, and repealing Directive 2009/22/EC (COM/2018/0184 final), dated 11 April 2018.

for provisional measures and the EAPO regulation is also clear; the "essential" nature of the documents whose translation may be required has its origin in the case law of the Court of Justice in the *Weiss und Partner* case,[51] in the same way as it is in the *ProRail* judgment[52] where the origin of the proposal regarding expert investigation abroad is to be found. It is evident, then, that the progress in the construction of a European civil procedural law is not based on disconnected impulses; on the contrary, there is a framework of pre-existing rules, case law and good practices that are being fed back.

If successful, an initiative with this content – or any similar one – would have a harmonising effect on national civil processes. Some provisions may be no more than the reflection of realities already existing in a common way in all Member States, because they are logical rules or because they are the result of a more or less spontaneous harmonisation that has been developing as over time in a slightly perceptible way.[53] For other matters the minimum standards are so general that Member States may not need to develop specific implementation measures to comply with them. But the proposal also addresses issues in relation to which the starting situations are different in the Member States, so that their transposition could force modification of certain sectors of some national legal systems. It should also be noted that there are several aspects of cross-border civil procedure that are potentially harmonisable but that are not addressed: one may miss a more clear focus on the rights of the defendant in cross-border settings, like the deadline to reply to the claim,[54] to react against an enforcement carried out abroad, or a definition of the cases in which fictitious notifications are allowed in cross-border litigation.

Therefore, despite this transformative potential, the proposal is still far from representing the means for a deep harmonisation of civil procedure. And, of course, it is even further from offering the design of a common European civil procedure for cross-border cases, equivalent to the European small claims procedure. It is obviously just a first step and it is logical that first steps be cautious. But, even being cautious in the content, the proposal is daring insofar as it clearly opens a door that until now was rather closed.

Moreover, the fact that the European institutions begin to make visible their interest in advancing more decisively on the path of approximation of laws in civil procedural matters entails the activation of a competence that until now had not been used openly, and the belief that European regulatory action has become necessary due to the dysfunctions associated to the procedural

---

51 Above n. 38.

52 Above n. 24.

53 On this phenomenon, see also C.H. van Rhee, "Harmonisation of Civil Procedure: An Historical and Comparative Perspective" in X.E. Kramer/C.H. van Rhee (eds.), *Civil Litigation in a Globalising World*, Asser Press, The Hague, 2012, 39–63.

54 See on this, again, F. Gascón Inchausti/M. Requejo Isidro (above n. 13) 112.

autonomy of Member States. Of course, it would also break the situation of relative tranquillity at this point between European and national law-makers, which, for now, is only sporadically shaken by the Court of Justice, but not by the Council or the Parliament.

An absolute approximation of civil procedural legislation would be, at least in the immediate future, a disproportionate measure from the point of view of subsidiarity, which would have no European constitutional support.[55] The assessment would be different in case of a more limited intervention, involving the harmonisation of some elements of civil proceedings, such as first service of proceedings, the linguistic dimension of proceedings or other factors directly associated with its cross-border nature. It would even be possible for the European law-maker to create the model of a cross-border civil procedure, similar to the European small claims procedure, but without claim value limits and with a much more detailed regulation that would leave less room to national procedural law:[56] although the use of such a proceeding should be restricted, we should count on the expansive force of these hypothetical European rules, if they turn out to be "better" or more effective than the internal ones with which they would have to compete.

In any case, procedural harmonisation, by itself, cannot be seen as a panacea,[57] either for cross-border litigation, or for the effectiveness of national civil justice systems[58] – first of all, because experience shows that not even the most exhaustive and detailed regulations can be applied in a homogeneous manner and without imbalances in all Member States.

But it is not just a matter of effectiveness. It would also mean recognising that the European law-maker has the capacity to force the insertion in national systems of decisions and solutions that could have been previously rejected by them. Therefore, from a more political perspective, harmonisation of civil proceedings – more or less intense – can raise in itself strong reluctance, both among European authorities and among Member States, including highly organised professional sectors. The Union itself seems to be well aware of this

---

55 B. Hess, "Ein einheitliches Prozessrecht?" (2016) 1 *International Journal of Procedural Law* 55–85.

56 See also B. Hess (above n. 7) 9–10.

57 As stated, "simply latching on the promise of harmonization may not lead us to a functional regulatory strategy" [E. Storskrubb (above n. 47) 23].

58 A strong – and very interesting – criticism to harmonization in the field of civil procedure, from a law and economics approach, can be found in L. Visscher, "A Law and Economics View on Harmonisation of Procedural Law" in X.E. Kramer/C.H. van Rhee (eds.), *Civil Litigation in a Globalising World* (above n. 52), 65–91. According to this author, procedural harmonisation would not serve to reduce transaction costs, but would deprive legal operators of the ability to choose justice systems according to different preferences, would reduce the capacity for legal systems to learn from each other and would leave the legislator in a position of greater vulnerability in the face of pressures from interest groups.

and that it could generate strong tensions in a hypersensitive matter, given the close link between jurisdiction and civil justice with the sovereignty and cultural idiosyncrasy of each country.[59]

It should be remembered, in this regard, that Article 67.1 TFEU expressly recognises that the construction of the European area of freedom, security and justice must be done with due respect for "the different legal systems and traditions of the Member States". Diversity of legal-procedural cultures, therefore, also deserves to be preserved, except in what is truly essential for the maintenance of the architecture of the European Area of Justice.

59 In a similar vein, see M. Tulibacka, "Europeanization of civil procedures: in search of a coherent approach" (2009) 46(5) *Common Market Law Review* 1527–1565, esp. at 1565, insisting on the need to be very aware of the close link between civil procedure and national legal culture.

THE 2017 PROPOSAL OF THE EUROPEAN PARLIAMENT ON COMMON MINIMUM STANDARDS OF CIVIL PROCEDURE

Vincent RICHARD*

1. INTRODUCTION

On 4 July 2017, the European Parliament adopted a resolution "with recommendations to the Commission on common minimum standards of civil procedure in the European Union". This project is a proposal for a directive and contains 28 articles on diverse aspects of civil procedure. The proposal deserves some attention because it represents the latest step towards procedural harmonisation in the EU. Procedural harmonisation in Europe has come a

* The author would like to thank Martina Mantovani and Stephanie Law for their helpful comments. All remaining errors are the author's sole responsibility.

long way since the famous "Storme Commission's report" of 1993.[1] This report is, nowadays, widely known among European procedural comparatists but, in 1993, it went largely unnoticed, especially by the EU legislator.[2] This "delayed glory" can be explained by the fact that, in 1993, the European Union had no direct competence to legislate on civil procedure and the Member States' governments did not consider the field of civil justice as a political priority.

Both factors changed with the signature of the Amsterdam Treaty in 1997 and the Tampere Council conclusions of October 1999,[3] where the Council expressed its wish to set up a "Genuine European Area of Justice" with "greater convergence in civil law".[4] With this political mandate, the European Commission started to work intensively in the field of civil and commercial disputes. The first step was the "communautarisation" of the Brussels Convention of 1968 with the Brussels Regulation,[5] followed by the adoption of the Insolvency Regulation[6] and several other instruments, mostly focusing on international competence and enforcement of foreign judgments.[7] In the meantime, the Commission proposed to adopt genuine European procedures and published a green paper in 2002 on a European order for payment procedure.[8] In this document, the Commission mentions the Storme Commission's report and describes it as a "valuable point of reference and source of inspiration".[9]

Since 2002, the European agenda on civil procedure has been well fulfilled and many instruments have been adopted, enhancing judicial cooperation and

1 M. Storme, *Approximation of Judiciary Law in the European Union*, Kluwer, 1994 and M. Storme, "A single civil procedure for Europe: A Cathedral Builders' Dream", *Ritsumeikan Law Review* no. 22, 2005, p. 87.

2 K. Kerameus, "International Procedural Harmonisation and Autonomous Interpretation" in T. Einhorn and K. Siehr, *Intercontinental Cooperation through Private International Law, Essays in memory of Peter E. Nygh*, T.M.C. Asser Press, 2004, pp. 177–186.

3 COM(2002) 261 final.

4 Presidency conclusions of the Tampere European Council of 15 and 16 October 1999.

5 Council Regulation (EC) No. 44/2001 of 22 December 2000 on jurisdiction and the recognition and enforcement of judgments in civil and commercial matters.

6 Council Regulation (EC) No. 1346/2000 of 29 May 2000 on insolvency proceedings and Regulation (EU) 2015/848 of the European parliament and of the Council of 20 may 2015 on insolvency proceedings (recast).

7 Notably Council Regulation (EC) No. 2201/2003 of 27 November 2003 concerning jurisdiction and the recognition and enforcement of judgments in matrimonial matters and the matters of parental responsibility, repealing Regulation (EC) No. 1347/2000; Council Regulation (EC) No. 4/2009 of 18 December 2008 on jurisdiction, applicable law, recognition and enforcement of decisions and cooperation in matters relating to maintenance obligations and Regulation (EU) No. 650/2012 of the European Parliament and of the Council of 4 July 2012 on jurisdiction, applicable law, recognition and enforcement of decisions and acceptance and enforcement of authentic instruments in matters of succession and on the creation of a European Certificate of Succession.

8 Green paper on a European order for payment procedure and on measures to simplify and speed up small claims litigation Brussels, 20.12.2002, COM(2002) 746 final.

9 COM(2002) 746 final, p. 12.

facilitating cross-border disputes.[10] Yet, European Union law has barely affected domestic procedures because of the absence of general legislative competence on this matter. EU procedural law also lacks a holistic regulation of civil procedure, at least nothing that comes close to the initial "European Judicial Code" idea that was the basis for the Storme Commission's report. Moreover, in the last years, it seemed that the EU Commission had halted its reflection on procedural harmonisation in order to wait for the publication of the final report of the ELI/UNIDROIT project on Transnational Principles of Civil Procedure.[11]

These considerations explain why the European Parliament proposal of July 2017 on Common Minimum Standards of civil procedure came as a surprise for many observers. Indeed, it was the first time that an EU institution took up the idea of drafting norms with the sole purpose of harmonising national civil procedures with a general approach. However, this 2017 document has attracted little attention[12] and the Commission's reaction to this proposal has been rather cautious so far.[13] The Commission underlines that many procedural rules can be found in EU Regulations and Directives and that it is currently working on the recast of the Evidence and Service regulations. The Commission also mentions that several studies have been conducted (or are ongoing) on the topic and that it is currently in the process of analysing the results of the studies carried out[14] and examining the first results of the ELI/UNIDROIT project. It is also interesting to note that the response of the Commission does not discuss at all the procedural standards proposed by the Parliament. This silence, and the general tone of the answer lead one to think that the Commission is quite sceptical on the content of the proposed directive – an opinion probably shared by many scholars.[15] In this author's opinion, this proposal is indeed of debatable quality, in the sense that

---

10 See notably Council Regulation (EC) No. 1206/2001 of 28 May 2001 on cooperation between the courts of the Member States in the taking of evidence in civil or commercial matters and Regulation (EC) No. 1393/2007 of the European Parliament and of the Council of 13 November 2007 on the service in the Member States of judicial and extrajudicial documents in civil or commercial matters (service of documents), and repealing Council Regulation (EC) No. 1348/2000.

11 See the contributions of E. Silvestri (Chapter 9), M. Stürner (Chapter 10) and C.A. Kern (Chapter 11) in this volume.

12 See however E. Guinchard, "Chronique Espace judiciaire européen en matière civile – Vers un code de procédure civile européenne", *Revue Trimestrelle de Droit Européen.* (*RTD Eur.*) 2017, p. 852.

13 See document SP(2017) 539 – Follow up to the European Parliament resolution of 4 July 2017 with recommendations to the Commission on common minimum standards of civil procedure in the European Union – 2015/2084 (INL).

14 See notably *An evaluation study of national procedural laws and practices in terms of their impact on the free circulation of judgments and on the equivalence and effectiveness of the procedural protection of consumers under EU consumer law* made by a consortium of universities led by the MPI Luxembourg in 2017 (JUST/2014/RCON/PR/CIVI/0082) and the project *Planning the future of cross-border families: a path through coordination (EUFam's)* (JUST/2014/JCOO/AG/CIVI/7729).

15 At least the few who decided on the title of this panel "*The 2017 Proposal of the Parliament: much ado about nothing?*"; see also E. Guinchard, "Chronique Espace judiciaire européen en matière civile Vers un code de procédure civile européenne", *RTD Eur.* 2017, p. 852.

its direct and immediate implementation would not bring much added value to domestic procedures and could actually be detrimental to the functioning of the whole system. This does not mean that the proposal doesn't have its merits. Rather, it constitutes a step in the right direction, as there is no doubt that "dynamics are working in the direction of further approximation".[16]

The movement towards procedural approximation in Europe is going quite slowly, but this pace is a necessary consequence of the many pitfalls such an endeavour encounters (section II). These obstacles can be overcome, but we believe that it would require a slight change of point of view, as well as a precise re-examination of the purpose of such standards. Thinking about the end goal, it is our opinion that, more than many Common Minimum Standards, EU procedural law rather needs a few detailed bespoke rules (section III).

2. PITFALLS OF ESTABLISHING COMMON MINIMUM STANDARDS IN EU PROCEDURAL LAW

The idea of procedural harmonisation in Europe has been around for nearly 30 years. So far, the project has been driven by two main actors: legal scholars and EU institutions. On one hand, comparative scholars compare national procedures and this task leads them naturally to think about harmonisation. The scientific task is indubitably interesting and useful because it often permits readers to have a glimpse of the functioning of a foreign procedural system. Harmonising different national procedures would also have the added value of greatly simplifying our work, as procedural comparatists.

The second actor is the European Union legislator. Its concern for harmonisation starts from the point of view of the Common Market and the Area of Freedom, Security and Justice. Goods, services, companies, citizens and judgments will circulate more easily if the rules affecting them are harmonised. However, it should not be forgotten that the EU institutions are not impartial actors in this context because they also want harmonisation to justify their action; as a token of their utility.

What is important to bear in mind from the above is that both actors do not concern themselves too much about the dangers of harmonisation. As a scholar, harmonisation is never more than a scientific project; it is harmless as long as it does not create binding rules, and scholars do not have this power. Their lack of concern is therefore understandable. As for the EU institutions, they have very little interest in putting these dangers forward as they face enough criticisms and resistance from various stakeholders. Doing so would feed arguments to their detractors.

---

[16] T. Andersson, "Approximation of procedural law in Europe" in M. Storme (ed.), *Procedural Laws in Europe – towards harmonisation*, Maklu, 2003, pp. 55–65.

This chapter will firstly examine the potential risk of creating common minimum standards in Europe. The aim is not to refuse any procedural harmonisation in Europe but to underline that such a project should be carefully carried out in order to really improve the life of European citizens. These concerns mostly stem from the fact that in the last two decades, the European legislating activity has created a normative labyrinth in the field of EU procedural law (section 2.1) where some problems result from the excess of norms and procedures. In that set-up, there is an inherent risk with the adoption of more legislation (section 2.2).

2.1. THE NORMATIVE LABYRINTH OF EU PROCEDURAL LAW

The European legislator has adopted a multitude of norms which, directly or indirectly, affect the conduct of litigation in Europe. These rules will mostly apply in cross-border disputes but can also influence purely domestic procedures. It is far from an easy task to describe the current European normative landscape in the field of procedure. The following overview is therefore non-exhaustive and the classification could be highly debated. Its purpose here is solely to provide an overview of European legislation in the field of civil procedure. To that end, we divided European norms into three main types of procedural rules: rules related to cross-border litigation (section 2.1.1), rules adopted as accessories to sectorial harmonisation of substantive EU law (section 2.1.2), and rules that can be considered as a first step towards a more general approach to harmonisation (section 2.1.3).

2.1.1. Procedural Rules Designed to Facilitate Cross-Border Litigation

The action of the Community in the field of procedure started with international civil procedure, i.e. private international law rules, with the signature of the Brussels Convention in 1968. This instrument did not primarily intend to provide for procedural rules besides rules on international jurisdiction. However, the Convention contained some rules that can be classified as purely procedural, such as Article 20 on the stay of proceedings in case the defendant does not appear.[17] Moreover, the operation of the Brussels Convention showed that a minimal harmonisation of some procedural concepts was absolutely necessary to ensure a smooth functioning of the rules affecting cross-border litigation. The amendments made to Article 30 of Regulation 44/2001,[18] defining when a court is deemed seised for the purpose of the *lis pendens* rule, is a good example of this need to harmonise procedural laws in Europe, even if on a small scale.

[17] Art. 26 Reg. 44/2001; Art. 28 Reg. 1215/2012.
[18] Art. 32 Reg. 1215/2012.

The Brussels Convention constituted the first instrument in what is nowadays sometimes referred to as the "the Brussels Regime" which encompasses several regulations covering cross-border litigation in civil and commercial matters,[19] and family law.[20] Since 2004, the European legislator has also adopted two genuine European procedures: the European Order for Payment Procedure (EOP)[21] and the European Small Claims Procedure (ESCP),[22] as well as a European Enforcement Order for Uncontested Claims (EEO).[23] These instruments were also the first ones to provide for "minimum standards", related to the service of summons. The Service,[24] the Evidence[25] and the European Account Preservation Order[26] Regulations can also be placed in this category, as they are tools solely designed to facilitate cross-border disputes resolution. Finally, it is possible to include in this category of cross-border procedural rules, instruments that are related to information and practical cooperation among actors in cross-border disputes,[27] such as the Council decisions creating the European judicial network in civil matters.[28,29]

Most of these regulations establish specific procedural rules for European disputes with a limited material scope and they replace the corresponding domestic rules of international litigation. Consequently, there is a multiplicity of procedural regimes applicable to European disputes whereas they represent

19 Most notably Reg. 44/2001 and Reg. 1215/2012.

20 Reg. 2201/2003 and Reg. 4/2009.

21 Regulation (EC) No. 1896/2006 of the European Parliament and of the Council of 12 December 2006 creating a European order for payment procedure.

22 Regulation (EC) No. 861/2007 of the European Parliament and of the Council of 11 July 2007 establishing a European Small Claims Procedure.

23 Regulation (EC) No. 805/2004 of the European Parliament and of the Council of 21 April 2004 creating a European enforcement order for uncontested claims.

24 Regulation (EC) No. 1393/2007 of the European Parliament and of the Council of 13 November 2007 on the service in the Member States of judicial and extrajudicial documents in civil or commercial matters (service of documents), and repealing Council Regulation (EC) No. 1348/2000.

25 Council Regulation (EC) No. 1206/2001 of 28 May 2001 on cooperation between the courts of the Member States in the taking of evidence in civil or commercial matters.

26 Regulation (EU) No. 655/2014 of the European Parliament and of the Council of 15 May 2014 establishing a European Account Preservation Order procedure to facilitate cross-border debt recovery in civil and commercial matters.

27 H. Boularbah, "Le cadre général des règles communautaire en matière de procédure civile" in M. Storme and G. De Leval, *Le Droit Processuel & Judiciaire Européen*, La charte, 2003, pp. 167–193.

28 Council Decision 2001/470/EC of 28 May 2001 establishing a European Judicial Network in civil and commercial matters, OJ 2001, L 174, as modified by Decision 568/2009/EC of the European Parliament and of the Council of 18 June 2009, OJ 2009, L 168.

29 A more refined classification of this category could be perfectly sensible as it contains a large number of instruments. It is notably possible to distinguish between classic Private International Law instruments (Brussels I, II bis, Maintenance etc.), instruments solely related to judicial cooperation (the Evidence Regulation, the judicial network decisions) and instruments creating an harmonised procedure or title (EEO, EOP and ESCP). For the purpose of this chapter this category is kept as a whole because these instruments deal exclusively with cross-border disputes.

a very small fraction of litigation. For example, a judge dealing with exequatur proceedings in the EU has to handle more than a dozen set of rules to enforce foreign judgments, as each regulation prescribes its own regime(s).[30] Similarly, a European creditor seeking to enforce his small commercial claim against a European defendant can choose to use one of the two European procedures (European Small Claims Procedure or the European Order for Payment), a national payment order procedure or any other national procedural avenue.[31]

2.1.2. Procedural Rules as Accessory to Sectorial Substantive Harmonisation

The next category of European procedural rules is harder to identify. These are procedural rules that have been sporadically added to European instruments harmonising specific parts of substantive law. In this field, the "*acquis communautaire*" is mainly composed of directives in the field of consumer law[32] including the 2013 Directive on consumer ADR.[33] These directives aim at harmonising substantive consumer law but also contain a few rules that affect national procedures involving consumers, even when the dispute has no cross-border element. The consumer ADR Directive is quite different because it focuses on dispute resolution but it can still be classified as a sectorial harmonisation as it deals only with consumer disputes. The same approach has been adopted in other legal areas such as the enforcement of intellectual property rights,[34] in labour law,[35] in competition law[36] and recently in the field of data protection.[37]

---

30 As an example, the Maintenance Regulation (Reg. 4/2009) and the Brussels IIbis regulation (Reg. 2201/2003) each contain two different regimes to enforce foreign judgments.

31 As Paulien Van der Grinten writes, "If we end up with a bowl of well-intended, yet fragmented regulations and procedures, this may in fact result in a practical obstacle for the accessibility of the court within the meaning of Article 6 ECHR (European Convention of Human Rights) as nobody will know which scheme applies to his or her situation and which procedure he or she should use." P. Van der Grinten, "Challenges for the Creation of a European Law of Civil Procedure", *Tijdschrift voor Civiele Rechtspleging* [*Civil Justice Review*], 2007, no. 3, pp. 65–70.

32 Council Directive 93/13/EEC of 5 April 1993 on unfair terms in consumer contracts, OJ L 95/29; Directive 2009/22/EC of the European Parliament and of the Council of 23 April 2009 on injunctions for the protection of consumers' interests, OJ L 110/30.

33 Directive 2013/11/EU of the European Parliament and of the Council of 21 May 2013 on alternative dispute resolution for consumer disputes and amending Regulation (EC) No. 2006/2004 and Directive 2009/22/EC, OJ L 165/63.

34 Directive 2004/48/EC of the European Parliament and of the Council of 29 April 2004 on the enforcement of intellectual property rights, OJ L 157/45.

35 Council Directive 2000/78/EC of 27 November 2000 establishing a general framework for equal treatment in employment and occupation, OJ L 303/16 (see notably, arts. 9 and 10).

36 Directive 2014/104/EU of the European Parliament and of the Council of 26 November 2014 on certain rules governing actions for damages under national law for infringements of the competition law provisions of the Member States and of the European Union, OJ L 349/1.

37 Regulation (EU) 2016/679 of the European Parliament and of the Council of 27 April 2016 on the protection of natural persons with regard to the processing of personal data and on the free movement of such data, and repealing Directive 95/46/EC, OJ L 119/1.

This legislative technique has sometimes been classified as "a vertical approach" to harmonisation[38] and results from the direct effect of the substantive rules[39] which need to be effectively implemented. However, this approach is difficult to apprehend comprehensively because it requires looking in detail at substantial rules in specific fields in order to understand how the procedural environment of these rules is being affected. This list is therefore most likely not exhaustive and it is worth noting that this is also the consequence of the "servant nature" of procedural law. More importantly, this sectorial approach brings about fragmented procedural rules which may regulate the same issue in different ways depending on the substantive law concerned. On a procedural level, it can also sometimes be difficult to have a clear coordination between rules that apply because of the substantive issue at hand and rules that apply because of the cross-border nature of the dispute.[40] This can be a problem if we take into account the fact that most judges in EU Member States are not specialised. They can preside over a consumer case in the morning and over an intellectual property right dispute in the afternoon. The more different the procedural rules are, the more likely it is that a mistake will be made in their implementation.

2.1.3. *Horizontal Procedural Harmonisation Rules*

The last category of European procedural norms is composed of two directives on legal aid[41] and mediation,[42] as well as the non-binding Recommendation on Collective Redress.[43,44] This category is harder to define: it concerns rules which

---

38 See point J. of the European Parliament resolution of July 2017; see also B. Hess, *Harmonized rules and minimum standards in the European law of civil procedure: in-depth analysis for the JURI committee*, June 2016, p. 5; A.-M. Van den Bossche, "L'espace européen de justice et le (rapprochement du) droit judiciaire" in M. Storme et G. De Leval, *Le Droit Processuel & Judiciaire Européen*, La charte, 2003, pp. 1–23, p. 8.

39 T. Andersson, "Approximation of procedural law in Europe" in M. Storme (ed.), *Procedural Laws in Europe – towards harmonisation*, Maklu, 2003, pp. 55–65.

40 On the question of the coordination between the GDPR and the Brussels I bis regulation and notably on the implication of recital 147 of the GDPR, see P. Franzina, "Jurisdiction regarding Claims for the Infringement of Privacy Rights under the General Data Protection Regulation" in A. De Franceschi (ed.), *European Contract Law and the Digital Single Market – The Implications of the Digital Revolution*, Intersentia, 2016, p. 81.

41 Council Directive 2002/8/EC of 27 January 2003 to improve access to justice in cross-border disputes by establishing minimum common rules relating to legal aid for such disputes, OJ L 27/41.

42 Directive 2008/52/EC of the European Parliament and of the Council of 21 May 2008 on certain aspects of mediation in civil and commercial matters, OJ L 136/3.

43 Commission Recommendation of 11 June 2013 on common principles for injunctive and compensatory collective redress mechanisms in the Member States concerning violations of rights granted under Union Law (2013/396/EU), OJ L 201/60.

44 In the framework of the New Deal for Consumers, the Commission has published two proposals for directive that could also be included in this category once they are adopted. See COM(2018) 184 final and COM(2018) 185 final.

are not primarily sectorial, meaning that they cover more than one specific type of dispute and are not exclusively concerned with cross-border litigation. Once again, this classification is debatable as the Legal Aid Directive and the Mediation Directive were aimed at facilitating cross-border disputes but their effect in national laws led to some concrete reforms even in purely domestic settings.[45] A similar remark could be made about the 2013 recommendation on collective redress because it concerned violations of rights granted by Union law, which could be considered a vertical/sectorial approach, albeit a very broad one. There is also no doubt that the recommendation was mostly targeting consumer disputes but this was not its sole focus. This category of procedural norms has sometimes been referred to as "horizontal rules",[46] as opposed to the vertical/sectorial approach described above.

It is worth noting that legal aid and mediation were regulated by binding instruments, i.e. directives whereas the recommendation on collective redress is a non-binding instrument. Yet there is no doubt that this recommendation has a very substantial impact in some Member States' laws notwithstanding its non-binding nature.[47] Overall, this approach, although horizontal, still only provides for piecemeal harmonisation,[48] firstly because these instruments do not regulate the procedural area concerned in a comprehensive manner and secondly because, as directives, they leave some leeway to Member States to enact national legislation.

Finally, this classification would not be complete without mentioning the role of the CJEU. It could be argued that the case law of the CJEU represents a fourth category of procedural norms within the classification made. There is no doubt that the case law of the Court of justice had many consequences at procedural level, most notably through the use of the principles of equivalence and effectiveness in consumer law.[49] For the purpose of this chapter, the CJEU case law is rather envisaged as an additional layer of rules within each category, as most of its decisions in these fields are given through the preliminary ruling procedure, which means that the CJEU is interpreting one of the European norms already described. In that regard, this author would prefer to classify each CJEU decision in the category corresponding to the instrument that it

---

45 See G. De Palo et al., *'Rebooting' the mediation directive: assessing the limited impact of its implementation and proposing measures to increase the number of mediations in the EU*, study for the European Parliament, 2014.

46 R. Manko, *Europeanisation of civil procedure – Towards common minimum standards?*, European Parliamentary Research Service, 2015, p. 21.

47 B. Hess, *Harmonized rules and minimum standards in the European law of civil procedure*, n. 38 above, p. 16.

48 See point K. of the European Parliament proposal of July 2017; see also R. Manko, n. 46 above.

49 Y. Chaput and G. De Leval, "L'harmonisation par la procédure: vers un 'procès européen'", *Gazette du Palais*, 21 August 2008, no. 234, p. 28.

is interpreting rather than adopting a new category.[50] However, this approach runs the risk of ignoring some particular trends in CJEU case law that affect several legal areas and notably the few overarching principles it has developed. Within the discussion on harmonisation of civil procedure in Europe, there is no doubt that the CJEU interpretation of the principles of effectiveness, non-discrimination, mutual trust and the right to a fair trial play a foundational role.[51] The same remarks could be made about the case law of the ECtHR because although it is not part of EU law, it certainly affects all European Member States.

This short classification of the diverse EU procedural rules could probably be debated, as it is hard to come up with a clear and exhaustive overview of all the current European procedural rules. It is anyway not the goal of this chapter, which is rather designed to firstly highlight that the current legal landscape is incredibly messy.[52] In this context, it is easy to understand that adopting more legislation in this field is inherently risky.

2.2. INHERENT RISK OF ADOPTING MORE LEGISLATION

Even in a purely domestic setting, excessive legislation carries some risk. It takes time for lawyers, judges and other legal professionals to be acquainted with all the rules. The more rules there are, the harder this task is and the more likely that these rules can contradict each other. Moreover, for most legal practitioners, cross-border litigation represents a very small percentage of their activity. There is therefore a risk that they will make mistakes when the case at hand involves cross-border issues, governed by rules that are different from the domestic ones which these practitioners are used to applying. This is important to understand because it means that harmonisation of procedural rules in Europe has to address this discrepancy between domestic and cross-border disputes. It should also be added that it is not only a problem of legal divergence between domestic litigation and European litigation. International litigation has to be taken into account as well. The issue is not only to decide whether the dispute is domestic or not, but whether the dispute is domestic, international or European.

This problem is directly linked with the issue of the scope of the European procedural rules. The adoption of EU law procedural rules with a limited scope

---

50 According to the European parliament: "the contribution of the CJEU should ultimately be seen as a standard-interpreting rather than a standard-setting", see point 2. of the European Parliament proposal of July 2017.

51 H. Boularbah, "Le cadre général des règles communautaires en matière de procédure civile: coopération judiciaire, droit judiciaire européen et droit processuel commun" in M. Storme et G. De Leval, *Le Droit Processuel & Judiciaire Européen*, La charte, 2003, pp. 1–23, pp. 167–193.

52 See also T.M. De Boer, "Jurisdiction and enforcement in international family law: a labyrinth of European and international legislation" (2002) 49(3) *Netherlands International Law Review* 307.

only exacerbates this problem. The European Parliament was clearly aware of this issue when drafting the proposed common minimum standards. In that regard, Article 3 of the proposed directive is worth looking at, as it tries to push for a broader interpretation of the notion of "cross-border disputes", notably to include disputes where

> both parties are domiciled in the same Member State as that of the court or tribunal seised, provided that the place of performance of the contract, the place where the harmful event takes place or the place of enforcement of the judgment is situated in another Member State.

The intention is commendable but such broad criteria run the risk of creating more litigation on this issue of scope.[53]

The heart of the problem results in the limited competence of the EU in the field of procedure. In essence, the EU has created a normative area that is distinct from both international and domestic law. Because it can legislate only within that legal area, it is powerless to solve the problem resulting from the coordination of the three areas (domestic – European – international). In other words, the EU does not have the legislative competence to solve the problem it has created. We can detect an admission of this powerlessness in the recitals of the EU proposal for a directive. In recital 13, it is written that

> the hereby proposed common minimum standards of civil procedure would lead to further efficiencies if Member States extended their scope of application not only to matters falling within the scope of Union law, but in general to both cross-border and purely internal cases.

Moreover, the analysis of some of the rules included in the proposal shows that the EU Parliament could not limit itself to cross-border litigation, even broadly defined. Some standards that are presented, for example in Article 9 on "*General principles for direction of proceedings*" are not, should not, and probably cannot be limited to specific disputes. It would make little sense to ask that cases are managed "at a reasonable speed and cost" only for certain disputes.[54]

The current European normative landscape could be described as a labyrinth for two reasons. Firstly there is a plethora of norms originating from different legal sources and secondly these norms have limited scope, meaning

---

53 See recital 12 of the proposal where the Parliament "Underlines that the current interpretation of the notion 'matters with cross-border implications' is rather narrow and results in the creation of two sets of rules and two categories of litigants that might lead to further problems and unnecessary complications; stresses that a broader interpretation should therefore be adopted".

54 See the contribution of F. Gascón Inchausti (Chapter 12) in this volume.

that different rules are applicable to the same issue. Therefore, attempting to harmonise cross-border litigation across the board does not avoid the discrepancy with domestic or international procedures and will therefore be only of a limited added value. These concerns do not lead one to reject the project of common minimum standards entirely, but when the time comes to adopt binding procedural rules at the European level, the EU legislator is advised to be very cautious in its approach. The goal would be to identify the precise problems that affect cross-border disputes and to adopt rules only so far as it is necessary, because in the current normative labyrinth, there is a very fine line between superfluous and detrimental.[55] Moreover, when possible, the goal should be to provide for rules applicable to all disputes regardless of their domestic, international or European character. Finally, it is hard to find major problems in the field of European civil procedure; at least until a decision is rendered.[56] There is therefore no urgency in adopting common minimum standards in European procedure and the enterprise is risky. Particular attention and time should thus be devoted to studying which procedural standards are needed in Europe.

3. FROM COMMON MINIMUM STANDARDS TO DETAILED BESPOKE RULES

Section 2 underlined the risks and pitfalls of procedural harmonisation in Europe. It should not be understood as a criticism but as an encouragement to think further about these procedural standards before adopting more legislation. Yet, there is not enough debate about the precise purpose of these standards which should be, firstly to improve cross-border litigation and secondly, to improve litigation in general (section 3.1). Once the purpose has been clearly defined, each standard has to be carefully assessed against it, and at the end of this process, it seems that the European Union will only need few bespoke rules (section 3.2).

---

55 It should be taken into account that any introduction of a new procedural rule will be followed by legal dispute on this issue to determine whether certain national rules or practice are compatible with the newly adopted rule. In that regards, if the rule has no particular beneficial effect in one system, its introduction will foster litigation and therefore be detrimental.

56 Y. Chaput and G. De Leval, "L'harmonisation par la procédure : vers un 'procès européen'" *Gazette du Palais* 21 August 2008, no. 234, p. 28; *An evaluation study of national procedural laws and practices in terms of their impact on the free circulation of judgments ...*, Evaluation Study, General Report, Strand 1, n. 14 above, p. 140; The adoption of Regulation (EU) 655/2014 on the European Account Preservation Procedure is a major step towards improving cross-border enforcement and the success or shortcoming of this procedure will be of utmost importance to assess the need for further legislation in the field of enforcement.

3.1. THE PURPOSE OF COMMON MINIMUM STANDARDS

The harmonisation process is a complex and a slightly dangerous endeavour and it therefore requires very precise assessment of what the aim of such project is. Looking at the European Parliament proposal and its preamble shows that the justifications given are very general. For the European Parliament, harmonisation of civil procedure should be pursued for two main reasons. Firstly, it should be pursued for the sake of harmonisation itself because procedural differences between Member States may constitute "disturbance to trade and can deter businesses and consumers from exercising their internal market rights".[57] In that regard any difference can be seen as a problem and the end goal is a European Code of civil procedure[58] which would harmonise "the balance between the claimant's right of access to justice and the defendant's rights of defence".[59] Secondly, providing for common minimum standards is also a way to set "a minimum level of quality of civil proceedings across the Union"[60] and to provide for "a more deeply rooted general feeling of justice, certainty and predictability throughout the Union".[61] This subsidiary goal is therefore to improve conduct of proceedings in every European Member State whether they are cross-border or not. The twofold aim can be summarised as such: harmonisation of civil procedure in Europe is needed to improve the free circulation of goods, services and citizens, and constitutes an opportunity to improve national systems of justice. These two goals can be reconciled through standards that are both common to every Member State and minimum in nature, in order to allow some Member States to offer a better level of protection. Yet, we find a natural opposition between these two goals, if Member States can go beyond the rules proposed, these rules are not common anymore. Conversely, if Member States agree on common rules, it is quite possible that the level of protection decreases in Member States that were providing the most protection. There is therefore a choice to make between common standards and minimum standards (section 3.1.1). Moreover, if the end goal is to improve litigation and to simplify the normative landscape, it is doubtful that general principles are needed and we therefore need standards with a high degree of precision (section 3.1.2).

3.1.1. Common or Minimum

The rules can be common or minimum but they cannot be both. The European Union has used the concept of minimum harmonisation for a long time, mostly

57 Point Y. of the European Parliament proposal of July 2017.
58 Point Z. of the European Parliament proposal of July 2017.
59 Point F. of the European Parliament proposal of July 2017.
60 Point Y. of the European Parliament proposal of July 2017.
61 Point 20. of the European Parliament proposal of July 2017.

because it is the easiest way to obtain a political consensus on some policies. In the field of consumer law, the minimum harmonisation technique has been a solution to improve consumer protection in some Member States while refraining from lowering the protection in others. It has also allowed Member States to continue to adopt legislation improving consumer's rights knowing that EU law in this field works only as a ratchet effect. However, in the field of consumer law[62] or in criminal law,[63] this minimum harmonisation technique has sometimes been abandoned precisely because it contradicts uniformity. If, as the European Parliament wrote, any procedural difference is an obstacle to the proper functioning of the internal market, minimum standards are not a solution to solve this problem.

Moreover, this idea of a "minimum" standard is often an illusion, especially when one tries to apply it to civil procedure, an area which is inherently about balance. The idea of minimum standards is politically seductive but is often hard to translate in legal terms. It is conceivable for some procedural rules but not for all of them. For example, when it comes to time limits, it could be possible to decide on a minimum number of days in which to reply to the summons or to make an appeal, and leave Member States free to adopt a longer deadline. The same could be said about limitation periods. The EU could decide that the limitation period for a tort claim could not be less than two or three years while letting Member States enact a longer limitation period. These two examples are simplified, in the sense that such harmonisation would also require harmonising the starting point of these deadlines, which is another complex problem. However, enacting such rules would do little for harmonisation across the EU, as national laws would still contain different limitation periods. It is also necessary to keep in mind that these limitation periods cannot be extended indefinitely without affecting defendants' rights or the overall efficiency of the system. Moreover, if this change, in a given Member State, leads to different limitation periods for rights derived from EU law or different time limits for cross-border disputes, this discrepancy with domestic law will still be a source of problems for legal practitioners and foster litigation on the scope of the rules. It should also be taken into account that some Member States have adopted very short time-limits in order to cope with a slow justice system. In that regard, the idea that harmonisation is feasible without "financial implication"[64] and without affecting

---

62 See Directive 2011/83/EU of the European Parliament and of the Council of 25 October 2011 on consumer rights.

63 CJEU, 26 February 2013, *Stefano Melloni v. Ministerio Fiscal*, ECLI:EU:C:2013:107; Alex Tinsley, "Note on the Reference in Case C-399/11 *Melloni*" (2012) 3 *New Journal of European Criminal Law* 19; N. De Boer, "Addressing rights divergence under the Charter: *Melloni*" (2013) 4 *CMLR* 1083–1103; D. Ritleng, "De l'articulation des systèmes de protection des droits fondamentaux dans l'Union", *RTD Eur.* 2013, pp. 267–292.

64 Point 26. of the European Parliament proposal of July 2017.

"the judicial organisation of the Member States or the principal characteristics of the manner in which civil litigation is conducted"[65] seems optimistic.

Regarding some other rules of civil procedure, the minimum idea is simply incomprehensible. When it comes to the role of the judge to direct proceedings[66] or to encourage parties to settle disputes,[67] it is quite hard to grasp what a minimum rule would be. If the goal is an across-the-board harmonisation, the rules cannot be minimum ones and in most cases, the right balance between claimants' and defendants' rights has to be set and agreed by all Member States. Leaving room to Member States to always improve the defendants' rights leaves them room to decrease the claimants' right of access to justice or the overall efficiency of their justice system. Once again, civil procedure is about balance, not about an ever-increasing protection of defendants or weaker parties. And because this balance has to be carefully set, general principles should be avoided.

3.1.2. Standards, Rules and Principles

The semantic choice to use the word "standard" by the EU legislator leaves some uncertainty on whether these standards should be principles or rules.[68] In the latest proposal of the European Parliament, it seems to be a conscious choice to encompass both.[69] It is hard to trace a precise distinction between principles and rules but there is no doubt that civil procedure contains some very general principles and some precise rules. The issue here is that general principles are rarely directly useful when it comes to regulating the details of civil procedure. The area is marked by its need to carefully balance the rights of the parties and therefore the principles have to be balanced as well. The tip of the scale has to be precisely placed to balance the rights of the defence and the efficiency of the process. A good procedural rule is a rule that manages to balance both imperatives correctly in a given situation.

Moreover, civil procedure in Europe is not lacking in principles. The case law of the Court of Justice and especially the case law of the ECtHR on Article 6

---

65 Point AA. of the European Parliament proposal of July 2017.

66 See Art. 9 of the proposal: "*General principles for direction of proceedings*: 1. Member States shall ensure that courts actively manage the cases before them in order to ensure fair, efficient disposition of disputes and that it is done at a reasonable speed and cost, without impairing the freedom of the parties to determine the subject-matter of, and the supporting evidence for, their case ...".

67 See Art. 12 of the proposal: "*Settlement of disputes*: 1. Member States shall ensure that at any stage of the proceedings and having regard to all the circumstances of the case, if the court is of the opinion that the dispute is suitable for a settlement, it may propose that the parties make use of mediation in order to settle or to explore a settlement of the dispute ...".

68 B. Hess, *Harmonized rules and minimum standards in the European law of civil procedure: in-depth analysis* for the JURI committee, European Parliament, June 2016, p. 8.

69 Point W. of the European parliament proposal of July 2017 ("a system of Union common minimum standards in the form of principles and rules").

have provided European judicial systems with a large number of principles. Given this normative landscape, it is doubtful that the introduction of more overarching general principles of civil procedure can be of much use. The only exception would be to establish a principle that is clearly not present in the ECHR, in the Charter or in the case law of either European court. One example could be the right to have translation and interpretation in civil lawsuits, where one of the parties is domiciled in another Member State. This right has not been derived from the Charter or from Article 6 of the ECHR and would substantially change the conduct of cross-border litigation in Europe.[70] Save for such principles that would be specific to European (cross-border) litigation; it is hard to see how the introduction in a European directive of some well-known principles would have any beneficial effect. Moreover, there are always exceptions to these general principles and the exceptions would be questioned if the principle is reaffirmed in a directive. Provisions such as Article 8 on the notion of reasoned decisions[71] seem to reiterate a principle that is well known in all Member States' civil procedures and its introduction would lead to questioning of the compatibility of most payment order and default judgment procedures in Europe with the said principle. We doubt that this change would constitute progress.

Finally, the European Parliament's proposal also includes some principles that are more detailed[72] and some provisions contain precise rules giving rights to EU litigants.[73] Compared to general principles of civil procedure, it is easier to see the added value of introducing relatively detailed norms in Member States' civil procedure.

3.2. IDENTIFICATION OF DETAILED BESPOKE RULES

It is easy to criticise a project as ambitious as the European Parliament's proposal of July 2017. It is much harder to convincingly decide what should be done in the field of EU civil procedure. In this chapter, we try to show that, because of the plethora of norms in the current European normative landscape, it is crucial to introduce as little legislation as possible and only rules that could actually improve the conduct of litigation in Europe. Moreover, these rules should have a large scope, including at least European and international litigation, especially if we want to avoid litigation on the issue of scope. The European legislator is well

---

70 We would argue that the cost outweighs the value of such reform but it is beside the point.

71 Art. 8: "Member States shall ensure that courts or tribunals provide sufficiently detailed reasoned decisions within a reasonable time in order to enable parties to make effective use of any right to review the decision or lodge an appeal."

72 See for example Art. 18 of the proposal on the right to a lawyer in civil proceedings.

73 See Art. 15 of the proposal on Legal Aid.

aware of this issue of scope; however, the European Parliament's proposal fails to critically assess the need for each of the proposed rules.

Several projects are running concurrently and the success of procedural harmonisation in Europe depends on a proper and coordinated use of these projects. On one hand, some academic projects, financed by the Commission, are looking at potential problems in cross-border proceedings.[74] If it is relatively easy to identify one problem in a given Member State, it is sometimes difficult to understand the scale of the problem, which is to understand whether the problem is specific to some judges, to the whole of a particular Member State or to several Member States. After all, it is much harder to come up with a useful solution without causing more problems. On the other hand, some projects have been focusing on procedural harmonisation and propose solutions in the form of principles and rules. That is the case of the 2017 European Parliament's proposal, but it was also the goal of the Storme' Commission's report of 1993 and the ALI/UNIDROIT project of 2004. Recently, the European Law Institute has also been involved with UNIDROIT in order to draft rules more specifically applicable to European litigation.[75]

It is crucial to take these two approaches together; that is to pinpoint the problems identified by the studies and decide if it can be remedied by one of the harmonised rules that are proposed. The implementation of new procedural rules in each Member State has to be done in a surgical way, taking only what is necessary to improve the system.[76] If the analysis concerning the scale of the problem is correctly done, it will give some guidelines on the scale of the solution. It is likely that the best solution will be to inject a precise rule in some Member States' law and not in Member States where the particular issue is not problematic. In that sense, the rule has to be adapted to a specific legal system in order to foster harmonisation without implementing redundant rules in legal systems that do not need them.

We can try to apply this approach to the issue of service of judicial documents. This legal area is a good example of the current normative labyrinth because, although the topic is covered by one specific European Regulation,[77] rules pertaining to service of documents can be found in other non-specific

---

74 For the most recent projects, see, among others, the evaluation study conducted by the MPI in 2017 and the EUFAM's project, n. 14 above. See also The IC2BE Project (Cross-Border Enforcement in Europe: Civil Justice Framework, National Courts and the Court of Justice of the European Union – (JUST-AG-2016-02)) and the ERC consolidator grant awarded to Prof. X. Kramer for her project "Building EU civil justice: challenges of procedural innovations bridging access to justice (2017–2022)".

75 The progress of this project can be followed at: https://www.unidroit.org/work-in-progress-eli-unidroit-european-rules.

76 P. Van der Grinten, "Challenges for the Creation of a European Law of Civil Procedure", n. 31 above.

77 Reg. 1393/2007.

EU instruments.[78] Moreover, the Service Regulation is primarily designed to coordinate different national laws and practice on service, and does not harmonise them. Although some of the problems identified in the studies can be remedied through the ongoing recast of the Service Regulation,[79] most of them stem from divergent national laws and practices that are not covered by the EU instrument. There is therefore no doubt that, in this area, some harmonisation of domestic rules regarding service of judicial documents could be beneficial. Several precise issues can be identified. For example, acknowledgements of receipt are not always used for the transmission of documents and it could be useful to introduce the principle of a "scaled system" of service,[80] meaning that methods of service without acknowledgement of receipt could only be used if service with acknowledgement of receipt has failed or is deemed impossible. This hierarchy is envisaged by the European Parliament proposal (Article 17) and it would be a sensible principle to have, both in national and European law.[81] Another example would be the question of who can be served instead of the defendant[82] especially if the defendant is a legal entity. The proposal seems to accept that service can be effectuated on any employee of the defendant present at the business premises. Again, if such rule is adopted, some Member States laws should be adapted but not all of them. More importantly, the length of time limits to answer the first summons is not harmonised in Europe and it may constitute an obstacle to the recognition of the subsequent judgment if the enforcement judge considers that the defendant did not have a sufficient time to organise his defence. This question is not covered by the European Parliament proposal but it was envisaged by the Storme group and they proposed a uniform time limit of 30 days if the defendant is domiciled in another Member State.[83] This constitutes an adequate basis for further consideration, provided that the question of the starting point of this time limit is also envisaged.

---

78 See notably, Art. 26(2) Reg. 44/2201, Art. 18 Reg. 2201/2003, Art. 11 Reg. 4/2009, Art. 16 Reg. 650/2012 and Art. 28(2) Reg. 1215/2012. Rules relating to service of documents can also be found in the EEO Regulation (Arts. 13 to 19 Reg. 805/2004); in the EOP (Arts. 13, 14 and 15 Reg. 1896/2006) and in the ESCP (Art. 13 Reg. 861/2007).

79 See *Proposal for a Regulation of the European Parliament and of the Council amending Regulation (EC) No 1393/2007 of the European Parliament and of the Council on the service in the Member States of judicial and extrajudicial documents in civil or commercial matters (service of documents)*, COM(2018) 379 final.

80 F. Gascón Inchausti, "Service of proceedings on the defendant as a safeguard of fairness in civil proceedings: in search of minimum standards from EU legislation and European case-law" (2017) 13(3) *Journal of Private International Law* 475–518.

81 It is interesting to note that this hierarchy is only explicit in the ESCP Regulation (Art. 13(4) Reg. 861/2007 amended by Reg. 2015/2421) and not in the other EU instrument including the Service Regulation. See CJEU, 9 February 2006, *Plumex v. Young sports NV*, C-473/04, ECLI:EU:C:2006:96; *Rev. Procédures* n°4, Avril 2006, comm. 66, obs. R. Perrot.

82 Evaluation Study, General Report, Strand 1, n. 14 above, pp. 56 ff.

83 Rule 8.2 of the Storme's working group, see M. Storme, *Approximation of Judiciary Law in the European Union*, Kluwer, 1994, p. 138.

The task is far from easy because it requires a strong collaboration between many experts that are familiar with the laws and legal cultures of several Member States. If the goal is to truly improve litigation in Europe, the final rules need to be tailored to each Member State and relatively detailed.

4. CONCLUSION

European procedural law is currently at a crossroads. The legislative activities of the European Union during the last 20 years have mostly focused on European cross-border litigation. This has created a distinct set of rules that functions rather well but struggles when it comes to coordination with domestic laws. Concurrently, the adoption of sectorial procedural rules has managed to address specific problems sporadically but has resulted in a very fragmented legislative landscape. Both approaches are not sustainable in the long term and there is no doubt that a more holistic framework is needed, but it needs to address domestic laws as well in order to really improve the functioning of the system. This task is hard to accomplish because of its sheer complexity and because of the absence of clear competence of the EU to regulate domestic procedures. It is this author's view that procedural scholars should not focus too much on the issue of legislative competence. Firstly because European lawyers and institutions are better armed to deal with it and secondly because this issue of competence should not prevent scholars from discussing procedural rules and their potential usefulness. The goal is to improve litigation and particularly cross-border litigation. Considering the current normative labyrinth and the risk of multiplying disputes related to the scope of the rules, the adoption of procedural minimum standards has to be evaluated carefully. It would also make sense to simplify the current normative landscape in European procedural law which could be envisaged through consolidation of the current regulations. Such consolidation would represent a good opportunity to isolate the few procedural rules that are contained in these instruments and to regulate them altogether in a separate one.[84]

Although the European Union should adopt a more general approach towards regulation of civil procedure, this does not mean that this would be best achieved through a single instrument. The issue will be to amend each Member State's law precisely in order to put it in line with the European rule. Member States' laws should be amended as little as possible and this surgical work can

---

[84] On this discussion, see M. Fallon, P. Lagarde and S. Poillot-Peruzzetto (eds.), *Quelle architecture pour un code européen de droit international privé ?*, P.I.E. Peter Lang, 2011 and X. Kramer, M. Rooij et al., *A European Framework for private international law: current gaps and future perspectives*, study for the European Parliament's Committee on Legal Affairs, 2012.

only be achieved through coordination between national legislators and the European institutions.[85] The task is daunting, but in contrast to many other political issues, harmonisation of civil procedure is not a pressing one. Scholars and EU institutions have plenty of time to think about how to introduce useful harmonised rules that would act as an Ariane's thread in the current normative labyrinth.

[85] We would therefore agree with the European parliament when it writes that "a robust and systematic supervisory process on the part of the Commission should be established for that purpose", Point 8. of the European Parliament proposal of July 2017.

A FINAL COMMENT ON THE FUTURE EVOLUTION OF CIVIL PROCEDURE IN EUROPE

Elisabetta SILVESTRI

I must confess that I am a bit sceptical and pessimistic as far as the harmonisation of national rules of procedure, reached via the initiatives of EU institutions, is concerned. I do agree that on a few basic principles of civil procedure (such as access to justice, fairness, equality of arms) the differences between domestic procedural systems are not so remarkable; certainly, though, there are areas in which the differences are truly striking. But before addressing this point, I would like to review a question, one that other contributors to this book, too, pose in their chapters: What does "harmonisation" mean? Certainly harmonisation is an "ambiguous and imprecise" concept, just like the synonym of harmonisation "approximation" is: both terms, besides the obvious reference to the idea of an alignment of national legislations to the *acquis communautaire*, leave much room for defining which kind of harmonisation has taken place in the EU, a spontaneous one or a policy-driven one.

But this is not the first point on which I would like to expand. The first point is encapsulated in the following question: To what level is harmonisation desirable and, most of all, to what level is it practically feasible? My impression is that these days, more now than in the past, the push to harmonisation is often perceived as a push to homologation, and this is something that a few Member States fear or, more simply, dislike. In 1997, Professor Lowenfeld wrote an essay titled: "The Elements of Procedure: Are They Separately Portable?"[1] He underlined that, contrary to the conventional wisdom – according to which procedural law plays a secondary role since it is simply ancillary to substantive law – the rules of procedure are the very ones that better embody the history, the culture, the societal developments and the values of a given legal system, well beyond the traditional divide between the civil law tradition and the common law tradition. This might explain why, in my opinion, harmonisation in the field of civil procedure is often seen as an attempt at homologation, and again

1 See A.F. Lowenfeld, "The Elements of Procedure: Are They Separately Portable?" (1997) 45 *American Journal of Comparative Law* 649.

something that a few Member States do not support, fearing that this will deprive them of their national identity. Maybe my ideas are influenced by the fact that I come from a country in which nationalism is on the rise, as the 2018 elections have demonstrated. But since Italy is not the only Member State following this trend, I venture to say that I do not foresee a bright future for harmonisation of national legislation (whether procedural or of any other nature) unless the general attitude towards the Union, its purpose and its political role changes so that a breath of fresh air allows European Union citizens to see the EU institutions as something more than a super-bureaucracy far removed from what really interests the general public.

My last comments deal with the future. Let me go back to what has been done so far by the enactment of a variety of EU directives and regulations aimed at fostering judicial cooperation among Member States. Here I see one monumental problem, which is the cross-border character of the matters falling within the scope of the rules that, according to the powerful definition given by Fernando Gascón,[2] make up the *corpus iuris processualis europaeum*. Cross-border relevance, cross-border implications and so on: it is a sort of mantra that EU directives and regulations repeat as if only the relationships (and therefore the disputes) between citizens of different Member States mattered and deserved the benefit of rules that quite often are better and more efficient than the rules provided for domestic disputes of the same kind. Of course, we all know why the EU institutions are obsessed with cross-border cases: it is necessary to create a level playing-field so as to make the European market smooth and customer-friendly, to ensure that competition is not distorted by different levels of efficiency of judicial systems, and so on. But are we sure that cross-border litigation deserves so much attention? I do not have statistical data at hand to support my assertion, but – at least with reference to my own country, Italy – I do understand that cross-border litigation is a small percentage of the caseloads of courts; so small that it is completely neglected by the legislators, who do not even bother to take into account the solutions devised by EU directives or regulations that are applicable to cross-border litigation when they ponder reforms aimed at improving domestic proceedings. So much for the cross-fertilisation and the inspiration to be drawn from cross-border litigation and its instruments.

Harmonisation goes hand in hand with mutual trust; the famous mutual trust and its apotheosis in the Brussels I recast.[3] In the present political

---

2 See above, Chapter 4 of this volume.

3 On mutual trust, see, for instance, E. Storskrubb, "Mutual Trust in Civil Justice Cooperation in the EU" in A. Bakardjieva Engelbrekt et al. (eds), *Trust in the European Union in Challenging Times* (Palgrave Macmillan-Springer, 2019), 159–180; E. Storskrubb, "Mutual Trust and the Dark Horse of Civil Justice" [2018] *Cambridge Yearbook of European Legal Studies* 1; M. Zilinsky, "Mutual Trust and Cross-Border Enforcement of Judgments in Civil Matters

situation, I must subscribe to what other scholars have said: mutual trust is just a 'grandiloquent proclamation' concealing, in reality, a creeping distrust that a few Member States nurture in their relationships with other Member States, most of all with those that are deemed (and often rightly so) 'rogue states'.

In a chapter of the book *EU Civil Justice. Current Issues and Future Outlook*, Burkhard Hess expands on EU law-making having a direct impact on domestic procedures.[4] At first this would appear to be the most direct and successful form of harmonisation. Professor Hess mentions the Directive on the enforcement of intellectual property rights,[5] as well as the Consumer ADR Directive,[6] and the Recommendation on Collective Redress.[7] Potentially, these instruments (the first two, in particular, since the Recommendation is not binding) could change domestic procedures in a relevant way: potentially, because in practice such a result is not guaranteed. I think it depends on the attitude of Member States and on the policy choices each Member State is inclined to make. I am not an expert in the field of IP rights, and therefore I cannot tell you much about the implementation of the IP Directive in Italy, but I can assure that the transposition of the Consumer ADR Directive has not had any effect on the domestic procedures (either judicial ones or out-of-court ones) that consumers can rely on; nor has it made the life of consumers easier, since the landscape of the ADR instruments available to consumers is at present more confused than ever.[8] What I want to emphasise here is that even the mandatory implementation of the Directive does not guarantee real harmonisation, since national legislators can demonstrate a different level of deference to the will of the EU institutions. The same can be said with reference to the guidance coming from the case law of the European Court of Justice: often national legislators as well as national courts do not pay tribute to it as they should.

In conclusion, my personal view on the influence of the European Union on the procedural law of Member States is that a global and coherent vision is

---

in the EU: Does the Step-by-Step Approach Work?" (2017) 64 *Netherlands International Law Review* 115; M. Weller, "Mutual Trust: In Search of the Future of European Union Private International Law" (2015) 11 *Journal of Private International Law* 64.

4 B. Hess, "The State of the Civil Justice Union" in B. Hess, M. Bergström and E. Storskrubb (eds), *EU Civil Justice. Current Issues and Future Outlook* (Hart Publishing, 2016) 1.

5 Directive 2004/48/EC of the European Parliament and of the Council of 29 April 2004 on the enforcement of intellectual property rights (Text with EEA relevance) [2004] OJ L157/45.

6 Directive 2013/11/EU of the European Parliament and of the Council of 21 May 2013 on alternative dispute resolution for consumer disputes and amending Regulation (EC) No. 2006/2004 and Directive 2009/22/EC (Directive on consumer ADR) [2013] OJ L165/63.

7 Commission Recommendation of 11 June 2013 on common principles for injunctive and compensatory collective redress mechanisms in the Member States concerning violations of rights granted under Union Law [2013] OJ L 201/60.

8 See E. Silvestri, "Too Much of a Good Thing: Alternative Dispute Resolution in Italy" (2017) 21 *Nederlands-Vlaams tijdschrift voor Mediation en conflict management* 77.

still lacking, and that even in the field of civil justice Europe is going through an identity crisis, essentially due to the political and economic tensions that threaten to tear apart the very construction of the Union. Yet, I should like to end with a "pearl of wisdom" intended to infuse the debate with a hint of optimism. The quotation is by Heraclitus of Ephesus, the renowned pre-Socratic Greek philosopher:

> Opposition brings concord. Out of discord comes the fairest harmony.

INDEX

ABOUT THE EDITORS

Fernando Gascón Inchausti is Professor of Procedural Law at the Complutense University of Madrid and Director of the Institute for European Law and Regional Integration. He is particularly interested in European civil and criminal procedure, from the perspective of the cooperation and coordination of legal systems, but also of the impact of European procedural regulations on domestic justice systems. He has published widely on this topic and has been actively involved in several research projects, at national and European level, namely the "Luxembourg Study on European Civil Procedure".

Burkhard Hess is Executive Director of the Max Planck Institute Luxembourg for Procedural Law and Professor of Law at the Universities of Heidelberg and Luxembourg. He is an Associate to the Institut de Droit International. His interests relate to European civil procedural law, comparative procedural law and the interfaces between private and public dispute resolution. He has published widely on these topics and has been engaged in many research projects for the European Commission, the European Parliament and national law makers. He is, namely, co-editor of the Luxembourg Study on European Civil Procedure.

www.ingramcontent.com/pod-product-compliance
Ingram Content Group UK Ltd.
Pitfield, Milton Keynes, MK11 3LW, UK
UKHW051921100926
8556IPUK00021B/1296

9 781780 688596